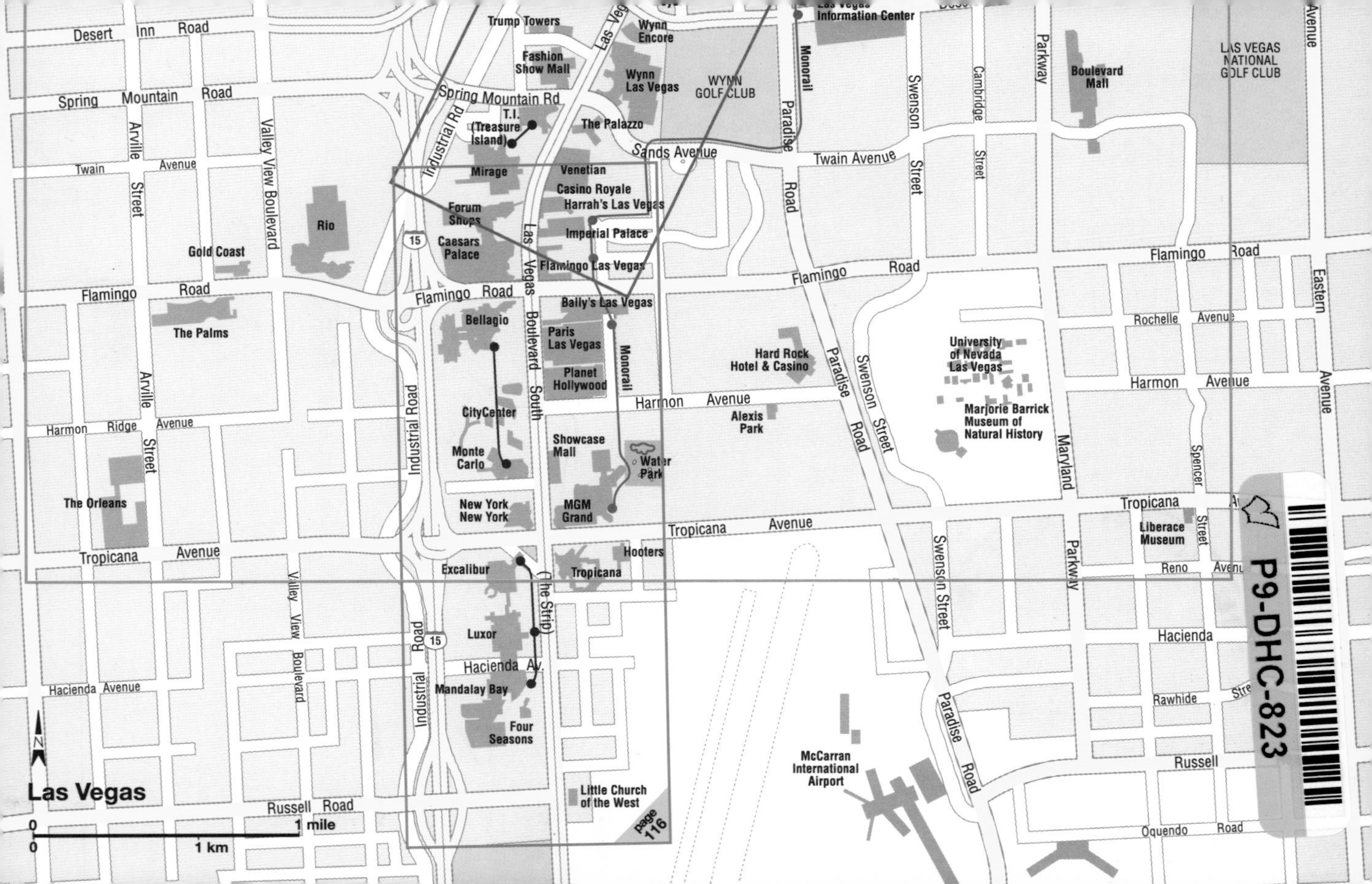

Las Vegas
Desert Inn Road
Trump Towers
Fashion Show Mall
Wynn Encore
Wynn Las Vegas
Wynn Golf Club
Las Vegas Information Center
Monorail
Las Vegas National Golf Club
Boulevard Mall
Spring Mountain Road
Spring Mountain Rd
Industrial Rd
T.I. (Treasure Island)
The Palazzo
Sands Avenue
Twain Avenue
Paradise Road
Swenson Street
Cambridge Street
Maryland Parkway
Eastern Avenue
Arville Street
Valley View Boulevard
Mirage
Venetian
Casino Royale
Harrah's Las Vegas
Imperial Palace
Flamingo Las Vegas
Forum Shops
Caesars Palace
15
Rio
Gold Coast
Flamingo Road
The Palms
Bellagio
Bally's Las Vegas
Paris Las Vegas
Planet Hollywood
Las Vegas Boulevard South
Hard Rock Hotel & Casino
University of Nevada Las Vegas
Marjorie Barrick Museum of Natural History
Rochelle Avenue
Harmon Avenue
Alexis Park
Harmon Ridge Avenue
Industrial Road
CityCenter
Monte Carlo
Showcase Mall
Water Park
MGM Grand
New York New York
The Orleans
Tropicana Avenue
Spencer Street
Liberace Museum
Reno Avenue
Excalibur
(The Strip)
Tropicana
Hooters
Luxor
Hacienda Av.
Hacienda Avenue
Hacienda
Mandalay Bay
Four Seasons
Rawhide Street
Russell Road
McCarran International Airport
Little Church of the West
page 116
Oquendo Road
0
1 mile
1 km
N
P9-DHC-823

INSIGHT GUIDES

LAS VEGAS

Discovery
CHANNEL

INSIGHT GUIDES

LAS VEGAS

Project Editor
Martha Ellen Zenfell
Picture Manager
Steven Lawrence
Art Editor
Ian Spick
Cartography Editor
Zoë Goodwin
Production
Kenneth Chan
Series Editor
Dorothy Stannard

Distribution

United States
Langenscheidt Publishers, Inc.
36–36 33rd Street 4th Floor
Long Island City, NY 11106
Fax: (1) 718 784-0640
UK & Ireland
GeoCenter International Ltd
Meridian House, Churchill Way West,
Basingstoke, Hampshire, RG21 6YR
Tel: (44) 1256 817987
Fax: (44) 1256 817988
Australia
Universal Publishers
1 Waterloo Road
Macquarie Park, NSW 2113
Fax: (61) 2 9888 9074
New Zealand
Hema Maps New Zealand Ltd (HNZ)
Unit 2, 10 Cryers Road
East Tamaki, Auckland 2013
Tel: (64) 9 273 6459
Fax: (64) 9 273 6479
Worldwide
Apa Publications GmbH & Co. Verlag KG (Singapore branch)
38 Joo Koon Road, Singapore 628990
Tel: (65) 6865 1600.
Fax: (65) 6861 6438

Printing

Insight Print Services (Pte) Ltd
38 Joo Koon Road, Singapore 628990
Tel: (65) 6865 1600.
Fax: (65) 6861 6438

First Edition 2003
Second Edition 2004
Third Edition 2009

www.insightguides.com
In North America:
www.insighttravelguides.com

ABOUT THIS BOOK

What makes an Insight Guide different? Since our first book pioneered the use of full-color photography used creatively in travel guides in 1970, we have aimed to provide not only reliable information but also the key to a real understanding of a destination and its people.

Now, when the internet can supply inexhaustible (but not always reliable) facts, our books marry text and pictures to provide that more elusive quality: knowledge. To achieve this, they rely on the authority of locally based writers and photographers.

This book turns the spotlight on a city that not only never stops, but lures people to visit again and again, in the hope that their wildest dreams just might come true. They probably won't, but Vegas is built on illusion, and that's a magic spell no one wants to break. Part fantasyland, part DisneyWorld for adults, there's also a hard-working heart behind the glitz and the glamour. *Insight Guide: Las Vegas* covers all this, and more, with an edge and an attitude worthy of the city itself.

CONTACTING THE EDITORS

We would appreciate it if readers would alert us to errors or outdated information by writing to:

Insight Guides, P.O. Box 7910, London SE1 1WE, England.
Fax: (44) 20 7403-0290.
insight@apaguide.co.uk

THE CONTRIBUTORS TO THIS BOOK

The guiding hand behind this book was that of **Martha Ellen Zenfell**, who has been the project editor of most of Insight Guides' North American titles. One of Zenfell's first tasks was to recruit **Catherine Karnow**, her favorite photographer and visual collaborator on several Insight books.

Zenfell and Karnow ran around the Las Vegas Strip in 110°F (43°C) heat like a pair of dervishes, and got busted for jaywalking when Karnow spied the perfect shot in front of the Monte Carlo Hotel *(see page 133 for the result)*. Karnow was also given unique access to take pictures in the gaming rooms of Bellagio, The Venetian, Caesars Palace, and Paris Las Vegas. Later, Insight flew in hard-working lensmen **Richard Nowitz** and his son **Abe Nowitz** to document America's best-known playground for adults.

Meanwhile, **Gina Cunningham** of the Las Vegas Convention and Visitors Authority smoothed the way for Zenfell to go through what seemed like hundreds of boxes of archive pictures to illustrate the history section, selecting images that for the most part have rarely been published.

At the same time, principal writer **John Wilcock**, who has worked on many Insight projects, was pounding away on the keyboard. Little of city life escaped his scrutiny. **David Whelan**, too, proved a dab hand at the typewriter, while polishing his techniques at the tables.

Other articles were penned by **Mike** and **Linda Donahue**, who live just outside Valley of Fire State Park, and **Richard Harris**, author of several books on Sin City. **Sylvia Suddes** proofread the guide, **Helen Peters** compiled the index, and **Mary Pickles** fine-tuned the layout.

THE GUIDE AT A GLANCE

The book is carefully structured both to convey an understanding of the city and its culture and to guide readers through its attractions and activities:

◆ The Best Of section at the front of the book helps you to prioritize. The first spread contains all the Top Sights, while Editor's Choice details unique experiences, the best chefs or other recommendations.

◆ To understand Las Vegas, you need to know something of its past. Sin City's history and culture are described in authoritative essays written by specialists in their fields who have lived in and documented the city for many years.

◆ The Places section details all the attractions worth seeing. The main places of interest are coordinated by number with the maps.

◆ A list of recommended restaurants is printed at the end of each chapter.

◆ Photographs throughout the book are chosen not only to illustrate geography and buildings, but also to convey the moods of the city and the life of its people.

◆ The Travel Tips section includes all the practical information you will need, divided into five key sections: transportation, accommodations, shopping, activities (including nightlife, shows and sports), and an A–Z of practical tips. Information may be located quickly by using the index on the back cover flap of the book.

◆ A detailed street atlas is included at the back of the book, complete with a full index, on which you will find all the restaurants and hotels plotted for your convenience.

PLACES AND SIGHTS

Color-coding at the top of every page makes it easy to find each neighborhood in the book. These are coordinated by specific area on the orientation map on page 110.

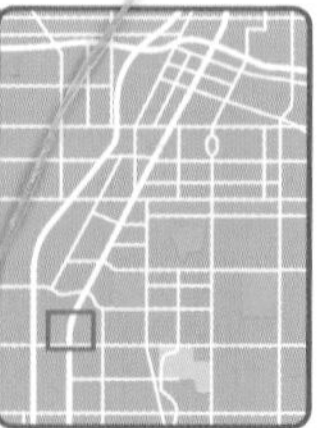

A locator map pinpoints the specific area covered in each chapter. The page reference at the top indicates where to find a detailed map of the area highlighted in red.

Margin tips provide extra little snippets of information, whether it's a practical tip, a whimsical quote, an historical fact or advice on shopping and eating.

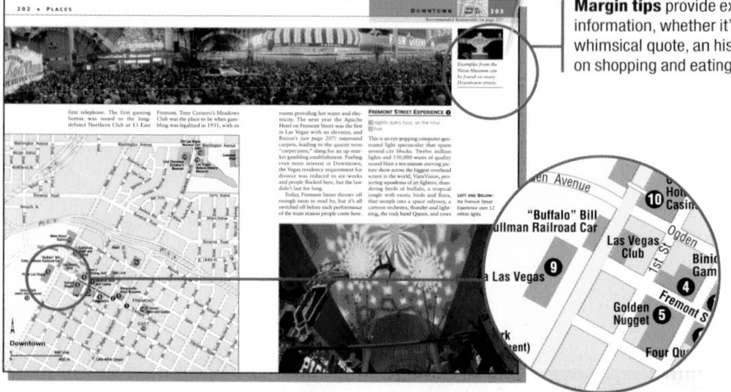

A four-color map provides a bird's-eye view of the area covered in the chapter, with the main attractions coordinated by number with the main text.

PHOTO FEATURES

Photo features provide magazine-style visual coverage of some of Las Vegas's major attractions. Topics covered include Cirque du Soleil, Shopping, Nightlife, and the 18b Arts District.

RESTAURANT LISTINGS

Restaurant listings feature the best establishments within each area, giving the address, phone number, opening times and price category followed by a useful review. The grid reference refers to the atlas at the back of the book.

Binion's Ranch Steakhouse
Binion's Gambling Hall
702-382-1600 D daily **$$$** [p278, B2]
Casino owner and rancher Benny Binion, who dominated the downtown

TRAVEL TIPS

Sightseeing

Limousines

Cruising the Las Vegas Strip in a limousine is an exciting way to see the sights. As with taxis, the limousine service in Las Vegas is strictly regulated. However, limousines are not metered. The cost is agreed at the time of rental.
A Luxury Limo Referral Service. Tel: 702-737-8899.
Ambassador Limousine. Tel: 702-362-6200.

Advice-packed Travel Tips provide all the practical knowledge you'll need before and during your trip: how to get there, getting around, where to stay and what to do. The A–Z section is a handy summary of practical information, arranged alphabetically.

Contents

Best of Las Vegas

Top Sights 8
Bellagio **144**
Caesars Palace **149**
Cirque du Soleil **72**
Fashion Show Mall **169**
Fremont Street Experience . . . **203**
Grand Canal Shoppes **168**
Paris Las Vegas **140**
Stratosphere Tower **183**
The Venetian **167**
Wynn Las Vegas **173**

Editor's Choice 10

Introduction

Guide at a Glance...................... **4**
A Delirious Desert City **21**
Viva Las Vegas **23**

History

Decisive Dates........................ **28**
The Making of Las Vegas.......... **33**
Players, Desert Palaces, and the Rat Pack.................. **43**
Modern Las Vegas **55**

Features

Behind the Spectacle **65**
Dicing With Lady Luck **75**
Vegas in the Movies **86**
Going to the Chapel **90**
Spectacular Sports **95**

Insights

Mini Features:
How to Win **84**
Pawn Shops **206**
What Price Power? **154**
Grand Canyon West **239**

Photo Features:
Cirque du Soleil....................... **72**
Shopping............................. **100**
Nightlife **162**
18b Arts District **198**

Places

Orientation **109**
- Mandalay Bay to the Tropicana **115**
- New York New York to CityCenter **127**
- Planet Hollywood to Bellagio **137**
- Caesars Palace to Casino Royale **149**
- Mirage to Fashion Show Mall **165**
- Wynn Las Vegas to Stratosphere Tower **173**
- Beyond the Strip **187**
- Downtown **201**
- Red Rock Canyon Loop **221**
- North of Las Vegas **227**
- Henderson and Boulder City **233**
- Lake Mead and Hoover Dam **241**

Restaurants

- Mandalay Bay to the Tropicana **125**
- New York New York to CityCenter **135**
- Planet Hollywood to Bellagio **147**
- Caesars Palace to Casino Royale **161**
- Mirage to Fashion Show Mall **171**
- Wynn Las Vegas to Stratosphere Tower **185**
- Beyond the Strip **197**
- Downtown **217**

Travel Tips

TRANSPORTATION

Getting There **248**
Getting Around **248**
Public Transportation **249**
Car Rental **250**

ACCOMMODATIONS

Where to Stay **251**
What to Know **251**
Booking a Room **251**
The Strip **252**
Downtown **253**
Beyond the Strip **255**
Beyond Las Vegas **257**

SHOPPING

Best Buys **258**
Shopping Malls **258**
Resort Shopping **259**
Clothes Chart **260**
Specialist Shops **260**
Art Galleries **261**

ACTIVITIES

Nightlife **262**
Comedy **262**
Headliners **262**
Tickets Online **262**
Live Entertainment **263**
Nightclubs **263**
Cocktail Lounges **264**
Tribute Shows **264**
Sport **264**
Camping and Hiking **266**

A–Z of PRACTICAL INFORMATION

268

Maps

Las Vegas **front flap** and **112**

Orientation map **110–11**

Map Legend **273**

Street Atlas, Restaurants and Accommodations Atlas **274**

Southern Strip **116**
Northern Strip **166**
Beyond the Strip **188**
Downtown **202**
Excursions **222**
Las Vegas and the Desert **back flap**

The Best of Las Vegas: Top Sights

At a glance, everything you can't afford to miss in Glitter City, from the soaring Stratosphere Tower and the neon dazzle of the Fremont Street Experience to sumptuous resorts and acrobatic, sensuous circuses

▷ **Bellagio**
This lavish resort has fountains that dance to music several times a night. *See page 144.*

▷ **Stratosphere Tower**
With thrilling rides and dazzling views, on a clear day you can see as far as Arizona and California from here. *See page 183.*

◁ **Wynn Las Vegas**
A man-made mountain and an award-winning golf course make the Wynn a luxurious oasis in the desert. There's elegant dining, too. *See page 173.*

▷ **The Venetian**
With its Campanile Bell Tower, Doges Palace, frescoed celings and Piazza San Marco, this resort really does feel like Venice. *See page 167.*

△ **Fremont Street Experience**
Twelve million lights are projected onto the largest overhead screen in the world. *See page 203.*

▽ **Cirque du Soleil**
Six resident shows of unique character enthrall Vegas audiences. *See page 72.*

▷ **Fashion Show Mall**
With 250 stores, a to-die-for location on the Strip, and fashion shows most weekends, this is a place to spend time and money. *See page 169.*

▽ **Caesars Palace**
One of the original old-school resorts, Caesars still feels up to the minute. *See page 149.*

▷ **Grand Canal Shoppes**
Performers and gondoliers make shopping here a grand experience. *See page 100.*

▷ **Paris Las Vegas**
Oo-la-la! Paris has scaled-down models of the Eiffel Tower, the Arc de Triomphe, great food and good shopping. *See page 140.*

The Best of Las Vegas: Editor's Choice

Lions, pyrotechnics, and a roller coaster are among the indoor spectacles. Outside are sea battles, a volcano, and a Sphinx. Here are our must-see attractions of the desert

Best Acts and Spectacles

Our choice of the dazzling highlights from this place of fantasy and extremes. Be sure to see or experience:

- Cirque du Soleil's astonishing **O show** *(see pages 72–3)* is in a purpose-built theater, with lake, at Bellagio.
- The **Colosseum** entertainment venue at Caesars Palace *(see page 152)* was built for Celine Dion's show, and refined by Elton John. Now Cher and Bette Midler take their turn on the spectacular stage.
- **Dale Chihuly's** 50-foot (15-meter) high chandelier of stained glass over Bellagio's lobby *(see page 144)*.
- **Acrobats** hang from the rafters day and night at Circus Circus *(see page 178)*.
- The pine-filled, man-made **mountain** and nearby **lake** in the desert at Wynn Las Vegas *(see page 173)*.
- A glittering galaxy of super-star turns at the Imperial's **Legends in Concert** show *(see page 157)*.
- The **Carnival World Buffet**, at the Rio *(see page 197)*, is consistently rated by locals as the best of Vegas's famous serve-it-yourself feasts.
- Stone-faced and slow-eyed heavyweights square up for big money at the **World Series of Poker**, which began at Binion's *(see page 207)* and now plays in one of the casinos owned by Harrah's *(see page 158)*.
- Go for blinding glitter and major bling at the **Liberace Museum** *(see page 190)*. You may need sunglasses.
- **In-pool blackjack** is the name of the game at the fun Tropicana *(see page 123)*.
- With more magic in Vegas than you can wave a wand at, **Penn & Teller's** show *(see page 163)* at the Rio is among the best.
- Tiger Woods is a regular at **Rio Secco** *(see pages 98, 265)*, one of the world's premier golf resorts.
- The giant pyramid and the enigmatic 100-foot (30-meter) Sphinx of **Luxor** *(see page 119)* cannot fail to impress.

- **First Fridays** in the trendy 18b Arts District *(see pages 198–9)* is the place to see and make the scene.
- The **Hoover Dam** *(see page 244)* is one of the engineering marvels of the USA.
- The **Red Rock Canyon Loop** *(see page 221)* is a stunning drive through the desert; try to be there at sunset to watch the rocks change colors.
- Walk the sky at **Grand Canyon West** *(see page 239)*, a glass walkway with breathtaking views.

BELOW: some of the bright lights and biggest spectacles of the most exciting city in the US.

ONLY IN VEGAS CAN YOU...

- **Walk** on a Picasso. Claude Picasso, son of the artist, designed the carpets for a fine restaurant in Bellagio *(see page 147)*.
- **Feel** rain in the desert at the Palms Rain Las Vegas nightclub *(see page 194)*.
- **Stand** by a curbside volcano as it erupts, four times every hour *(see pages 165, 167)*.
- **Watch** a perfect dawn and splendid sunset – indoors; every hour at the Forum Shops *(see page 152)*.
- **See** the world's biggest golden nugget at the Golden Nugget casino, Downtown *(see page 208)*.
- **Ogle** a double-sized David. The statue of David at Caesars *(see page 149)* is twice the size of Michelangelo's original sculpture.
- **Marry** in the place that Britney Spears wed Jason Alexander, in the Little White Chapel *(see page 91)*. Hopefully, though, you'll stay together a bit longer.
- **Plight** your troth on a bungee jump, in a drive-thru chapel, in the back of a limo with hot tub, or over the Grand Canyon *(see page 90)*.

GAMBLING TERMS

Comp: complimentary, or free of charge.
Drop box: a box below a casino game table where dealers deposit paper money through a slot on top of the table.
Eye in the sky: mirrors or concealed video cameras used to monitor table games (dealers and gamblers) so as to prevent cheating.
Pit boss: the person overseeing table games from behind the dealer.
Shoe: the small box on the gaming table from which poker cards are dealt.
Shooter: the player rolling the dice at a craps game.
Toke: a tip or gratuity.
Whale or **high roller:** a customer with the bankroll to bet large sums of money. Whales may arrive in Vegas by private jet courtesy of the casino, and be given comp food and suites.

ABOVE: Caesars Palace's Garden of the Gods pool area has marble statues, secluded areas, and a distinct aura of sybaritic luxury.

BEST SPAS AND POOLS

- The huge **Canyon Ranch SpaClub** at The Venetian *(see page 167)* is one of the largest spas in the US. With gorgeous roof-top pools, the spa offers over 30 types of massage, and a variety of treatments.
- **Spa Bellagio**, at Bellagio *(see page 144)* offers hydrotherapy treatments and fine waxing. Massages include aromatherapy and tandem.
- **The Spa** at the Four Seasons *(see page 118)* has 16 treatment rooms, a hydrotone capsule and eucalyptus steam, Balinese and Javanese body rituals, facials and massages.
- **Wet Republic** at the MGM Grand *(see page 129)* has the only saltwater pools on the Strip.
- **Bellagio's** pools, set among gardens of vines, offer cabanas with a dressing area, lounge chairs, TV, phone, air mister and a stocked fridge.
- **Caesars'** Garden of the Gods pool area *(see page 150)* has marble statues, shrubs and umbrellas; three pools and two outdoor whirlpool spas.
- **The Hard Rock** *(see page 187)* has a trendy beach club, with wave pools and underwater music. Beach parties here are wild.

CELEBRITY CHEFS

More than 50 renowned restaurateurs are enhancing their fame in Sin City. Here are a few:

- **Alessandro Stratta** at Alex, Wynn Las Vegas has been awarded a 5-star rating by the Mobil Travel Guide.
- **Joel Robuchon** at the Mansion, MGM Grand, is another recent 5-star winner.
- **Emeril Lagasse** is at Delmonico's in The Venetian, and at his own New Orleans Fish House at the MGM Grand.
- **Wolfgang Puck,** the first of Vegas's star stirrers, now operates six establishments in Glitter City.
- **Charlie Palmer** transplanted the chic Aureole from NYC to the Mandalay Bay, and opened Charlie Palmer Steak at the Four Seasons.
- **Nobuyuki Matsushia** prepares world-famous sushi at Nobu in the Hard Rock.
- Steve Wynn lured **Julian Serrano** to serve food among the Cubist originals and preside over Picasso at Bellagio.
- **Jean-Georges Vongerichten** cooks beautifully at Prime in Bellagio.
- **André Rochat** at André's Downtown, has been consistently voted the best in Las Vegas since 1980.

ABOVE: thrills and cheers at New York New York.
LEFT: celebrity chef Wolfgang Puck.

THRILL RIDES

- The Stratosphere Tower hosts three of the world's highest rides by erecting them on the tower's landmark needle:
- **Big Shot** catapults riders at high speed to the top of the tower's mast, 1,000 feet above ground.
- **X Scream** dangles frightened guests in the air more than 800 feet above ground.
- **Insanity** spins dizzy riders around at the force of 3Gs.
- **Manhattan Express** at New York NewYork: as well as the usual flips and loops, this roller coaster twists and spins dizzyingly around the replicated towers of Manhattan.
- **Canyon Blaster** at Circus Circus gives a 60-foot drop, a spiral spin around a mountain and three upside-down spins as it whips riders around and up to 45 miles per hour. All of this takes place indoors.

VEGAS FOR FAMILIES

- **Circus Circus** *(see page 178)*. Children under 16 stay for free, and cribs are available. The Adventure-Dome and a children's playground are on the premises, too.
- Kids under 12 also stay free at the **MGM Grand** *(see page 129)*, where admission to the Lion's Habitat is free.
- **The Sahara** *(see page 181)*. The NASCAR Café is inside the resort, making this a good place to stay with older children, especially teenagers.
- The **Stratosphere Tower** *(see page 183)* lets children under 10 stay free, and also offers cribs. Three of Vegas's best thrill rides are at the top.
- **Excalibur** *(see page 121)* has many kids' activities, and under 12s stay here free.

VEGAS FOR FREE

- The **sea battle** at T.I. *(see page 169)* is a roadside engagement between scantily clad Sirens and a crew of renegade pirates. The sea battle takes place several times each evening.
- The **Conservatory at Bellagio** *(see page 146)* showcases lilies, orchids, ferns and rare tropical flowers around water features that seem impossible in the desert. Seasonal themes, too.
- At **Ethel M. Chocolates** *(see page 233)*, around a ton and a half of these local chocolates are produced on each employee's shift. On the way to Henderson.
- **Lion Habitat** at MGM Grand *(see page 130)*. The home of the descendants of Metro, MGM studio's signature lion. Walk underneath a glass roof and watch them prowl or sleep.
- **M&M's World** *(see page 132)* in the Showcase Mall has four floors of interactive exhibits, souvenirs, and a candy store to make your eyes pop out.
- The fine **Marjorie Barrick Museum** *(see page 189)* is a natural history museum with live lizards, exhibits, and in the back, the Xeric Garden, with cacti and a bird-watching platform.

ABOVE: sea battles, pirate ships, and sexy Sirens are all part of a night's work at the free spectacle in front of Treasure Island (T.I.).

THEMED DINING

- **ESPN Zone Sports Bar** in New York New York *(see page 128)* offers diners 150 screens featuring nothing but sport.
- **Harley Davidson Café** on the Strip has around 15 custom-made motorcycles including Elvis Presley's. As the latest Harleys pass by on a conveyor belt, eat tasty American road food.
- **House of Blues**, Mandalay Bay *(see page 125)* is a Southern and blues-themed restaurant offering regional cuisine including Creole and Cajun staples. A Sunday gospel feature has live music and a country-style buffet brunch.
- **NASCAR Café** at the Sahara, *(see page 182)*. This two-level restaurant features NASCAR stock cars, and huge screens showing the best races. Drag-race mechandise is on offer, along with American food.
- **Roundtable Buffet** and the **Sherwood Forest Café,** Excalibur *(see page 121)* have Merrie Old England themes and "all you can feast."

MONEY-SAVING TIPS

Free gaming lessons Whether you're new or just want to brush up on some skills, casinos will teach you for free. At Mandalay Bay they've got poker covered, while Imperial Palace offers classes in blackjack, craps and roulette.

Avoid gas stations on the Strip Head east or west for cheaper gas.

Lunch it Lunchtime buffets can be identical to the evening's offerings, but will cost you much less.

Book ahead Reserving tours in advance, say online, saves money.

Player's Card Sign up for one at every casino to get food discounts, etc.

Website specials Check out the Tourist Board's Special Offers pages for up-to-the-minute deals: www.visitlasvegas.com/vegas/special-offers

Discount coupons Hunt out these coupons, offering reductions on shows and attractions, in your hotel lobby or make enquiries with the desk clerk.

EXCALIBUR

NEW YORK
HOTEL &
JVC

Las Vegas and the Desert
0
20 miles
0
20 km
N
Reno
Nellis Air Force Bombing and Gunnery Range
Rhyolite Ghost Town
Beatty
Nevada Test Site
Amargosa Desert
Amargosa Valley
Mercury
Stovepipe Wells
Panamint Range
Amargosa Range
Furnace Creek
Ash Meadow National Wildlife Refuge
8218
Death Valley National Park
Skidoo
Devil's Hole (Death Valley National Monument)
8756
Death Valley Junction
Ash Meadows Rancho
Death Valley
-282
Badwater
Dante's View
Black Mts
Pahrump
Wildrose Canyon
11049
Telescope Peak
Ballarat
Shoshone
Tecopa
Ashford Mill
Trona
Trona Pinnacles
Searles Lake
Westend
Kingston Pk 7323
Las Vegas
Lake Mead National Recreation Area
Lake Mead
0
10 miles
0
10 km
Pearce Ferry
Colorado
Toll Booth
Black Mountains
Henderson
Hoover Dam
Temple Bar
Skywalk
Boulder City
Grand Canyon West
Nevada
Eldorado Mnts
Colorado
Black Mtns
White Hills
Grand Wash Cliffs
Hualapai Indian Reserve
Arizona
Pierce Ferry Road
Red Lake
Lake Mead National Recreation Area
Dolan Springs
California
Mojave
Baker
Soda Lake
Zzyzx

RESTAURANTS

American

Aureole 125
Bradley Ogden 161
The Burger Bar 125
Charlie Palmer Steak 125
Company 125
Dick's Last Resort 125
Harley-Davidson Café 135
I Love This Bar and Grill 161
Margaritaville 161
Monte Carlo Brew Pub 135
NASCAR Café 182, **185**
Roxy's Diner 185
Spago 161
Stripburger 171
Table 10 171
THE Steak House 185
Top of the World 185
Triple 7 Restaurant and Brewery 217
Wolfgang Puck Bar and Grill 135

Asian

Ah Sin 147
Fusia 125
Lillie's Noodle House 217
Red 8 185

Barbecue

Tony Roma's 217

Brazilian

Pampas Churrascaria 147

Buffet

Carnival World Buffet 197
Wynn Las Vegas Buffet 185

Cajun

Delmonico Steakhouse 171
Emeril's 135
House of Blues 125

Caribbean

Margaritaville 161

Chinese

Chinois 161
Ming 161

Continental

André's 135

Delicatessen

Shrimp Bar and Deli 217

French

Alex 185
Alizé 197
André's Las Vegas 217
Eiffel Tower Restaurant 147
Joël Robuchon 135
Le Cirque 147
Mon Ami Gabi 147
Pamplemousse 197
Picasso 147

German

Hofbräuhaus 197

International

Cravings 171
DJT 185
Sensi 147
Sushisamba 171

Irish

Nine Fine Fishermen 135

Italian

Battista's Hole in the Wall 197
Chicago Joe's 217
Fiamma Trattoria 135
Onda 171
Osteria del Circo 147
Penazzi 161
Postrio 171
Ristorante Italiano 185
Wolfgang Puck's Trattoria del Lupo 125

Japanese

Benihana Village 197
Hyakumi 161
Koi 147
Pink Taco 197
RA Sushi 171

Mediterranean

Olives 147

Mexican

Blue Agave 197
Diablo's Cantina 135
El Sombrero Café 217

Russian

Red Square 125

Spanish

Café Ba-Ba-Reeba! 171

Steak/Seafood

Bally's Steakhouse 147
Binion's Ranch Steakhouse 217
Blue Agave 197
Golden Steer Steak House 197
House of Lords Steak House 185
Hugo's Cellar 217
Kokomo's 171
Seablue 135
The Steakhouse at Bill's 161

Thai

Lotus of Siam 197

Vietnamese

Pho 171

Silverman, Charles L. 123
Simpson, Weldon 122–3
Sinatra, Frank 45, 57, 67
and the Mob 50–1
and Rat Pack 43, 48–50
wedding 90
Sinatra, Nancy 49
Sirens of T.I. 59, 66, **169**
skiing 227, 267
skydiving 267
Skywalk (Grand Canyon) 239
slot machines 39, 76, 79–81, 207
Slots-A-Fun 181
Smith Center for the Permorming Arts 213
Smith, Harold 39
smoking 271
Snake War 35
Snakes & Dragons 116
Spa Tower 144
Spacey, Kevin 78
spas
Canyon Ranch 167
JW Marriott Las Vegas Resort & Spa (Summerlin) 225
Mandra 139
Qua 151
Red Rock Casino Resort & Spa 225
Wynn Las Vegas 174–5
Spears, Britney 90, 120
specialist shops 260–1
"Speed – The Ride" 182
Sphinx 119
sport 95–9, **264–7**
Caesars Palace 151, 152
Sports Books 82, **85**, 120–1
Spring Mountain Ranch 222–3
Star Trek: The Experience 88, 192
Stardust Hotel 45, 47, 61, **180**
Statue of Liberty 127
Stewart, Helen 36, 37
Stocker, Harold 69
Stocker, Mayme 37
Stomp Out Loud 138
Stone, Sharon 89
Stratosphere Tower 58, **183–4**, 253
Street of Dreams 133, 260
Streisand, Barbra 51
strikes 59
The Strip
accommodations 252–3
"Stripping" 169
Strom, Brian 26
Summerlin 225
Sunset Station Hotel Casino (Henderson) 235, 257
Super Bowl 82, 96
swimming pools
Garden of the Gods 150
Hard Rock Hotel 188
Mandalay Bay 115
Swingers 87

T

Tabbish, Rick 56
tax 271
taxis 249
telephone numbers 272
television 270
tennis 99, 151, 266
Texas Hold 'em 85
theater 26
Theater Paris Las Vegas 141
Theater for the Performing Arts at Planet Hollywood 26, 138
THEhotel 118–19
Thomas & Mack Center 190
Thornton, Billy Bob 91
Thunder from Down Under 122
T.I. (Treasure Island) 169, 253
tickets, for shows 193, 262
tigers 66, 165–6
time zones 271
Times Square 27–8
tipping 272
Tobin, Phil 38
Toiyabe National Forest 228
tour operators 250
tourist information 272
Tournament of Kings 122
Tower Shops 184
Tower Suites 174
Town Square 120, 121
Transport Workers Union 143
transportation 248–50
travelers' checks 271
Treasure Island *see* **T.I.**
Trevi Fountain 152
tribute shows 132, 264
trolleys 249
Tropicana 123–4, 253
Truman, Harry 44
Trump International Hotel and Tower 60, **170**, 253
Tyson, Mike 96

U

UFOs 230
Union Park 212–13
University of Nevada 189
Performing Arts Center 26
Uston, Ken 78

V

V Bar 168
V Theater 139
Valley of Fire State Park 230–1, 244
Venetian 59, 60, **167–9**, 253
Venezia Tower 168
Versailles Theater 176
Very Bad Things 87
Via Bellagio 145, 260
video poker 81
Villamor, Mike 34
Viva Las Vegas 86, 182
Volcano (Mirage) 59, 70, 165, 167
Vongerichten, Jean-Georges 146
VooDoo Lounge 194–5, 263

W

Ward, Kenric F. 34
Warner, Jack 49–50
Water Reclamation Facility (Henderson) 236
water-skiing 267
Wayne, John 157
weddings 90–4
weights and measures 272
WET Design 70, 145
What Happens in Vegas 87
The Who 189
wildlife 66
Duck Creek Trail 242
Flamingo Garden 155, **156**
Las Vegas Natural History Museum 215–16
Las Vegas Wash 242
Lion Habitat 130
Pahranagat National Wildlife Refuge 230
Shark Reef 66, **115–16**
Siegfried & Roy's Secret Garden & Dolphin Habitat 166–7
Snakes & Dragons 116
tigers 66, 165–6
Water Reclamation Facility (Henderson) 236
Wilkerson, W.R. 40
Williams, Don 55
wine 168
Woods, Tiger 98
World of Coca-Cola 132
World Market Center 213
World Series of Poker 159, 208
Wynn Art Collection 174
Wynn Las Vegas 58, 60, **173–5**, 253
Wynn, Steve 57–8, 208–9
Bellagio 58, 65
Wynn's Picasso 199

X

X Scream 184
Xeric Garden 190

Y

Young, Brigham 35, 214
Young Scientists Center 216
Yucca Flat 229
Yucca Mountain 61, **229**

Z

Zumanity 59, 73, **128–9**

COIN WINNERS
2
COIN WINNERS
400
250
200
150
80
1,000
500

BALLYS
BALLYS

A DELIRIOUS DESERT CITY

Chancers, dreamers, gangsters, and entrepreneurs – all have been lured across the scorching desert to try their luck at games of chance

Desert springs watered Las Vegas, and the hot-house canopy of arid isolation nourished the town's primary business, which was best conducted away from the prying eyes of the outside world. Since 1920, when Mayme Stocker opened the first casino, chancers and gangsters have been lured across the desert to try their luck at games of chance.

The lights, the shows, the fortunes turning on the roll of a die – Las Vegas is a world of neon fantasy and eye-popping architectural illusion. Enticements include an indoor parody of the ancient wonders of Egypt, hourly sea-battles, and surreal reincarnations of Venice and Paris. Lush and lavish pools surrounded by Italian gardens, and museums with treasures from the ancient and modern world provide, among other things, a breeding colony for a rare human sub-species – the Elvi, otherwise known as the people earning a living impersonating the Mississippi rock 'n' roller.

The character of modern Las Vegas has been most obviously shaped by three groups: the casino visionaries, a handful of world-class singers, and the arcane masters of magic and illusion. All of them brought innovations that shaped the way Vegas has evolved by drawing their own crowds of devotees from across the States and beyond.

The gaming entrepreneur who reinvented Vegas hospitality was Jay Sarno. His Caesars Palace was the first of the casinos designed as an integrated, themed fantasy. From the world of entertainment, Frank Sinatra set the tempo, singing songs for swinging lovers in Las Vegas lounges. And then there's magic. Magic is such an integral part of Vegas that no fewer than four museums here are dedicated to the art. The city is itself a vast showcase of sleight-of-hand, and it's no coincidence that the magicians' most basic, intimate illusions often involve the manipulation of playing cards, only the throw of a die away from the gaming tables.

For although 78 percent of visitors claim to be attracted to Sin City by something other than gambling, somehow 84 percent of people find time to play the tables or slots during their stay, contributing an average of $555 each to the casinos' coffers. ❑

PRECEDING PAGES: the Vegas skyline inspires amateur photographers day and night; the Liberace Museum; she's a winner!
LEFT: the fountains of Bellagio and Paris Las Vegas.

HOT PENNY SLOTS
CASH BACK COMPS
VIVA VISION
Straight Up
Country
2007

VIVA LAS VEGAS

The city is built on illusion and dreams, on fortune and fun-filled fantasy. The people who live and work here buy into these dreams just as much as visitors

Las Vegas is truly a 24-hour city. Most modern cities make that claim, but it is almost impossible to get served a decent meal at 4am in any of them. Here, night and day really are almost indistinguishable. At any hour of the day or night you may need to and you can, without difficulty: buy clothes and jewelry, get married, hire an attorney, get divorced, or engage an Elvis impersonator.

Just ordinary stars

In other ways Vegas is a city just like any other – ordinary folks live here and go about their business, albeit with a larger percentage of entertainers and workers in the demimonde of nightlife. The casinos and hotels employ a total of 166,000 Las Vegas residents. For many, Vegas is their last stop – a place to work at that final job before retiring. But it's not only the aging butchers, bakers, or cabinet-makers who will settle in Sin City. For others it seems like a natural home. Musicians, comics, dancers, and other performers who have spent a part of their working lives here develop an affinity with the place.

People come to Vegas for weddings, sports, conventions, vacations – there are scores of reasons to visit Glitter City. The best reason of all? PARTY!

LEFT: New Year's Eve in Fremont Street.
RIGHT: a dream come true – kissing Elvis.

Professional athletes – tennis players, golfers, football, and baseball stars – may also have earned some of their living here, and for many of them, gambling may not be an unfamiliar pastime. Wild-haired Don King and his fellow promoter Bob Arum have chosen to live in this city where boxing plays such a large part. Defeated heavyweight and ex-convict Mike Tyson keeps a home here, too.

World-champion basketball star Shaquille O'Neal has a home reputedly just five minutes from the Strip. The multiple Grand-Slam winner Andre Agassi, still ranked as a world-class tennis player, enjoys family life here with wife Steffi Graf and their two children. Agassi was born in Las Vegas, and founded a school for children with special needs in his hometown.

Basketball star Greg Anthony, who got his start playing on the Las Vegas campus of the University of Nevada, played for several professional teams in his career, and is now a respected sports broadcaster. He maintains a home locally, as does Las Vegas-born Marty Cordova, well-known as a left fielder for the Baltimore Orioles. Former Boston Red Sox second baseman Marty Barrett ended his career with the San Diego Padres, and came back to support local youth baseball players and provide TV commentary for the Las Vegas 51s. Kevin Elster settled here after his career with the New York Mets, and former city councilman Frank Hawkins was a professional football player with the Oakland Raiders.

Stars of stage and screen

Stage and television stars who have set up home in Las Vegas include the former teen heart throb David Cassidy (the brains and money behind the smash hit *The Rat Pack is Back*), actor and artist Tony Curtis, and singers La Toya Jackson, Gladys Knight, Steve Lawrence and Eydie Gorme, Tony Orlando, and Sheena Easton. Comics Rita Rudner,

HIGH-SEASON DAYS AND HOLIDAYS

Las Vegas is high on most people's lists of places to celebrate, and every three-day weekend, spring break, Columbus Day, Christmas, New Year's Eve, and Valentine's Day, Vegas hotel rooms are in their highest of high-season demand. Every imaginable occasion is celebrated here. Martin Luther King, Jr's birthday is marked with a parade, marching bands, floats, and an awards ceremony. Cinco de Mayo and the Day of the Dead both have carnival parades, mariachis, marches, and mole. Come for the Fourth of July and you'll see skyfuls of the brashest, most exuberant fireworks displays anywhere. For Halloween, bring a very special costume (or rent one locally), especially if you plan to join an adult-themed party like the Fetish and Fantasy Halloween Ball at the Sports Center. And when it comes to sports, January's Superbowl weekend is one of the biggest of the year in Vegas, and the atmosphere in the Sports Books at every casino is electric. Come in May or June for the World Series of Poker, come for the most memorable New Year's Eve ever. Just come. Come soon and celebrate.

David Brenner, Rich Little, and Jerry Lewis have settled in the Las Vegas Valley, as has the venerable bluesman BB King.

Performers Debbie Reynolds and Wayne Newton have turned their hands to businesses here, much like magicians Lance Burton, Penn & Teller, and Siegfried & Roy. Elton John, Bette Midler, Cher, and Barry Manilow live in the area while performing their long-running shows on the Strip, following a trend started by Celine Dion, who took a house on Lake Las Vegas while starring in her ground-breaking show at Caesars Palace's Colosseum.

Celebrity draws

"Trying to identify all the celebrities who live here is difficult," said Sonya Padgett, who compiled a list for the *Review-Journal*. "Many prefer to keep a low profile… (and) while we think our hospitality and favorable weather are selling points, it's just as likely celebrities decide to move to southern Nevada for the tax advantages."

One disadvantage, however, might be the commuting problems. Nevertheless, it's not every town where Meals on Wheels might be delivered by a nationally known racing-car driver in his souped-up speedster, which is what happened the day that NASCAR Busch Series driver Larry Foyt kicked off the casino Harrah's sponsorship of the program to feed needy seniors. Often praised for its community outreach, Harrah's donated a refrigerated Meals on Wheels delivery van to the Catholic Charities of Southern Nevada and, through its many casinos in 12 states, is still a national corporate sponsor of the program.

It takes 216,510 bulbs to illuminate the faux Christmas tree that heralds the festive season at Caesars Palace.

Like anywhere else, but maybe for different reasons, people arrive in Las Vegas for a visit and just never leave. The city is also a mantrap. After Alaska – which has a ratio of 107

LEFT: spas, pampering, and to-die-for swimming pools are all part of a modern Vegas visit.

ABOVE: Oscar Goodman, the popular, ebullient mayor (seen here at the Golden Nugget casino), is a champion of downtown Las Vegas.

men to every 100 women, Las Vegas has the second highest man-to-woman ratio, 103.9 men to 100 women. Nationally, there are said to be 143.4 women to every 100 men.

Cultural affairs

Las Vegas revolves around tourism, but there is a rich local social and cultural life, including two active theater companies, concerts, and a winter season by the Las Vegas Philharmonic (a 2008 highlight was a concert with Placido Domingo at Planet Hollywood's Theatre for the Performing Arts.) A community center screens art-house movies as well as staging both jazz and classical concerts.

The Univerity of Nevada's Performing Arts Center hosts ballet, chamber orchestra and jazz concerts. The city itself turned over an old Mormon facility it had been using as a city hall while a new one was built, and the building, renamed the Reed Whipple Center after one of the commissioners who brokered the deal was designated for performance and the arts. "It's rare that a municipality seeks out the arts," said Jody Johnson, who brought a children's theater she started with local playwright Brian Strom, the Rainbow Company, to the Reed. Almost immediately, the troupe was recognized by the Children's Theater Association of America as the best in the US, and many graduates now have successful theater careers.

Local artist Patricia Marchese runs the town's vigorous cultural affairs program. Las Vegas's "Queen of Culture," as a local paper called her, is pleased by the privatization of the arts. "The arts are not going to make it in this town till the casinos get into the business. And now they have. You have top Broadway shows here, Cézanne here, priceless jewels here, all in casinos.

"I would hope that this would turn into an enlightenment that will lead people to greater support of the local arts. Any time people are exposed to high-level arts, it engenders a desire for more," she said.

SHIFTING POPULATION

"In the past few years, Las Vegas's homeless population has doubled to 12,000, but for many, Las Vegas is the American dream come true – affordable housing, no state income tax, and well-paying jobs that don't require much education," ran an *Associated Press* story.

"Only three states have fewer college graduates, but the median household income for the greater Las Vegas area is almost $50,000. Valet car attendants can easily bring in that much. Card dealers on the Strip can make more than that and don't need a high school diploma."

A stripper in a local bar might make $400 on a good night, and one just off the Strip could make almost three times as much.

But locals may be tiring of the caravan of newcomers. In 2008, Marc Furman, president of the Southeast Regional Council of Carpenters, told the *Las Vegas Sun* "There's no point in encouraging more people to come." Mr Furman didn't say how long he'd been resident in Nevada.

Locals live here, too

A few years ago, Syl Cheney-Coker moved to Las Vegas from Sierra Leone with her husband. At first she was frustrated, trying to find the "city." She wrote in *Las Vegas Life* that the initial impression was surreal.

She talked about "the architectural madness," which she said, "sometimes reminds me of bad opera in which the libretto and the music do not harmonize… try to imagine what this place would be like if only more poets, painters, writers and other artists moved in to create the right atmosphere… It is crying out to be an artist area like Soho or the Village in New York. All it needs are the cafés, bookstores, studios, and art galleries."

Having been the fastest-growing city in the US for most of the last decade, even in these uncertain times, Las Vegas is still the fourth most rapidly expanding.

And in fact, they are coming – to an extent. The city has declared a run-down 18-block area between the Strip and Downtown an art-studio zone – the 18b Arts District. But with the exception of the Arts Factory on East Charleston Boulevard (which has around 15 studios), galleries are often closed to the public in the heat of the day. The best time to visit is on the evening of the monthly First Friday, when all the arts centers open their doors, street entertainers duck and jive, and a festive air prevails.

LEFT: music at the Venetian and dining at Paris Las Vegas. **ABOVE:** go for a thrilling ride at the Stratosphere Tower, or admire 1,000 dazzling costumes in the long-running show at Bally's, *Jubilee!*

But the arts still have a way to go, as the city concentrates on what it does best – commerce. After the sale of 1,900 acres (769 hectares) by the US Bureau of Land Management, a further 5,000 homes are projected in the downtown area in North Las Vegas. There has also been a huge increase in development along the Strip since 2005, with over 80 projects completed or about to be completed – most of them upscale and glittering.

City of dreams

Las Vegas is still a fast-growing city of dreams. Barbara Brent, a sociologist at the University of Nevada Las Vegas said that the city "is built on illusion and dreams. Its whole goal to tourists is to sell fantasy. In some ways that spills over into people who see it as a place where they can fulfill things that they couldn't do elsewhere."

Maybe it's the glamor of the 24-hour twilight zone, this town with no sense of time. ❑

DECISIVE DATES

300 BC
The Anasazi tribe are thought to have discovered and inhabited the territory located about 60 miles (96km) north of present-day Las Vegas.

1829
Mexican trader Antonio Armijo's party, probably directed by Paiute or Ute tribesmen, discovers the local region and names it Las Vegas, Spanish for "the meadows," or the fertile plains.

1830
Caravans of traders begin trekking along the Old Spanish Trail through native Paiute land, camping without permission.

1844
Noted explorer John C. Fremont, leading an overland expedition, camps at a site that as a tribute to him years later becomes known as Fremont Street, in downtown Las Vegas.

1848
The US acquires the region by treaty after winning the Mexican War.

1855
Mormons build an adobe fort in what is today downtown Vegas, to protect the mail route from Los Angeles to Utah. They abandon it three years later.

1859
Three white men are killed by Paiutes. An expedition from Fort Tejon, California, kills five Paiutes and leaves bodies hung from the gallows "as a warning."

1864
Nevada is admitted into the Union during the American Civil War. The capital of the new state is not Las Vegas, but Carson City.

1866–68
US troops suppress the Paiutes in the "Snake War." In the end, 1,000 Native Americans are force-marched across the desert to Fort Tejon.

1905
The San Pedro, Los Angeles, and Salt Lake Railroad (later to be known as the Union Pacific) makes an inaugural run, and land lots are auctioned locally.

1908
The first phone wires are erected on Fremont Street, and water lines are added soon after.

1910
In the first of what were to become many policy changes, gambling is outlawed throughout the state of Nevada.

1911
The city of Las Vegas is incorporated. Noted ranch owner Mrs Helen Stewart deeds 10 acres (4 hectares) of her land "for the use of Paiute Indians."

1920
Mayme Stocker opens the first legalized Las Vegas gaming hall, the Northern Club, on Fremont Street in what is now Downtown.

1922
Westside School is built for the children of Old Town, the original town site on Washington Avenue along the railroad tracks.

1923
The Hitching Post wedding chapel is built at 228 Las Vegas Boulevard South.

1926
Western Airlines lands its first commercial flight in Las Vegas.

1928
Herbert Hoover, as secretary of commerce, steers the enactment of the Boulder Canyon Project Act, making way for the Boulder – later Hoover – Dam.

1931
The legislature passes a gambling bill by rancher Phil Tobin to raise taxes to build more public schools. Construction begins on the Hoover Dam.

1935
President Franklin D. Roosevelt presides at the dedication of Hoover Dam.

1941
Tommy Hull builds the influential El Rancho Vegas on land opposite today's Sahara Hotel. El Cortez Hotel opens Downtown.

1942
The Last Frontier Hotel opens, later to be called the New Frontier. The Basic Magnesium plant, employing 3,000 workers, opens at Basic, a community south of today's town of Henderson.

1946
The state levies gaming taxes for the first time. Mobster Benjamin "Bugsy" Siegel, a member of the Meyer Lansky crime organization, opens the Flamingo Hotel. He is murdered six months later, allegedly for "skimming the take."

1949
The *Las Vegas Review-Journal*, incorporating earlier newspapers, is born,

FAR LEFT: petroglyphs discovered northeast of Las Vegas. **MIDDLE LEFT:** the Mormons established a fort in what is now downtown Vegas in 1855. **LEFT:** explorer John C. Fremont. **ABOVE LEFT:** legalized gaming began in 1920. **ABOVE:** Hoover Dam, completed in 1935. **RIGHT:** the Frontier hotel, which operated from 1942 to 2007.

followed the next year by the *Las Vegas Sun*.

1950
The population of Las Vegas reaches 24,624.

1951
Vegas Vic, the huge Downtown neon icon, is erected on Fremont Street.

1952
The Sahara Hotel opens on the Strip, wooing movie stars from Hollywood and making Las Vegas a fashionable destination.

1955
The nine-story Riviera Hotel is the first high rise. Heavyweight champion Joe Louis is co-owner of the Moulin Rouge, but black entertainers must live off the premises. The Gaming Control Board is established.

1959
In an attempt to control gambling, the state legislature creates the Nevada Gaming Commission.

1960
The El Rancho Vegas burns down. Las Vegas's population reaches 64,405.

1966
Howard Hughes arrives to buy casinos and live reclusively in a penthouse on top of the Desert Inn Hotel.

1967
Nevada's state legislature decides to allow publicly traded corporations to obtain gambling licenses, opening up the market.

1970
Las Vegas's population doubles.

1977
The gaming revenues in Clark County – in which the city of Las Vegas is situated – exceed $1 billion.

1989
The Mirage casino and hotel opens with 3,039 rooms for gamblers.

1990
Las Vegas's population doubles again in just a decade to reach 258,295.

1992
The success of Warren Beatty's movie *Bugsy* prompts the Flamingo Hilton to open the Bugsy Celebrity Theater.

1993
The Dunes' owner, Steve Wynn, demolishes Bugsy Siegel's office to make way for a new resort. Treasure Island and the Luxor casinos opened. The MGM Grand opens as the world's biggest resort, with 5,009 guest rooms, 12 restaurants, and a 33-acre (13-hectare) theme park.

1995
Clark County's population tops 1 million. Clark County casino gaming revenues are $5.7 billion – 78 percent of the US total. The Fremont Street Experience opens to woo visitors to the downtown area.

1996
Siegfried & Roy celebrate their 15,000th Las Vegas performance. The Stratosphere Tower opens on the Strip, changing the look of the boulevard. The Sands Hotel is imploded.

1997
New York New York opens, initially welcoming 100,000 visitors a day.

1998
A 66-year-old Las Vegas resident wins $27 million at the Palace Station Hotel Casino. Bellagio opens, billed as the most expensive hotel in the world.

2000
The Venetian Hotel opens. Las Vegas now has 19 of the world's 20 biggest hotels.

2002
Nevada is the fastest-growing state in the nation. The US Government gets approval to ship nuclear waste to a burial site in Yucca Mountain, 100 miles (160km) north of Vegas, (now delayed until 2013.)

2003
Roy of Siegfried & Roy is mauled on stage by one of the magicians' famous tigers. Treasure Island resort rebrands itself as the adult-oriented "T.I."

2004
The monorail is unveiled, running from the MGM Grand to the Sahara. Planet Hollywood makes a successful bid for the Strip's Aladdin Hotel.

2005
Wynn Las Vegas opens.

2007
The Stardust is imploded in March, to make way for Echelon, a "mini-city" of hotels, shops, and entertainment places. The second-oldest casino on the Strip, the Frontier, is imploded later that year.

2008
Major projects are completed, including Trump International and Palazzo, sister property to the Venetian. Work continues on the CityCenter complex – which includes a 4,000-room hotel, a casino, and sculptures by famous artists.

2009–10
CityCenter, Echelon, and the Fountainebleau are scheduled to open.

FAR LEFT: the Sahara attracted Hollywood celebrities. **TOP LEFT:** the only way to travel. **LEFT:** the Luxor opened in 1993. **ABOVE LEFT:** Vegas favorites Siegfried & Roy, until Roy was mauled by one of his tigers in 2003. **ABOVE:** the Stratosphere Tower changed the face of the Strip. **RIGHT:** the first of two Trump hotel-condo towers was completed in 2008.

THE MAKING OF LAS VEGAS

Native Americans had lived in the desert for centuries. Then came the Spanish Trail, the railroad and, with the building of the Hoover Dam – Sin City

Las Vegas – Spanish for "the meadows," or fertile plains – grew around an oasis in the desert, but the valley wasn't always as harsh and arid as it is today. In 1993, construction workers in Nevada uncovered the remains of a Colombian woolly mammoth and the beast, anywhere from 8,000 to 15,000 years old, showed that in prehistoric times the terrain nourished life in relative abundance. Known to the Native Americans, the Las Vegas Valley oasis was hidden from others by the harsh and unforgiving desert.

The semi-nomadic Paiute tribe adapted over centuries to survive the barren terrain by careful husbandry, planting corn and squash in the well-watered areas, timing their return to harvest the crops. Remains at Tule Springs in the northwest of the valley indicate that they also hunted caribou, mammoth, and bison.

Petroglyphs are ancestors of modern writing, carved or etched into rock. They are found all over the world, except for Antarctica, from as long as 12,000 years ago.

Prehistoric

There are traces, too, of the so-called Archaic Indians, a foraging culture of hunters who harvested mesquite and cholla fruit. As early as 300 BC, the Anasazi settled about 60 miles (96km) north of present-day Las Vegas, along the Muddy and Virgin rivers, and were known for basket-making.

LEFT: trapping a woolly mammoth; in 1993 a prehistoric mammoth was discovered in the Nevada desert.
RIGHT: many petroglyphs have been found locally.

The prehistoric Native Americans were hunter-gatherers who collected seeds and pods from cacti, yucca, and agave, and hunted rabbits, coyotes, and rodents in the desert, heading into the mountains after deer and bighorn sheep. Annual expeditions led to still higher elevations to collect pinon nuts.

The first non-native person known to have discovered the springs was a young Mexican scout, Rafael Rivera, who came along the Spanish Trail with the Mexican trader Antonio

Armijo. Rivera was an experienced scout, and in search of water. The exact date of the find is unknown, but he is thought to have left the party around Christmas 1829 and made his momentous discovery soon after. The abundant spring water at Las Vegas eased the rigors for Spanish traders – and hastened the rush west for California gold – but it didn't make the journey much less arduous. For the preceding hundreds, maybe thousands of years, the region had been covered in marshes with vegetation nurtured by the water, but the marsh receded and gave way to desert. Rivers disappeared below the surface, and the once teeming wetlands transformed into an unforgiving baked landscape, though underground water did surface to nourish luxuriant plants and create welcome oases.

The incursions of the pioneers were, of course, disastrous for the native Paiute. Traders and travelers camped without permission at Paiute sites by springs and streams, and by the 1830s, were becoming a menace. They shot the game, and sometimes shot the locals too, and their stock damaged the crops. The Paiutes raided mines, settle-

MORMONS IN THE MODERN ERA

By the 21st century, when nearly one quarter of local jobs were in casinos, Mormons – prized for their integrity – filled top posts. John Marz, vice president for corporate marketing at Mandalay Resorts, said: "People just wouldn't be here without these jobs. For me it came down to 'can you function in the job and still be a good Church member?'"

In his book *Saints in Babylon: Mormons and Las Vegas* Kenric F. Ward said that "While Church leaders remain queasy about gambling – regularly denouncing it as a pernicious pastime and fighting its importation into other states – Latter Day Saints in Nevada have played a major role in regulating the business, and in some cases promoting it." In 1959, Senator Jim Gibson helped create the Nevada Gaming Commission. Don Shaw, who ran the Castaways Hotel casino said, "As long as you're ethical and honest in your dealings, that's what counts." His partner Mike Villamor, who converted to Christianity when he was 21 and married in the Las Vegas Temple, said, "Yes, I've seen people lose their life savings in casinos. I've also seen a man die from overeating in a restaurant."

Still there are hold-outs, including the prominent Marriott Corporation which operates several Vegas hotels – all free of slot machines or spinning wheels, but with a Book of Mormon sitting in most guest rooms.

ments, and stagecoaches. Native Americans attacked the intruders and in 1859, troops mounted a punitive expedition from Fort Tejon, near what is now Los Angeles. The "Snake War" followed from 1866 to 1868, and the Paiutes were finally forced onto a reservation at Fort Tejon.

The US acquired the region after winning the Mexican War in 1848, and seven years later the Mormons arrived. Leader William Bringhurst established a fort with 30 settlers, dispatched by Brigham Young to protect the mail route between Los Angeles and Salt Lake City. Their fruit trees and vegetables failed, and a mining venture at nearby Mount Potosi also failed for lack of water to process the ore.

Mining began in Nevada long before the discovery of the Comstock Lode in 1859. Just a few miles from the adobe pueblos, salt was mined by local inhabitants using stone tools.

LEFT: Mormons preaching in the wilderness, 1853. **ABOVE:** this fort near modern-day downtown Las Vegas was established by the Mormons in 1855.

Mormon settlement

The Mormons' adobe brick fort had stone foundations and thick walls 14ft (4 meters) high and 150ft (46 meters) long. Nails were scarce, so rawhide thongs and wooden pegs were used. The Mormons abandoned it after three years, partly because of raids by native peoples, but more to pre-empt a threat from the Federal government to march on Salt Lake City. The portion of the Mormon Fort that survived, with some reconstruction, is maintained as a historic site in downtown Las Vegas *(see "Downtown," pages 214–5)*.

Members of the Church of Jesus Christ of Latter-Day Saints (the Mormons) currently make up about 12 percent of the southern Nevada population, and in December 1989 a Mormon temple was dedicated in Las Vegas; temple spires are visible in the foothills of Sunrise Mountain east of the city. LDS leaders were originally opposed to gaming, but they now accommodate it *(see box on page 34)*.

On May 13, 1844, the well-known explorer, John C. Fremont, led an overland expedition heading west, and camped at Las Vegas Springs, and thousands of copies of the map he drew were freely distributed. His name is today not only in museums and history books

but also glowing in neon. The Fremont Hotel-Casino and Fremont Street in downtown Las Vegas both bear his name.

Railroads and mines

Helen Stewart eventually came with her husband, Archibald, to be the biggest landowner in the area with 1,800 acres (728 hectares), including the site of the old Mormon fort. Her husband was shot and killed by a neighbor, but she operated this enourmous ranch for 20 years or so afterwards. Mrs Stewart sold land for the railroad to Senator William Clark in 1902 for $55,000, and she later deeded around 10 acres (4 hectares) "for the use of Pauite Indians."

The region's largest ranch was called Los Vegas Rancho by the owner, Octavius Gass, to avoid confusion with the settlement of Las Vegas, New Mexico.

From some tented shacks, saloons, stores, and boarding houses, the town's population grew to 1,500 when the railroad was completed in early 1905. The railroad gave free rides to town for a big land auction, and 175 lots sold almost immediately for $450 each. The land finally raised $265,000, five times what Helen Stewart had been paid for it. On January 20, 1905, trains made the inaugural run from California to points east.

The railroad yards were at the birthplace of a partly paved, dusty Fremont Street. Today, the Plaza Hotel, at Main and Fremont streets in downtown Las Vegas, occupies the site of the original Union Pacific Railroad depot.

After the turn of the 20th century, mining in the region still thrived. A camp at Searchlight, established by George Colton in 1907, produced $7 million in gold, silver, and other precious metals.

Personal disputes were often settled with guns, and duels were not unknown. Mugging was common in Searchlight, and embezzlement was, if not the norm, then certainly widespread. In 1906, newspapers followed the case of postmaster W.B. Atwell, who admitted stealing $5,730 in government funds. The most common of the lesser crimes was "high-grading" – smuggling ore out of a mine in clothes, hair, or a lunchbox.

When miners worked high-grade ore, owners required them to shower and change clothes after shifts, but men found endless new and ever more ingenious ways to smuggle, using hollowed-out ax handles, double-crowned hats, or extra pockets sewn into trouser legs.

Nevada is still the US's leading producer of silver, and yielded more than 8 million ounces (227,000kg) of gold at the beginning of this century, but most of the Searchlight mines were closed long ago. Today, Searchlight is little more than a stop for travelers on US 95 from Needles to Las Vegas or Lake Mojave.

Early in the 20th century, Nevada outlawed gambling, as many other states had, but the activities simply went underground, and everybody knew somebody who knew the right door to knock on. No-one had any trouble joining a game.

Pioneers

When the city of Las Vegas was incorporated on March 16, 1911, it was hardly a pretty sight. Newcomer Mayme Stocker from Reading, Pennsylvania said, "Anyone who lives here is out of his mind." Her husband came for work as an engine foreman at the railroad yards. Many years later, Mayme said "There were no streets or sidewalks and there were no flowers, lawns, or trees." In spite of this, she stayed, and in 1920 opened the Northern Club on Fremont Street, and for it was granted Las Vegas's first casino license.

The first man to be known as "Mr Las Vegas" was Robert Griffith. He helped his father to build a home at the southwestern corner of 2nd and Fremont streets, where the Golden Nugget now stands. At the age of 26 as postmaster, he was instructed to prepare for an airport. He leveled a site in the desert, near today's Sahara and Paradise roads, and the first flight landed on April 17, 1925, taking letters which were hand-stamped to mark the occasion on the 2½-hour flight back to Los Angeles. The next year, Western Airlines inaugurated passenger flights into Vegas.

The following years saw many artesian wells drilled for water, but after an initial boom the town remained more or less isolated until the building of the Boulder (later Hoover) Dam in the early 1930s.

FAR LEFT: mountainman and a Paiute chief in the 1860s. **LEFT:** early railroad depot. **ABOVE:** a Nevada silver-mining camp in 1894.

THE RAILROAD WEST

The late-19th century was a lawless time. An early historian, Hubert Bancroft, wrote in an 1890 book that there were 400 murders in Nevada between 1864 and 1890, a huge number, considering how sparse the population was at that time.

By the last decade of the 19th century, railroad developers had determined that the water-rich Las Vegas Valley would be a prime location for trains to stop. The town, along with the ranch and vineyard on the old Mormon site, was eventually acquired by Senator William Clark's railroad, in the purchase he made from Helen Stewart *(see page 36)*.

When Clark's San Pedro Los Angeles Salt Lake Railroad (later the Union Pacific) advertised for workers, they offered $2 per 10-hour day for white men, $1.75 for Mexicans and Native Americans, with teamsters (union members) promised $40 a month, including board.

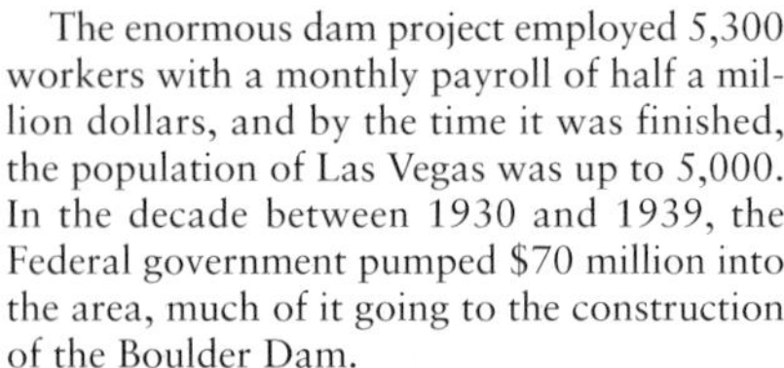

The enormous dam project employed 5,300 workers with a monthly payroll of half a million dollars, and by the time it was finished, the population of Las Vegas was up to 5,000. In the decade between 1930 and 1939, the Federal government pumped $70 million into the area, much of it going to the construction of the Boulder Dam.

HOOVER DAM

At its completion, two years ahead of schedule in 1935, the Boulder Canyon project had produced the world's biggest electricity generator, and the world's largest concrete structure. Herbert Hoover was the Federal government's representative to a commission, formed in 1922 to oversee the adjacent states' use of the Colorado River's waters, and he signed the appropriation of funds for the dam as US president in July, 1930.

Still referred to by some as the "Boulder Dam," the project was finally sited 8 miles (13km) downstream from Boulder Canyon, and was named, in the tradition of great US projects, after the president in office. Boulder City was built expressly for the dam's laborforce.

In August 1931 the workers went on strike complaining about heat prostration from the 130°F (54°C) temperatures, poor food and drink, and the lack of safety precautions. The "muckers," who did the most dangerous job of shoveling up dynamite-loosened rock to be hauled away, were the lowest paid.

The Great Depression

Legal gambling returned to Nevada in 1931 during the Great Depression, legitimizing a small but lucrative industry. Phil Tobin, a northern Nevada rancher who had never visited Las Vegas, persuaded the Nevada legislature to pass a gambling bill to raise funds for public schools, an idea so durable that today nearly one-third of Nevada's current $2.7 billion annual state budget comes from the taxes on casino winnings.

Local businessmen had operated most of the gambling halls, with enforcement handled by the sheriff. Later, the state set up the Nevada Gaming Board and the Tax Commission.

Originally, Las Vegas had been envisioned as a resort city, for visitors who came to see Boulder Dam (later renamed Hoover Dam) and go boating on Lake Mead, but the nation-

wide crackdown on illegal gambling benefited the state. An ex-carnival barker named Harold Smith, spread the Nevada gambling message around the world with no less than 2,300 signs advertising his Lake Tahoe club as far afield as Casablanca and the Antarctic.

Boulder City was a federally run enclave, built to house the dam workers in a place where liquor, gambling, and prostitution could be banned. Cars were searched and impounded if liquor was found. Naturally, off-duty residents flocked to Vegas to enjoy themselves. Boulder City is still one of only two town in Nevada that outlaws all forms of gaming, including slot machines.

Ernie Cragin, a former insurance salesman and unashamed racist, was then mayor of Las Vegas, and his police rigidly enforced segregation in a town where most of the casinos and nightclubs refused to serve blacks. In World War II, when black military officers guarding the dam came to town, there were gun battles with the local police. It took two decades for things to improve, by which time NAACP lawyer Charles Kellar instigated protest marches on the Strip, and civil rights lawyer Ralph Denton helped Governor Grant Sawyer to get elected.

LEFT: conditions during the construction of the Hoover Dam were primitive and damaging to its workers' health. **ABOVE:** opening ceremonies for the Hoover Dam.

El Rancho

By 1941, with a population of about 8,000 people, a group of local businessmen invited Tom Hull, owner of a chain of El Rancho motor inns, to town. Hull chose a site just outside town where Highway 91 intersected San Francisco (now Sahara) Avenue for El Rancho Vegas. With cheap land taxes and water, he built a 65-room motor inn with a swimming pool. The casino was an afterthought. Later expanded to 125 rooms, El Rancho Vegas became popular for banquets and wedding parties. It was also headquarters of the valley's first radio station, an ABC affiliate named

> *The first one-armed bandit in a Vegas casino was the Liberty Bell, built in 1887 by Charles Fey in San Francisco. Three bells won the maximum payout of $10.*

KENO. The station's owner, Maxwell Kelch, sold the town as a product. He never ran for office or invested in a casino. He told his son, "there's two businesses you don't get involved in. One's liquor and the other's gambling." The venerable El Rancho Vegas was destroyed by fire in 1960.

In 1948, the El Cortez Hotel was built at Fremont and 6th streets. Among its partners were Meyer Lansky and Benjamin "Bugsy" Siegel. Lansky invested $60,000 for his 10 percent stake, and left Siegel to run it. In their youth the pair had worked a New York protection racket, preying on bootleggers. Siegel went to Los Angeles to consolidate the rackets there, and on to Las Vegas to handle the Mob's race book wires and gambling. In Manhattan, Siegel lived at the Waldorf Astoria and traveled with bodyguards. Out west, he soon made friends with members of Hollywood's movie colony.

Growth of gambling

In December 1942, movie chain mogul R.E. Griffith introduced a western motif at the Last Frontier, with Pony Express lanterns hanging from wagon wheels, Texas cattle horns, leather bar stools shaped as saddles, and a bullet-riddled mahogany bar. The hotel, later renamed the Frontier, offered horseback and stagecoach rides into the desert. Frontier Village was established with buildings rehabilitated from old Nevada ghost towns.

The Last Frontier also came up with and implemented the idea of "the junket," gaming tours arranged by the operator of a small airline, a tycoon named Kirk Kerkorian.

The Fremont Street area grew in the late

BUGSY SIEGEL

"He was a frustrated actor who secretly wanted a movie career," actor George Raft said, "but he never quite had nerve enough to ask for a part in one of my pictures." Once on the West Coast, Benjamin "Bugsy" Siegel muscled his way into illegal gambling, including Tijuana's Agua Caliente racetrack in Mexico. He also helped to import narcotics from Mexico, and took a cut from a huge prostitution ring.

His big break in Vegas came with the arrival of a Hollywood entrepreneur named W.R. Wilkerson. Wilkerson had begun betting on the World Series and at the track while he was at college. He founded the influential *Hollywood Reporter* in 1930, and played regularly with $20,000 chips at movie mogul Sam Goldwyn's weekly poker game. An obsessive gambler, he would charter a plane to fly from Los Angeles to Las Vegas, and soon thought of owning his own hotel in the desert resort in order to entertain his movie-star friends. That was the genesis of the Flamingo Hotel which – through amply documented chicanery – came to be known as Siegel's place.

1940s and early 1950s with the Golden Nugget and the Monte Carlo Club. Then came Benny Binion, a Texas gambler with big, white cowboy hats and a buffalo-hide overcoat. Binion had twice been convicted of bootlegging, and once got a jailor drunk and stole a truckload of liquor right out of the jail. In Dallas in the late 1930s, he operated craps games in hotel rooms, taking tables in and out disguised as beds. In 1947 Binion and a partner opened the Las Vegas Club on Fremont Street. Four years later, he opened the Horseshoe with a $500 limit on craps – ten times the other casinos' limit.

In Manhattan, Bugsy Siegel traveled in a bulletproof limousine. Out West, the mobster made friends with Clark Gable, Cary Grant, and Jean Harlow.

Benny Binion's principle was "giving a lot of gamble for the money." True to this motto, Binion's casino is still open.

In 1946, when the *Hollywood Reporter* publisher, W.R. Wilkerson's initial investment of $1.5 million ran out *(see box on page 40)*, "Bugsy" Siegel took over the incomplete Flamingo Hotel. Siegel took his eye off the business and costs soared.

By the opening night on December 26,1946, the still-unfinished Flamingo Hotel had cost $6 million, and since the hotel rooms weren't ready, the few celebrities that braved the dreadful weather to attend, crossed the street to El Rancho Vegas or the Last Frontier to stay over and bet.

The Mob was displeased by the venture's losses, and Meyer Lansky discovered that Siegel had been skimming the Flamingo building fund, sending his girlfriend Virginia Hill to deposit large sums in a Swiss bank account. In June, as Siegel sat in the window of Miss Hill's Beverly Hills home, a single shot blasted through the glass, and Bugsy Siegel was dead.

Hill was in Europe at the time of the murder, probably on the advice of his killers. ❑

FAR LEFT: the Dice Girls of El Rancho, an influential casino in the early days of Vegas entertainment. **TOP LEFT:** the Flamingo was both a dream and a disaster for mobster Bugsy Siegel. **ABOVE:** Fremont Street in 1950.

PLAYERS, DESERT PALACES AND THE RAT PACK

Las Vegas was an oasis of mobsters and showgirls, wire-taps and wild publicity stunts – then the crooners made way for the tycoons

On a New York spring morning in 1957, Frank Costello, the "Prime Minister of the Mob," was cut down by a volley of gunshots in the paneled lobby of his apartment building in Central Park West. The injured mobster was rushed to the hospital and in the bustle, a quick-thinking cop checked the pockets of Costello's tailored suit. A hand-written note among the contents read, "Gross Casino Win as of 4-26-57... $651,284," tallying the first 24 days' takings from the Las Vegas gaming house, the Tropicana Hotel.

Memo from the Mob

The Costello memo was the first solid evidence of Mob ties to Vegas casinos since the hearings into organized crime headed by Tennessee senator Estes Kefauver in 1950 and 1951. This was also the year that Alan Dorfman, son of one of Al Capone's soldiers, started getting loans to finance casino construction from the Teamsters Union's western states pension fund.

Allegedly, Frank Sinatra never liked the name the Rat Pack, preferring instead The Summit or The Klan. Needless to say, Pack member Sammy Davis, Jr was unhappy with the second.

LEFT: the Rat Pack were the "greatest, cool, hippest entertainers around." Front row: Sammy Davis, Jr. Back row: Frank Sinatra, Dean Martin, Peter Lawford, Joey Bishop. **RIGHT:** Frank Costello, the "Prime Minister of the Mob."

During the proceedings, Nevada's lieutenant governor Cliff Jones was asked about "undesirable characters with bad police records," who had been engaged in gambling in the state. He conceded that there had been such occasions, but Jones, himself a part owner of the Thunderbird casino said, "...people who came here when the state started to grow – they weren't particularly school teachers or anything like that. They were gamblers."

After Kefauver concluded his hearings into Mob connections, he proposed a 10 percent federal gaming tax, which was averted through persistent efforts by Nevada senator Pat McCarran. A defense lawyer and later district

attorney, McCarran lost many races before being elected senator in 1932, and had served for 20 years when he halted the move to tax gaming. "It isn't a very laudable position for one to have to defend gambling," he said. "One doesn't feel very lofty when his feet are resting on the argument that gambling must prevail in the state that he represents. The rest of the world looks upon him with disdain."

Four years after Estes Kefauver's exposures of Mob involvement in Vegas, a Gaming Control Board was established to regulate and legitimize the industry. Gambling had already become the state's greatest source of income.

On a roll

The whole southern Nevada region was on a roll by the early 1950s, largely due to the efforts of publicity man Steve Hannagan *(see box on right)*, who had promoted the Indianapolis Raceway and Miami Beach before he was hired to promote the city of Las Vegas. A Hannagan protegeé, Harvey Diederich, gained massive coverage from a stunt in the 1956 US presidential election. A scantily clad showgirl, "Miss Bea Sure 'N Vote," held a campaign poster for Dwight D. Eisenhower in her right hand and one for Adlai Stevenson in her left. "Cold Turkey," was the caption for another girl, posed astride an ice turkey, carved by the Topicana Hotel chef. "Publicity far exceeds the value of advertising," said Diederich. "It's more believable."

Downtown continued its rapid growth when Texan Benny Binion opened the legendary Binion's Horseshoe, the first off-the-Strip casino with a carpet, as well as the first to offer free drinks not only to high rollers but to slot-machine players, too. He also had customers collected by limousine at the airport. "If you wanna get rich," Binion said, "make little people feel like big people."

Around that time, the Atomic Energy Commission started conducting above-ground nuclear test explosions at test sites about 100 miles (160km) northwest of Las Vegas. President Harry Truman declared the valley, "a critical defense area," which did wonders for

SELLING THE SIZZLE

Publicist Steve Hannagan never lived in Las Vegas, rarely visited, and ran the town's public relations for less than two years. In that time though, he transformed the city's image. Photographer Don English, who worked for Hannagan from 1949, said, "Every morning, we would go to all the hotels – there were about four of them at the time – and look for attractive couples.

The idea was to take a photo of people vacationing and send it back to the subject's local newspaper. It would run the picture of this couple sitting by the pool, and a neighbor would see someone he knew and say, 'If the Joneses can afford to go to Las Vegas, then we can, too.'"

"Outside writers on the land of Sodom and Gomorrah made Las Vegas known as a gambling resort, [but Hannagan] wanted to diversify the other images in order to entice wives and families to come," said writer Perry Kaufman in his book, *City Boosters, Las Vegas Style*.

Vegas's economic well-being. In 1951, the first year of testing, the commission's construction payroll was more than $4 million.

The Desert Inn

The idea for the Desert Inn, with its lavish golf course, came from a former San Diego bellboy named Wilbur Clark. "It was Wilbur's dream," his widow Toni said. "He always said the bubble would never burst in Las Vegas and he was right. It was all class then. People used to dress every night." Frank Sinatra's first singing engagement in Las Vegas was at the Desert Inn, on September 4, 1951, while he was still getting over his break up with actress Ava Gardner.

With his Cleveland partners, Moe Dalitz, "a smart, brilliant man," according to some, owned three quarters of the Desert Inn. During prohibition, Dalitz allegedly bootlegged liquor with Meyer Lansky across the lake from Canada, and in 1958 kept union interference from his chain of Midwestern laundries with hoodlum strong-arms. Dalitz's business acumen raised $8 million from the Teamsters Union's pension fund to finish the Stardust Hotel.

FAR LEFT: showgirl and friend at the opening of the Dunes casino. **LEFT:** Estes Kefauver's investigation into organized crime in 1950–1 exposed Mob connections. **ABOVE:** singer Phyllis McGuire, seen here with Desert Inn owner Moe Dalitz, was a girlfriend of Mafia boss Sam Giancana.

Government investigations showed that the Teamsters Union's investments in Nevada casinos eventually exceeded $238 million. Dalitz got out, but years later the mobsters who still owned it were jailed for skimming the profits. "Conspiracy to defraud the government of taxes through illegal and unreported income," was how the rap sheet put it.

> *According to the* New York Times, *in 1953 a first-class hotel in Vegas charged $7.50 a day, while a motel charged $3.*

In his book, *Gamblers' Money*, Wallace Turner said, "In Cleveland, Moe Dalitz was a bootlegger but in Las Vegas he stands as an elder statesman of what they call the gaming industry," and *Las Vegas Review-Journal* columnist John L. Smith said, "How did a former bootlegger and illegal casino operator… go about gaining respectability? Dalitz took

the same approach that many other American capitalists did. He donated generously to political causes and wrapped himself in the tailored suit of corporate citizenship."

Dalitz himself told an interviewer in 1975, "I was never a member of any gang. I never considered myself a gangster or a mobster. I was always in a business that threw me into meeting all kinds of people." When he died in 1989, the foundation that he had set up distributed $1.3 million to charities, and the 300 mourners at his funeral included politicians, judges, and other influential figures.

Atom-bomb tests began in 1951, and a Las Vegas PR said, "The angle was to get people to think the explosions wouldn't be anything more than a gag."

High rise

Until 1955, the Desert Inn offered guests the highest unobstructed panorama of the Las Vegas Valley from the resort's third-floor Skyroom – cocktail and dancing favorite of visitors, residents, and celebrities. Soon after, the Riviera Hotel rose to nine stories and became the city's first high-rise building.

That same year, the Moulin Rouge opened across the city, at a time when blacks were still unwelcome at Strip casinos, and black entertainers were required to live off-premises while entertaining. The hip, interracial after-midnight crowd at the Moulin Rouge's club attracted showgirls and performers from so many other casinos that some threatened to dismiss any cast members seen there.

The Moulin Rouge starred former world heavyweight boxing champion Joe Louis as owner-host, and singer Bob Bailey from the Count Basie Orchestra produced the stage show. The club had a rocky ride, closing and re-opening many, many times, and when Bailey moved his show onto KLAS-TV, he had to go back to using the service entrance. Bailey worked to get Grant Sawyer elected governor in 1958. "He indicated that if he was elected governor, certain changes would be made. He struck me as a man you could believe." Three years later, a state commission was established on the subject of discrimination.

Joe Louis moved on to become a much-

loved casino host at Caesars Palace. The Moulin Rouge was declared a national historic site in 1992, but in 2003 the boarded-up casino was permanently damaged by arson.

In 1955, casinos were going up right and left, and the city's population was on the verge of an increase, from 45,000 to 65,000 residents, but Governor Sawyer hated how the industry was in the sway of hoodlums. He helped to set up the Nevada Gaming Commission Board to license and police the scene.

The Black Book

Then, and for a decade afterwards, Nevada law required all casino owners to be individually licensed, preventing ownership by public companies with multiple stockholders. The law changed in the late 1960s, and investors were allowed to own less than 10 percent of a casino's stock without individual licenses.

Sawyer also wanted a list published of disreputable characters to be barred from casinos. To his surprise, the US Federal Court upheld the state's right to a List of Excluded Persons, known since as "the Black Book."

Some of the "disreputable characters" were, of course, already established in management *inside* the casinos. Hidden FBI microphones at the Fremont Hotel in 1961 picked up one of the owners, Ed Levinson, discussing what seemed to be a casino skimming operation involving Meyer Lansky. Las Vegas telephone records show that from 1961 to 1963, they leased 25 lines to the FBI, for concealed listening devices in hotels including the Desert Inn, the Stardust, the Fremont, the Sands, the Dunes and the Riviera. Later, the FBI uncovered skimming at the Flamingo; apparently the New York office was the beneficiary of gambling debts which were omitted from the casino's Las Vegas book. The owners pleaded guilty to skimming $36 million.

In the late 1950s, community leaders

LEFT: Marlene Dietrich, seen here in 1953, was a frequent guest and performer in Vegas. **ABOVE:** the Sahara, one of the few old-time resorts still on the Strip. **ABOVE RIGHT:** the domed convention center opened in 1959.

SHOWGIRLS AND DONN ARDEN

The Stardust Hotel brought in the *Lido de Paris* stage show, which ran for years. The topless revue was produced by legendary showman Donn Arden.

"There's a certain way a girl can walk, particularly when crossing a stage," he once explained, somewhat painstakingly. "By simply twisting the foot it swings the pelvis forward, which is suggestive and sensual. If you twist right and swing that torso, you get a revolve going in there that's just right. It isn't the way a woman should walk necessarily unless she's a hooker. You're selling the pelvis. That's the Arden walk."

Arden went on to choreograph *Jubilee*!, which is still playing at Bally's casino.

thought of a convention facility to fill the hotel rooms during the months when tourism was slack. Commissioner George Albright, who was no fan of gambling, lobbied hard for the center, and a site one block east of the Strip was chosen. In April 1959 the 6,300-seat, silver-domed rotunda with adjoining exhibition hall opened.

THE REGULATION OF GAMING

The Nevada Gaming Commission and the Nevada Gaming Control Board were both set up by the Nevada state legislature in 1959 with the aim of regulating the practice of gambling, and regulating ownership and management of casinos.

Prior to that, in the 1950s and 1960s, casino ownership was an ever-shifting mosaic of names and faces, holding and mysteriously transferring percentages fairly anonymously. The gaming profits and their beneficiaries were practically untraceable, and operations were very much in the hands of organized crime.

The commission required all casino shareholders to be openly declared, and to hold gaming licences in their own rights, thus being what the commission decreed "fit persons." This meant as well as licencees having (relatively) unblemished records themselves, they were also not associated with "undesirables."

A crooner, a king, and an aviator

Three men cast such long, shimmering shadows over Las Vegas that the town bears their marks to this day. Sinatra brought high-society elegance into the lounges. Elvis brought the mass market to the Strip. And Howard Hughes brought the appearance, at least, of respectability to the business of owning and running casinos.

Jack Entratter, formerly the general manager of New York's Copacabana Club, brought entertainers Lena Horne, Danny Thomas and others out west to the Sahara Hotel. In 1952, Entratter booked a crooner named Frank Sinatra, and, soon, Frank was on a roll. He won an Oscar for the movie *From Here to Eternity*, and released an album, *Songs For Young Lovers*, which became a bestseller.

Veteran lounge singer Sammy King said, "He was actually the king of Las Vegas because the minute he stepped in town, money was here. He drew all the big-money people. Every celebrity in Hollywood would come to Las Vegas to see him."

Sinatra bought 2 percent of the Sands for $54,000 and within a decade owned 9 percent, by which time the Rat Pack – a loose association

of singers, actors, and comedians – was the hottest thing in town. One night, as her version of the story goes, actress Lauren Bacall was on her way to watch Noel Coward perform at the Desert Inn. Spying Humphrey Bogart, Frank Sinatra, Judy Garland, David Niven, Angie Dickenson, and agent Swifty Lazar, she said, "You look like a goddam rat pack." In true Vegas style, it was heisted by Sinatra, Dean Martin, Sammy Davis Jr, actor Peter Lawford, and comedian Joey Bishop as their moniker.

The Rat Pack's era began when Sinatra joined Dean Martin on stage at the Sands in January 1959, and lasted loosely through 1963. Typically, the group would perform two shows a night in the Copa Room, followed by a friendly and less formal gathering in the lounge, getting together in the daytime for filming. When they were scheduled to appear, there wasn't a hotel room to be had anywhere which, according to some estimates, benefited Sin City to the tune of an extra $20 to 30 million a week. As a group, the Rat Pack never recorded an album or released a single, although some live recordings survive.

LEFT: ex-president and entertainer Ronald Reagan at the Last Frontier, an early Vegas club. **ABOVE:** Pack members Frank Sinatra and Peter Lawford with Lawford's brother-in-law, Robert Kennedy.

> *In* Movin' With Nancy, *a 1967 NBC special, Nancy Sinatra and Sammy Davis, Jr. greeted each other with one of the first black-white kisses on US television.*

Sinatra and the broads

Tony Badillo, a long-time dealer at the Sands, said, "Back in those days we used to let Frank and Sammy and those guys deal the game. Of course, with the Gaming Control Board you couldn't do that now. Frank was a pretty good gambler (but) sometimes he'd get angry. Like if a woman at the table didn't laugh at his jokes he'd say, 'Tony, get that broad off my table... '"

In 1959, Pack member Peter Lawford discovered a movie script about a group of World War II veterans who rob several Vegas casinos simultaneously. When Jack Warner gave the green light to what became *Ocean's 11*, Sinatra said, "We're not setting out to make *Hamlet* or *Gone With the Wind*." Warner himself is claimed to have said, "Let's not make the movie. Let's pull the job."

Looking back at the movie 41 years later – in light of the George Clooney remake – *Las Vegas Life* called it, "a time capsule of a Las Vegas that no longer exists," and said that director Milestone, "would have been better off shooting the Rat Pack's nightly performances."

FILMING *OCEAN'S 11*

Filming on *Ocean's 11* was scheduled to coincide with the Rat Pack's January 1960 "Summit at the Sands," and was as loose as the group's image. Veteran director Lewis Milestone, an Oscar winner for *All Quiet on the Western Front* (1930), was only able to assemble the entire cast once during the five-week shoot. Sinatra turned up, usually late in the afternoon, on only nine days. The others also turned up late, restricting Milestone to a day's shoot of only about three hours. Peter Lawford said, "Frank would tear handfuls of pages out of the script and allow (Lewis Milestone) only one take."

Sinatra and the Mob

Joseph Kennedy asked his actor son-in-law, Rat Pack member Peter Lawford to throw his support behind his son John F. Kennedy's 1960 presidential bid. In the process, Lawford got Sinatra involved in a murky political campaign. Two weeks after announcing his race for the presidency, JFK allegedly collected a $1 million donation from Sinatra's friend, Mafia boss Sam Giancana. "(Jack) loved his brief visits to Las Vegas," Michael Herr said in *The Money and the Power: the Making of Las Vegas and Its Hold on America*. "He was the most star-struck of stars... and his Vegas friends arranged everything for him, especially seeing to it that his privacy would be respected."

Giancana boasted that he had bought a president, and had been promised by Sinatra that Bobby Kennedy's investigation into organized crime would be stopped. Frank felt betrayed when the new attorney general's attacks resumed, Giancana topping the list.

In 1963, two months before President Kennedy was assassinated, Sinatra battled with the Gaming Control Board. The FBI discovered Sam Giancana's presence at Sinatra's Cal-Neva Lodge in Lake Tahoe, where Marilyn

Monroe had spent the week before her suicide.

The FBI suspected Jimmy Hoffa had made a loan from the Teamsters Union's pension fund for improvements to Sinatra's lodge. Investigations showed that Hoffa had in fact turned down the loan. Still, the FBI's findings were reported to the Nevada Gaming Commission and Sinatra's gaming license was suspended. He had been a public partner, Giancana a secret partner. A girlfriend of Giancana's, singer Phyllis McGuire, said of Sinatra, "He'd been friends with the boys for years, ever since he needed to get out of his contract with (band leader) Tommy Dorsey."

> *They were style with substance, swing with swagger, a nonstop party that everyone wanted access to.*
> *Player* Magazine on the Rat Pack

The Gaming Control Board ordered an appearance from Sinatra, but instead he gave up his casino interests and let the license go.

LEFT: the Sultan of Swing, with personal harem, in 1955. **ABOVE:** the Desert Inn casino had excellent Rat Pack connections. **ABOVE RIGHT:** Elvis and Liberace swap instruments and jackets, 1956.

The boy from Mississippi

Elvis Presley's first Las Vegas gig was in April 1956 at the Frontier. He was 21, billed as "the atomic-powered singer," and opened a show for comic Shecky Greene. *Newsweek* magazine reported that the audience was "underwhelmed," and made comparisons to "a jug of corn liquor at a champagne party."

Shecky said, "The presentation was terrible. He wasn't ready. He walked out with three or four guys. It looked like a rehearsal hall." After that, "Colonel" Tom Parker kept Elvis away from the stage and in Hollywood for 12-years of high-yield movie-making, most of which the singer loathed. The Colonel earned well, however, and made some money for the boy from Tupelo, Mississippi.

In 1969, Kirk Kerkorian, then owner of the Flamingo, opened the International (now the Las Vegas Hilton) and talent agent Bill Miller contacted Parker about having Elvis perform. Elvis had married Priscilla Beaulieu at the Aladdin two years before and was a big Vegas fan. "Parker didn't want him to open in that big 2,000-seat theater. He said we'd have to put somebody else in to open and Elvis would follow." Miller booked Barbra Streisand.

Presley was nervous. He studied other performers in showrooms, and particularly took Tom Jones as his model, for the way the Welsh singer aroused a female audience. But on opening night, Elvis was a sensation. He delivered a relaxed show, rated by many as among the best of his career. He referred to his time in Hollywood as, "ten years with my top lip curled." The following day Parker wrote a contract with the International's general manager (according to the late Nevada newspaper writer Kenneth Evans), for Elvis to play four-week gigs twice a year, for $125,000 a week. By the end of the singer's first four-week stint, the showroom had generated more than $2 million in revenue. Evans said that Elvis's contract was for a "piddling sum," because Parker wanted to be in Vegas, where he became one of the highest rollers, often losing $50,000 a night. Evans called Parker a "degenerate gambler," as did others at the time.

THE AUTOBIOGRAPHY THAT WASN'T

In 1972, novelist Clifford Irving made publishing deals with McGraw Hill and *Life* magazine with what he claimed was the autobiography of billionaire Howard Hughes *(right)*. Mike Wallace interviewed Irving about the book on CBS's show *60 Minutes*. Hughes was so reclusive that it took months for the manuscript to be exposed as a fake, Hughes himself finally giving a telephone press conference. *60 Minutes* called Irving "Con Man of the Year," and he admitted, "I was filled with the success of my fairy tale." He repaid the $765,000 advance, was convicted of fraud, and served 14 months in jail. Years later, Irving published the story in *The Hoax*, which was filmed in 2006 with Richard Gere as Irving.

Howard Hughes

Early one morning, on or around Thanksgiving Day in 1966, Howard Hughes was carried by a stretcher to the Desert Inn's ninth-floor penthouse. The windows were blacked out with drapes, armed guards stationed by the elevator, and seven Mormon personal aides worked around the clock, catering to Hughes' needs. He checked in for 10 days, stayed four years, and never once left his far-from lavish room. He took daily codeine injections for spinal injuries sustained in an airplane crash, and subsisted, it's said, on Campbell's chicken soup and banana-nut ice cream. He sealed his urine in glass jars and, despite his phobia of germs, the room was not cleaned during the whole of the four years.

Hughes hired Robert Maheu as his liaison to the outside world. Maheu did not meet Hughes when he was hired, nor during his four-year employment, nor ever afterwards. Stories of Hughes are legion. Apparently, the reclusive tycoon hadn't checked out in time for Christmas, and high rollers were booked in. The Desert Inn's owners were furious, but so

was Hughes – he wasn't ready to leave. Hughes's man Maheu contacted John Rosselli, the Mob's Vegas liaison. (Maheu and Rosselli reputedly met collaborating on a CIA plot to kill Fidel Castro.) Maheu also called Jimmy Hoffa, as the resort's owner, Moe Dalitz, was part financed by the Teamsters Union pension fund. Dalitz agreed to sell the resort and after much quibbling, Hughes took the Desert Inn on April 1, 1967 for $13.2 million.

Lord of the valley

Hughes saw Las Vegas's potential, and also that it would take only money for him to become lord of the valley. Nevada had no income, inheritance, or state corporate taxes. "We can make a really super environmental city of the future here," he wrote. "No smog, no contamination, efficient local government where the taxpayers pay as little as possible and get something for their money." He sold his TWA stock and acquired the Frontier for $14 million, and the land now occupied by the Mirage and T.I., which he never developed. He bought the lot where the Fashion Show Mall now stands, then the Silver Slipper, adjoining the Frontier, although he was unable to buy the Stardust Hotel. Still, he bought the Sands. Along with a TV station, North Las Vegas airport, large lots on the Strip, the Landmark, and a small airline, Hughes's Vegas shopping spree cost him a total of $300 million.

On November 5, 1970, Howard Hughes was carried from the Desert Inn, still on a stretcher, and put on a plane to the Bahamas. He died five years later, aged 70. ❑

> *Before the popularity of video recorders, Howard Hughes bought the Las Vegas TV station, KLAS-TV, so that he could choose which late-night movies to watch.*

FAR LEFT: Howard Hughes "changed Las Vegas forever." **LEFT:** Jimmy Hoffa was president of the Teamsters Union and helped friends like Moe Dalitz purchase casinos by embezzling from the union's pension fund. **ABOVE TOP AND BOTTOM:** Vegas veterans, including part-time Packer, comedian Milton Berle. **ABOVE RIGHT:** Elvis ties the knot with Priscella Beaulieu at the Aladdin, 1967.

MODERN LAS VEGAS

The opening of Caesars Palace heralded the era of fantasy writ large, and mega-palaces like Bellagio, Paris Las Vegas, The Venetian, and Wynn Las Vegas took it to another level

Entrepreneur Jay Sarno's visions were studies in excess. It's rumored that he wanted the fountain pool of a restaurant at Caesars Palace stocked with piranhas, to be fed a pig at mealtimes. The Health Department banned the stunt. His deputy at the Circus Circus casino, Don Williams, said, "His insights all came from his own appetites. Get prettier girls. Build bigger buildings, get better restaurants, have bigger gamblers around. All those things came from his loins, not his brain."

Hail Caesar

The opening of Sarno's Caesars Palace in August 1966 heralded the modern Las Vegas era of fantasy writ large. The white palace of illusion with Greek- and Roman-style edifices set the tone for the giant spectacles lining the Strip now. In the 1960s, Jay Sarno owned a chain of hotels and visited Vegas to play craps, at which he consistently lost. He later admitted losing $1 million over two years. Sarno may have been a lousy gambler, but he had a vision, and he found the hotel casinos dull.

In 1962, Kirk Kerkorian bought a plot on the Strip for $960,000. Jay Sarno rented the lot to build Caesars Palace. In six years, it made Kerkorian $9 million.

LEFT: the implosion of the Sands Hotel in 1966 marked the beginning of the Venetian Hotel.
RIGHT: Steve Wynn, architect of modern Las Vegas.

His daughter September said, "He was building slick, gorgeous hotels and making a living. Then he saw modest hotels here making money hand over fist. He realized he wasn't building the wrong kind of hotels, he was building them in the wrong place." Former *Nevada Journal* editor A.D. Hopkins said that Sarno's philosophy was for, "an island of fantasy in a mundane world." Sarno traveled to photograph columns, pilasters, and flying buttresses in Europe.

Inspired by Italian baroque, with an approach dotted with fountains and its staff dressed as gladiators, Caesars Palace was a sensation. The restaurant was called Bacchanal,

and wine goddesses massaged diners as they ate. "People would travel from faraway places just to get a shoulder and neck massage from these goddesses," September said.

Three years later Sarno sold Caesars Palace for $60 million, double what it had cost, and planned an even more ambitious casino, Circus Circus, targeted at high-rollers. For Sarno, though, Circus Circus was a bust. Money was wasted flying a pink-painted elephant on an overhead track. Patrons descended by fireman's pole or a waterslide into the casino, but too many drunks were nearly injured, and gamblers were distracted by the overhead show. There were no hotel rooms to keep customers on the premises, but the fatal flaw was probably the admission charge.

Sold out

After five years of losses, Sarno sold out to new owners, who turned Circus Circus around. It was successfully marketed to a middle-class audience. *Las Vegas Life* writer Greg Blake Miller called Jay Sarno, "The Freud and Ford

A Modern Tale of Sex, Drugs, Death, and Buried Treasure

Ted Binion succeeded his father Benny in running the family businesses, including Binion's Horseshoe *(right)*, the landmark casino in downtown Vegas. He kept lots of cash, and buried silver worth $6 million in a desert vault. Ted had drug problems and a stormy affair with a lap-dancer, Sandy Murphy, 26.

On September 17, 1998, Sandy called for an ambulance at Ted's Las Vegas ranch. Paramedics found Binion lifeless in his den, among drugs and drug paraphernalia. Police decided Ted died from a self-inflicted overdose.

Ted's lawyer, James J. Brown, told police of a call from Binion the previous day. "Take Sandy out of the will if she doesn't kill me tonight," Binion said. "If I'm dead, you'll know what happened." Ted's associates were amazed no cash or items of value were discovered when the ranch was searched. The next night, police found Murphy's "companion," Rick Tabbish, unearthing Binion's silver stash in the desert with a truck and a mechanical digger. Following a lengthy trial, Murphy and Tabbish were found guilty of Binion's murder by "Burking" (smothering the victim with a pillow, named after William Burke, a 19th-century Scottish murderer). Attorneys, however, successfully appealed the convictions and won a new trial, at which the pair were found not guilty of murder. The case was the subject of a made-for-TV movie, and was fictionalized for an episode of *CSI*.

of Las Vegas. The first in town to fully realize the link between our dreams and our appetites. The central assumption of his career was that we wanted the same things he did."

Howard Hughes's stay from the 1960s to 1970 had changed the casino business. His acquisition of six casinos, generating about a quarter of Vegas's gaming revenues, marked the shift to corporate ownership, and the influence of the Mob is said to have virtually vanished. Today, monitored by the state gaming authority and tax watchdogs, the gambling business seems outwardly respectable.

The 1970s and '80s saw Vegas become a fabulous playground to the stars – whether they were appearing on stage, gambling in the casinos, or working it off on the golf courses. Everyone who was anyone came to Sin City: Liz Taylor and Richard Burton, Sonny and Cher, and the Beatles.

Steve Wynn came to US television viewers when the youthful casino boss appeared with Frank Sinatra in TV commercials in the 1980s. The world's most famous crooner had a three-year contract to appear at the Golden Nugget, of which Wynn was president.

In 1978, 11 million visitors to Las Vegas spent a total of just over $3.2 billion dollars. In 2008, 39 million people together brought $4 billion in local trade.

Wynn's winners

In 1989, Wynn built The Mirage. With a waterfall, an active "volcano," and white tigers, it made a $44 million profit in the first quarter, and 17 or 18 percent in its first year, at a time when Caesars Palace, its next-door neighbor, declined by 43 percent. Ever the self-publicizing showman, Wynn conducted a video tour of the hotel in all 3,044 guest rooms. He followed this in 1993 with Treasure Island, and filled the sidewalk with spectators who gawked at its nightly "naval battle."

At the time,Wynn's annual salary of $34.2 millon made him the highest-paid executive in the USA. In 1992 he paid $75 million for

LEFT: Jay Sarno was, according to a local writer, the "Freud and Ford of Las Vegas." **ABOVE TOP:** Jay Sarno's Circus Circus. **ABOVE BOTTOM:** Steve Wynn's Mirage. **ABOVE RIGHT:** Kirk Kerkorian, money-maker.

the Dunes, and spent another million blowing it up, with a huge fireworks display for an audience of 200,000 on the Strip. He promised that Bellagio, its replacement, would be the "most extravagant hotel ever built on earth." Choreographed fountains sprayed colored water 160ft (49 meters) into the air, Dale Chihuly's gigantic chandelier *(see page 144)* graced the lobby, and Wynn's boast was fulfilled.

Wynn sold all of his holdings in March 2000 to Kirk Kerkorian's MGM Grand Inc. for $6.4 billion to fund a new spectacle: Wynn Las Vegas, for which he bought and demolished the 50-year-old Desert Inn. In 2001, Wynn said "My new hotel has been the most wonderful experience of my life. It's about our desert and the southwestern United States." Wynn Las Vega opened in 2005.

> *Clark County's annual gaming revenue is around $10.8 billion, and with $6.8 billion of its own, Vegas's contribution accounts for a huge portion of the take.*

The MGM Grand was the biggest hotel in town, and both incarnations of this casino were owned by former charter airline operator, Kirk Kerkorian. The first MGM Grand opened in December, 1973 with 2,100 rooms. It suffered a disastrous fire in November 1980, in which 87 people died and 700 were injured. When the hotel was sold to the Bally Corporation in 1985, one fifth of the price – $110 million – was reserved for settlements that were still pending from this fire.

Kerkorian's MGM connection came about like this: already owner of the Flamingo Hotel, in 1967 he began work on the International. This was so successful that his $16.6 million investment was soon worth $180 million. When he sold the International and the Flamingo to the Hilton hotel group, Kerkorian became a majority stockholder in both MGM and United Artists Studios.

"I think it's better to keep your business private," he told writer Dave Palermo. He expressed admiration for his rival Howard Hughes. "I liked him. He was a helluva guy. If you take him early in his career he didn't get the credit he deserves." Of Kerkorian himself, a stock analyst said, "Every shareholder who has participated with him has doubled or tripled his money. That's a record few men have."

Extravaganzas

In 1994 the 1,500 room hotel-casino New York New York was announced. It opened three years later to 100,000 visitors each day. Vegas construction inspector Sue Henley was a satisfied customer: she won $12.5 million at a slot machine, the biggest jackpot up to then.

Downtown casino owners watched their competitors on the Strip with awe and envy, and in 1994 fought back, breaking ground for the Fremont Street Experience, a six-block section of the main street with an elaborate canopy to present giant animation shows.

In the closing years of the century, still greater expansion came to the Strip. The first tunnel under the Strip was completed; the Monte Carlo and the Stratosphere Tower both opened; and in quick succession to Steve Wynn's Bellagio, came the even larger Venetian; Paris Las Vegas with its replica of the Eiffel Tower; and the Mandalay Bay, where the owners, Circus Circus Enterprises, went so far as to change their name to the Mandalay Resort Group. MGM Grand's acquisition of Mirage Resorts Inc. from Steve Wynn was the largest corporate buyout in gaming history. And Las Vegas was attracting 32 million visitors per year.

But urban growth brought urban problems, like street gangs. A *Washington Post* story suggested that some locals yearned for the bad old days. "Those punks wouldn't have dared show their faces when Bugsy was around," one said.

Trouble in paradise

Through the last three decades of the century, the Strip had its share of labor problems. Unions voted for strike action on March 11, 1970, known locally as Black Wednesday. The Desert Inn, Las Vegas Hilton, and Caesars were hit. The Frontier suffered a 75-day strike in 1985, and an action began in 1991 lasting six years and four months. Strike action loomed again in April 2002, over lay-offs and falling working conditions after a downturn in trade followed September 11, 2001. Also in 2002, a bartenders' strike hit Downtown.

FAR LEFT: Treasure Island's sidewalk pirate battle, championed by Steve Wynn, was a huge success.
LEFT: Vegas has suffered from strike action.
ABOVE: the opulent Desert Passage mall was an artistic, but not a commercial, success.

NOT SO FAMILY-FRIENDLY

The choreographed "pirate battle" outside Treasure Island, the volcano in front of The Mirage, and the spectacular water shows from the fountains of Bellagio all literally stopped traffic on the Strip every day. New York New York's Coney Island rides, Excalibur, Circus Circus, and Luxor were all built with the family holiday firmly in sight. But after the millennium, things changed. New York New York mounted an adult-oriented Cirque du Soleil show, *Zumanity*, and Treasure Island re-branded with the sexy "sirens" battling in the galleons on the Strip. Vegas marketers recognized that families didn't spend money, and started to gun for those old enough to gamble.

About a quarter of Vegas's visitors each year were first-timers, and this was one of the first groups to decline when people stopped traveling after September 11. To entice them, as well as the veterans, a $13-million eight-week campaign was themed by a never-before-released Sinatra song, *It's Time for You,* licensed by Tina Sinatra. By 2008, though, still only about 19 percent were first-time visitors.

A vital component in the city's – and particularly the Strip's – plans for the future, is the Las Vegas monorail, a public-transportation system substantially funded by the private sector. It is claimed to be the first such project "in the world," but that's probably just Vegas talk.

Travel by monorail

A link between the MGM Grand in the south and Bally's/Paris was opened in 1995 at a cost of $25 million, using two trains purchased from Walt Disney World. The monorail extended the route in 2004, to the Sahara in the north, along a 4-mile (6.5km) route, taking passengers between the Flamingo, the Hilton, Harrah's/Imperial Palace, and the Convention Center. The nine automated four-car trains can carry up to 5,000 passengers per hour in both directions. The monorail is designed to be upgraded with more trains to take 20,000 passengers per hour. Present estimates are that the railway will reduce traffic around the Strip by 4.4 million journeys per year, cutting annual carbon emissions by 135 tonnes. Ultimately, the monorail is hoped to extend

THE RISE AND RISE OF NEW DEVELOPMENTS

After the waves of new concept and theme resorts during the 1990s and the early millennium, new developments at the end of the first decade are often extensions or siblings to existing properties. Wynn Las Vegas has extended with 2,000 more rooms in the Encore Suites; the Venetian produced The Palazzo, a 3,000-room sister property in January 2008; and Caesars Palace is gaining a $1-billion 650-room tower. Las Vegas's often overlooked McCarran Airport is benefitting from a $4-billion expansion.

There are new projects, of course: on the old Stardust site, Echelon will house boutique hotels – a Delano, a Mondrian, and a Shangri-la – in a new resort complex, although there is no firm date for completion. Trump International is a non-gaming tower of 1,300 suites and residences. Opening on the Strip in 2009 is a cousin to the famous Miami landmark, the Fountainebleau, and the new CityCenter "city-within-a-city" resort, which features art, including sculptures by Claes Oldenburg and Jenny Holzer.

The average Vegas visitor spends 3.2 nights, 's 48 years old, and if the purpose is to gamble, drops $555 on the tables and slots. Under 21s make up 10 percent of the visiting population.

as far as Downtown and the airport, but only the airport extension seems still under discussion; current projections are that this will be completed by 2011, but anything could happen.

The US Government stopped nuclear tests at its Nevada site in 1992, but atom power exploded passions six years later when Yucca Mountain, 90 miles (144km) northwest of Vegas, was chosen as a dump for the entire nation's nuclear waste. Congress picked the mountain to hide 77,000 tonnes of radioactive rubbish that would remain deadly for thousands of years. The plan, furiously opposed by Nevadans, was for the site to begin storing the nuclear waste in 2010. Nevada governor Kenny Guin vetoed the plan, claiming that the nuclear industry had spent $120 million supporting the proposal. The veto was overridden by the House and Senate. The license for the US Energy Authority was approved, but delays and budget cutbacks mean that the battle is still going strong, with a new date set for 2013.

FAR LEFT TOP: the public monorail along the Strip. **FAR LEFT BOTTOM:** Loews Resort, Lake Las Vegas. **LEFT:** the Venetian's Palazzo opened in 2008. **ABOVE:** Paul McCartney and Ringo Starr are joined by Ringo's wife and the widows of George Harrison and John Lennon at the one-year anniversary of Cirque du Soleil's *Love*, 2007.

New projects

And still the projects continue *(see box on left)*. Lake Las Vegas, a resort, residential, and leisure complex on the way to Lake Mead, has grown up around its shores, with condos, golf courses, glitzy hotels, and celebrity residents.

In early 2004, the Planet Hollywood group made an offer for the Aladdin Hotel and its opulent mall, the Desert Passage. These are now part of the Planet Hollywood empire, and are known as Planet Hollywood and the Miracle Mile Shops respectively. In 2007, the venerable Stardust Hotel was imploded to clear space for the upcoming "multi-city" Echelon, and the second-oldest of Vegas's casinos, the Frontier, was also demolished. ❑

EXIT
EXIT

BEHIND THE SPECTACLE

Round-the-clock surveillance, sex that sells, transporting tigers through rush-hour traffic – keeping Vegas running to schedule is big-time business

Of the apparent paradoxes in quantum physics, Albert Einstein said, "God does not play dice." Maybe he does, maybe he doesn't, but if he did, Vegas would be a good place to roll the bones. Every aspect of this most modern of cities has paradox embedded, nowhere more than in the landscape of illusion, facade, and trompe l'oeil. Indoor rivers, canals, and sunsets, erupting volcanoes – everything here has a sprinkle of stardust.

The zany architecture, of course, is the first thing visitors tell their friends back home about, but being Las Vegas even something so obvious is rarely what it seems. In the words of one commentator, "it's the only place in the world where they try to make buildings look smaller." Writing in *The Atlantic*, Richard Todd said it was hard to believe people who visited such casinos really thought they were having a New York or Paris or Venetian experience. "We like this architecture, if we do, for its ingenuity, not its realism. We are gratified that someone has gone to such lengths to entertain us: it's performance architecture."

n keeping with the city's love of innovation, he Lou Ruvo Alzheimer's Institute, in the new Union Park development, has been ommissioned from architect Frank Gehry.

PRECEDING PAGES: a night out at LAX, in the hotel Luxor. **LEFT:** the Las Vegas spectacle at its best. **RIGHT:** last stop for dreamers and drifters – a pawn broker.

Illusion by effort

Bellagio is spectacular by any standard, but spokesman Alan L. Feldman said the theme, unlike Excalibur's for instance, is understated.

"The theme we had in mind was just 'romance.' We had thought of classical French styling but we had also thought of something very modern. In fact, we had a design and announced a hotel built in the shape of a great wave. But then Steve Wynn went to Italy and he was sailing on Lake Como and he looked back at the shore and said, 'This is the most romantic place I've ever seen. Let's build this.'"

What visitors don't see is how much behind-the-scenes work the "effortless illusion" takes.

Spectators who filled the street to watch Treasure Island's daily battles between pirates and sexy sirens had no idea how far the designers scoured the world for the cannons and cauldrons to create the ship's fake 18th-century authenticity. Craftsmen and designers from Hollywood were delighted to create something that wouldn't be destroyed when filming ended.

Personnel usually come from amusement parks or theaters where they have learned technical skills like pyrotechnics, hydraulics, audio, and lighting. Every step is well-rehearsed, with remote switches to stop the action if need be.

Horticulturists need to rappel and climb to reach plants in the rocks and lagoons of the pirate-village waterfront. Less visible are the scuba-diving plumbers maintaining the waterfalls at the neighboring Mirage, and 17 round-the-clock florists working to pamper the 60ft (18-meter) palms, banana trees, and orchids.

Stars at Mandalay Bay's Shark Reef are the diver-aquarists, most with biology degrees, who dive into the tank with headsets to answer visitors' questions. Sea turtles like to nibble on the divers' ears but sharks usually keep their distance. Brine shrimp are served to the jellyfish, and crocodiles are fed with long poles.

Tigers take a trip

Animals play a surprisingly large role in everyday Las Vegas life. Rick Thomas is one local who, when not touring the country, uses his tigers in his magic act at various casinos. Thomas and his family live with tawny tigers Zeus, Maximilian, Morpheus, Rocky, and white tigers Samson and Kira on a property north of town, and the trainer has to drive in and out of Las Vegas most days. "People don't see the work that goes into this," he says. "They're animals; they're not potty trained."

Up at 11am for bathing and primping, an air-conditioned trip into town, a nap in the dressing room adjoining the showroom, then two 10-minute afternoon shows are on the agenda before Rick drives all of them home to a dinner of 5lb (2kg) of steak tartare. "The cats are not just a prop," said Thomas. "The moment I make a cat appear on stage, I'm no longer a magician. I'm a trainer."

MARITAL DILEMMA

Conferences and conventions are part and parcel of many businesses now. But if your firm sends you to Vegas on business, and you don't take your spouse along, what will they think? Or what will they spend if you do? Either way, for a happy business trip, seasoned conventioneers suggest leaving the kids at home.

Stage-door Johnnies

Backstage of certain shows, usually the ones featuring showgirls, have always held a certain attraction for what were once known as "Stage Door Johnnies." John F. Kennedy loved to watch the girls perform, both before and during his presidency, and Frank Sinatra sometimes courted the leggy beauties by sending flowers backstage with amorous notes.

Las Vegas casino dealers have to complete a minimum of a six-week training course, then gain experience in one of the smaller clubs, before earning tips on the Strip.

Rich gamblers who made extravagant promises were occasionally hooked into marriage but officially, dancers and showgirls are not permitted to fraternize with the audience or in the casino.

FAR LEFT: unlike this man, most casino security takes place out of sight and undercover. **TOP LEFT:** parenting the parrots. **ABOVE:** snatching a phone call home in between shifts.

After more than half a century, however, the mystique of the showgirls remains, and misconceptions abound. The classic showgirl, tall, stoic, slim, and poised, must not be so overly endowed as to offend wives and girlfriends, and these days topless shows are usually confined to the late performances. Dancers, who rarely appear topless in production shows, tend to be shorter and originally were "saloon girls," hired to spruce up a casino. Then legendary producer Donn Arden brought in a group of dancers to the Desert Inn's Painted Desert Room, which began the tradition of runway models.

Beauty and skill

One of the first showgirls was Dorothy Dandridge, a beauty and a skillful dancer at the famed Club Bingo in the late 1940s. Dandridge won a Best Actress nomination in 1954 for her part in *Carmen Jones*. *Minsky's Follies*, which opened at the Dunes in 1957, was the first topless production show. The *Follies* ran for more than four years, and set show attendance records. The Sands never went topless. The "Texas Copa Girls" or "Pony Girls" were 16 beauty queens brought from Texas expressly to entertain Texan big spenders in the late 1950s. The girls were not trained dancers, nor had they any show experience.

In the 1980s and 1990s, Las Vegas was marketed as a resort for young families and seemed to see an important part of its future in family vacations. Though there are still many entertainments for children and a number of hotel casinos have been themed around family-friendly motifs, the resort is turning back to its earlier market.

Hip place

The *Las Vegas Review-Journal*'s Dave Berns wrote, "Marketeers of the desert city, *circa* 2000, have made an aggressive push to reposition the town as an adult getaway." He said it is "a hip place Frank Sinatra would have enjoyed, a setting where people can leave their day-to-day lives behind in Des Moines, Iowa, or Des Plaines, Illinois and chase drink, song, money and sex." Casino executives focus on the demographic of the middle-aged baby boomer, because their average age is 49 and up. As the Mandalay's president Glenn Schaeffer said, "For the next decade, one American will turn 50 every 11 seconds."

Promise and enticement

Sex is a major component in the Las Vegas spectacle, and the visible part is barely the tip of an iceberg. In a city whose very essence is promise and enticement, the sex trade flourishes. Some visitors find themselves victimized by sex-tease clip joints where women hustlers extort huge sums for drinks with the

SEX

Sex in Las Vegas still makes national headlines. When Melissa Farley, a San Francisco researcher, self-published her book, *Prostitution and Trafficking in Nevada: Making the Connections*, *New York Times* columnist Bob Herbert took it as a jumping-off point for an article in which he said, "There is probably no city in America where women are treated worse than in Las Vegas." UNLV sociologists Barb Brents and Kate Hausbeck spent more than 10 years researching Nevada's prostitutes, and said that some women choose to sell their bodies. Like all Las Vegas stories, the true picture is more complex than a headline can encompass.

promise of action "later." These operators prey mercilessly on the unwary and the mistaken belief that prostitution is legal in Las Vegas. Reputedly, they charge anything up to $6,000 for a bottle of non-alcoholic "champagne," and the "non-alcoholic" part is the giveaway.

Sex-tease clubs are tolerated, but they aren't given liquor licenses, so if you find yourself, for any reason, in a bar with no beer, you may want to leave smartly.

High expectations

Prostitution is illegal in Vegas, but nobody pretends it doesn't happen. Out on the Strip, countless freesheets and flyers offer phone numbers for an exotic range of services in your hotel room. Like any city in the world but Las Vegas style – with much glitz and show.

Expectations are high because of the seemingly inexhaustable number of glamorous women, anxious to make a living by any means necessary. This goes for men, too; a growing market in Sin City is the male striptease revues, catering to women on "gal pal" weekends.

LEFT: sex and the city. **ABOVE:** transporting cargo through the heavy Vegas traffic is not always easy.

Pressure to legalize prostitution dates back almost as far as the city itself. Harold Stocker, son of Mayme *(see page 37)*, a former dealer and bootlegger who went on to chair the state's Republican Party in the 1950s said, "They're trying to lay all this crime we have today on hookers and pimps. Well, if that's the problem, why the hell don't they legalize (prostitution) so they can regulate it? Regulating it is all you can hope to do because they have never succeeded in eliminating it in a thousand years of trying."

In 2006, after a 10-year investigation, the Crazy Horse Too gentlemen's club was closed. Owner Rick Rizzolo, a convicted racketeer, pleaded guilty – to tax evasion.

Nevada state law prohibits brothels in counties with more than 400,000 inhabitants. The closest legal brothels to Las Vegas are in Nye County, particularly in the desert town of Pahrump about 60 miles (96km) away.

It's not surprising that the euphemistically styled "adult entertainment" industry chooses the Las Vegas Convention Center for its annual

trade show – the Adult Entertainment Expo. This in turn attracts "Porn Pastor" (his description) Craig Cross of xxxchurch.com, a Vegas-based crusade against the porn and flesh trade. "If Jesus were walking the earth today," said Cross, in his early thirties, "he'd be here, too. After all, he hung out with prostitutes and stuff." They work with a church, whose pastor said, "It is very near to our hearts to help people overcome sexual addiction and to help them have healthy sexual boundaries with other people." And surely, God would love Las Vegas as much as any of us. Referring to Einstein's quote, cosmologist Stephen Hawking said, "God plays dice all the time."

Surveillance

Not many gamblers glance upwards as they navigate the aisles, but most of them are aware that their every move is watched through the cameras and one-way mirrors mounted in the casino walls, catwalks, and ceiling.

The video cameras are programed to zoom in automatically on any unusual activity. Recording audio contravenes the Federal laws against wiretapping, but visual surveillance goes on around the clock on games where illicit activity is suspected.

Dealers and pit bosses are never above suspicion, and casinos also have a habit of monitoring their own security staff. *Review-Journal* columnist John L. Smith said that gaming establishments, "have a long tradition of employing convicted card and slot

WET Technology

WET Design are the company responsible not only for the new volcano and lake at The Mirage, but also for those spectacular fountains at Bellagio. These make water dance 460ft (140 meters) high, from 1,214 spouts, across the 8.5-acre (3.5-hectare) lake.

The fountains are maintained seven days a week, 365 days a year by a staff of 38. As well as cleaning the fountains, the crew fit and take care of the shooters, pumps, and water compressors, the purification equipment and a fog system so powerful that it could cover much of Las Vegas Boulevard. The computer program that runs the fountains compensates automatically for wind and weather conditions, and the fountains themselves use only about 10 percent of the water that the Dunes Hotel golf course required, when it occupied the same site.

The free aquatechnic spectacle attracts and entrances huge crowds, every 30 minutes between 3pm and 7pm, and then every 15 minutes until midnight on weekdays. The shows start at noon on weekends.

cheaters to catch those still practicing the racket."

Nevada Gaming Control Board agents have full access at all times, and the power to demand any videotape they want. Officials are unwilling to give details, but all the videotape of both play and players is said to be collected daily and stored in a warehouse. Tapes are usually saved for seven days but in certain areas, the law mandates 30-days' retention. Cameras are equipped with infra-red and ultraviolet imaging to detect concealed devices, as well as face-recognition.

Hidden cameras

Surveillance cameras have been known to pick up almost invisible beams of infra-red light from a hidden miniature video camera. In one instance, it was in the purse of a woman sitting by a blackjack dealer, and it transmitted a picture of his hole card as he peeked at it before taking players' bets.

Back when microphones were allowed, supposedly, some customers used to "audition for the lounge shows" by singing into the mics mounted at gaming tables. Today, though, the only microphones allowed in casinos are those that monitor audio in the count rooms, where the sound of money can be very important.

Surveillance cameras pick up more than just casino cheats. Apparently, videotapes of people having sex in the elevators are particularly popular.

Magazine writer Sergio Lalli says that five people are likely to be in the count room at one time, and each of them has to be authorized by the Gaming Control Board. They are not subject to casino authority.

In his book *Loaded Dice,* self-confessed "casino cheat" John Soares recounts years working with a team switching the dice in craps games. Soares repeatedly points out the risks inherent in cheating – when failure might have resulted in death and a burial in the desert – but he claims that he and his team ripped off millions without any serious setbacks. ❑

LEFT: dinner with the Rick Thomas family.
ABOVE: Anthony, Caesar, and Cleo take the weight off their sandals.

Cirque du Soleil

Sensual, elegant acrobats and magicians, martial artists, dancers, swimmers and divers weave the distinctive Cirque magic

The story of Cirque du Soleil began in 1980, with a troupe of street performers called Les Echassiers (the waders) in the artist-friendly Quebec community of Baie Saint-Paul. Crowds and praise came to the dazzling circus of choreographed acrobats, dancers, high-wire, trapeze, and magic acts, but they struggled for finance for the first few years. By the end of the decade, though, the human-only, no-animal circus with their highly original music, costumes, and lighting, were performing in Europe and the USA as the Cirque du Soleil (Circus of the Sun).

In 2007 alone, Cirque performed in front of almost 10 million spectators, and currently presents 18 different shows around the world. There are six resident shows in Las Vegas, with a seventh opening in 2010.

Above: incorporating fire and water, the name of *"O"* at Bellagio has a double-meaning; the circle, O, for infinity, and the French *"eau,"* meaning water.

Left: *Mystère* was Las Vegas' first permanent Cirque du Soleil show, in a theater built to the company's specification at T.I. (Treasure Island).

Below: the gravity-defying *KÀ* at the MGM Grand is presented on a massive custom-built stage, which rotates a full 360°.

Above: the one-year anniversary of the *LOVE* show at The Mirage was attended by Beatles Sir Paul McCartney and Ringo Starr, and the Beatles' legendary producer, George Martin.

BEHIND THE BIG TOP

All of Cirque du Soleil's performing artists begin their association with the company in Montreal, training at the Creation Studio. Here, everyone is schooled in acrobatics and dance, as well as in percussion and acting. Swimmers, gymnasts, tumblers, dancers, singers, and musicians all gain from the multi-discipline induction into the family of almost 1,000 artists from 40 nationalities who make up this unique troupe. Behind-the-scenes staff swells this number to around 3,500 people.

The company's initial success was based on its touring shows, where tutors are often provided for children who accompany their parents on the road. With the huge success of the resident shows in Vegas, there are now permanent Big Tops in Orlando, Florida, Dubai, Tokyo, and Macao.

ABOVE LEFT: *Criss Angel Believe* is a marriage of Cirque du Soleil's other-worldly illusion and dance, and the remarkable displays of Angel, the modern *enfant-terrible* of illusion.

ABOVE: when New York New York wanted to re-brand itself in the post-family style of Las Vegas, they began by commissioning the adult-themed show, *Zumanity*, which explores more deeply the sensual side of Cirque.

RQUE DU SOLEIL SHOWS TIMELINE

2010 *Elvis* opens at CityCenter
2008 *Criss Angel Believe* opens at Luxor
2006 *Love* premiers at the Mirage
2005 *KÀ* opens at the MGM Grand
2003 *Zumanity* opens at New York New York
1998 *O* – first shows at Bellagio
1993 *Mystère* opens a new venue at T.I.
1992 *Nouvelle Expérience* begins a year-long residency, in a big top outside Vegas's The Mirage
1990 *Nouvelle Expérience* premieres in Montreal
1984 Named Cirque du Soleil for a Canadian tour
1980 Troupe formed in Baie Saint-Paul, Quebec

BELLAGIO
$25,000
BACCARAT
LAS VEGAS NEVADA
50
25
20
10
5
6
5

DICING WITH LADY LUCK

Hope springs eternal in the human breast, and nowhere is this more evident than on the floor of a gaming hall

In a book on the subject, Alan Wykes said, "Gambling is a way of buying hope on credit." Or, as Alexander Pope put it, "Hope springs eternal in the human breast." Everyone dreams of leaving Vegas richer than when they arrived.

The 2007 Las Vegas Visitor Profile reported that 78 percent of the city's tourists citing the primary purpose for their visit was other than gambling, but closer examination reveals that 84 percent actually had a little flutter. For some it was no more than quarters in a slot machine, but the average number of hours spent gambling was four, and the average budget for gaming was $555.

A Godfather speaks

Mario Puzo, author of *The Godfather*, wrote from his own experience. "A gambler should never write a check or sign a chit," he said, "gambling only with the money he brought with him, if he wants to stay out of trouble." He discussed what he calls the "ruin factor," less important when you have nothing to lose, but, "now I have too much to lose, and the ruin factor is decisive. Of course, I had to lose a great deal of money… before I could figure this out. Gambling education is not cheap."

Casino Royale was reported, in 2008, to be the only casino on the Strip to offer blackjack games dealt from a single deck, rather than from a multi-deck shoe.

Once upon a time in America, government policy was to discourage or even prohibit gambling, but that was another age. Today, more and more states not only allow, but encourage, gaming. Politicians seem to have fallen under the spell of easy revenue, almost as much as the casinos and the punters.

The latest change on the green-baize map has been the growth of gambling on Native American reservations. As semi-autonomous regions, indigenous nations are able to run

LEFT: more than $1 million in chips at Bellagio.
RIGHT: cheats often attempt to substitute dice weighted on one side to favor a given number.

casinos even in states which otherwise prohibit it. Of America's 561 tribes recognized by the Federal government, 108 are in California. Las Vegas casino owners were alarmed by the competition so nearby, and spent $20 million fighting to prevent Native American gambling businesses, until a Californian legal decision allowed it in 1988. Las Vegas claims that Native American casinos in California are currently taking 10 percent of their business – more than $1 billion a year. In an acceptance of the new reality Harrah's partnered with the Rincon Reservation near Escondito in California for a co-managed casino resort.

CITY OF SLOTS

There are a few non-gambling oases in Vegas, but slot machines seem to pop up in more places all the time. In 2000, the Gaming Commission allowed drugstores and grocers to install slots if they were walled off from the rest of the store, but they also made specific exceptions: new liquor stores, gas stations, no-booze restaurants, car dealerships, motels, and sandwich shops. Tourists at McCarran Airport find slot machines as much of a lure as the shops. Contrary to the myth that machines outside the casinos seldom pay off, within a two-week period, there were two million-dollar winners on McCarran's slots.

It's a gamble

From high rollers like radio host Howard Stern, who tried to place a $1-million bet on a blackjack hand, to the nickel-slots players, gambling cuts across social and economic classes. Gambling has been studied from just about every angle, and in minute detail.

The percentage of women gamblers has, as reported by the Connecticut Council on Problem Gambling, with a huge increase in calls to its hotline. Statistically, men and women carry similar gambling debts, but men have a greater average lifetime loss. Independent studies suggest that compulsive gambling may be higher among teens than adults. For teenagers, gambling may begin with friendly wagers on sports events, penny-ante card games, or the lucky "gift" of a lottery ticket.

To their credit, the casinos do not sweep the problem of compulsive gambling under the rug. Eight gaming companies are represented on the Council on Problem Gambling, which develops treatment resources and displays large posters exhorting, "Know when to stop." The posters also give a 24-hour-a-day helpline number to call (1-800-522-4700).

Compulsive gambling is described as "an emotional illness that remains hidden until the consequences begin to affect the financial and emotional security of the gambler and his family." Early warning signs, according to the leaflet, include: losing time from work or family, borrowing money to gamble, gambling to escape worry, selling personal possessions to

get gambling money, and lying about the time and money spent on gambling.

"In a gambling addiction," writer Joseph Epstein said, "one tends to bet on anything – from the gestation period of a gerbil to different lengths of two paper clips."

One thing that might help is the Innovative Gaming Corporation of America's technology, which allows gamblers to program a set limit on their ATM cards at a casino kiosk, then use them in slot machines that "lock up" for five to 10 days when the limit is reached.

The history of blackjack

Also known as "Twenty-One" or *vingt-et-un*, blackjack is a descendant from the French game of *chemin de fer*, as is baccarat. The game was played in French casinos as far back as the early 1700s. It arrived in the US in the 1800s, and got its modern name from the frontier practice of paying extra on a hand of an ace with the jack of spades, i.e. "blackjack."

LEFT AND ABOVE: compulsive gambling is described as "an emotional illness that remains hidden until the consequences begin to affect the financial and emotional security of the gambler and his family."

The natural house edge is around 3.5 percent, but a skilled player can reduce it to 1 percent or less, still the best odds in the casino.

Avery Cardoza, a gambling author and publisher said, "Blackjack is a game of skill that can be beat. However, to win, you must learn the game properly." The game is played against the house, and the object is to beat the dealer by drawing a higher hand than the dealer without going over 21 – "busting" – or by not busting when the dealer does. The top hand, an ace and either a 10 or a picture card is called blackjack. The house pays evens (1-1) to a winner, and 3-2 for blackjack.

> *Statistically, men and women are said to carry similar gambling debts, but men have a greater average lifetime loss. Women may gamble, in secret, on the Internet.*

There are innumerable systems for blackjack which all promise to tip the odds in favor of the player. The system known as "card counting," however, is still treated as cheating by Nevada casinos. Widely regarded as the

world's greatest blackjack player, Ken Uston gave up his post as a senior vice-president of the Pacific Stock Exchange in order to organize teams of card counters.

Kevin Spacey starred in the 2008 movie, *21,* based on a true story about a group of MIT students who set up a successful blackjack card-counting ring in the 1990s.

Poker ploys

Regardless of status, motive, or method, most of us make unconscious revelations through body language. In poker, this can be the difference between winning or losing. Tics, twitches, nervous laughs, or facial expressions can be crucial giveaways. Andy Bellin discussed these "tells," as they are called, in an article in *Atlantic* magazine.

"Having a poker tell can be disastrous (although) overcoming a tell is as difficult as changing any other habitual aspect of your personality." Often, he says, a player will slump in his chair when he has nothing, or jump to flip the cards over when he has a good hand. "The more attention you pay to the body language of your opponents, the less money you'll leave on the table."

New Yorker reviewer Joseph Epstein says that poker is not a game for delicate souls. "Good players always beat less-good players over the long haul, but in poker the short haul can kill you." He identifies aggression as the key characteristic in poker players – "the instinct for the jugular." Newer games like Let It Ride, Caribbean Stud, Casino War, and Spanish 21 are played against the dealer. "The intimidation factor has been diminished a lot," says Barney Vinson of Caesars Palace.

The odds of winning in these specialty games are lower than in standard casino games. The house edge on craps and blackjack can be 1 percent or less, but it's about 3.5 percent in Let It Ride and around 5 percent in Caribbean Stud. Casinos claim that it takes longer for the house to make a profit, and the games are popular in part because the hands take longer to play out.

> “ *Improvement can be due to only one thing: to character, which as I finally begin to improve myself a bit, I see that the game of poker is all about.*
> Playright David Mamet ”

The noisiest, rowdiest places in a casino are usually the craps tables. Play is fast and generates a great deal of excitement. The stickman calls the shots like a carnival barker, and two dealers handle the bets, with a boxman who supervises the game and settles disputes. The dice move from one player to another, and bets can be made either for or against the "shooter" making his target, or "point."

Dice games date back to the Bible, and craps is traced back to before the 1700s, when it came to the USA from Europe. Benny Binion introduced craps to casino gaming in Texas, and brought it to Vegas when he opened Binion's Horseshoe, the Downtown casino.

Kirk Kerkorian, founder of the MGM Grand, was known as the "Perry Como of the craps table" for his style and equanimity in regularly winning – or more often losing – from $50,000 to $80,000 in an evening. Legend has it that he and a buddy were down to their last $5, and the buddy suggested they buy breakfast. Kerkorian took the $5 bill to the craps table, returning half an hour later with $700. When he had his own casinos, Kerkorian reputedly stopped playing craps.

Granddaddy of all slots

The century-long history of the slot machine began with the original three-reel machine which emerged from Charles Frey's San Francisco workshop in 1898. The German-born inventor pioneered many coin-operated gaming devices, most of which went into San Francisco's Barbary Coast gambling clubs.

LEFT AND ABOVE: slot machines, also known as "one-armed bandits," presently bring in about 70 percent of Las Vegas's gambling revenue.

The basic design of "Liberty Bell," the granddaddy of all American slot machines, is still used today, although the simple trio of reels have evolved into microprocessor-controlled machines, with up to five spinning reels holding hundreds of symbols. By the time Bugsy Siegel added slot machines to his Flamingo Hotel in the late 1940s, they had

CONTROLLED AGGRESSION

British writer, poet, and poker tournament player Al Alvarez said, "Poker is a game of many skills. You need card sense, psychological insight, a good memory, controlled aggression, enough mathematical know-how to work out the odds as each hand develops, and what poker players call a 'leather ass' – patience! Above all, you need the arcane skill called money management, the ability to control your bankroll and understand the long-term implications of each bet so that you don't go broke during the session." Alvarez, who was educated at Oxford University, has also written on other topics, like suicide.

already spread across the USA as a way to entertain the wives and girlfriends of high rollers. Soon they were making more revenue than the table games combined. Slot machines now generate two-thirds of Nevada casinos' take, with the nickel slots producing $1 billion annually. The machines are programed for a jackpot rare enough to make a big pay off, but leaving a tidy profit for the casino. Pay outs are between 83 and 98 percent, and vary from casino to casino. Nickel slots pay out significantly less than the higher-stake machines, though Gary Thompson, speaking for Harrah's, said this was not the reason for the increase in nickel slots. "We're not tightening the slots," he said, "the customers are opting to go for the nickel games."

Phenomenal popularity

The popularity of slot machines is doubtless because they require no skill and the pace is set by the player, driven by the illusion that a machine will be ready to pay off after a certain amount of play. The machines are driven by random generators, making new selections every 1,000th of a second, with no reference to what went before, so in reality the machines are never "ready to hit."

Some machines don't even pay a jackpot on one single coin, but the three-coin jackpot often pays 150 percent of a two-coin win. Theoretically costing a quarter or a dollar, they only pay out substantial sums if two or three coins are deposited instead of one, but

CARDS COUNT

The United States Playing Card Company have made cards since 1867. Their "Bee" cards have been a popular brand since 1892, which is why they bear the number "92" on the ace of spades (the standard poker deck is now known as deck type 92).

"Bee"s are widely used in casinos, and have a diamond-patterned back, usually blue or red, and casinos often have their logo on the back. Casino cards also have the back pattern right up to the edge, making it easier to see if a card is face up in a deck.

At the 2007 World Series of Poker, USPC debuted their "PokerPeek" cards, with the rank and suit printed on all four corners of the face, at a 45-degree angle to the card's edges, so players can read face-down cards, but making it harder for others to read.

Players found the new cards unfamiliar, and they were mostly withdrawn from the tournament, but the design was integrated into the Bicycle Pro casino-quality cards which are aimed at the home market, and are available from retailers.

LEFT: Caesars Palace slots. **ABOVE:** New York New York – the greatest city in Las Vegas.

less than half of slot players play more than one coin at a time, says Crevelt in his book *Video Poker Mania*. He advises, "always play the maximum number of coins because there is a bonus when you win (which) can be up to 5 percent of the payback, which doesn't apply if you are not playing to the full extent." Playing a single coin at a time leaves the casino an extra advantage.

Multiple-coin slot machines were soon followed in the USA by video machines, which substituted screens for the old-fashioned reels. This enabled other games like poker, keno, blackjack, and craps to be played on them instead of just at the table. William Silas "Si" Redd developed video poker machines when he bought Fortune Coin Co. and converted the early Pong machines for poker.

Casinos were quick to capitalize on the explosive growth of video poker, and in a short time they were taking the place of the original slots. More than 15 percent of Harrah's 1,760 slots are now devoted to video poker, and the percentage is increasing. The video poker machines far outrank the table games in popularity, especially among women; almost three quarters of visitors to Las Vegas play slots as opposed to the 29 percent of players who opt for table games such as blackjack or craps. But playing the slots can also lead to other games. "A lot of people have learned to play poker on the video poker machines," says Alan Abrams of the El Cortez casino. "Now they enjoy the camaraderie of a table game where people interact with each other."

> *The biggest Las Vegas penny-slot payout was for $10.8 million at Wynn Las Vegas in 2006. The largest slots jackpot ever was $39.7 million, at Excalibur in 2003.*

The 3,000-year-old game

Keno evolved from a Chinese game which is at least 3,000 years old. The modern game makes a slightly inclined bow in China's direction in the "Yin-Yang" symbols on most tickets. Keno runners, like many casino workers in Vegas, count on tips for most of their income, so

they're usually easy to find and eager to help. The game is to predict as many numbers as possible of the 20 picked in a random draw. There are about half a dozen combination tickets, the bets tend to be small, and payouts can be up to $50,000. The odds are too poor for serious gamblers, but for a frivolous flutter, there is a game about every 20 minutes in most casino hotels, often in the bars or coffee shops.

> *When the Rolling Stones came to town, the Hard Rock casino issued a series of commemorative chips featuring the British rockers.*

Super Bowl and other sports

Every January, the handful of men known as the Las Vegas Sports Consultants meet in a three-story building near McCarran Airport to establish the "line," (ie set the gaming odds) on the USA's Super Bowl American football game. The Sports Books in Las Vegas, and in other casinos around the country, await the official word, the yardstick from which bets are figured. Super Bowl weekend betting is about three times the average in the National Football League season and includes not only low-stake tourists, but the high rollers – who tend to stick around town for a while, and the "wise guys" – professional sports gamblers who stay only long enough to win or lose big.

Georgia-born Billy Baxter, winner of seven World Series of Poker bracelets, bets about $1 million that weekend, half on Saturday college football games, the rest on Sunday pro football.

LVSC has 14 odds-makers for sports, all of them licensed by the Nevada Gaming Control Board. After the Super Bowl, the NCAA basketball tournament is the single biggest gambling event. "Blink at the wrong time," says a Sports Book manager, "and you can easily lose six figures."

Cards, chips, and cheats

The accoutrements of games – dice, cards, and chips – have to be as tamper-proof as human skills can make them. Early dice were made from the knucklebones of sheep; today those used for craps are crafted to a tolerance of one ten-thousandth of an inch.

Most of the thousands of decks of cards used annually in Las Vegas are supplied by the US Playing Card Company of Cincinnati, Ohio, whose Bicycle brand – and the Bee brand for casinos – are the most widely used cards in the country. The Bee, introduced over a century ago, has the highest content of rag, giving the card a good "memory," the term for how well a card snaps back after being bent.

Collectable chips

Commemorative chips are a winning move for casinos, because many gamblers take the chips home without redeeming them. Chipco International of Raymond, Maine, specializes in designer graphics with what is termed a high "walk factor." Their canny SmartChip, however, can be tracked by computer and trips a sensor-activated alarm if a chip is taken from the casino.

Since in one way or another the house nearly always wins, some determined casino customers are constantly devising new ways to cheat. "Some cheaters will place a stack of $5 chips in the betting circle and angle the chips slightly towards the dealer... an attempt to block the dealer's view of the bottom chip," says George Joseph. And then, "if the cheater gets a good hand he will slide a higher value chip underneath."

LEFT: downtown Vegas is good for gaming souvenirs.
ABOVE: betting can be fast and furious, which is how many gamblers like it.

Magic skills

The sleight-of-hand used by magicians is much the same as that employed by casino cheats. "They're magicians, too," says writer Deke Castleman. "They're expert at diverting attention while they pull off their scam. The quickness of the hand deceives the eye." So, do the casinos cheat, too? Mario Puzo said not. "I reluctantly came to the conclusion that Vegas has honest casino gambling." ❑

JACKPOT!!

The highest ever payout on a Las Vegas slot machine was to a 25 year-old visitor in 2003. In town for the NCAA basketball tournament, he rolled $100 into the slots at Excalibur, and won £39.7 million, which he collects as $1.5 million per annum over 25 years.

The record for a nickel slot was a nearly $3.2 million hit in 2005 by an off-duty cab driver in Las Vegas. Elmer Sherwin was a 92 year-old second-time jackpot winner. He had won $4.6 million, 21 years before, and was content with that and with his life, so he decided to donate the whole of his second, $21 million payout, to victims of the Hurricane Katrina disaster.

How to Win

There is one sure-fire way to make money from a casino – buy one. If you play the slots, the tables, or the Sports Book in Las Vegas, do it to have fun. You may have Lady Luck at your shoulder and win a fortune at the tables. Then again, you may not. Tåhe golden rule for happy gambling is to set a limit beforehand and not exceed it. If you can manage that, the other motto is "quit while you're ahead." Serious players pre-calculate a stake range – highest to lowest bet – by multiplying the number of hours they intend to play by the number of games per hour, and dividing their "bankroll" by the result, to set a maximum stake. A low stake is then set at around 20 percent of the maximum, or less. Low bets are made until a winning streak is hit, then stakes are progressively raised. This way, losses are kept small and winnings are maximized.

It's a good idea to ride a winning streak. If you strike it lucky, put a profit to one side, then raise your stakes and go for it. If you start to lose, cut back or – better still – walk away. Playing comfortably low stakes offers more fun in the long run. Betting $5 a hundred times and winning some of the time gives more hours of entertainment than playing $500 and maybe losing, once.

Blackjack

Blackjack offers some of the best odds in the casino. The house's natural edge is between 3 and 5 percent, and skilled players can narrow that to 1 percent with betting and playing combinations.

The object is to get a hand of cards closer to 21 than the dealer. Cards take their face value, except for pictures counting as 10, and aces, which the player can value as 1 or 11. The top hand, an ace with a 10 or a picture, makes 21 – "blackjack."

Blackjack deals are from a six or eight-deck plastic "shoe." Some casinos, mostly Downtown, play with a single deck, giving the player much better chances to predict the remaining cards.

Craps

A craps game may look daunting, but is really fairly simple. It also offers good odds to players; the house edge on a simple "pass line" bet is only 1.4 percent. Bets are made for and against a dice roll, called "right" or "wrong" bets. The dice pass around the table. No-one has to roll, but the thrower must bet on his own game.

At the first, or "come out" roll, a throw of 2, 3, or 12 is known as craps. This is a win for bets on the "don't pass" line, or wrong bets. The numbers 7 or 11 are automatic winners for "pass-line," right bets. Any other number rolled establishes the shooter's "point." The aim then is to roll the point again before hitting a 7.

Keno

Keno is hugely popular because it is so simple to play, and a $50,000 payout is possible on a $1 bet. All you need do is pick some numbers on a ticket and wait. It's easy, and it's fun. It's also among the lowest player odds in the house, with a casino edge of 20 to 30 percent.

Due to a mystery of Nevada gaming regulation, keno is not, technically, a lottery. Payouts must be collected immediately after each game, and before the next game starts, or they are forfeited. Take a place at the bar or café and call a keno runner over, pick your lucky numbers and wait for the draw. Any number of tickets can be bought for each game, and there are endless combinations to mark the numbers, which the runner will happily show you. If the runner returns with winnings, it is polite to tip.

Roulette

The wheel spins, the ball spins against it. The ball drops, and clatters. It bounces once, twice, and comes to rest in number 7. The dealer places the white marker next to your chip on the 7, and your $100 bet is joined by $3,500 in chips. Or not.

Payout is a dizzying 35 to 1 on a single number, but the 0 and 00 make the odds 38 to 1 against you predicting correctly. If the ball falls on 0 or 00, all bets lose, except for those predicting that exact outcome. This makes the overall house edge 5.26 percent, and about the poorest table odds in town.

The safest bets on the wheel are the outsiders; the "dozens" (first 12, second 12, third 12, or one of the three "columns"), which pay out 2 to 1. Otherwise, 1 to 1 payouts are offered by "red or black," "odd or even," or "first or last 18."

Sports Books

In the Sports Book, players back their expertise in predicting sports events. Odds are offered on football, baseball, Indy car races, and championship boxing. But the main event in the book is horse racing, still the largest spectator sport in the US. A horse's previous performance, or "form," is a guide, and the simple bets – "win" or "place" – are the most profitable.

The Sports Book is the one place in a casino you are guaranteed to find a clock.

Poker

A tip from one professional poker player is this: sit down at the table and spot the sucker. If you haven't made them within five minutes, get up and leave. It's you. The ability to read other players at the table can be as important in poker as getting the best cards. In the betting rounds, the players who think they have the strongest hand will try to lure money into the "pot." But players who believe they have weaker cards may bluff, to scare others out of the game. Poker is the only game where play is against other gamblers and not against the house. Instead, the house makes its living from a cut – usually around 5 percent – off the top of each pot.

A common form of poker in Las Vegas is "Texas Hold 'em." Each player is dealt two cards, face down. Through progressive

betting rounds, five "community cards" are dealt, face up. Each player then makes the highest five-card hand they can from the seven cards available.

Advice from the pros

Serious and professional players consider whatever is in front of them as their own money – not the house's – and safeguard their chips accordingly.

The house plays most games with what seems like a tiny advantage. Over time, though, the odds are likely to attract your bankroll across the table. The main thing that you can do is to slow the roll. ❑

LEFT: the best way to win – own a casino.
RIGHT: money – that's what I want.

VEGAS IN THE MOVIES

The fantasy facades of Sin City offer endless opportunities for movie-makers. The fact that Vegas is just a short hop on a Lear jet from Hollywood also helps

Las Vegas magic is the magic of illusion, and many of its spectacular displays are the work of designers, set builders, and special-effects experts from the movie business. The puffy clouds and sunsets inside shopping arcades like the Forum Shops, the millions of megawatts of artificial light outdoors, the pyramids and volcanoes, and the sea battles of T.I. (Treasure Island) make the town like a Hollywood blockbuster set. The gold and the glitter, the instant flips of fortune, and the fantasy facades also offer endlessly rich plot potential. All this has kept Sin City in the movies and in the business of movies. The fact that Vegas is just a short hop in a Lear jet from Hollywood helps, too.

Made in Vegas

Since movies were silent, Las Vegas had starring roles in movies like *The Hazards of Helen* and John Ford's 1932 film *Airmail*. Edwin L. Mann's 1946 film *Lady Luck* was a moral tale about the lure of gambling. In 1960, Marilyn Monroe and Clark Gable both played their last movie roles in John Huston's *The Misfits*, much of it filmed in the Nevada desert. Arthur Miller's script was uncannily prophetic of the Monroe-Miller marriage.

Ocean's 11, also made in 1960, was the famous Rat Pack film, directed by Lewis Milestone in the time Frank Sinatra, Dean Martin, Sammy Davis Jr, and Peter Lawford could spare from carousing. Though the film wasn't rated by critics, it made respectable enough ticket sales for a follow-up, *Robin and the Seven Hoods*. *Ocean's 11* was remade in 2001 with George Clooney, Matt Damon, Andy Garcia, and Julia Roberts topping a stellar bill, and with interiors shot in Bellagio. The same team came back to town, though perhaps less successfully, in 2007's *Ocean's 13*.

Elvis Presley wooed Ann-Margret from the Sahara all the way to Lake Mead and Mount Charleston in *Viva Las Vegas* (1964), a famous pairing rumored to have continued off screen.

In 1971, Sean Connery went Downtown to Fremont Street as James Bond in *Diamonds Are Forever*, which critic Leonard Maltin described as a "colorful comic book adventure." Dustin Hoffman won an Oscar for his role in *Rain Man* in 1988, which co-starred fresh-faced Tom Cruise, and featured a scene filmed in the Pompeiian Fantasy Suite of Caesars Palace. Actor

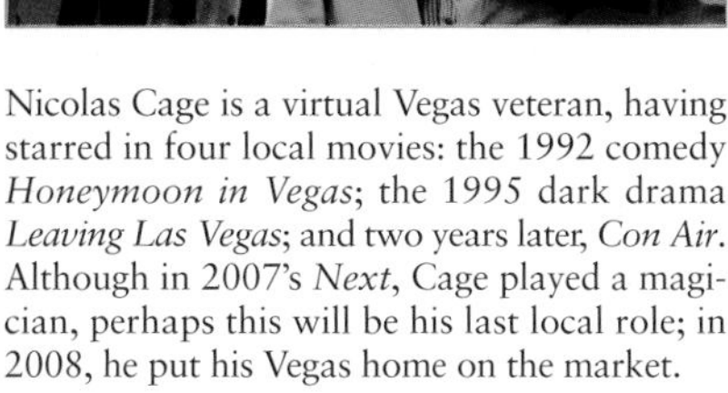

Nicolas Cage is a virtual Vegas veteran, having starred in four local movies: the 1992 comedy *Honeymoon in Vegas*; the 1995 dark drama *Leaving Las Vegas*; and two years later, *Con Air*. Although in 2007's *Next*, Cage played a magician, perhaps this will be his last local role; in 2008, he put his Vegas home on the market.

In the 1995 movie, Leaving Las Vegas, *the bartender who wipes blood from Nicholas Cage's face is Julian Lennon, son of John Lennon.*

High-rolling Redford

Lavish high-roller suites and turns of the tables provided the setting for Adrian Lynn's *Indecent Proposal* (1993), where Woody Harrelson rashly encouraged screen wife Demi Moore to spend a night with tycoon Robert Redford for a million dollars, and lived to regret it – until the last reel, of course.

Johnny Depp took lots of narcotics and trashed a hotel room as a reporter covering a prosecuters' war-on-drugs convention in the 1998 film of Hunter S. Thompson's *Fear and Loathing in Las Vegas*, filmed partly in the Riviera, Circus Circus, and Stardust hotels.

LEFT: William H. Macy's character in *The Cooler* has the ability to ruin other gamblers' good runs. **ABOVE TOP:** Howard Hughes presents *The Las Vegas Story.* **ABOVE BOTTOM:** the updated *Ocean's 11* team. **RIGHT:** Sean Connery as James Bond makes Fremont Street safe for the world in *Diamonds are Forever.*

The venerable Stardust, which was demolished in 2007, was the best thing about the 1995 melodrama *Showgirls*, often ranked among the worst movies of all time. The casino was the scene for a more charming film, the hit indy movie *Swingers* (1996), when Vince Vaughn and Jon Favreau spend a womanizing weekend in Sin City. Favreau returned to Vegas two years later in the darker *Very Bad Things*.

Drawn from the true-life tale in the best-selling book *Bringing Down the House*, *21* (2008) follows six gifted MIT students, who, with their professor and mentor, take on Vegas as card-counters. Most of the casino scenes were filmed in Planet Hollywood. That same year's silly rom-com *What Happens in Vegas* spends only the first few minutes in Sin City.

The low-key comedy *St John of Las Vegas* (2009) is about an ex-gambler lured back to the game by an insurance-fraud investgator. John is played by the always-reliable Steve Buscemi.

Sci-Fi on the Strip

The Amazing Colossal Man (1957) saw Las Vegas attacked by a soldier who grew to 60ft (18 meters) after surviving an atomic blast. *Mars Attacks*, Tim Burton's 1996 sci-fi fantasy featured a galaxy of stars including Pierce Brosnan, Annette Bening, Tom Jones, two roles for Jack Nicholson, and the Las Vegas Strip spectacularly demolished. That year, the only stars of *Independence Day* to survive with reputations intact were the special effects. In 1998, Klingons visited Sin City, aiming to kidnap guests from the Las Vegas Hilton, foiled by the crew of the Starship Enterprise in *Star Trek: The Experience*.

Rick Moranis reprised the goofy scientist from *Honey I Shrunk the Kids* in *Honey I Blew Up the Kid* (1992), as his two-year-old son grew 150ft (46 meters) high and even

FILM FESTIVALS

In a short history, beginning in 1998 at Bally's, the CineVegas festival (www.CineVegas.com) has hosted the premieres for a number of breakout movies, including *Star Trek: Insurrection*.

Along with a "Best of the Fests" feature, cannily harvesting winners and highlights to showcase from other film festivals around the globe, CineVegas aims to provide a platform for artists and art lovers, shown amid the unique, unpredictable, and intoxicating environment that is Sin City. Actor Dennis Hopper is on the board.

The festival is currently held in showrooms and convention spaces in Paris Las Vegas. The festival also holds a *La Proxima Ola* section, highlighting new independent films that are produced in Mexico.

The "CineVegas From the Vault" screening series is a year-round festival presented by the CineVegas Film Festival and the Las Vegas–Clark County Library District, showcasing films that the festival has either premiered or featured throughout its brief but august history. The screenings are free and open to the public, and are held on the first Thursday of every month at 7pm, at the Clark County Library, which is at 1401 East Flamingo Road.

For those who appreciate the very special art of short films, the historic Boulder Theatre (1225 Arizona Street, Boulder City) is the venue in February for the Dam Short Film Festival, founded in 2003 by Lee and Anita Lanier, who developed a love of short films from their times at film festivals in the US, Canada, and Europe.

larger near electricity. In Las Vegas – well, you can easily imagine.

Gangsters and godfathers

In 1972 and 1974, parts 1 and 2 of Francis Ford Coppola's *The Godfather* trilogy were partly filmed and set locally. Between them, the two films won 13 Oscars and 11 Golden Globe awards for their stars and the mercurial director. The saga of the Corleone family includes references to the Mob's attempts at legitimacy in the Nevada gaming business. The movie also features the now-legendary tale of a Hollywood producer who finds the head of his favorite horse tucked up in his silk sheets as encouragement to release a certain skinny, Italian-American crooner from an engagement.

Warren Beatty played a highly romanticized Benjamin "Bugsy" Siegel, and conducted an on-screen romance with his soon-to-be wife Annette Bening in Barry Levinson's *Bugsy* in 1991. After the movie's success, the Flamingo's owners opened the Bugsy Celebrity Theater. Martin Scorsese's *Casino* (1995), starred Robert de Niro and Sharon Stone in a brutally comic tale of mobsters hustling into Vegas.

> *During the making of* Showgirls, *the only times actresses were uncomfortable were, they said, the scenes with the monkeys, who stared fixedly at their bare breasts.*

William H. Macy plays the unluckiest man alive in *The Cooler*, a gritty, violent yet charming meditation on the nature of luck in old-time Vegas. For his role as a mobbed-up casino boss, Alex Baldwin was nominated for both an Oscar and a Golden Globe award in 2004.

Feature films bring in up to $100,000 a day for goods, services, and local talent. And, sometimes, movie money gets spread around unexpectedly: a scene in *Rush Hour 2* scattered millions of dollars of fake money, some of which was gathered up by onlookers and reportedly passed off later as real currency. In Vegas, like the movies, nothing is ever as it seems. ❑

LEFT: the Flamingo was coy about its associations with mobster Bugsy Siegel until the 1991 movie *Bugsy*, starring Warren Beatty, became a hit. **ABOVE:** Sharon Stone and Robert de Niro in the 1995 movie *Casino*, directed by Martin Scorsese.

GOING TO THE CHAPEL

Britney Spears did it; Mickey Rooney did it eight times in the very same chapel. The neon nirvana is a mecca for couples bent on matrimony

Las Vegas is a destination not only for gambling and conventions, but also as a paradise of promises, a Valhalla of vows. Here, each year, 120,000 troths are pledged.

In 1943 when the Little Church of the West was at the New Frontier, Betty Grable and trumpeter and band leader Harry James exchanged their vows. The *Las Vegas Review-Journal* reported that more than 100 locals went in the middle of the night to the train station, hoping for a glimpse of Grable as she waited for James to return from Mexico with his divorce papers. The wedding took place not long before dawn and after the ceremony, the couple drove right back to Los Angeles.

Here come the brides

Celebrity weddings have always been fashionable in Sin City. Zsa Zsa Gabor married actor George Sanders in 1949 at the Little Church of the West. Zsa Zsa purred through another seven marriages, but she didn't try her luck at love in Vegas again. In 1949, Rita Hayworth married singer Dick Haymes at the Sands. Hayworth had been married to Prince Ali Khan, and to Orson Welles, and her partnership with Haymes lasted only two years. On July 19, 1966 Ol' Blue Eyes married Mia Farrow at the Sands, Sinatra's second home for nearly a decade.

Mickey Rooney married Ava Gardner at the Little Church of the West in January, 1942. Over the next three decades he made seven return trips to the same chapel, concluding with a marriage to January Chamberlin in 1978. Rooney is definitely in line for frequent-matrimony miles.

More recently, in January 2004, singer Britney Spears married hometown honey Jason Allen Alexander at the Little White Chapel; the marriage was annulled 50 hours later. Later that same year, Nicky Hilton, sister to the more famous Paris (also in attendance) wed money manager Todd Andrew Meister; local

> *Princess Leia, Chewbacca, and Darth Vader from Star Wars can all be on hand to witness your vows, along with, of course, Elvis impersonators.*

lore has it that Tinkerbell, Paris's dog, wore a tiara and carried the ring on a pillow. That union, too, was over two months later. The co-star of Paris's infamous sex video, Rick Saloman, married former *Baywatch* babe Pamela Anderson in 2007. Two months later they filed for an annulment, both parties citing fraud.

Little White Chapel

The Little White Chapel was also the venue for Michael Jordan and Juanita Vanoy in 1989. Bruce Willis and Demi Moore married there, and the chapel beams weddings live over the web via its wedding cam onto the Discovery Channel's website. The chapel displays Joan Collins' and Michael Jordan's name in lights. Joan Collins told owner Charlene Richards "Charlotte, when I leave this place you can tell the world if you like."

Billy Bob Thornton married Angelina Jolie at the oldest wedding chapel in Vegas, the Little Church of the West on May 5, 2000. Both stars wore blue jeans. According to the Little Church's owner Greg Smith, most big-name stars want quiet, unpublicized ceremonies. When Richard Gere and Cindy Crawford wed in 1991 he didn't know who the bride and groom were until they arrived.

"They said it would be a celebrity wedding and if they saw any press hanging around outside they wouldn't come in," said Smith when pressed for details. "Both were dressed casually and said they were dining in Los Angeles when they got talking about it.

LEFT: I heart a Las Vegas wedding. **ABOVE:** keep your head in the clouds with a wedding at the Stratosphere Tower. **ABOVE RIGHT:** a sign of the times: ceremony organized off-site by Chapel of the Flowers.

"They just got on one of Disney's planes and came here and did it." The couple had photos taken, but took the negatives when they left.

Las Vegas has hosted 500 celebrity weddings or more, according to Dan Newburn who officiated at the Treasure Island wedding of former boxing champion Ingemar Johansson. Of the public appetite for celebrity splicings, he said, "I think basically people have a latent voyeuristic streak in them and they like to peek in on other people's lives."

Invitation to impulsiveness

Vegas has about 50 wedding chapels open daily from 8am to midnight, including holidays. The invitation to impulsiveness is taken up by about 60,000 couples every year, with Valentine's Day weekend understandably the busiest time of the year (New Year's Eve is also popular). Clark County issued 108,963 marriage licenses in 2007, which cost $55 each. This must be paid for in cash, and the correct change is appreciated. Some legal identification is required, like a driver's license, passport, or birth certificate, as well as divorce papers if either party has previously wed. Same-sex marriages are not allowed. Betrothed couples often fly friends, well-wishers, and families to Vegas as a starting point for the adventure.

Married by Merlin

Excalibur offers medieval-themed ceremonies, the Las Vegas Hilton provides Intergalactic Federation regalia and *Star Trek* characters as witnesses. Most resorts will arrange nuptials by their pools, and more exotic settings include Wild West weddings on horseback, ancient Egyptian or pirate ship themes, the Las Vegas Motor Speedway, the floor of the Grand Canyon, and weddings under water. Ceremonies are also conducted at the top of Paris Las Vegas's Eiffel Tower.

MAGIC NUMBERS FOR MATRIMONY

The well-known genealogy website, www.ancesty.com, launched a section dedicated to their 9 million records of Nevada marriage and divorce data, facts, trivia, and statistics.

The most popular wedding dates in Las Vegas (aside from the perennial favorites of Valentine's Day and New Year's Eve) are dates with repeating numbers (1/01/01, 2/02/02, 3/03/03, for example). One of the most popular wedding dates of all time, 7/07/07, was a big day in Las Vegas due to its implied luckiness (it's the ultimate gaming jackpot) and the fact that it landed on a Saturday.

Even though it fell on a Monday, August 8, 2008, was massively popular with the highly number-conscious Chinese Vegas visitor, who favors the number eight most highly. Though the reasons for this are obscure, it is reputedly because the number eight is pronounced in Chinese in a way that sounds very similar to a most propitious word meaning "fortune."

Drive-thru venue

One wedding chapel provides a convenient ceremonial drive-thru window, so the bride and groom don't even need to leave their car. For the up-market autophile, hire a limo, take it to the scenic backdrop of your choice – and get married in the back of the stretch. Some limousines are equipped with whirlpools and hot tubs, so the happy couple can bubble and betroth simultaneously.

Those with a taste for the extreme (for whom marriage itself isn't scary enough), can marry on a bungee jump, during a roller-coaster ride or, for even whiter knuckles, parachute-jump or sky-dive during a wedding. Ceremonies can be officiated in a helicopter hovering over the Strip, the Grand Canyon, or the Hoover Dam. For more serene mid-air matrimony, a hot-air balloon is available with a basket large enough for the bride, groom, and assembled company.

The 3-millionth wedding in Las Vegas was celebrated at the Imperial Palace's We've Only Just Begun Wedding Chapel in July 2001, and coincided with the 92nd anniversary of the first recorded wedding in Clark County in 1909. The couple, Alberto and Marian Recio of Miami, Florida, renewed their vows in Spanish, serenaded by Elton John, Elvis, and Wayne Newton lookalikes from the hotel's *Legends in Concert* show.

The Clark County Recorder's office has made marriage records available on the internet, and certified copies can be bought for a small fee. Requests for duplicate certificates come in from around the world.

> *More than 120,000 marriage licenses are applied for each year in Las Vegas, which has minimal requirements; proof of age, a social security number, and $55. In cash.*

And then, just in case the marriage doesn't work out exactly as planned, a remedy is conveniently close at hand. About 446 miles (718km) north of Sin City in Reno, Nevada, a divorce can be arranged, almost as easily as a Las Vegas wedding. ❑

LEFT AND ABOVE: you can choose to be married by a wizard or a medieval minstrel, on a bungee jump, or under water. Elvis may participate or even officiate.

NASCAR
WWW.NASCAR.COM
LIGHT
40
Lite
2

SPECTACULAR SPORTS

Tennis aces, golf pros, maniacal motorcycle riders, heavyweight boxers – everybody wants to flaunt their physical prowess in Vegas

Hundreds of years before non-Native Americans reached the Las Vegas Valley, the Southern Paiute tribes played and wagered on a game involving several small sticks. The game, which is still played by the local tribes around the Las Vegas area, takes skill, courage and, of course, luck. Spectators crowd to watch the players' finesse and daring. Fortunes, relative to the era and values of the time, are won and lost by players and spectators alike.

Although the game, whose exact rules are still closely guarded by the Southern Paiutes, bears little similarity to the games of chance

asketball star Jason Kidd told an Arizona ewspaper he planned to give his 2008 lympic gold medal to Elaine Wynn. If so, it ill probably end up being displayed in her usband's Wynn Las Vegas casino.

played in the big casinos, it could be seen as the beginning of the multimillion dollar industry of sports and sports-betting in Las Vegas.

Headline sports

In trade and value, Las Vegas is a world sports capital, but the city has yet to support a professional sports team of any kind. Attempts have been made to seed professional hockey, basketball, football, soccer, and baseball franchises in southern Nevada, but no team has manged to inspire Clark County's 1.7 million inhabitants to the point of putting up the money.

LEFT: NASCAR racing at Las Vegas Motor Speedway.
RIGHT: the nearby suburb of Summerlin has several high-class golf courses.

In spite, or perhaps because of this, the city's sports are guaranteed to make headlines. There was, for instance, the-late Evel Knievel's 1967 attempt to jump over the fountains of Caesars Palace, a stunt that landed him in the hospital for 31 days. Or his failed jump over Snake River Canyon in the desert in a souped-up rocket bike called the "Skycycle."

Twenty-two years later, son Robbie Knievel drew equally large crowds when he effortlessly sailed over Caesars' fountains (with no hands

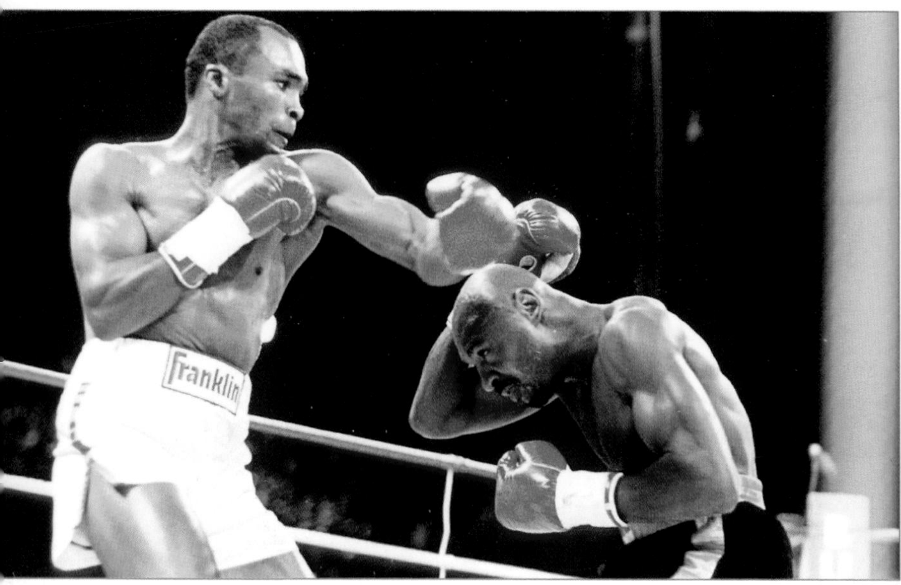

on the handlebars), and later, when he made a successful jump in the Grand Canyon. And who can forget the Flying Elvi, those Elvises in pompadours and white catsuits who regularly parachute out of airplanes and took a stirring role in the movie *Honeymoon in Vegas*?

Spectacular sports, live-action sports, sports in general, and sports betting in particular are prime draws for visitors to Sin City. On Super Bowl weekend (usually late January), Vegas swells to capacity as more than 200,000 fans converge for raucous parties, and to bet millions of dollars on America's football championship. Resorts host lavish invitation-only bashes to lure the highest of high-rollers to their casinos to drink, party, and put up as much of their money as they dare.

Big-ticket boxing

Probably the best-known live sport in Las Vegas is boxing. The city hosts many world championship bouts, bringing in millions of dollars for both the city and the contenders. The big-ticket ringside seats are coveted by the social, entertainment, and sports elite, male fans often in black tie and tuxedo, their female consorts in long evening gowns and sparkling with jewelry.

Las Vegas was world-renowned as a boxing venue long before defeated and disgraced heavyweight boxing champ Mike Tyson chewed Evander Holyfield's ear (literally) in 1997. Most, if not all,

Championship Boxing

Las Vegas has hosted boxing world championship title bouts since 1960, when the world welterweight title was taken by **Benny Paret**, who beat **Don Jordan**. That decade, **Cassius Clay** (who changed his name to **Muhammad Ali**), **Sonny Liston**, and **Floyd Patterson** fought at the silver-domed Convention Center.

In the 1970s, big **Ali**, **George Foreman**, **Ron Lyle**, **Ken Norton**, and **Roberto Duran** fought here, most of them at Caesars Palace. Las Vegas's place in the center of the boxing world was secured in 1980, when **Larry Holmes** crushingly defeated **Ali**, and two years later when **Holmes** beat **Gerry Cooney**.

In the 1980s, Las Vegas was the setting for some of the sport's most memorable moments, through the skills of **Sugar Ray Leonard**, **Thomas Hearns**, and **Marvin Hagler**. In the 1990s, **Mike Tyson** and **Evander Holyfield** were followed by **Oscar De La Hoya**, who was involved in five of the top 10 grossing fights in the history of Las Vegas boxing. Tickets for his match at Mandalay Bay with Felix Trinidad fetched $12 million.

of the great fighters in the modern boxing world have fought in Las Vegas rings, including Sugar Ray Leonard, George Foreman, Oscar de la Hoya, Riddick Bowe, Lennox Lewis, and Muhammad Ali. Heavyweight champion Joe Louis became a casino "greeter" at Caesars Palace after his long and illustrious boxing career ended, and he called Las Vegas home for many years.

Lennox Lewis

Convicted rapist Mike Tyson maintains a multimillion-dollar house in the south of the valley. Tyson was knocked out cold in his 2002 fight with heavyweight champion Lennox Lewis. The fight was scheduled for Las Vegas, but Nevada's Athletic Commission denied Tyson a license to fight in the state, saying that his image wasn't what Nevada boxing is all about. Before the two met in the ring, Tyson bit Lewis on the leg in front of the cameras during a news conference in New York City.

LEFT: Sugar Ray Leonard defeats Marvin Haglar for the World Middleweight title, April 6, 1967.
ABOVE: Floyd Patterson and Cassius Clay in the World Heavyweight title bout, November 22, 1965.

Singers and swingers

Golf is another sport long associated with Las Vegas. In the early years – the 1940s, '50s, and '60s – the casino builders saw golf as an aspirational game, a sport for those a cut above the common man. Nearly every casino on the Strip sported acres of posh green fairways.

> “ *If you watch a game it's fun. If you play at it, it's recreation. If you work at it, it's golf.* Comedian Bob Hope ”

The Tropicana, the Dunes, the Sahara, and the Desert Inn all maintained lavish courses, often with fairways right outside the casinos. Many legendary performers played Las Vegas showrooms at night and cleared their heads of cobwebs with a daily round on a Las Vegas course. The legendary drivers and putters roster included Dean Martin, Bob Hope, Bing Crosby, Debbie Reynolds, the McGuire Sisters, Willie Nelson, Joe DiMaggio, Burt Bacharach, and others too numerous to mention.

In the early 1990s, however, the landscape began to change for Las Vegas golfers. Strip-resort entrepreneurs realized that the grass and sand traps around their casinos would be more valuable covered by a casino, a parking lot, or an amusement arcade. Many courses sank below the creeping concrete carpet.

In June 2002, Wynn closed the last course on the Strip, at the Desert Inn. But to appease his high-end guests, Wynn opened an 18-hole, par-70 extravaganza with lush green elevations designed by Tom Fazio, just steps from his Wynn Las Vegas resort. Otherwise, you have to travel to play golf, which most are prepared to do.

> *I'm not trying to kill myself. I don't have a death wish. If you make the jumps and stay alive, it's all worth it.*
> Daredevil rider Robbie Knievel

Las Vegas courses are still celebrity-packed, and it's not unusual to run into the elite from the worlds of sports, politics, or entertainment. Golfing phenomenon Tiger Woods won his first major tournament in Las Vegas in 1996, and he still plays on local courses. Woods' long-time coach Butch Harmon has opened a golf school at the Rio Secco Golf Club, with indoor and outdoor practices. Former president Bill Clinton was known to play golf every time he visited Vegas, and was one of the first to play Southern Highlands Golf Club when it opened in April 2000.

Celine Dion, George Clooney, Eddie Van Halen, Smokey Robinson, Will Smith, Lou Rawls, and Joe Pesci are regularly seen on the greens. At least a dozen former and current PGA Tour players live in or have ties to Las Vegas, and Jeff Gallagher, Craig Barlow, Chad Campbell, Bob May, Edward Fryatt, Robert Gamez, Skip Kendall, Stephanie Keever, John Riegger, Chris Riley, and Eric Meeks are often seen teeing off, or relaxing after a game.

NASCAR action

One of the most popular spectator sports in the US is NASCAR, and about 10 miles (16km) north of the city, Las Vegas has one of the country's largest and best racing tracks. Every year the Sam's Town 300 is held at the Las Vegas Motor Speedway. Tens of thousands of supporters flock to the track to cheer and bet on their favorite drivers. Since the early 1970s, southern Nevada has also been the home of an off-road vehicle race sponsored by SCORE International, the nation's oldest established major desert-racing organization. And the Mint 400 is one of the longest-running off-road vehicle races in the country. Enthusiasts race anything from big-wheeled motorcycles to huge custom-built trucks. The vehicles scream, scramble, and slide around a 50-mile (80km) track.

Tennis aces among the dice

Andre Agassi, the tennis phenomenon of the 1980s and 1990s, was born and raised in Las Vegas. He and his wife Steffi Graf still live here with their two children. Agassi's older sister, Rita, was married to the late tennis legend Pancho Gonzales. In 1995, when Gonzales died in Las Vegas, Agassi paid for his funeral. For years, Las Vegas has hosted tournaments showcasing great names of the game like Arthur Ashe, Rod Laver, Chris Evert, and Martina Navratilova.

The Nevada desert has served as a sports ground for as long as man has lived here. From the games the Native American inhabitants played to the world-title boxing matches, and the roar and scream of the NASCAR vehicles, its popularity shows no sign of declining. ❑

LEFT: Rachel Sproul in the barrel-racing round at the National Finals Rodeo, held in Vegas's Thomas & Mack Center. **ABOVE:** Evel Knievel's "Skycycle," used in a failed attempt to jump Snake River Canyon in 1974.

RODEOS

"His eyes dart like a hawk's, his head swivels like an owl's. In his hand is a stopwatch." Shawn Davis, the general manager of the National Finals Rodeo, produces the sport's richest and most prestigious show. Every December, Las Vegas's western roots are on show when the city hosts the final event in the Pro-Rodeo Cowboys Association calendar.

Broncos are ridden and steers are broken in pursuit of the hotly contested cowboy title, World Champ All-Around Cowboy. Only the top 15 cowboys from the national rankings are invited into the competition, and fighting is fierce for tickets and hotel rooms.

Shopping

Retail therapists storm the stores of Vegas for high-end fashions, poker toys, vintage va-va-voom, and major bargains in bling

Bling and bliss. Glamour and great bargains. Outdoor malls with waterfalls, or indoor specialty shops with fashions that show up in films. This is retail reality, Vegas style. In a hot, open-air city, cool clothes are second only to buffed, naked skin in the "look-at me" sweepstakes.

Most stores are concentrated on the Strip. Leading the way is the Fashion Show Mall, with 250 retail outlets and runway shows most weekends. Some casino-resorts come complete with their own malls, like Grand Canal Shoppes at The Venetian, and Miracle Mile at Planet Hollywood; Wynn Esplanade at Wynn Las Vegas even has its own Ferrari-Maserati dealership.

If your luck at the tables doesn't run to such extravagance, try an outlet mall, like the Las Vegas Outlet Center beyond the southern Strip, or Las Vegas Premium Outlets, near Downtown. More dash than cash? Head for The Attic, in the 18b Arts District. This is a vast emporium of vintage clothing famous for supplying photo shoots starring couples like Brad and Angelina.

For more shopping, see pages 258–61.

Top: glide to the shops in a gondola and be serenaded at the sales when you visit The Venetian's Grand Canal Shoppes, which culminate in a scaled-down version of the Piazza San Marco.

Above: designer labels and sexy showrooms share floorspace with the gods of antiquity at the Forum Shops, a chichi arcade complete with columns, fountains, and a simulated-sky dome.

Left: in Vegas, you're never far from a store servicing a gambler's every need.

RIGHT: vintage clothing on a vast scale.

BELOW: a sprawling shopping mall styled with the look and feel of a small town, Town Square breaks down into easily identifiable zones – such as children, teens, and jewelry.

ABOVE: the grandeur of Ancient Rome – here in the shape of a replica of the Trevi Fountain – is a fitting backdrop to those upscale Forum Shops.

ABOVE: Fashion Show Mall's sheer size and its state-of-the-art runway shows should keep fashion fiends happy.

ABOVE: bring on the bling – whether it's jewelry or gifts, the glitziest of wishlists meets its match in Las Vegas.

planet
Flamingo
Flamingo
Harrah's
MADAME
TUSSAUDS

CAESARS
THE MIRAGE
CASINO & RESORT

BALLYS

FIVE
DOLLARS

Le CHAMPAGNE SLOTS
Le CHAMPAGNE SLOTS

PLACES

A detailed guide to Las Vegas and its surroundings with the main sites clearly cross-referenced by number to the maps

Las Vegas is a twinkling, flashing, glittering, lop-sided crown, jutting irregularly out of the desert. It soars and scrambles upwards, stranded in an arid dust-bowl. When approached at night from the air, it beckons like a seafront arcade from the wilder edges of science fiction. Arriving after dark on the road, it pulsates and looms ever larger, defying belief. Closer up, the giant neon glare evolves into shapes, signs, and pictures, and the spectacle of the world's most lavish playground unfurls in the car windshield.

When most people think of Las Vegas, the part they usually have in mind is the four-mile (6km) stretch of Las Vegas Boulevard South known as the Strip, which is lined with America's biggest and most famous casino resorts. In any of these, almost impossible show-business dreams are made flesh – the carpet, the decor, and the dress of the staff tell you instantly where you are. Circus Circus is a glittering merry-go-round; New York New York is as you would expect from the Big Apple. Among the ambitious new projects are Echelon Place, CityCenter, and the twin-towered Trump International, slated for completion between 2009 and 2011 at a cost of billions of dollars apiece.

Large resort hotels have also been built within a mile or two east and west of the Strip. The trend started in 1969 with the building of the International Hotel near the original Las Vegas Convention Center, east of the north end of the Strip. More recent off-Strip development has focused on areas near the southern Strip: along Paradise Road, home to the hip Hard Rock Hotel and the well appointed non-gaming Alexis Park Resort, and south of Mandalay Bay, with the opening of Town Square shopping mall.

Formerly nicknamed "Glitter Gulch" until the city fathers tried to shed its dubious reputation by renaming it "the Fremont Street Experience," Fremont Street is the center of the action in downtown Las Vegas. Many serious gamblers prefer Downtown casinos for their lack of touristic distractions.

Whatever your taste in post-millennial recreation, roll up, roll up, ladies and gentlemen, it's all here, just waiting for you. Step right in. ❑

PRECEDING PAGES: the Strip; Bellagio fountains; the casino of Paris Las Vegas.
LEFT: the Fremont Street Experience.

Las Vegas Top Sights

Caesars Palace
pgs 149–153

Fashion Show Mall
pgs 169–170

Wynn Las Vegas
pgs 173–75

Fremont Street Experience pgs 203–4

Stratosphere Tower
pgs 183–84

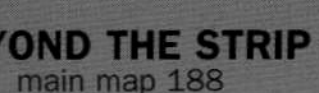

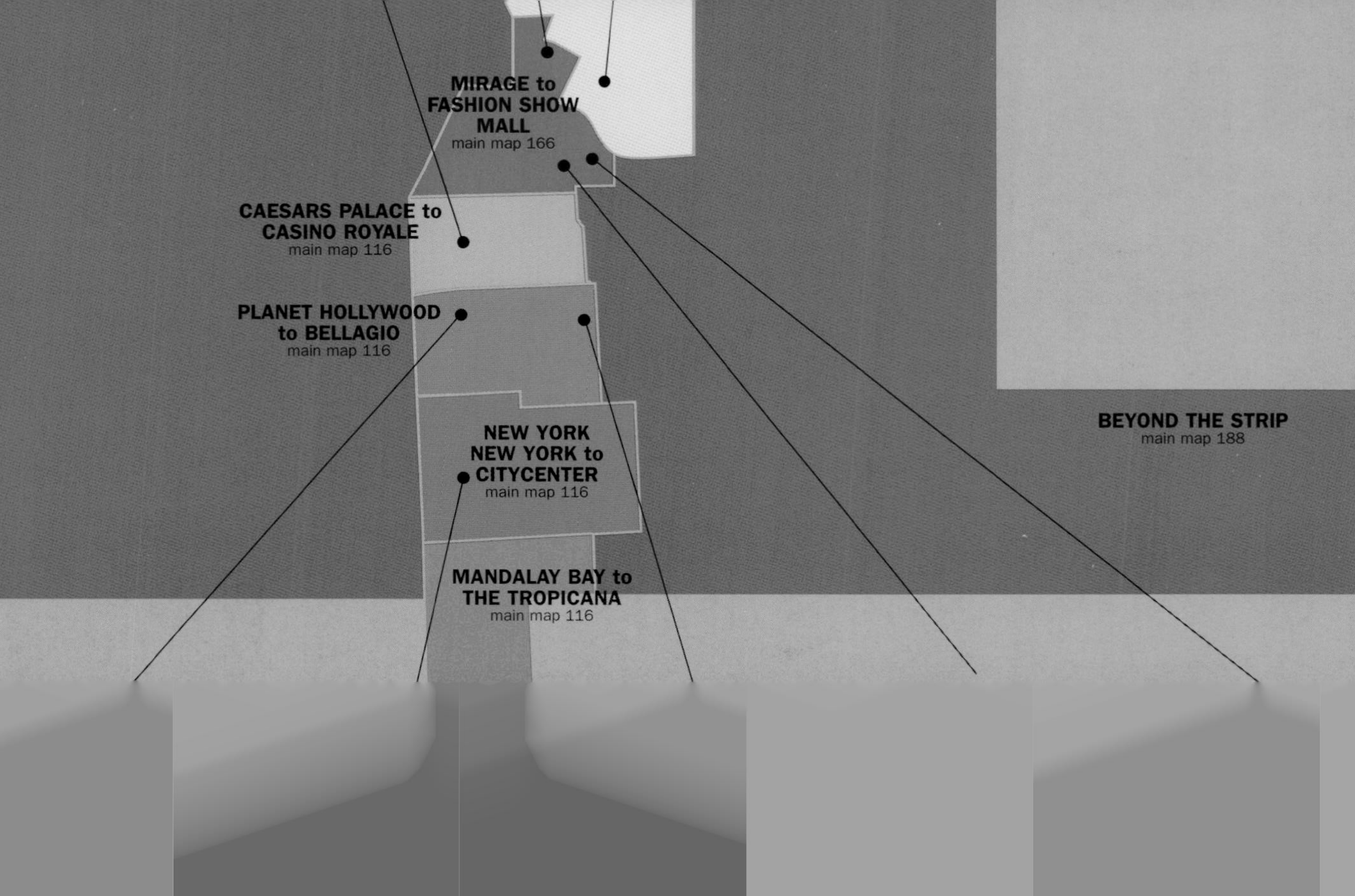
MIRAGE to FASHION SHOW MALL
main map 166
CAESARS PALACE to CASINO ROYALE
main map 116
PLANET HOLLYWOOD to BELLAGIO
main map 116
NEW YORK NEW YORK to CITYCENTER
main map 116
MANDALAY BAY to THE TROPICANA
main map 116
BEYOND THE STRIP
main map 188

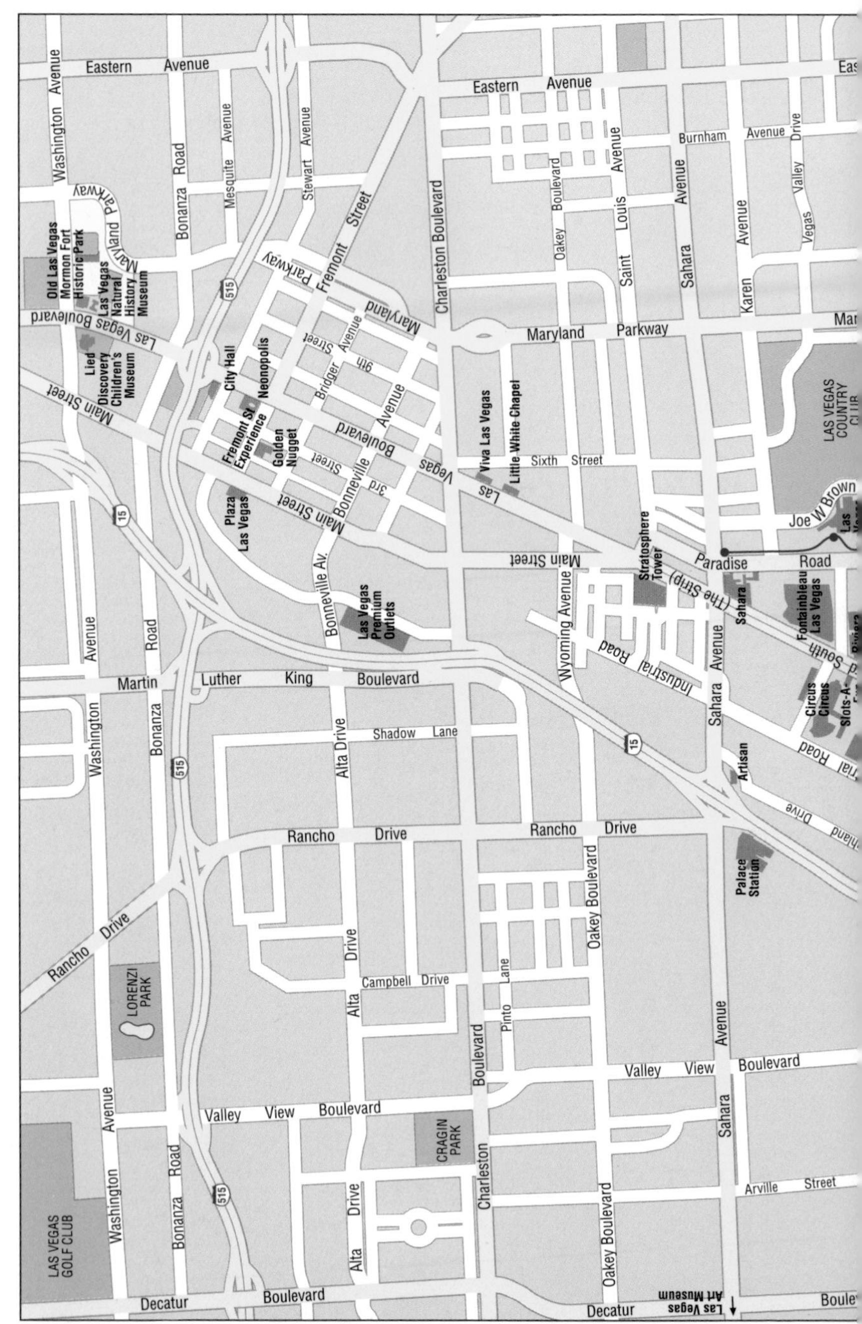
Old Las Vegas Mormon Fort Historic Park
Las Vegas Natural History Museum
Lied Discovery Children's Museum
City Hall
Neonopolis
Fremont St Experience
Golden Nugget
Plaza Las Vegas
Las Vegas Premium Outlets
Viva Las Vegas
Little White Chapel
Stratosphere Tower
Sahara
Fontainbleau Las Vegas
Circus Circus
Artisan
Palace Station
LAS VEGAS COUNTRY CLUB
LORENZI PARK
CRAGIN PARK
LAS VEGAS GOLF CLUB
Las Vegas Art Museum
Eastern Avenue
Washington Avenue
Bonanza Road
Mesquite Avenue
Stewart Avenue
Fremont Street
Maryland Parkway
Las Vegas Boulevard
Main Street
Charleston Boulevard
Oakey Boulevard
Saint Louis Avenue
Sahara Avenue
Karen Avenue
Burnham Avenue
Vegas Valley Drive
Bridger Avenue
9th Street
6th Street
3rd Street
Sixth Street
Bonneville Avenue
Bonneville Av.
Joe W Brown
Paradise Road
(The Strip)
Wyoming Avenue
Industrial Road
Martin Luther King Boulevard
Shadow Lane
Alta Drive
Rancho Drive
Campbell Drive
Pinto Lane
Valley View Boulevard
Arville Street
Decatur Boulevard
15
515

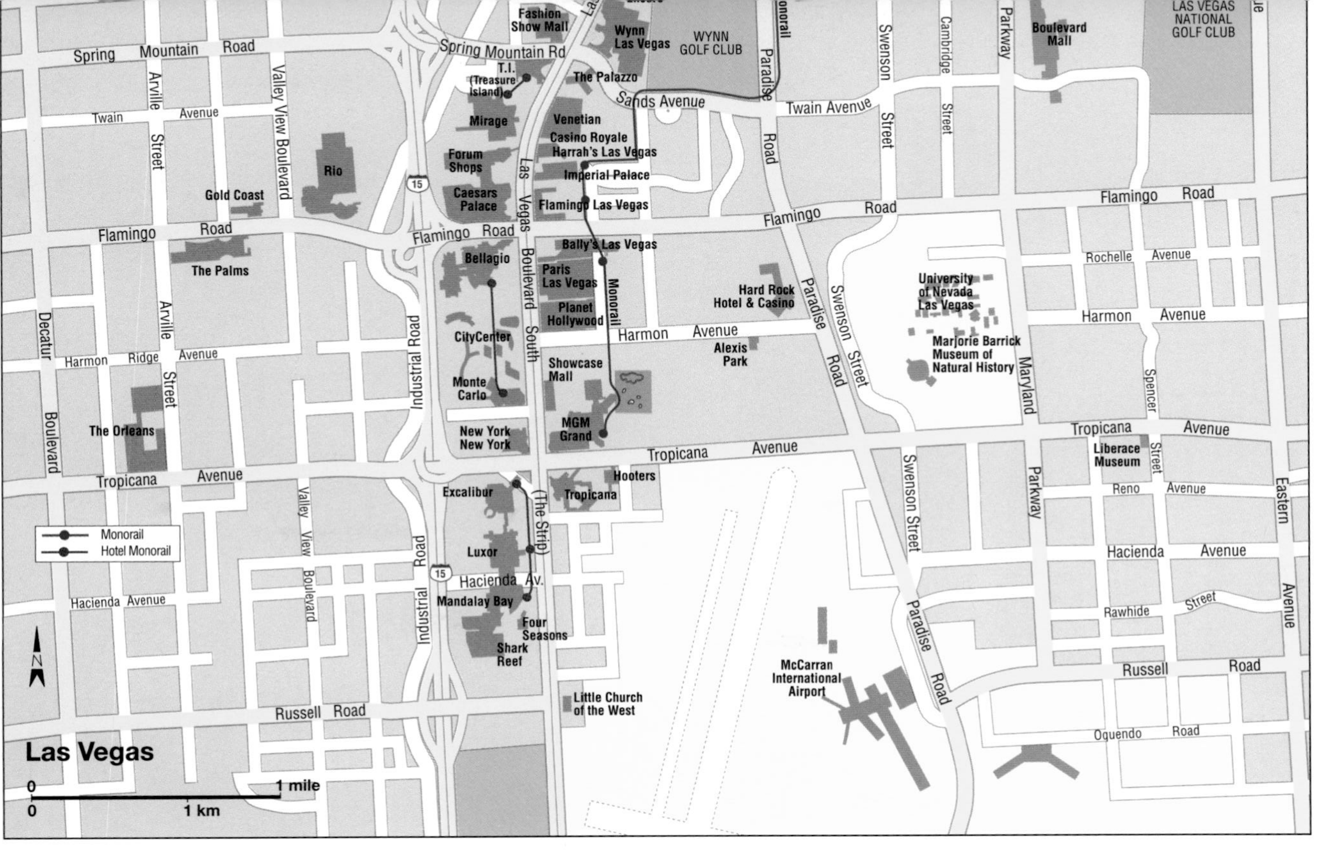
Las Vegas
LAS VEGAS NATIONAL GOLF CLUB
Boulevard Mall
WYNN GOLF CLUB
Fashion Show Mall
Wynn Las Vegas
The Palazzo
T.I. (Treasure Island)
Mirage
Venetian
Casino Royale
Harrah's Las Vegas
Imperial Palace
Forum Shops
Caesars Palace
Flamingo Las Vegas
Bally's Las Vegas
Bellagio
Paris Las Vegas
Planet Hollywood
Monorail
CityCenter
Showcase Mall
Monte Carlo
MGM Grand
New York New York
Excalibur
Hooters
Tropicana
Luxor
Mandalay Bay
Four Seasons
Shark Reef
Little Church of the West
Rio
Gold Coast
The Palms
The Orleans
Hard Rock Hotel & Casino
Alexis Park
University of Nevada Las Vegas
Marjorie Barrick Museum of Natural History
Liberace Museum
McCarran International Airport
Spring Mountain Road
Spring Mountain Rd
Sands Avenue
Twain Avenue
Paradise Road
Swenson Street
Cambridge Street
Maryland Parkway
Flamingo Road
Rochelle Avenue
Harmon Avenue
Spencer Street
Tropicana Avenue
Reno Avenue
Eastern Avenue
Hacienda Avenue
Rawhide Street
Russell Road
Oquendo Road
Arville Street
Valley View Boulevard
Decatur Boulevard
Harmon Ridge Avenue
Industrial Road
Las Vegas Boulevard South
(The Strip)
Hacienda Av.
15
Monorail
Hotel Monorail
N
0
1 mile
1 km

MANDALAY BAY
MANDALAY BAY
MANDALAY BAY

Recommended Restaurants on page 125

MANDALAY BAY TO THE TROPICANA

Tropical luxury is found beside Merrie Old England, while the Sphinx next door shoots laser beams from its eyes. Where could you be but Las Vegas?

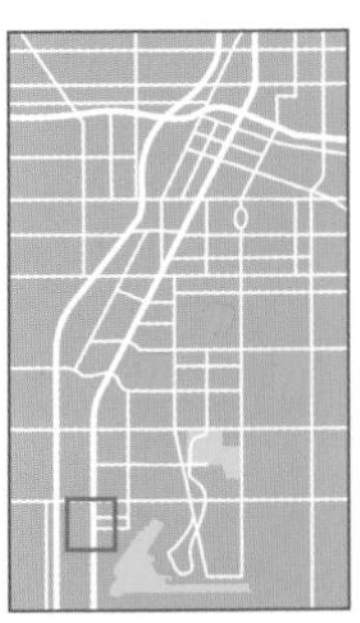

Main attractions

- MANDALAY BAY
- SHARK REEF
- MAMA MIA!
- THE FOUR SEASONS
- THEHOTEL
- LUXOR
- TOWN SQUARE
- EXCALIBUR
- CASTLE WALK
- THE TROPICANA
- LEGENDS DELI
- FOLIES BERGÈRE

Theme casinos on the Strip have the inscrutable sphinx guarding the pyramid of Luxor and nearby, minstrels guard damsels in distress – well, these aren't so rare in Sin City. Bordering these endangered theme resorts are tropical paradises at both ends of the scale. The elegant Mandalay Bay has two adjoining, classy, non-gaming hotels, while the area ends with a flourish of brash, old-style Vegas at The Tropicana.

MANDALAY BAY ❶

3950 Las Vegas Boulevard South, www.mandalaybay.com
702-632-7777 or 877-632-7800

Mandalay Bay is a luxurious, tropically themed resort on a lagoon, with its own rum distillery and a pool with a sandy beach. The beach is swept by waves from a giant machine that can generate 6ft (2-meter) breakers for body surfing. Visitors can see the pool through windows near the entrance to Shark Reef, but only hotel guests are allowed to swim here.

In its evaluations of Strip pools, *Where Las Vegas* magazine gave top marks to the Mandalay Bay's sandy shore. Luxor and the MGM Grand, each with five pools, received mentions. Noted also was Caesars Palace's Garden of the Gods, inspired by Rome's Baths of Caracalla. The beach club at the Hard Rock Hotel is gaining attention, too, as its extensive wave pool hosts bigger and wilder parties.

Shark Reef (open 10am–11pm, charge) is a huge indoor aquarium holding more than 1,200 marine animals. Installed after the hotel opened, it is extremely popular.

LEFT: Excalibur, Luxor, and Mandalay Bay light up the Strip at night.
RIGHT: glitzy club LAX in Luxor was opened by pop princess Britney Spears.

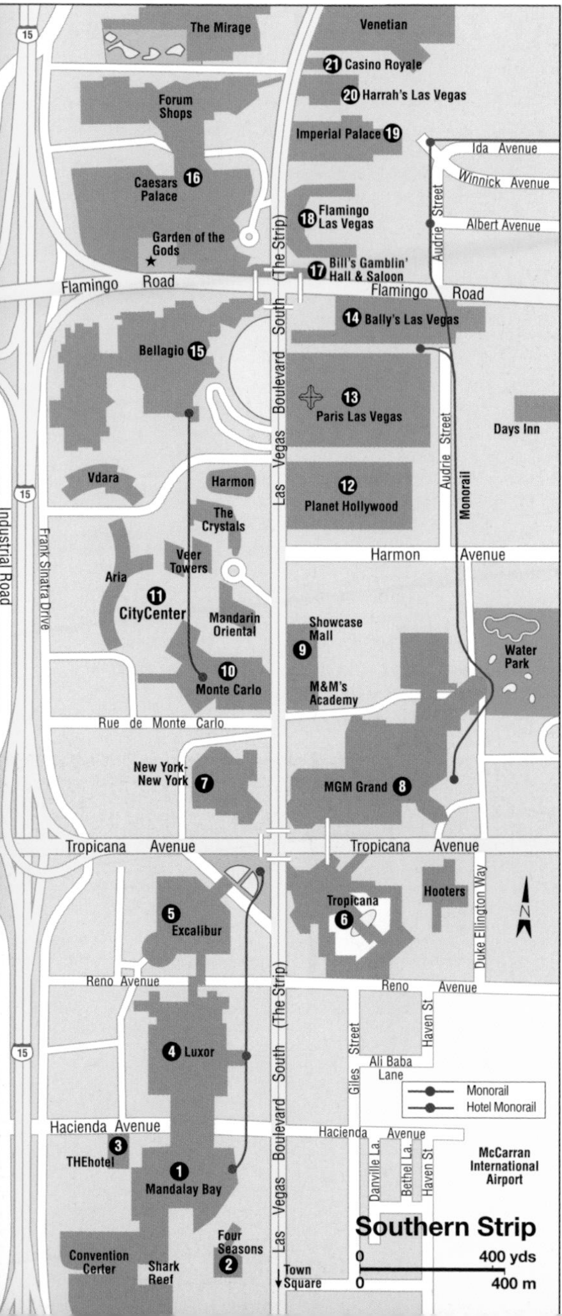

Sunken temples, statues, old stone stairways, and a ship are entombed in 1½ million gallons (5,676,000 liters) of water that is home to aquatic creatures of all shapes and sizes.

Baby shark

The exhibit has a dozen species of shark, ranging from a baby Port Jackson shark, only 10ins (25cm) long to a 12ft (4-meter) nurse shark which, in its coral-reef habitat, sucks its prey out of holes in the rocks. The exhibit points out that despite their fearsome reputation, millions of sharks are killed every year for every human killed by a shark.

Another exhibit is **Snakes & Dragons**, the former being pythons, and the latter fish and reptiles. A recent addition is a Komodo dragon, the largest species in the lizard family. An endangered species from Indonesia, the Komodo relies on its sense of smell to find its prey.

Visitors carry "narration wands" that describe the golden crocodiles from Thailand and the green tree pythons. At the touch pool they can put their hands in the water to stroke horseshoe crabs and baby stingrays.

The **Mandalay Bay Events Center** sits on 17 adjoining acres (7 hectares), which the company hopes will tap into the billions of dollars that conventions bring to the city each year. Concerts and boxing events fill the seats when there is no convention.

Mama Mia!

Mandalay Bay's restaurants *(see page 125)* offer many cuisines and suit all pockets, especially the ever-popular **House of Blues**. Permanently on show in the resort's theater is ***Mama Mia!***, the feel-good musical based on the songs of Abba. The Mandalay Bay also has a gift shop, with upscale crafts and clothes from around the world, and a vaguely tropical theme. One timely purchase is a parasol from Thailand, which comes

Recommended Restaurants on page 125

Underwater god at Mandalay Bay's Shark Reef.

in very useful when trawling the Strip during the 100°F (37°C) -plus heat during June, July, and August.

The Four Seasons ❷

3960 Las Vegas Boulevard South, www.fourseasons.com
702-632-5000 or 877-632-5000

Occupying the top five floors (36–39) of Mandalay Bay is the Four Seasons, an opulent hideaway which is one of the few major hotels on the Strip not to offer gaming. In similar luxurious style to others in the chain, this is a peaceful sanctuary in shades of gold, green, amber, and purple. Furnished with antiques and a Renaissance painting, the Four Seasons has its own private driveway, three private elevators, and a separate lobby so that guests can avoid the

Left: Shark Reef is enormously popular.
Below: a free monorail connects Mandalay Bay with Luxor and Excalibur.

ABOVE: enjoy the high life at the Four Seasons and THEhotel.
BELOW: inside Luxor's atrium.

casino in the Mandalay Bay if they wish, a luxury many will pay for if only to avoid the ear-jangling, nerve-shattering, and ever-present Las Vegas theme tune, the burble of the slot machines.

Excellent service is guaranteed by a ratio of two staff members per guest, and there are little touches such as Evian water in the bathrooms, and chilled grapes served at the poolside. Traditional Balinese and Javanese body rituals are a regular feature of the spa, where cucumber slices are dispensed to cover the eyes.

The concierge desk stands ready to book guests into any of the numerous golf courses in the area, or on trips into the Nevada wilderness. In winter, they will find and arrange a slot for you to ski at the Las Vegas Ski and Snowboard Resort, 45 minutes away on Mount Charleston. Very little is too much trouble at the Four Seasons.

THEHOTEL ❸

✉ 3950 Las Vegas Boulevard South, www.mandalaybay.com ☎ 702-632-7777or 877-632-7800

THEhotel is also part of Mandalay Bay, but whereas the sophistication of the Four Seasons appeals to an older crowd, THEhotel caters to visitors who actually live (or aspire to) Carrie Bradshaw's view in *Sex and the City*. Be sure to pack those Manolos, as this is definitely a fancy-shoe type of place, with lots of cream, brown, and tan walls to offset the fabulous frocks you'll either bring with you or buy in Vegas. Like the Four Seasons, there's a separate entrance and no gaming, but with

Map on page 116
Recommended Restaurants on page 125

the Strip only steps away, it's easy to escape the hushed atmosphere and plunge into the hurly-burly of normal Las Vegas life.

LUXOR ❹

✉ 3900 Las Vegas Boulevard South, www.luxor.com
☎ 702-262-4000 or 800-288-1000

Luxor, like the pirate-themed casino formerly known as Treasure Island farther down the Strip, is suffering from an identity crisis. When it opened in 1993, the Egyptian-themed resort caused a sensation, its spectacularly engaging architecture and moderate room rates making it a hit with families on a budget.

And Luxor's architecture certainly is striking: the 30-story, glass-paneled pyramid's atrium is said to be spacious enough to park nine Boeing 747s, and the beam of light from its summit shines 10 miles (16km) into the sky, running up an electricity bill of over $1 million a year. (It's said the beam can be seen from outer space, but that's likely just Vegas talk.)

Two smaller pyramids were added with courtyards, terraces, and low-rise villas, and Luxor was linked to the adjacent Excalibur by moving walkway. Another walkway still leads to Mandalay Bay through a small shopping center.

The 100ft (30-meter) **Sphinx** can project a 55ft (17-meter) -high hologram of King Tut's head on to a water screen with laser beams from its eyes, but the Federal Aviation

Be alert, but be aware, too, that a car is necessary only if you plan to stray from the Strip or downtown Vegas.

LEFT: pyramid power.
BELOW: Luxor.

Administration requested the lasers be switched off after complaints from airline pilots. Its attractions, too, were family-friendly – an indoor "Nile River" ferried guests by boat to the elevators, and a shopping arcade called the Giza Galleria sold Egyptian-styled knick-knacks.

A fun thing still to do at Luxor is to visit someone in a guest room, accessed by elevators called "inclinators" which turn sideways and run along rollers at 39 degrees at the upper floors, with views down to the fourth floor.

But after the millennium, visitors with kids in tow were found to spend less time and less money at the gaming tables, and Vegas turned into Sin City once again. Which left the Luxor with a puzzle: how to "de-theme" a casino where the theme is defined by the very shape of the building?

ABOVE AND BELOW: Town Square is ranged along low-rise outdoor streets with Spanish and Mediterranean architectural accents.

Adults? Kids?

Although this is an ongoing transition, at present the Luxor is a kiddie palace with adult attractions. Playing in the theater is ***Fantasy***, which bills itself as "the Strip's most seductive dance show." The controversial exhibition "**Bodies**" (open 10am–10pm; charge) displays the bodies of real human beings, sprayed with a kind of plastic. Thirteen whole-body specimens and more than 260 organs and partial body specimens are on display. The red-hot club **LAX**, opened by Britney Spears in 2007 to worldwide coverage, brings the pretty people to party.

Definitely popular with the grown-ups is Luxor's Sports Books. Sports Books date back to Bugsy Siegel's innovation of the Trans-America Wire Service, which had a monopoly on relaying all horse-race information in the US directly from the racetrack. No bookie could oper-

Town Square

Aimed at local residents as much as tourists, Town Square, south of Mandalay Bay, is a shopping mall styled with the ambiance of a small town. The 17-acre (7-hectare) development is arranged within easy shopping zones with specific areas for teens, children, clothes and jewelry. European fashion giant H&M has an enormous store on-site, with a spa in which to soak those retail-weary bones.

Among the 150 stores are famous names like Armani Exchange, Abercrombie and Fitch, Banana Republic, and Wholefoods. This is also one of the few places with a bookstore (other than the airport), so if you're after a good read by the pool, go to the large Borders, and you may just catch a book-signing session. There are at least 10 places to eat and drink, from pizza palaces to martini bars. Town Square is open from 10am–9.30pm, 11am–8pm on Sundays. Catch a cab from Mandalay Bay.

Recommended Restaurants on page 125

ate without this information, and so Siegel could charge pretty much what he liked. Today, the rates are set by a state commission.

EXCALIBUR 5

3850 Las Vegas Boulevard South, www.excalibur.com
702-597-7777 or 877-75-5464

Excalibur, with its multicolored spires like a Disney World castle, has kept its kiddie roots (adding an adults-only swimming pool, just so parents don't go crazy). Alighting from the monorail, visitors are greeted by a sign setting the tone: "Welcome to the medieval time of your life." Across the moat and drawbridge, the resort itself is filled with heraldic motifs, plastic knights bearing battle-axes, the Steakhouse at Camelot, and giggling couples being photographed with their heads in sets of wooden stocks.

Through the endless, heavily carpeted corridors, the first thing to reach is the **Sherwood Forest Café** (open 24 hours), then the casino itself. Few visitors look up to notice the colored-glass windows and intricate cornices decorated with statues. Inside, it is almost as impressive as the startling exterior, assuming you have a liking for *faux* England.

The resort was opened in 1990, covering 57 acres (23 hectares). With twin 28-story towers holding more than 4,000 rooms, it was, at the time, the world's largest hotel-casino. Some floors are given over to family-friendly non-gambling enter-

Town Square shopping mall has a well-regarded Children's Park. Attractions include a tree house inside a live oak tree, a maze with interactive animal toparies, and a theater with storytelling Wednesdays from 11am to noon.

LEFT: a dragon knight, poised to charge.
BELOW: Excalibur is one of the best resorts for families.

The Las Vegas Outlet Center is just a short cab ride south of the Strip *(see page 221)*. Featuring 130 stores and savings up to 50 percent off, it's worth the trip, especially if you combine it with a visit to Town Square *(see page 120)*. Anyone with a lot of time can hop aboard a double-decker Deuce bus from the Strip.

ABOVE: be king for a day at Excalibur's spa. **BELOW:** Excalibur's Regale restaurant.

tainment. Excalibur nevertheless serves 1.2 million alcoholic drinks every month.

Castle Walk ("shoppe til you drop") continues the medieval theme, containing stores with names like Dragon's Lair, selling Camelot-inspired goodies, and Kids of the Kingdom, selling fairytale items. From time to time, performers garbed in medieval costume play period arrangements on mandolin, flute, and harp, to accompany mimes and magicians, while other costumed figures and strolling minstrels parade in the area and provide entertaining merriment.

Of those who choose one of Excalibur's two wedding chapels for their nuptials, about one-quarter opt to do so in medieval attire.

Staged entertainment comes in the form of the ***Tournament of Kings*** (jousting and dinner), or the very grown-up Australian male striptease, **Thunder from Down Under**, the place where "at night our knights shed their armor."

Excalibur's designer, Weldon Simpson, was also responsible for the original Luxor and the MGM Grand. Simpson said, "Las Vegas is better than virtual reality, because in virtual reality you have to trick your mind into thinking that you are someplace else – many other places."

Eventually, though, he believes that slot players will be enclosed in private virtual-reality environments, allowing 3-D interaction in games that are based on the hotel's

Recommended Restaurants on page 125

medieval theme. The more the gambler plays, the further they will advance into the virtual world of the game. He also forsees "Second Life"-style avatars for players. "You will become one of the virtual-reality characters yourself," he says.

Charles L. Silverman, a designer of casino interiors for more than three decades, says that the customer base is not only the gambler any longer, "it is anyone who walks through our doors. If enough people come in, enough of them will gamble, so we are creating lavish palaces to attract them."

THE TROPICANA ❻

3801 Las Vegas Boulevard South, www.tropicana.com
702-739-2222 or 800-634-4000

The Tropicana is styled as "the island of Las Vegas." The concept began when a 22-story tower opened on a 5-acre (2-hectare) landscaped island among flamingos, parrots, cockatoos, and swans. Over the years more wildlife, more towers, and a walkway link were added, and the pool area expanded. Another island fronts the hotel. The land is home to two 35ft (11-meter) -tall sculptures of Aku Aku gods and a Polynesian house, which nestles in tropical landscaping.

More than 50 years old, the Tropicana still has a funky, old-fashioned charm, which some guests find refreshing and others find lackluster. The **Legends Deli** is where customers enjoy their favorite stars in the form of sandwiches; the Joey Bishop (pastrami on rye with a pickle), the Liberace (grilled prime rib on a French roll), Jerry Lewis (baked ham on a wholewheat baguette) or, of course, "the King" (grilled banana, peanut

ABOVE: cabs are the best way to reach the two shopping malls just south of the "tourist" part of the Strip.
BELOW: never let an opportunity go by at The Tropicana.

butter, and grape jelly on white toast). The hotel's main attraction is the long-running ***Folies Bergère*** show. With its origins in the demimonde of Toulouse Lautrec and Montmartre in the Paris of 1869, the show was brought to the Tropicana in 1959 by Lou Walters, father of the television interviewer Barbara Walters, and after preening and strutting through more than 25,000 performances, it really is a Las Vegas classic.

Entertainment abilities

Along with entertainment abilities, performers have to have a minimum height qualification to work here – 5ft 3ins (1.6 meters) for acrobats, 5ft 6ins (1.7 meters) for dancers, 5ft 10ins (1.8 meters) for showgirls. The cast's age ranges from 18 to about 40. These glamorous girls, who usually perform topless, receive plenty of opportunities for extra work (being decorative, but clothed) at Vegas's many conventions.

Topless showgirls arrived on the Strip in 1957 at the Dunes Hotel show, *Minsky's Follies*. Early shows were produced by Donn Arden, the man credited with the style of modern showgirls, at the Desert Inn.

Girls 5ft 8ins (1.75 meters) tall or above were hired, and today's showgirl is even taller. Dancers can be shorter and sometimes perform clothed. The showgirl style was followed successfully at the Stardust, where the *Lido de Paris* show was imported from France for a run that lasted 31 years. Both the Stardust and the Desert Inn have been imploded. ❑

The Tropicana experimented with a Folies performance suitable for children, ie with no nudity and no drinks. But since a Folies show was founded on the idea of bare breasts, this was not popular, and the resort has gone back to staging two "classic" shows most nights.

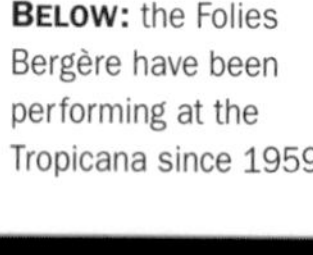

BELOW: the Folies Bergère have been performing at the Tropicana since 1959.

BEST RESTAURANTS

Price includes dinner for one and a glass of wine, excluding tip:
$ = under $20
$$ = $20–$30
$$$ = $30–$40
$$$$ = over $40

American

Aureole
Mandalay Bay 702-632-7401 D daily **$$$$** [p275, C4]
Celebrity chef Charlie Palmer's version of his New York classic is architecturally arresting (a three-story wine tower and a pond with swans). The excellent food is complemented by an outstanding wine list.

The Burger Bar
Mandalay Bay 702-632-9364 L & D daily **$–$$$$** [p275, C4]
A burger to suit all pockets, from the Kobe burger with foie gras and truffles to the dessert burgers with a donut base, topped off with cheesecake, yummy chocolate or peanut butter and jelly.

Charlie Palmer Steak
Four Seasons Hotel at Mandalay Bay 702-632-5000 D daily **$$$$** [p275, D4]
Charlie Palmer presents most of his signature dishes here, like succulent wood-grilled filet mignon. Seafood or family-style side dishes are available to non-carnivores. Clubby.

Company
Luxor 702-262-4852 D Wed–Sat **$$$** [p275, C4]
Log and sandstone decor creates a rustic setting for food that fuses American tradition with Japanese influences. Try the crispy *chipotle*-miso salmon, or the apricot soy-glazed pork chop.

Dick's Last Resort
Excalibur 702-597-7991 L & D daily **$$** [p275, C3]
From barbecued ribs to big buckets of southern-fried catfish, this family-friendly place prides itself on messy food served up by rowdy employees to the accompaniment of live rock'n'roll.

Asian

Fusia
Luxor 702-262-4000 D daily **$$$** [p275, C4]
An atmosphere of serenity pervades this ultra-modern restaurant. The cuisine spans the Pacific Rim from Japan to Indonesia. Appetizers come in extra-large portions, inviting guests to order an assortment to share around the table.

Cajun

House of Blues
Mandalay Bay 702-632-7605 B, L & D daily **$$** [p275, C4]
Creole and Cajun staples such as jambalaya and gumbo go down well here, as do other Southern-style regional dishes. Fri and Sat blues band. For Sun brunch, tuck into grits and hickory-smoked bacon to the sound of live gospel music.

Italian

Wolfgang Puck's Trattoria del Lupo
Mandalay Bay 702-740-5522 D daily **$$** [p275, C4]
Trattoria del Lupo means "restaurant of the wolf." This eatery is full of antiques and unique lighting fixtures and even includes an exhibition pizza station. Although known for pizzas, there are other delicious Italian dishes on the menu.

Russian

Red Square
Mandalay Bay 702-632-7407 D daily **$$$** [p275, C4]
A consistent winner in *Las Vegas Weekly*'s "dining with a scene" lists, Red Square is the place to dress up, roll up to the neon ice bar, and partake of as many Russian-influenced cocktails as possible. Afterwards, it's only a short walk to a table to dine on dishes like chicken Kiev.

RIGHT: Mandalay Bay's Red Square restaurant.

JULY
IV

Recommended Restaurants on page 135

NEW YORK NEW YORK TO CITYCENTER

Visitors from all over the globe congregate at the "Crossroads of the World" and the "performance architecture" reflects a surreal multinationalism

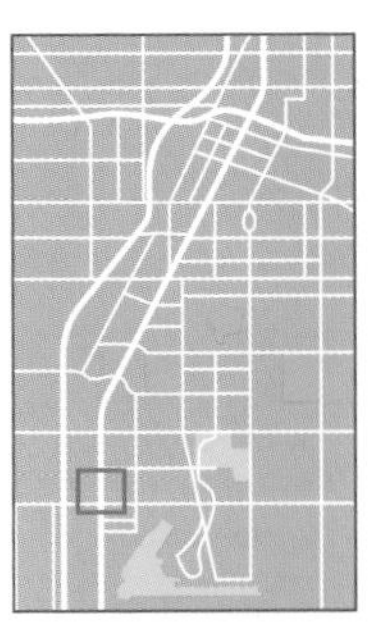

One of the busiest junctions in Las Vegas is where Tropicana Avenue crosses the Strip, connecting casino-hotels on all four corners. Everyday, thousands of pedestrians ride up and down elevators and escalators, and across the elevated pedestrian crossways. CBS Television calls this the "Crossroads of the World," and often recruits targeted audiences to test pilot shows at the junction.

As David Poltrack, CBS vice president for research and planning said, the location is perfect because "It is the one place in the country where you can get a socioeconomic cross section of America, with great geographic diversion."

NEW YORK NEW YORK ❼

✉ 3790 Las Vegas Boulevard South, www.nynyhotelcasino.com
☎ 702-740-6969 or 800-689-1797

Opened in January 1997, towering, 47-story New York New York was Nevada's tallest casino at 529ft (160 meters). Its 2,023 rooms were filled even before it opened, by previewers excited by the appeal of staying in the Big Apple without having to actually go there. ("New York New York "The Greatest City in Las Vegas" it proclaims above the casino floor.) Visitors can admire the world-famous skyline and visit replicas of landmarks such as the stately **Statue of Liberty** or a 150ft (46-meter) **Empire State Building.**

The resort's towers include the 40-story replica **Chrysler building** and the 41-story **Century building.** The large gaming area is surrounded by Park Avenue and Central Park, and adjoins **Times Square**, which has a terrific selection of fast-food

Main attractions

NEW YORK NEW YORK
ROLLER COASTER AT NEW YORK NEW YORK
ZUMANITY
MGM GRAND
LION HABITAT
MGM GARDEN ARENA
CBS TELEVISION CITY
SHOWCASE MALL
M&M'S WORLD
GAMEWORKS
MONTE CARLO
LANCE BURTON THEATER
CITYCENTER

LEFT AND RIGHT: New York New York – my kind of town.

You can grab a Broadway burger in a New York minute.

outlets. Visitors can cross the 300ft (90-meter) **Brooklyn Bridge**, spend time in the Coney Island-style amusement arcade, and stroll along a prettily graffitied **Lower East Side street** of shops and eateries. Thousands of coins are thrown into the "lagoon." These coins are periodically fished out and donated to the charitable Make a Wish Foundation.

Kids go crazy on the **Roller Coaster at New York New York** which offers thrilling views of the "Crossroads of the World" before a stomach-churning plunge down the track, followed by a series of dizzying corkscrew turns.

RIGHT: Big Apple check-in desk. **BELOW:** the roller coaster runs until 11pm during the week, and until midnight on weekends.

Successful

"The interesting thing to me about New York New York," says University of Nevada professor Dave Hickey, "is that visually, externally it really is a successful building. It solves the facade problem by multiplying facades, which also solves the scale problem."

The facade problem Hickey talks about is the trick of providing thousands of rooms in one complex, but giving all of them a desirable view. This is the reason that so many hotels on the Strip are built in "X" or "Y" shapes. The "scale problem" is that visitors could easily be overwhelmed by the vastness of the buildings in Las Vegas. Bellagio's canny architect addressed this by having each "window" actually cover four rooms, making the hotel appear only one quarter of its size.

Sports bar

The exterior of New York New York is esthetically better than the interior, but there is the **ESPN Zone** Sports Bar with 12ft (3-meter) screens and 160 TV monitors, of which a dozen are located in the *Guys* and *Dolls* washrooms so you need never lose track of the track. Las Vegas construction inspector Sue Henley won $12.5 million on a New York New York slot machine in 1997, at the time the biggest jackpot ever.

The owners of New York New York decided to spice up the resort's wholesome image, and commissioned ***Zumanity***, the third Cirque du Soleil show on the Strip. Taking its cue from the adult-oriented accent that is part of Vegas's post-millennium redefinition, one of the main ingredients of the show is sex.

Recommended Restaurants on page 135

Zumanity is, in fact, a circus of sexuality, from homoerotic to racy to kinky, offering g-strings, fetish wear, and nudity aplenty. The stage juts out suggestively into the audience, and there are scenes of naked people woven into the carpet.

The show should have been a winner. And although profits are acceptable, *Zumanity* has not reached the dizzy heights of popularity achieved by Cirque's other productions. Whether the adult-oriented theme carries over into more Soleil shows remains to be seen.

MGM GRAND ❽

✉ 3799 Las Vegas Boulevard South, www.mgmgrand.com
☎ 702-891-1111 or 877-880-0880

Las Vegas's biggest hotel, the 5,005-room MGM Grand has enough rooms and suites to offer a restless guest a different room every day for almost 14 years. Add to this the non-gaming **Signature at MGM Grand** towers, and you are talking big, BIG numbers. Guests at the original resort are greeted at 38 reception-desk windows and entertained as they wait by panoramic images of desert scenes, baseball stadiums, and advertisements on an 80-panel video screen.

As the world's biggest gambling operator, the MGM-Mirage company's assets include 12 Vegas casinos, including New York New York across the street, Bellagio, Mandalay Bay, and The Mirage. The corporation was

DRINK

Drinking and casual dining options are plentiful. In the Big Apple, try the pastrami in the café called America, or killer cocktails in Coyote Ugly. In the Grand, the chic option is Zuri, a martini bar with a selection of vodkas infused with flavors ranging from key lime to expresso.

LEFT AND BELOW: a Grand resort in the Nevada desert.

Buy your Crazy Horse tickets here.

BELOW: Crazy Horse Paris is an MGM Grand possibility for the evening. Another is discoing at Studio 54.

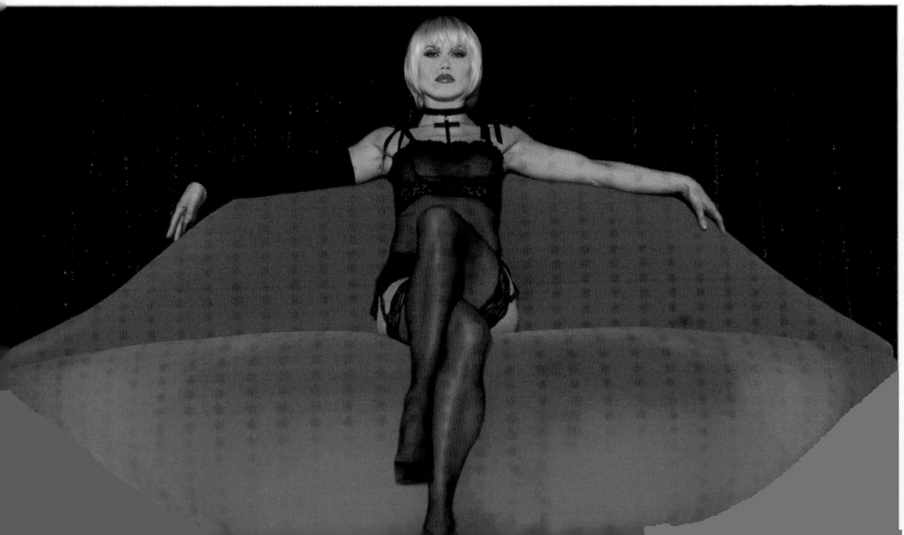

at one point headed by Kirk Kerkorian. A high-school drop-out who is now over 90 years' old, Kerkorian began his Las Vegas career piloting players between here and LA. He went on to build a series of hotels which were always the biggest in town. "He doesn't do it for the money, he has more money than he'll need in five lifetimes," said a friend. "He does it because he gets bug-eyed like a little kid when he goes through the place."

Giant screen

The MGM Grand's entrance is flanked by a 45ft (14-meter) -high lion, which is claimed to be the largest bronze statue in the United States *(see fact box on page 131)*. At the entrance on the Strip, a walkway from The Tropicana leads onto MGM's balcony over the casino floor. Over on the far side, a giant screen often shows live musicians and trailers projected from new movies. In the **Rainforest Café**, simulated thunderstorms, and animated monkeys, crocodiles, and birds surround and distract the diners.

Lions sleep here, too

On the casino floor to the right, visitors walking through the glass enclosure of the **Lion Habitat** (open 11am–10pm; free) discover lions sleeping above their heads or beneath their feet. The 450lb (204kg) beasts frolic with their trainer among waterfalls in a rocky African savannah enclosure. Usually, only a few lions are displayed at any one time, but there are 31 in all; Metro, Goldie, and Louis B, three of the resident pride, are said to be descendants of the MGM signature lion whose yawn-like roar was the company's movie logo.

MGM's casino is one of the biggest in town at 171,500 sq ft (16,000 sq meters) and significantly has 3,500 slots. Slot-machine betting, the fastest-growing game over the past decade, increased at the rate of about 12 percent every year, producing $1 billion a year for casinos from nickel slots alone.

The **MGM Garden Arena**, built to resemble Madison Square Garden, seats 17,000 people and has a reputation as a world-class venue

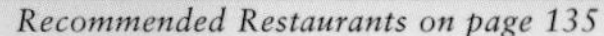
Recommended Restaurants on page 135

The MGM Grand's original entrance was through the open mouth of a gigantic lion (see photo far left). The resorts' many Asian gamblers were unhappy, as this was thought to bring bad luck, and the doorway was promptly changed.

for superstar concerts and world-championship sports events.

The **CBS Television City** research center is where visitors are recruited to attend the free screenings of pilot TV shows, to give their opinions and help shape the coming schedules. In return they are offered discount certificates that can be used in the adjoining Television City gift shop. Tests are conducted all day, and shows last about one hour, including the time to gather reactions. There is rarely a wait of longer than a few minutes for a show.

Previewed shows do sometimes offer good entertainment, and the venue has become CBS's most important test market. "People come here for the nightlife and try to figure out what to do during the day," one participant said after a show. "This is a place where people have time to spare."

Above Left and Right: a lion is the MGM logo.
Below: a sporting chance to win a fortune.

ABOVE: Showcase Mall.
BELOW: Elvis lives (and lives and lives).

SHOWCASE MALL 9

3785 Las Vegas Boulevard South
702-597-3122

Just north of the MGM Grand is the Showcase Mall. An elevator takes visitors up the 100ft (31-meter) high Coca-Cola bottle so they can enjoy the view of the Strip from above. The bottle is the most visible sign of the **World of Coca-Cola**, where exhibits and souvenirs of the global brand can be purchased. Another sweet-toothed favorite also has a busy outlet here. Four stories of **M&M's World** is the place for "designer versions" of the US's best-known candy – with interesting oddities like silver, gold, purple, or turquoise-colored M&Ms.

A joint venture between Universal Studios and Sega Enterprises, **Gameworks** has over 200 state-of-the-art arcade games. There are vintage attractions like pinball machines here, too. If the screeching of the machines and the screaming of the fans gets too much, head upstairs to The Loft. Dim lighting and soft sofas provide a serene respite, while a viewing platform allows parents to keep an eye on the main floor and their kids' highjinks.

MONTE CARLO 10

3770 Las Vegas Boulevard South, www.montecarlo.com
702-730-7777 or 888-529-4828

From the outside, the Monte Carlo is low-key by Vegas standards, with arched domes, marble floors, ornate fountains, and gas-lit promenades. It is modeled after Monaco's Place du Casino. The resort's marble registration area overlooks the pool, which

Impersonators and Tribute Shows

This city of illusion and fantasy is a spiritual home for impersonators. After all, many of the buildings on the Strip are replicas of famous landmarks. Elvis is impersonated in so many forms and guises here that they literally drop out of the sky. As well as the 35 Flying Elvises, featured in the 1992 movie *Honeymoon in Vegas*, there are thought to be more than 85,000 Elvi worldwide. A *Naked Scientist* article estimated that by 2019 they will make up a third of the world's population.

A pretty sizeable roster of impersonators have found their niche in the casts of *The Rat Pack is Back*, *Legends in Concert*, *American Superstars, Country Superstars Tribute, Fab Four Live, Barbra & Frank, A Neil Diamond Tribute*, and *An Evening with Dean and Friends.* Impersonators also proliferate in the songbook shows *Mama Mia!* (Abba), *Jersey Boys* (Frankie Valli and the Four Seasons), and *Hitzville* (Motown). Imitating Madonna, Coty Alexander said, "Right before I go on stage I feel like Madonna. When you're impersonating, you're acting. Sometimes you're really into it and the character overcomes you."

Perhaps we should all stop fighting it and impersonate someone.

Recommended Restaurants on page 135

is able to produce waves up to 30ins (75cm) in height.

The **Monte Carlo Pub & Brewery** produces 8,000 gallons (250 barrels) of beer each month. Varieties of ale include Winner's Wheat, High Roller Red, and Jackpot Pale, the last clocking 5.2 percent of alcohol by volume. Beer is brewed here every two or three days and aged from 14 to 60 days. Because it is not pasteurized and no artificial preservatives are used, the beer is best kept refrigerated. Huge glass windows show the giant copper tanks, each holding 620 gallons (2,350 liters).

For those who want to drink and keep on going, outside is a Beer on Tap counter, sharing space on the

Street of Dreams shopping boulevard, and lit by old-fashioned gas lamps.

Lance Burton is a long-time Vegas headliner who has been starring in the **Lance Burton Theater** since 1996.

ABOVE AND BELOW: the Monte Carlo.

Map on page 116

His show ends a 10-year stint in 2009. As a kid, Burton spent his money at the magic shop, getting some of it back by doing shows and charging 5¢ admission. The amiable Burton's act includes ducks, Elvis the parakeet, and a seemingly endless flight of white doves.

CityCenter ⓫

North of the Monte Carlo is one of Vegas's most ambitious schemes to date – the $9.2-billion CityCenter. Located on 76 acres (31 hectares) of the Strip, this dazzling, vertical mini-city is scheduled to open at the end of 2009 or shortly after. The centerpiece will be the 4,000-room Aria Hotel, with a convention center and an all-glass casino at the top of the building. Designed by Pelli Clarke Pelli, the casino breaks with the tradition of ground-level, windowless gaming rooms, suspended in an unreal, timeless state.

World-class artists

Other CityCenter additions include the chic Mandarin Oriental Hotel and Casino, and The Crystals, a retail complex designed by Daniel Libeskind, best known for his World Trade Center tower now under construction. His high-end shopping arcade will be enclosed in a shimmering canopy. Dotted around the landscape and in view of the public will be sculptures from world-class artists like Frank Stella and Claes Oldenburg. Central to the layout of The Crystals is a theater with a new production from Cirque du Soleil, based on the music of Elvis. The show is scheduled to open in 2010.

CityCenter continues Vegas's trend of eco-building, with commitments to water conservation, high indoor air quality, and energy consevation measures built into the design. ❑

ABOVE RIGHT: Lance Burton. **BELOW:** the new CityCenter project is calling itself "one of the world's largest environmentally sustainable urban communities."

BEST RESTAURANTS

Price includes dinner for one and a glass of wine, excluding tip:
$ = under $20
$$ = $20–$30
$$$ = $30–$40
$$$$ = over $40

American

Harley-Davidson Café
3725 Las Vegas Blvd S ☎ 702-740-4555 ⊙ L & D daily **$–$$** [p274, C2]
Motorcycles upstage the big barbecue plates and classic cheeseburgers. A seven-times-life-size replica of a Harley soft-tail protrudes through the streetside facade, while the interior decor features custom bikes, rock-star memorabilia, and an American flag made entirely from motorcycle drive chains.

Monte Carlo Brew Pub
Monte Carlo ☎ 702-730-7777 ⊙ L & D Wed–Sun **$–$$** [p274, C3]
Food until 10pm; snacks until late. Good meals, great brews, and music from 9pm nightly in the first microbrewery in a Las Vegas resort. The casual atmosphere tends to attract a noisy but fun-loving crowd.

Wolfgang Puck Bar and Grill
MGM Grand ☎ 702-891-3000 ⊙ L & D daily **$$** [p275, C3]
Circular restaurant surrounds an open kitchen dishing up high-class pizza, steaks, and much more.

Cajun

Emeril's
MGM Grand ☎ 702-891-7374 ⊙ L & D daily **$$$** [p275, C3]
Celebrity chef and TV star Emeril Lagasse's Creole-Cajun seafood continues to pack them in. It's all good, but especially tasty is the barbecued shrimp.

Continental

André's
Monte Carlo ☎ 702-730-7955 ⊙ D daily **$$$$** [p274, C3]
Elegant dining in an upscale setting, featuring award-winning chef André Rochat's gourmet cuisine and world-class wine cellar. Great for a special occasion.

French

Joël Robuchon
MGM Grand ☎ 702-891-7925 ⊙ D daily **$$$$** [p275, C3]
The famed Parisian chef came out of retirement to open this elegant signature restaurant, his first in the US. Very pricey but divine six-course and 16-course tasting menus are available, as well as a limited à la carte menu.

Irish

Nine Fine Fishermen
New York New York ☎ 702-740-6463 ⊙ L & D daily **$$** [p275, C3]
Decorated like an Irish pub, complete with a long Victorian-era bar, this restaurant offers a great view of the Strip along with traditional grub such as shepherd's pie and bangers and mash. There are fine ales and stouts and live tenors. The "full Irish breakfast" isn't served until lunch time.

Italian

Fiamma Trattoria
MGM Grand ☎ 702-891-7433 ⊙ D daily **$$$** [p275, C3]
Fiamma puts a fresh, modern spin on traditional Italian recipes amid decor that blends free-form shapes and wood, steel, and marble textures into a feast for the eyes. A signature dish is lobster and portobello gnocchi.

Mexican

Diablo's Cantina
Monte Carlo ☎ 702-730-7979 ⊙ L & D daily **$$** [p274, C3]
Mariachis play and pink neon beer signs festoon the bright gold and purple walls of this big restaurant and nightclub right on the Strip in front of the hotel. Mexican standards such as fajitas and fish tacos are on the menu along with ribs, burgers, steaks and 32 kinds of tequila.

Seafood

Seablue
MGM Grand ☎ 702-891-7433 ⊙ D daily **$$$** [p275, C3]
The menu changes constantly depending on what fresh-catch seafood is flown in that day. Cooking is done on wood-fired grills and in clay ovens. Russian and Iranian caviar are available, as are such oddities as lobster corndogs.

ACADEMIE · NATIONALE · DE · MUSIQUE

Recommended Restaurants on page 147

PLANET HOLLYWOOD TO BELLAGIO

Sensual, sumptuous, lavish, and outlandish, the resort casinos along this section of the Strip – Planet Hollywood, Paris Las Vegas, and Bellagio – cater for the discerning sybarite

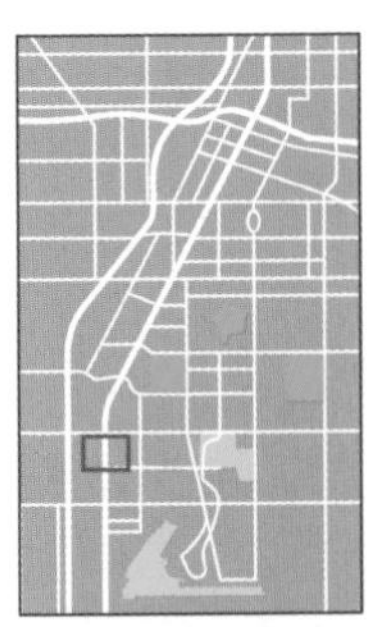

Main attractions
- PLANET HOLLYWOOD
- MIRACLE MILE SHOPS
- PARIS LAS VEGAS
- EIFFEL TOWER
- MONTGOLFIER BALLOON
- LE BOULEVARD
- BALLY'S
- JUBILEE!
- BELLAGIO
- FOUNTAINS AT BELLAGIO
- VIA BELLAGIO
- BELLAGIO GALLERY OF FINE ART
- CIRQUE DU SOLEIL'S *O*
- BELLAGIO CONSERVATORY AND BOTANICAL GARDENS

Planet Hollywood has landed on the Strip, and in its wake it brings some movie magic and red-carpet glamor to Glitter City. This little niche was already sparkling with the glitz and èlan emanating from the Napoleon Champagne bar in Paris Las Vegas, and the opulent fountains and stained-glass at Bellagio. But, in Las Vegas, there could never be such a thing as too much pizzazz.

PLANET HOLLYWOOD ⓬

3667 Las Vegas Boulevard South, www.planethollywoodresort.com
702-785-5555 or 866-919-7472

Planet Hollywood took over the Aladdin Hotel and extensively rebranded it with their signature Hollywood theme in 2007. The entrance to the property is now a long, waved, illuminated awning, with the distinctive edifice recalling touches of the older casino, but now white and simplified. The lobby has a dark, polished granite floor and a color-shiftimg backdrop. The sleek 100,000-sq-ft (9,290-sq-meter) casino has suspended lamps and illuminated walls – which also change color – and draped, illuminated columns. Drinks are served by cocktail waitresses in black leather go-go kit. An exotic gaming room called **The Pleasure Pit** features female blackjack and roulette dealers in slinky lingerie, with go-go dancers adding to the spicy atmosphere.

Movie memorabilia and tinseltown glitz adorn the casino, and unique pieces of actual movie history are in each of the 2,567 guest rooms.

Among the dozen restaurants and cafés are a **Spice Market Buffet**, a

LEFT: Paris Las Vegas.
RIGHT: neon margarita in the Mirace Mile shopping mall, Planet Hollywood.

24-hour coffee shop, **Planet Dailies**, the **Strip House** for steaks on the mezzanine level, and **Koi**, a popular LA restaurant and lounge. On the casino level is an **Earl of Sandwich**, and the Mexican cantina, **Yolos. The Living Room** provides a calm refuge from all the casino action in the leather couches and velvet drapery of a peaceful bar, with crackling fireplaces to complete the mood.

A new 1,500-seat showroom is home to the energetic production ***Stomp Out Loud***, an expanded version of their percussive spectacle, devised for Planet Hollywood and based on the exuberant Olivier award-winning show, *Stomp*. The raucous musical production uses cardboard boxes, garbage cans, boots, naturally, and other surprise instruments, played and stomped by the group from Brighton in the UK, now known all over the world. The $28-million venue has a movie screening system, technologically advanced as befits the Planet Hollywood name, and the showroom is also used for motion-picture premiers.

Concert venue

Planet Hollywood also has one of the best concert venues in Las Vegas, the **Theatre for the Performing Arts at Planet Hollywood**. The room has an ingenious curtain system, designed to vary the capacity between the maximum of 7,000 seats and a more intimate 2,000, for a range of headline shows.

Nightlife includes the club **Privé**, a night-time experience with a Miami vibe; the chic **Heart Bar** on the casino floor; and the **EXTRA Lounge**, where the crew and presenters of the TV show *EXTRA* mingle

ABOVE: a street in the Miracle Mile Shops.
BELOW: Hollywood teeth and smiles.

Recommended Restaurants on page 147

with and interview guests for inclusion in their weekday evening and Sunday afternoon broadcasts.

The Mandra Spa endeavors to ensure that guests luxuriate and feel suitably pampered by offering massage therapy, signature facials, custom spray tanning, teeth whitening, nail and hair and make-up salons, a fitness center, sauna, steam room, jacuzzi and the Alpha 2010 relaxation capsule.

The **Miracle Mile Shops** adjoins Planet Hollywood, on the site of the former, fantastically opulent but commercially unsuccessful Desert Passage shopping mall. Shops at Miracle Mile include European fashion giant H&M, exotic wear from Frederick's of Hollywood and Victoria's Secret, accessories by Swarovski, apparel for men and women at Urban Outfitters, Ben Sherman, United Colors of Benetton, and Gap, and dining and nightlife at Taverna Opa, Trader Vics and Hawaiian Tropic Zone.

Hollywood workout

Also in Miracle Mile, David Saxe follows the fashion for pole dancing and stripping and dishes it up as a fitness routine, offering a pulse-accelerating workout with boas and poles in the **V Theater** show, *Stripper 101*.

The resort has expanded already with the **Planet Hollywood Towers**. The two 50-story towers, which connect directly to the casino-hotel, have a tropical pool for residents, plus another exclusively for penthouse dwellers, 1,200 suites and 28 penthouses for timeshare tenants.

If all that shopping has made you teeter on your Jimmy Choos, consider investing in a "Shop and Spa" package from the Miracle Mile Shops. You can indulge in a "Sole Delight " foot treatment, complete with pedicure, then kick off those shoes over a reduced-price lunch or dinner. Revived, use the set of enclosed coupons to do even more shopping.

LEFT AND BELOW: Steve Wyrick performs in the theater that bears his name in the Miracle Mile Shops.

This replica of the Montgolfier balloon glows with night-time neon, and is a significant Strip landmark.

PARIS LAS VEGAS ⓭

✉ 3655 Las Vegas Boulevard South, www.parislasvegas.com
☎ 702-946-7000 or 888-266-5687

This gorgeous hotel-casino is modeled on the 800-year-old Parisian Hotel de Ville, the Paris City Hall. It is distinguished by one of Vegas's more prominent landmarks, a 50-story replica of the **Eiffel Tower**, thrusting through the roof of the casino and rising 540ft (165 meters) in the air, accompanied by a neon copy of the **Montgolfier balloon**.

A half-size scale model of the original, the tower offers panoramic views of the city from the 11th-story piano bar, one of eight restaurants at the casino specializing in regional French cuisine from Alsace, Burgundy, and Lorraine *(see page 147)*. Bastille Day (July 14) is celebrated annually at the two thirds-scale **Arc de Triomphe** in solidarity with ceremonies at the Parisian Arc.

No special celebratory cause is needed to indulge at **Napoleon's Champagne Bar**, where a collection of featured quotations includes one from the blind French monk Dom Perignon who first concocted champagne, "Brothers, come quick! I am tasting stars!"

Towering signs

The colossal legs of the Paris's Eiffel Tower are solidly planted inside the 85,000-sq-ft (7,900-sq-meter) casino, which houses an attractive fountain and a plethora of signs saying things like "Le Salon des Tables," "Les Toilettes," "La Réception," "Le Bell Captain," and "Les Artistes Steak House." A romantic, lamp-lit bridge straddles the casino high above the room but access is available only to those with a ticket to climb the tower.

The Paris especially touts its classy spa: "Long ago the French recognized the healing benefits of massage, spa treatment, and aromatherapy," offering facilities which include many styles of massage and body treatments. The larger hotel suites – ranging from 1,000 to 4,180 sq ft (93 to 388 sq meters), are given names to evoke Napoleon, St Tropez, and Charlemagne.

BELOW: at JJ's Boulangerie in Le Boulevard, eat pastries hot from the oven and be serenaded, too.

Recommended Restaurants on page 147

Aware that many visitors will be familiar with Paris itself, the architects here aimed to duplicate its landmarks "with pinpoint accuracy," by studying Gustav Eiffel's original 1889 drawings and covering interior facades with murals representing Parisian districts, before "aging" the buildings appropriately.

Fronted at the Strip by the massive **Academie National de Musique**, Paris Las Vegas's other replicas include the **Champs Elysées**, the **Louvre**, the **Paris Opéra**, and the **Palace of Versailles.**

The **Theater Paris Las Vegas** has showcased musicals and theatrical performances in the past, while currently *Anthony Cool's Uncensored Hypnotist* plays there most days.

Among the establishments along Le Boulevard is **JJ's Boulangerie**, where you might encounter "the singing breadman," a local opera singer who serenades visitors in any one of five languages. These chic, upscale little shopping streets include famous names like Cartier, Coach, Hunting World, Hermes, Gucci,

ABOVE, LEFT, AND BELOW: cruising up to eat, drink, and play in Rue de la Roulette.

Fendi, and Omega. Retail therapy continues in the avenue that connects this casino with its neighbor along the Strip, along the **Bally's-Paris Promenade.**

A knowledgeable but rather stingy local suggests that lunch patrons of the excellent Paris buffet time their visits just before it switches to dinner (at 5.30pm), when more expensive dinner items such as king crab legs are added to the menu. This is a canny strategy at other buffets around town, too, although many venues require a time break before introducing the more expensive dinner menu.

Paris is one of the Strip casinos that can be reached by its very own stop on the monorail, sharing it with the casino on its northern side.

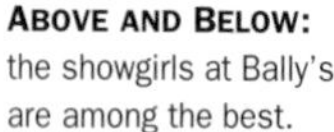

ABOVE AND BELOW: the showgirls at Bally's are among the best.

BALLY'S LAS VEGAS ⓮

✉ 3645 Las Vegas Bulevard South, www.ballyslv.com
✆ 702-739-4111 or 800-634-3434

The approach to Bally's from the Strip is fun, via 200ft (60-meter) long escalators flanked by cascading water, lighted pylons, and giant palm trees. Every 20 minutes the entry area erupts with a sound-and-water show involving a wave machine and blow-hole fountains. Water is very much in favor here; in the long-running show ***Jubilee!***, the *Titanic* sinks every night on stage.

Bally's has doubled the size of its baccarat room, to target players who are willing to wager hundreds of thousands of dollars on a single

Map on page 116

Recommended Restaurants on page 147

hand: "whales" in gaming parlance. Liberal odds and high-bet limits make baccarat a favorite with high rollers, and in one recent year, the Strip's 55 baccarat tables generated $594 million, compared with the $482 million yielded by almost 900 blackjack tables.

Unions

Bally's was one of six Vegas casinos, along with the MGM Grand, New York New York, the Monte Carlo, the Las Vegas Hilton, and the Riviera, which collectively voted against Transport Workers Union representation, by 1,564 to 554. As most dealers are paid only a minimum wage, they rely heavily on tips (or "tokes," in the parlance) to augment their income.

Shannon Bybee, a casino industry expert at the University of Nevada Las Vegas, said dealers may not want to change the status quo, despite pressure from colleagues to unionize: "They make good money in tips and they don't want to risk losing that in contract negotiations."

Nevertheless, in 2007, casino dealers in Caesars Palace and Wynn Las Vegas voted to join the union.

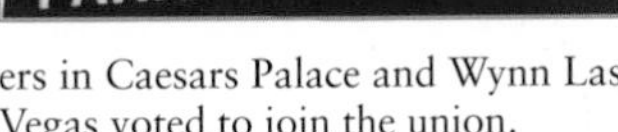

When the old MGM Grand opened on the Bally's site in 1973, it was the world's largest hotel, following a precedent Kerkorian had set in 1969 with his International Hotel, now the Las Vegas Hilton.

"We opened that hotel with Barbra Streisand in the main showroom," he said. "The rock musical *Hair* was in the other showroom

TIP

For a taste of old-style Vegas, try taking in the show at Bally's and then joining a backstage tour. Your guide is likely to be one of the hotel's showgirls, who gives inside tips on the glitz and the glamor of being a Las Vegas icon.

LEFT AND BELOW: although the monorail has had mixed reviews, it's a lifesaver during the summer heat.

TIP

Most Vegas ATM machines charge to take out money, but be sure to avoid the ones in the casinos – the fee can be astronomical. For a better rate, try to use an ATM off the Strip or at a convenience store.

and the opening lounge act was Ike and Tina Turner."

But the Grand was the scene of a disastrous fire in November, 1980 that killed 87 people and injured 700. In 1993, Kerkorian opened the present MGM Grand farther up the Strip.

Bally's showgirls are among the best. For a touch of old-style glamor, try the casino's backstage tour.

ABOVE RIGHT: the Bellagio Gallery of Fine Art. **BELOW:** Dale Chihuly's spectacular chandelier in Bellagio's lobby.

BELLAGIO ⓯

✉ 360 Las Vegas Boulevard South, www.bellagio.com
☎ 702-693-7111 or 888-987-6667

Superstar entrepreneur Steve Wynn's Bellagio, now owned by MGM-Mirage, was admired from the outset for raising the level of local sumptuousness. It is said to have cost $1.8 billion to build, requires $2.5 million a day to break even and has almost 9,000 employees. But only three years after opening, Bellagio was posting an annual profit of $323.5 million, making it the world's most profitable casino.

Splendor and success

Bellagio elevated its splendor to even greater heights a couple of years ago with the opening of the **Spa Tower**, providing 928 additional rooms and suites, some more lavish than in the original building. Success was sealed when it was discovered that the 2001 remake of the Rat Pack classic movie *Ocean's 11* was filmed using some of the gaming room interiors on Bellagio's casino floor.

Dale Chihuly: Man of Glass

Dale Chihuly, whose epic, glass-flower chandelier literally dominates Bellagio's lobby, was the first person from the United States to be accepted by Venice's Murano community as a master glass artist, and his work truly merits the overworked adjective "gorgeous." When the Las Vegas Art Museum exhibited hundreds of his pieces, the show was described by *Where* magazine as "a vibrantly colored veil of glass." The sculptor's works can be found in nearly 200 museums around the world, as well as in his native town of Tacoma, in Washington state. There the artist was recently in charge of contributing a pedestrian walkway, with countless displays and soaring crystal tower, to the city's Museum of Glass.

Chihuly himself, blinded in one eye years ago in an accident, says "Glass inspires me. As I work it becomes magical… the only material you can blow human breath down. Sun and light come through it. Glass can't be carbon-dated so you can't tell how old it is, how hard it is – there are so many mysterious things about it. It has its own category: it's not a solid, and it's not a liquid. They don't even know quite what it is except that it's the cheapest material in the world."

Recommended Restaurants on page 147

Visitors to the hotel are greeted by operatic arias soaring over the lake, where the **Fountains at Bellagio** dance to music (ranging from Pavarotti to Gene Kelly), all coordinated with jets as high as 240ft (73 meters), fading to clouds of mist in quieter interludes. The water, all 1.5 million gallons (5.5 million liters) of it, emanates from an aquifer via the resort's own treatment plant, which also fills the lagoons in front of The Mirage and Treasure Island.

Fire and water

The lake's design is by California-based company WET Design. They also created the glass cauldron which cradled the Olympic flame at the winter games in Salt Lake City, as well as the "new improved" water and fire volcanic action at The Mirage. "We work expressively with the water itself," said the group's founder Mark Fuller. "We don't do a traditional structure or something and then gush water over it."

Entrance to the resort is along a retail arcade, the **Via Bellagio**, which includes Tiffany & Co., Chanel,

Armani, Prada, and Hermes. By the reception desks is a refreshing garden below an iridescent work of glass by well-known sculptor Dale Chihuly *(see box, page 144)*.

The **Bellagio Gallery of Fine Art** (open Sun–Thur 10am–6pm, Fri–Sat 10am–9pm; charge) was Wynn's inspiration, and he bought three of

EAT

Located in the sweet-smelling Conservatory, Café Bellagio is open 24 hours a day, and has such fine pool and garden views, it's difficult to believe you're in the middle of a desert.

LEFT: Osteria del Circo, one of 20 different places to eat.
BELOW: the world-famous fountains dance to music ranging from Gene Kelly to Luciano Pavarotti.

Two of Bellagio's restaurants are the recipient of AAA Five Diamond awards, Le Cirque and Picasso. Michelin award-winning chef Michael Mina has his own establishment here, while four-star award-winning celebrity chef Jean-Georges Vongerichten presides over the Prime Steakhouse.

RIGHT: Via Bellagio has elegant, upscale shops. **BELOW:** the resort was modeled after a town on Italy's Lake Como.

the pictures back when he sold the hotel. The gallery became popular, despite a steep admission fee for all, which some guests of the hotel described as "rather cheesy," given the price of their room. The gallery exhibits high-quality touring exhibitions from domestic and foreign museums.

Fountains and flowers

In desert climates, water is prized, the very thing Wynn was after with the Bellagio fountains and also around the hotel; the water feature in the sweet-smelling Conservatory was imported from Italy.

Fountains and water are also the theme of the spectacular, **O**, the permanent show by Cirque du Soleil. It takes 74 performers to mount this unique melange of acrobatics, theatrical effects, diving, and swimming which takes place on, in, and under an indoor lake.

Roses, anemones, peonies, birds of paradise, and cherry blossom are lavishly distributed over Bellagio's Italianate decor. The floral display is most abundant just beyond the lobby, under the 50ft (15-meter) high glass ceiling of the **Bellagio Conservatory and Botanical Gardens**. The hotel employs 150 gardening and greenhouse staff alone. ❑

BEST RESTAURANTS

Price includes dinner for one and a glass of wine, excluding tip:
$ = under $20
$$ = $20–$30
$$$ = $30–$40
$$$$ = over $40

Asian

Ah Sin

Paris Las Vegas ☎ 702-967-4035 ⓒ D Wed–Sun **$$** [p274, C2]

In its indoor-outdoor location on the Strip, Ah Sin serves dishes from around the Pacific Rim. Offerings include *bulgogi* (Korean-style sesame pork ribs), tangerine-spiced beef, and Thai cashew chicken.

Brazilian

Pampas Churrascaria

Miracle Mile, Planet Hollywood ☎ 702-737-4748 ⓒ L & D daily **$$** [p274, C2]

Big slabs of juicy meat, spit-roasted on a brick rodizio grill, are the menu mainstays at this South American-style restaurant. Order sirloin, lamb, chicken, pork loin, *linguica* sausage, or a tasting plate of all of them, accompanied by black-bean stew or fried bananas.

French

Eiffel Tower Restaurant

Paris Las Vegas ☎ 702-948-6937 ⓒ D daily **$$$** [p274, C2]

Gourmet Gallic entrées in an elegant atmosphere, with a romantic view of the illuminated Strip from the 11th floor.

Le Cirque

Bellagio ☎ 702-693-8100 ⓒ D daily **$$$$** [p274, B2]

Coat and tie are mandatory for men. Le Cirque has creative gourmet entrées such as organic roast chicken with black truffles, salmon with Szechuan pepper and cardamom, and a "rabbit symphony" of ravioli, roast loin and braised leg with Riesling sauce. After all this culinary splendor, enjoy luscious desserts.

Mon Ami Gabi

Paris Las Vegas ☎ 702-944-GABI ⓒ L & D daily **$$$** [p274, C2]

Enjoy the passing crowds or the Bellagio dancing fountains from this charming French restaurant. The best dishes on le menu are classic *steak au poivre* or trout *grenobloise*.

Picasso

Bellagio ☎ 702-693-7223 ⓒ D Wed–Mon **$$$** [p274, B2]

A feast for the eyes and the stomach: French food is served in a room designed by Pablo Picasso's son, Claude, with paintings on the walls by papa estimated to be worth $50 million.

International

Sensi

Bellagio ☎ 702-693-7223 ⓒ L & D daily **$$$** [p274, B2]

Decorated with water walls and massive sandstone blocks, the restaurant surrounds an elaborate glassed-in kitchen where diners can watch chefs prepare four different cuisines – Italian, Asian, grilled, and seafood.

Italian

Osteria del Circo

Bellagio ☎ 702-693-8150 ⓒ L & D daily **$$$$** [p274, B2]

The younger and more casual sibling of Le Cirque, there's a lighthearted feel to this fine restaurant. Nevertheless, it's an idea to leave the kids at home, for the casual elegance and Tuscan dishes are best sampled without distraction.

Jananese

Koi

Planet Hollywood ☎ 702-454-4555 ⓒ D daily **$$–$$$** [p274, C2]

Polished wood and dramatic lighting set the stage for contemporary Japanese culinary creations. Signature dishes include rock-shrimp tempura and oysters on the half shell. There's a full sushi and sashimi bar.

ABOVE: Vegas buffet; Paris Las Vegas.

Mediterranean

Olives

Bellagio ☎ 702-693-7223 ⓒ L & D daily **$$$** [p274, B2]

Tasty Mediterranean food with one of the best views in town of Paris Las Vegas's Eiffel Tower.

Steak/Seafood

Bally's Steakhouse

Bally's ☎ 702-967-7999 ⓒ D daily **$$$** [p274, C1]

Dark wood panels, wainscoting, gilt-framed period paintings, and a tuxedoed staff strive hard for the ambiance of a New England-style hunt club. The fare includes thick steaks, prime rib and Chilean sea bass. Leave room for one of the spectacular desserts, such as the giant ice-cream sundae.

ESCADA

CAESARS PALACE TO CASINO ROYALE

The Garden of the Gods, Marilyn Monroe's convertible, Bugsy Siegel's hotel, and live penguins in a tropical garden are just a few of the attractions here

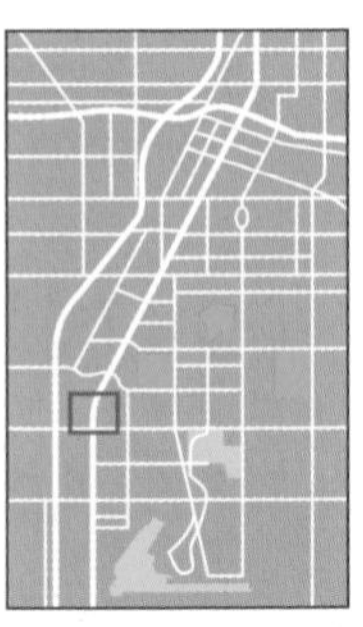

Main attractions

CAESARS PALACE
GARDEN OF THE GODS
FORUM SHOPS
COLOSSEUM
BILL'S GAMBLIN' HALL AND SALOON
FLAMINGO LAS VEGAS
FLAMINGO GARDEN
IMPERIAL PALACE
LEGENDS IN CONCERT
THE AUTO COLLECTIONS
HARRAH'S
CARNAVAL COURT
CASINO ROYALE

Gaming action, with a strong emphasis on the fun side, is what this area is all about. Harrah's is a burbling palace of slots, perfectly catering to those who come to play. When Caesars arrived, it cranked Vegas up a gear, with every nook and cranny packed with lavish entertainment. And the history of the Flamingo makes it, whether the owners admit it or not, a Las Vegas icon.

CAESARS PALACE 16

3570 Las Vegas Boulevard South, www.harrahs.com
702-731-7110 or 800-634-6661

Caesars Palace has provided the set for more than a dozen movies and 80 television shows. The fabulous and venerable facade dominates the western side of this portion of the Strip with 50ft (15-meter) cypresses shipped over from Italy, and a trio of eye-catching fountains that spray columns of water 35ft (10.5 meters) into the air. It is claimed that due to ingenious recycling, water usage is about the same as that used on an average-sized lawn.

Beside the reflecting pool into which 10,000 gallons (38,000 liters) of water pours, is a copy of Giovanni's 16th-century sculpture *The Rape of the Sabine Women* while nearer to the street is another famous statue, a good replica of the *Winged Victory* (300 BC) that hangs in the Louvre.

The approach is dominated by four gold-leaf horses and a charioteer, the fine *Quadriga* statue. The casino's entrance doors are flanked by more replicas of classical statues, including the *Venus de Milo*. Most famous of all, an 18ft (6-meter) high *David* dominates the **Appian Way**

LEFT AND RIGHT: Caesars Palace.

ABOVE: the resort was built in 1966.
BELOW: the Augustus Café is open 24 hours a day.

shopping arcade inside the casino. Carved from the same Carrara marble as the Michelangelo original but at twice the height, the replica weighs 9 tonnes (8,000kg).

Caesars Palace has had several owners since Jay Sarno completed it in 1966, but the look of it owes much to Sarno's belief in the magically relaxing properties of the oval. Jo Harris, the designer who later worked with Sarno on Circus Circus, attributes part of Caesar's success to its layout as a spoked wheel, with the gambling area as the hub, which is in view, wherever you walk.

The 5-acre (2-hectare) **Garden of the Gods**, named after the Baths of Caracalla frequented by ancient Rome's elite, has three swimming pools and two whirlpool spas, the whole complex landscaped with sweeping lawns, graceful fountains, and classically inspired statuary. Even the lifeguard stands are designed to resemble imperial thrones. A sign at the entrance reads, "European-style topless bathing is permitted at Caesars' pools. We prefer that this is restricted to the Venus pool area." The resort's top entertainment venue, the **Colosseum,** was designed with the ancient Roman original in mind, and was built specifically to showcase the talents of Canadian singer Celine Dion; now it plays host to some of showbiz's biggest names *(see page 152)*.

Tower power

The most desirable hotel rooms at Caesars Palace are those in the towers, and, cannily following the trend, the luxurious **Octavius Tower** opens in 2009. With 695 new rooms, three swimming pools, a garden wedding chapel, and a convention center, Caesars are hoping to capture even more of the top travelers to Vegas.

The 29-story **Palace Tower** houses around 1,100 de-luxe guest rooms and suites, all with huge whirlpool bathtubs and terrific views. The 24-story **Forum Tower** is comprised of two-story, four-bedroom apartments known as Fantasy Suites, themed in Roman or Egyptian style and designed for special guests who travel with families or retinues, or for honeymooners who hold their wedding at the hotel.

Caesar salads

Food in Las Vegas always comes in colossal amounts: 21 tonnes (19,000kg) of smoked salmon and 2,700 ounces (76kg) of caviar are consumed in the hotel's various restaurants *(see page 161)* every year, as well as 336,000 of the aptly chosen Caesar salads. The salad, incidentally, was first tossed by an Italian immigrant to the US, chef Caesar Cardini, and his 1924 recipe remains popular the world over.

Caesars is known for hosting sports events. Jimmy Connors and Martina Navratilova battled on the Palace courts, and Evander Holyfield and Sugar Ray Leonard have fought championship boxing matches on the premises.

LEFT: the Artic Ice Room at Caesars Palace's Qua spa. **BELOW:** at the Garden of the Gods, even the lifeguard stands are designed to resemble imperial thrones.

Slots with the allure of a mysterious queen of the desert.

Sports gods

Caesars has a long association with sporting events, and was the first hotel in Vegas with satellite equipment to relay races and matches into the casino. Former world heavyweight champion Joe Louis was employed here as the greeter, up to his death in 1981. Frank Sinatra and the Reverend Jesse Jackson delivered eulogies at his memorial service, and the former champ is remembered with a 7ft (2-meter) marble statue standing at the entrance to the Race & Sports Book, inside which are 90 video screens, hundreds of electronic panels and reader boards, and larger-than-life murals of famous performers.

More than 160 major boxing contests have been held here, including the bout between Larry Holmes and Muhammad Ali in 1980, which ended Ali's career. Other championship events have also been staged in the hotel's spacious grounds, including the hotel's very own Formula 1 Grand Prix, held in the early 1980s, and perpetually rumored to return.

Forum Shops

The classy arcade known as the **Forum Shops** features Dior, Versace, Gucci, Bulgari, Ferragamo, and other retail empires, and is always crowded. A domed ceiling emulates a changing sky over the arches of the central piazza, from sunrise to sunset about every 20 minutes. Columns, fountains, and Wolfgang Puck's Spago restaurant *(see page 161)* adjoin a pertty good replica of the **Trevi Fountain**.

One of the liveliest places late at night is the fun, floating cocktail lounge known as **Cleopatra's Barge** with furled sails, ostrich-feather fans, and stalwart waitresses dodging between the dancers, bringing drinks across the gangplank to spectators in the tiered seats.

Bacchus

At one end of the arcade, beneath a pale blue ceiling with puffy white clouds, is an enormous statue of Minerva. Bacchus presides over another piazza, on an elevated throne. Now and again the throne revolves, the god raises a beaker to

BELOW: Bette Midler at the Colosseum.

Stars and the Colosseum

Caesars' 4,000-seat Colosseum is designed to recall its ancient Roman namesake, and was purpose-built in 2003 as a showcase venue for Canadian singer Celine Dion. She agreed a $45-million contract to give five shows a week for three years. What convinced Celine to sign up to the Colosseum was, she said, seeing the spectacular Cirque du Soleil show, *O*, performed in their custom-built auditorium at Bellagio. "I knew that I wanted to have a show like this and have, like, 60 performers on stage with me, making every song a visual appearance," she says. "It's kind of impossible to travel with a show like this; the effects and the decor and the whole thing make it technically impossible without a base. We found that in Las Vegas." She certainly started a trend; singers Elton John, Cher, and Bette Mider have followed Dion into long residencies on that same stage.

Bette Midler said, after the opening of her highly acclaimed show, *The Showgirl Must Go On*, "I never wanted to play in Vegas before, because it seemed so much like the end of the line. That's all changed now, and it seems more like a beginning." Caesars seems to have innovated an era of the megastar no-road show.

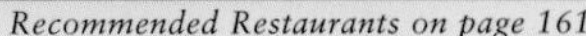
Recommended Restaurants on page 161

his lips and speaks, as laser-driven planets, stars, and constellations race through the sky above.

Plutus, god of wealth, controls the music and dancing waters, and Apollo strums a modern fiber-optic lyre. One attraction just off the magnificently decorated **Great Hall** is ***Race for Atlantis***, a convincingly scary ride, and pretty amazing even without the 3-D glasses.

Approaching the entrance from the **rotunda** with its **circular aquarium**, the arcade is filled with Aqua Massage tanks, while Japanese slot machines allow you to box and dance with partners on screen, and a photo booth will place you in front of scenes from around the world, or show you what your future child might look like.

BILL'S GAMBLIN' HALL & SALOON ⑰

3595 Las Vegas Boulevard South, www.billslasvegas.com
702-732-2100 or 866-245-5745

Bill's (formerly the Barbary Coast) stresses "Victorian charm and elegance," more or less sustained by chandeliers with big white globes, Art-Deco glass signs, and waitresses who wear red garters over black-net stockings.

Along with its decorative windows in the Victorian Room is what it claims is the world's largest "Tiffany-style" stained-glass mural. Some tables are set aside for *pai gow*, a form of poker adapted from an Asian domino game, and there is a poker machine played with gold coins which pays $250,000 for a royal flush, or just a free drink for two pairs.

Bill's Lounge is a classic casino lounge and the performance venue

DRINK

After an evening at Pure, Caesars' sexy nightclub, sophisticated sippers might like to head for the Seahorse Lounge, with its calming ambiance and chilled champagne. If you're in a mood to continue the party, head for the Shadow lounge, where women in skin-tight body stockings dance in silhouette, and the bartenders put on an acrobatic show.

LEFT AND BELOW: day and night at Caesars Palace.

What Price Power?

The new CityCenter project touts itself as a "sustainable community," but what about everywhere else?

A couple of years ago, one of the biggest resorts on the Strip had to close for a night, leaving thousands of guests to check in elsewhere. Bellagio was hit hard after a main power line failed, and although by the next day normal relations were restored, the incident was yet another example of Sin City's almost crippling dependency on power. And power means big bucks. "I guess I'll have to go to another casino to lose money," quipped one displaced guest – not the sort of comment any gaming establishment wants to hear.

Energy problems in the desert are a constant worry. A hotel-casino on the Strip can use up as much energy as 10,000 private homes, and rising electricity bills have come as a shock to the neon-happy resorts.

At the MGM Grand and other hotels, the 750 watts of light in many rooms has been reduced to 500. Motion sensors turn off the lights in empty offices. The current generation of slot machines are designed to consume 25 percent less electricity than their predecessors. Intelligent thermostats are reducing the air conditioning in empty convention rooms. CityCenter, the new mini-city on the Strip, has eco-friendly alternatives built into its design.

Seeing power bills rise so steeply, several casinos began to shut off exterior spotlights at 2am. The people behind Caesars Palace's new Octavius Tower consulted architects with LEED experience (Leadership in Energy and Environmental Design).

Luckily, the city's convention center was between shows when Nevada Power asked customers to "shed load." Lights in the building are now being replaced with low-wattage bulbs. To take advantage of off-peak rates, the Cashman Center delayed the start of its home baseball games, so that they began (at cheaper rates) at 7.15pm.

Nevada Power is one of the state's oldest companies, and at the same time has made itself one of the most unpopular. The state's Public Utilities Commission rejected almost half the $922 million the company sought in increased charges. Politicians blame the utility's troubles on bad public relations.

As of the last count, there were 15,000 miles (24,000km) of neon on the Strip. The Rio's 125ft (38-meter) -high marquee, voted the city's best neon sign, uses 12,930ft (4,000 meters) of neon tubing, and over 5,000 lightbulbs. The hotel recently installed a facility that generates electricity while providing heat that is captured for water heating.

The glare and glitter of the fantasy city in the desert is sacred to the casinos. One casino boss said, "Las Vegas has an image and a certain cachet that it has to live up to, and that includes the exterior lighting, the neon, and the marquee. It's what people come here to see, and reducing those would be the last thing we do."And so the search for sustainability continues. ❑

LEFT AND ABOVE: exhibits from the Neon Museum.

Map on page 116

Recommended Restaurants on page 161

for Pete "Big Elvis" Vallee, who once weighed near 900 lbs (400 kg), but lost almost half that amount and now bears an uncanny resemblence to the King.

FLAMINGO LAS VEGAS ⓲

✉ 3555 Las Vegas Boulevard South, www.flamingolv.com
☎ 702-733-3111 or 888-902-9929

The Flamingo of today is a far cry from the "carpet joint" of Bugsy Siegel's day. Almost the last traces of the mobster disappeared in 1995 when his bullet-proof casino office with elaborate escape routes, and his private villa, were bulldozed.

This was all part of a master plan which included razing the outmoded, motel-style buildings at the rear of the property and constructing a $104-million tower addition. The hoodlum might well have been forgotten by now but for the success of Warren Beatty's 1991 movie *Bugsy*, with himself in the title role. Though the movie was more fantasy than fact, it did kindle enough interest for the hotel to open the **Bugsy Celebrity Theater**.

Bugsy's bluff

Historians like to recount that, tough as he was, Benjamin Siegel did not faze everybody. Paying tax was not one of his top priorities, and he was once challenged by Robbins Cahill from the Nevada Tax Commission, who sent an employee to collect $5,000 owed in gaming taxes. "What'll you do if I don't pay?" the mobster asked. He was told that his license would be

TIP

The Flamingos' most charming attraction is the Flamingo Garden, which has wildlife, lagoons, and – of course – flamingos. If you'd like a peek before committing to the long journey down the hot Strip and through the clamoring casino, get off the monorail at the Flamingo/Caesars Palace stop, and just gaze down.

LEFT AND BELOW: night-time at the Flamingo Hotel.

ABOVE: Vegas meals are usually good value. **BELOW:** the Imperial's impressive collection of automobiles.

revoked, and replied, "You wouldn't dare." The employee reported back to Cahill who told the hoodlum, "Maybe you'd better try us." Siegel backed out of the challenge and wrote a check.

Six months later, in June 1946, Siegel was murdered at the Beverly Hills mansion of his girlfriend, Virginia "Flamingo" Hill. A plaque near the Flamingo's garden buffet pavilion wryly commemorates the mobster's demise, but that his "preoccupation with safety proved to be geographically misplaced." The late Las Vegas historian Frank Wright said that, "In a sense, Siegel's death was a great advertisement for the city of Las Vegas. It certainly brought attention, and created a sort of sense of illicit excitement."

The 15-acre (6-hectare) **Flamingo Garden**, with many plastic flamingos and several real penguins, is really very charming at night. Only steps away from the bright-heat roar of the Strip, it's filled with the sound of crickets. There are pools, waterfalls, a lagoon, and a turtle observation bridge, and an entire wildlife habitat, with koi, swans, ducks, and – of course – (real) Chilean flamingos. The garden is open to the public most days, to hotel guests at night.

IMPERIAL PALACE ⓳

3535 Las Vegas Boulevard South, www.imperialpalace.com
702-731-3311 or 800-634-6441

The Imperial Palace opened in 1979 with an Oriental theme, the roofs covered in blue tiles from Japan. Inside are carved dragons, giant wind-chime chandeliers, and bars called Geisha and Ginza.

Recommended Restaurants on page 161

Until his death in 2003, owner Ralph Engelstad was the only sole proprietor of a major Las Vegas casino, and earned himself an untold fortune. Currently the premises are operated by the Engelstad family trust. Engelstad was acclaimed for his friendly policies toward disabled people, who form 13 percent of the 2,600 employees here.

Legends

John Stuart's ***Legends in Concert*** has been running over a decade, with impersonations (of varying verisimilitude) of luminaries like Liberace, Michael Jackson, Madonna and, of course, Elvis. Stuart rotates a cast of about 100 lookalikes, who study videos of their models obsessively. "I loved everything about the way he wore his clothes, his hair, the way he sang. I would study myself doing his smile in a mirror," said Graham Patrick, who plays Elvis, complete with upper-lip curl.

The 2,700-room Palace has all the usual amenities, plus an Olympic-sized swimming pool, a business center, and a karaoke club. Gamblers should be alert for the sometimes short-lived promotions like the Imperial Palace's "New Member Mania." Under this plan, enrollees could qualify for a variety of freebies ranging from room vouchers to car-rental days, concert tickets, spa passes, free meals, and even airline credit vouchers. The only drawback seems to be a requirement for around six hours of straight gambling to qualify.

$50 million

Ralph Engelstad, was renowned for his antique cars, which are now on show as **The Auto Collections** (open daily 10am–6pm; charge). An animated figure of John Wayne stands beside the Duke's silver 1931 Bentley, welcoming guests to the impressive 250-car collection. Priceless motors include a $50-million array of 1930s Duesenbergs, Liberace's 1981 Zimmer with a candelabra hood ornament, Howard Hughes' baby-blue Chrysler, a 1929 Isotta Fraschini of the type seen in *Sunset Boulevard*, and a replica of Karl Benz's 1886 three-wheeler said to have reached speeds of up to 8mph (13kph).

In the 1950s, great motels on the Strip were commonplace, but now most of the originals have been pulled down.

BELOW: the Imperial Palace has its own karaoke club.

A big draw is the Imperial Palace's Dealertainer's Pit in the casino. From noon until 4am, fun impersonators deal backjack and then perform to an eager crowd.

Also on show are cars formerly owned by Hitler, Kruschev, and many US presidents. The blue-and-white 1976 Cadillac for which Elvis Presley paid $14,409 – including extras like brass hubcaps – and Marilyn Monroe's 1955 Lincoln Capri convertible, in which the screen goddess clocked up only 26,000 miles (42,000km), are cars that have motor-mad fans eating their room vouchers with envy.

HARRAH'S ⑳

3475 Las Vegas Boulevard South, www.harrahs.com
702-369-5000 or 800-214-9110

William Harrah was building casinos in the town of Reno and at Lake Tahoe as early as the 1930s, but Harrah's on the Las Vegas Strip dates back only to 1992, having opened 20 years earlier as the Holiday Casino.

Its famous riverboat facade was replaced – and lamented by some regulars – by a glitzy exterior with gold-trimmed harlequins, and celebrated its $200-million new look by mounting a daring, high-wire walk 100ft (30 meters) above the Strip by Tino Wallenda.

RIGHT AND BELOW: Alice and Marilyn will be your dealers for the evening.

Major player

Harrah's is a major player in gaming circles, having at one time or another owned or managed around 40 other casinos in the United States,

Recommended Restaurants on page 161

including properties in New Orleans and Mississippi. The company was also instrumental in partnering with California Native American tribes, particularly in the Escondito region.

In 2004, Harrah's stepped in virtually overnight to manage the venerable Binion's Horseshoe casino in downtown Vegas *(see page 207)* and transferred its famous World Series of Poker to the company's roster of casinos.

One of Harrah's lounges, with multicolored palm trees, illuminated rocks, and three-dimensional mural, evokes "a day at the beach," the fantasy enhanced by tropical drinks in exotic glasses. The glamorous comedian **Rita Rutner** performs most nights in the main showroom, while fresh young talents try out their acts at the smaller **Improv Comedy Club.**

Carnaval Court

Outdoors is a popular entertainment plaza, **Carnaval Court**, with cafés, stores, and performers. There is also a bar where bartenders are skilled in singing, dancing, juggling glassware, and the breathing of fire.

Among the shops are the Jackpot store selling magazines, newspapers, and books as well as fresh flowers

and Harrah's logo merchandise, and the Old Fashioned Chocolate Shop and Soda Fountain from San Francisco's Ghirardelli Chocolate Co.

The casino's happily named Fresh Market Square Buffet offers a good champagne brunch from 10am to 4pm on weekends.

Harrah's is an exuberant place, where the nickel video-poker machines are just inside the door. The Bally Pro Slot machines at Harrah's are advertised as having a noisy stainless-steel tray, to make pay offs even more exciting. The trays are even designed to prevent

TIP

It can be time-consuming without hailing a taxi to get to casinos off the Strip or that are not part of the monorail system, like the Rio, so jump on the free shuttle that connects the Harrah's properties to each other. The shuttle runs every half hour from 10am to the early hours of the morning.

BELOW: Harrah's is an exuberant place.

If money is tight, Casino Royale has low-risk bets that begin at $1.

RIGHT: welcome to Harrah's Carnaval Court. **BELOW:** Casino Royale is an affordable hotel at a convenient location.

coin cups being used in them, which could modestly deaden the sound.

Apparently, Bill Harrah was the first casino operator to emphasize slot machines over table games. He began the chain with a bingo parlor in Reno in 1937. The slot machines now typically account for 62 percent of a casino's winnings.

"Most casinos are getting on the slot-band wagon," says an employee. "They recognize that it's the most stable customer base. They are not trying to win real big, it's people who are there for fun. They'll be back if they have fun."

CASINO ROYALE ㉑

✉ 3411 Las Vegas Boulevard South, www.casinoroyalehotel.com
☎ 702-737-3500 or 800-854-7666

The bright blue-and-violet windows of the Casino Royale light the way to a 152-room hotel where affordablility and a convenient location (between Harrah's and the upscale Venetian, and across the street from The Mirage) are among its biggest draws. It's a good place for low-risk bets, as the casino has a variety of penny slots, and even some of the table games accept a minimum bet for just $1.

The Outback Steakhouse serves hearty meals, and the numerous fast-food restaurants (some open 24 hours a day) mean that you will never have to go far to be fed. ❑

BEST RESTAURANTS

Price includes dinner for one and a glass of wine, excluding tip:
$ = under $20
$$ = $20–$30
$$$ = $30–$40
$$$$ = over $40

American

Bradley Ogden

Caesars Palace 702-731-7410 D daily **$$$$** [p274, B1]
San Francisco celebrity chef Ogden's signature restaurant presents fare ranging from heirloom-tomato salad to bison tenderloin, with an emphasis on farm-fresh, organic ingredients. A tasting menu is also available.

I Love This Bar and Grill

Harrah's 702-697-2880 L & D daily **$$** [p274, B1]
Named for C&W singer Toby Kieth's hit, "I Love This Bar," the restaurant features country favorite foods like chicken fried steak, catfish po'boys and fried bologna sandwiches. Live music nightly. The outdoor Carnaval Court serves colorful cocktails whipped up by acrobatic bartenders.

Spago

The Forum Shops at Caesars Palace 702-737-9700 L & D daily; sushi bar 3–11pm **$$$** [p274, B1]
Named after Wolfgang Puck's first restaurant in Beverly Hills, this popular restaurant features an ever-changing menu of California nouvelle cuisine.

American/Caribbean

Margaritaville

Flamingo 702-733-3111 B, L & D daily **$$** [p274, B1]
Styled to resemble a beach-front *palapa* with a seaplane hanging from the ceiling, singer Jimmy Buffet's indoor-outdoor tropical restaurant offers jambalaya, Jamaican jerk salmon and, of course, Buffet's trademark "cheeseburger in paradise."

Chinese

Chinois

The Forum Shops at Caesars Palace 702-737-9700 L & D daily; sushi bar 3–11pm **$$$** [p274, B1]
Wolfgang Puck offers Chinese with a Gallic attitude. Specialties include Shanghai lobster with coconut curry sauce, stir-fried string beans, catfish, duck, and much more. A few steps away is a branch of Puck's California-inspired Spago.

Ming

Imperial Palace 702-731-3311 D daily **$–$$** [p274, B1]
In a hotel geared for an Asian clietele, this affordable restaurant presents familiar Mandarin and Cantonese fare as well as inventive dishes such as abalone with black mushrooms.

Italian

Penazzi

Harrah's 702-697-2880 D Wed–Sun **$$$** [p274, B1]
Simply decorated in earth tones, this restaurant serves gourmet Mediterranean fare such as scallops crusted with pistachios and filet of sole stuffed with crab meat in a tomato-caper sauce. There's also an oyster bar. The wine list is long and impressive.

Japanese

Hyakumi

Caesars Palace 702-346-4642 D daily; noodle and sushi bar 11am–4pm **$$–$$$$** [p274, B1]
Every type of sushi is available here.

Steak/Seafood

The Steakhouse at Bill's

Bill's Gamblin' Hall 702-737-2100 D daily **$$$** [p274, C1]
Mesquite-grilled steaks share the menu with lobster, ahi tuna and assorted pasta dishes. The atmosphere recalls the opulence of Victorian-era San Francisco, with deep red velvet upholstered booths, matching wallpaper and dark wood paneling.

RIGHT: scary drinks at Harrah's Carnaval Court.

NIGHTLIFE

There's glitz and glamour in Las Vegas's huge showrooms and in the intimate clubs, bars, and lounges of Glitter City

Conversation softens across the chink of glasses as the lights dim. Out on the stage steps Sinatra. Bette Midler. The Beatles. Donnie and Marie Osmond *(below right, at the Flamingo)*. The magician Rick Thomas with a series of performing animals. And, of course, a line of long-legged showgirls, shiny makeup covering more than their costumes do. Since the days of the Rat Pack at the Sands, Vegas nightlife has been a sparkling, glossy affair of world-class performers, or world-class imitators of world-class performers.

Resorts compete with each other to launch the latest, brightest and most luxurious clubs, employing cascading, indoor waterfalls, perspex sliding boards, and DJs in swimming pools. Elegant lounges hum with jazz and bonhomie, huge showrooms host top-line acts, and casino bars are opened by Hollywood starlets. That's Vegas after dark.

BELOW: one for the girls: a fast-growing market is male striptease, popular with women on "gal pal" weekends.

ABOVE: *Legends in Concert* is a big draw for the Imperial Palace, where the show started in 1983. Now, *Legends* is a brand, with tribute shows playing across the country.
BELOW: Vegas lounges have the perfect ambience for jazz.

MAGIC AND MAGICIANS

Las Vegas, built on illusion and fantasy, is a spiritual home for magicians. Magic is so much a part of the Vegas experience that in 1996, the Monte Carlo offered the master illusionist Lance Burton his own theater, with a contract running until 2009. Planet Hollywood has repeated the trick by building a theater especially for Steve Wyrick, and the Venetian has a museum dedicated to master showman Houdini.

Penn & Teller's residency at the Rio, and Criss Angel's show with Cirque du Soleil at The Mirage are edgy and controversial events. More intimate is Steve Dacri, a tireless, 30-year veteran who is a favorite with visiting celebs out on the town in Vegas. Dacri delivers close-up magic straight to diners at the Six Tables restaurant.

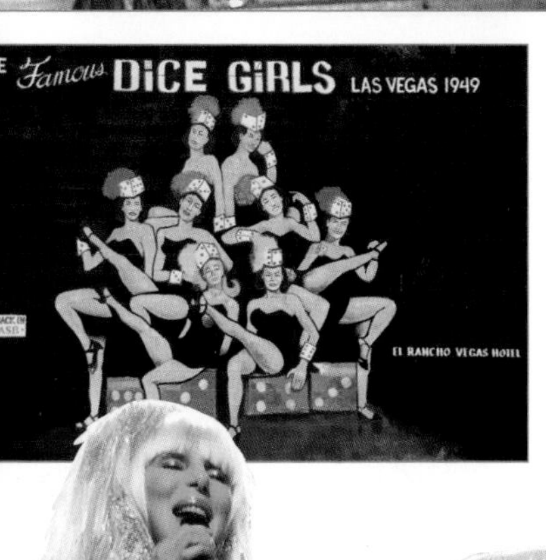

ABOVE LEFT: one of the first of the showgirl productions, the Dice Girls, opened at Rancho Vegas in 1949.

ABOVE: the Blue Man Group's enigmatic dance, mime, and multimedia show amazes audiences with themes of science, technology, and plumbing at the Venetian.

LEFT: Cher has been in the business since the 1960s, and her show of epic kitsch runs in tandem at Caesars Palace with Bette Midler's *The Showgirl Must Go On.*

RESERVED
BACCARAT

Recommended Restaurants on page 171

MIRAGE TO FASHION SHOW MALL

Sea battles and erupting volcanos, white tigers, leaping dolphins, one-armed bandits, a Trump, and The Venetian Hotel. Need we say more?

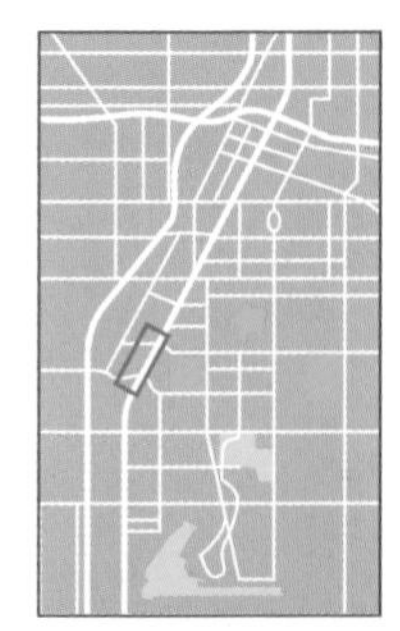

Main attractions

THE MIRAGE
SIEGFRIED & ROY'S SECRET GARDEN & DOLPHIN HABITAT
THE VENETIAN
GRAND CANAL SHOPPES
MADAME TUSSAUD'S
THE PALAZZO
THE SHOPPES AT THE PALAZZO
T.I. (TREASURE ISLAND)
SIRENS OF T.I.
FASHION SHOW MALL
TRUMP INTERNATIONAL HOTEL AND TOWER

Some of the largest, swankiest and fastest-expanding properties on the Strip are congregating at this select little corner. The Mirage has the distinction of being Steve Wynn's first venture on the Strip. The Venetian, having added the massive Palazzo, is soon to grow a timeshare tower, and Trump's signature tower is also due a twin.

THE MIRAGE ❶

✉ 3400 Las Vegas Boulevard South, www.mirage.com
☎ 702-791-7111 or 800-374-9000

In 1989, when he was about to open the Mirage, entrepreneur Steve Wynn said that there had been "a terrible sameness" to earlier Vegas casinos. "I wanted to take it to a new level. We presented this place as an alternative for people. I always knew others would follow, as they have, but it happened much faster than even I expected."

The Mirage certainly was different. From the erupting volcano just off the sidewalk to the tigers'glass-enclosed habitat in the arcade of smart shops underground, it drew huge crowds of curious spectators right from the beginning. Within three years, the casino was the biggest money-maker on the Strip. Even the need for more than a million dollars a day to break even never seemed to be a problem.

The spectacular appeal of the royal white tigers and their charismatic magician owners, Siegfried & Roy, filled the 1,500-seat showroom 480 times a year, the resort's biggest draw ever. But Roy was attacked and dragged off stage by one of his

LEFT: high rollers at The Venetian.
RIGHT: within three years of opening in 1989, The Mirage was the biggest money-maker on the Strip.

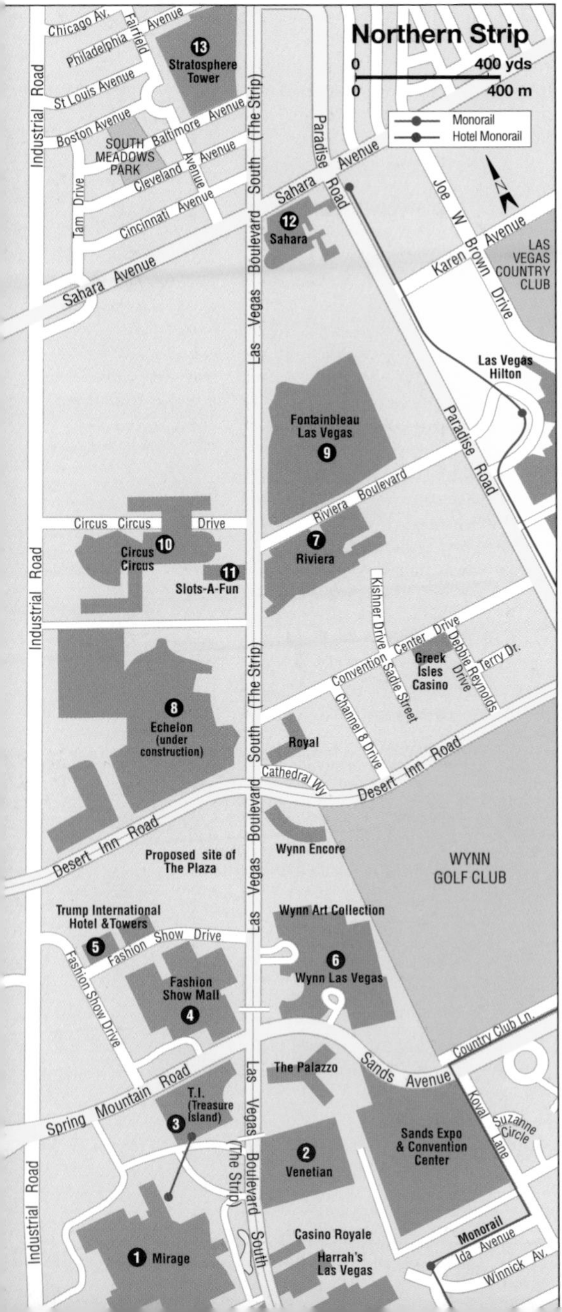

Northern Strip

0 400 yds
0 400 m
Monorail
Hotel Monorail
N

Chicago Av.
Philadelphia Avenue
Fairfield
St Louis Avenue
Boston Avenue
Baltimore Avenue
SOUTH MEADOWS PARK
Cleveland Avenue
Avenue
Tam Drive
Cincinnati Avenue
Sahara Avenue
Industrial Road
Las Vegas Boulevard South (The Strip)
Paradise Road
Joe W Brown Drive
Karen Avenue
LAS VEGAS COUNTRY CLUB
Las Vegas Hilton
13 Stratosphere Tower
12 Sahara
9 Fontainbleau Las Vegas
Riviera Boulevard
7 Riviera
Circus Circus Drive
10 Circus Circus
11 Slots-A-Fun
Kishner Drive
Convention Center Drive
Sadie Street
Greek Isles Casino
Debbie Reynolds Drive
Terry Dr.
Channel 8 Drive
8 Echelon (under construction)
Royal
Cathedral Wy
Desert Inn Road
Proposed site of The Plaza
Wynn Encore
WYNN GOLF CLUB
Wynn Art Collection
Trump International Hotel & Towers
5
Fashion Show Drive
6 Wynn Las Vegas
Fashion Show Mall 4
Country Club Ln.
The Palazzo
Sands Avenue
Spring Mountain Road
T.I. (Treasure Island) 3
Koval Lane
Suzanne Circle
Sands Expo & Convention Center
2 Venetian
Casino Royale
Monorail
Ida Avenue
Harrah's Las Vegas
Winnick Av.
1 Mirage

tigers in October 2003. He is not expected to fully recover, and the show is permanently closed.

Rare species

But the entertainers are remembered and the tigers are safe at **Siegfried & Roy's Secret Garden & Dolphin Habitat** (open 11am–5.30pm; charge). Past azure dolphin pools, rare or endangered species include white and black-and-white tigers. The Dolphin Habitat houses 10 Atlantic bottlenose dolphins in 2.5-million gallon (9.5-million liter) saltwater tanks. In a new program, kids are invited to stop being a tourist and become a trainer for a day. Exotic sea life swim in a

Recommended Restaurants on page 171

huge tank behind the registration desk, inside an atrium with palm trees and foliage. Cirque du Soleil's hot-ticket Beatles' show, *Love*, plays in the showroom.

THE VENETIAN ❷

3355 Las Vegas Boulevard South, www.venetian.com
702-414-1000 or 888-283-6423

The Venetian was conceived by maverick Sheldon Adelson, ebullient founder of the annual computer convention COMDEX. Adelson, the son of a Boston cabbie, financed the Venetian partly from the $900 million proceeds of the sale of COMDEX. Adelson and his wife Miriam, an Israeli doctor, spent their honeymoon in Venice and subsequently set a pair of historians to work compiling a photographic catalog of original Venetian artwork and architectural details.

Built to be beautiful

Built at a cost of $1.5 billion on the site of the former Sands Hotel, the Venetian has rooms almost twice as large as the average. The restaurants are served by chefs on the critics' Top-10 lists; the spa and fitness club is operated by the renowned **Canyon Ranch**; and the complex has enough marble-and-stone flooring to cover a dozen football fields. The resort adjoins a pool deck modeled after an Italian garden.

Viewed from the Strip, the lavish Venetian really does look like Venice, from the **Campanile Bell Tower** soaring 300ft (98 meters)

In 2008, The Mirage unveiled its new, even more volatile volcano, with sound effects provided by Grateful Dead drummer Mickey Hart.

FAR LEFT: the bell tower of The Venetian. **LEFT:** statue of Siegfried & Roy on the grounds of The Mirage. **BELOW:** a treatment room at The Venetian's Canyon Ranch spa.

Hotel bars along this part of the Strip offer different atmospheres to suit different tipplers. The Venetian's V Bar is so stylish, subdued, and minimal that people either love it or hate it. T.I.'s Kahunaville Party Bar, on the other hand, has dancing waitresses, dueling pianos, and show-off bartenders.

above the **Grand Canal** to the *gondolieri* in striped shirts. Like their Italian counterparts, they serenade their sometimes embarrassed passengers, but the gondola rides are at least cheaper than the originals. Adding to the "realism," pigeons have been trained to fly out and swirl around at least twice a day.

Grand Canal Shoppes

Along with the **Doges Palace** and **Rialto Bridge**, the resort sports a scaled-down **Piazza San Marco** in which jugglers, singers, and dancers seem to be continually performing. The square is the culmination of the **Grand Canal Shoppes** which begins with a colorful, awe-inspiring frescoed ceiling and segues into the bluest skies ever seen.

Contemporary celebrities are portrayed in wax at **Madame Tussaud's** (open 10am–11pm; charge) near the hotel's entrance. When the **Venezia Tower** opened with 12 stories of rooms and 10 stories of parking, it took The Venetian's total accommodations up to 4,049 rooms.

In 2008, the resort went through an even greater expansion with the unveiling of a fabulous new building next door, **The Palazzo**.

Sharing the facilities of The Venetian but with its own casino, stores, and restaurants, The Palazzo is meant to evoke the romance of the Italian countryside – with an upscale spin. **The Shoppes at The Palazzo** have 50 international boutiques selling gorgeous goods, but as they are

RIGHT: sushi for the famished. **BELOW RIGHT:** Playboy frenzy in a slot machine.

First-Rate Wine

Among Glitter City's gastronomic merits, Las Vegas has no fewer than 17 master sommeliers, more than any other US city. Las Vegas restaurants are as serious about wine as they are about the food they serve, and these days, that's pretty serious. The restaurant Aureole in Mandalay Bay, for instance, has a four-story, climate-controlled glass wine tower, and wines of distinction are fetched by "wine angels," under the patronly eye of master sommelier William Sherer. The wine cellar and tasting room at the Rio resort keeps a collection of 50,000 bottles, valued together at more than $10 million. Among these are an 1800 Madeira from the cellar of former president Thomas Jefferson.

The wine shop 55 Degrees Wine + Design at Mandalay Place stocks almost 2,000 wines ranging from $8 discoveries to a 1953 Bordeaux, as well as exclusive lines of glass and wine accessories. Napoleon's Champagne Bar at Paris Las Vegas serves more than 100 champagnes and sparkling wines.

Recommended Restaurants on page 171

under the same roof as the Grand Canal Shoppes, it's difficult to see where one mall ends and the next begins. As if it matters.

Until recently, The Venetian was also the home of the greatest art gallery in Las Vegas, the Guggenheim Hermitage Museum. The highly regarded museum, under a seven-year agreement with the Guggenheim Foundation, closed its doors in May, 2008. It will be missed by the city's lovers of high culture, of which there are more than you might expect.

T.I. (TREASURE ISLAND) ❸

3300 Las Vegas Boulevard South, www.treasureisland.com

702-894-7111 or 800-944-7444

T.I. (Treasure Island) shares a 100-acre (40-hectare) site with The Mirage, and like Luxor, has embarked on an only partially successful campaign to shed its family image and rebrand itself as the adult-oriented T.I. Out have gone the kids' costumes, in have come scantily clad girls and T-shirts saying "TI girl." Although the sign in front of the hotels says "T.I.," the logo at the top says "Treasure Island." So go figure.

In front of the resort, a vast lagoon is the scene of the ***Sirens of T.I.*** – a stand-off between a group of tempting sirens and a band of renegade pirates. The crowd is different from those that gathered to watch the now-defunct "historical" pirate battle. That audience was casual with kids; this audience is hip and eager to spend money.

T.I.'s showroom is the venue for the very first Cirque du Soleil show that came to Las Vegas, ***Mystère.*** Over 70 singers, dancers, jugglers, and acrobats deliver an athletic and metaphorical journey through life. Even after all these years, it's still fantastically popular, so be sure to book ahead for tickets.

A long pedestrian bridge crosses the Strip to connect T.I. with The Venetian, which is very useful when traffic is heavy.

"Stripping" was a term used a few years ago to describe the activity of frolicking from one Strip casino to the next to check out the showbiz lounge acts.

FASHION SHOW MALL ❹

3200 Las Vegas Boulevard South, www.thefashionshow.com

702-784-7000 Mon–Sat 10am–9pm, Sun 11am–7pm

LEFT AND BELOW: the sexy sirens of the sea battle that is enacted every night in front of T.I.

Who says you can't have everything? Sunburned Las Vegans, desperate for a little of the cold, white stuff, can go to Fashion Show Mall during the winter holidays and experience the thrill of a "snowstorm."

The best-located shopping center on the Strip is the Fashion Show Mall, whose recent $350-million expansion, which doubled its size, has added Nevada's only Nordstrom's to make seven flagship retail giants, including Bloomingdales, Neiman Marcus, and Saks Fifth Avenue. There are 250 stores in all.

The eye-catching retail space has a movable stage with retractable runways, state-of-the art video, and lighting and sound equipment to enhance runway fashion shows. A canopy area known as **The Cloud,** onto which images are projected after dark, stretches along a major part of its Strip frontage. The mall houses several bistros and sidewalk cafés, and is easy to access via a (free) underground garage.

Trump

At 200 Fashion Show Drive is the gleaming **Trump International Hotel and Tower** ❺ (www.trumplasvegashotel.com; tel: 702-982-0000). This non-gaming complex (said to be encrusted with 24-carat gold glass) opened in 2008 at a cost of $600 million dollars, and is planned to be one of two identical towers on the site (whether the ecomonic situation encourages the bulding of the second tower remains to be seen.)

Inside are 1,300 non-smoking residences, some of which are condos. Guests can snooze in a cabana by the pool, or eat fantastically well at DJT Restaurant, amenities that presumably contribute to Trump's promise that each hotel guest will have "a personal attaché service." ❑

RIGHT AND BELOW: Fashion Show Mall stages runway shows most weekends.

BEST RESTAURANTS

Price includes dinner for one and a glass of wine, excluding tip:
$ = under $20
$$ = $20–$30
$$$ = $30–$40
$$$$ = over $40

American

Stripburger
Fashion Show Mall ☎ 702-258-1211 ⌚ L & D daily **$** [p276, B4]
Outdoor seating surrounds the enclosed kitchen at this upscale fast-food joint. The menu showcases blue-cheese-burgers, green-chile burgers, and hickory bacon burgers, all, ground fresh throughout the day. Beer and cocktails are also served, as well as alcoholic milkshakes.

Table 10
The Palazzo ☎ 702-607-6363 ⌚ L & D daily **$$$** [p276, B4]
Celebrity chef Emeril Lagasse ventures beyond his Louisiana roots in this new venture, which focuses on organic grass-fed meats, just-caught seafood and farm-fresh produce. Specialties include lobster pot pie and rotisseried *kurobuta* pork loin.

Cajun

Delmonico Steakhouse
The Venetian ☎ 702-414-3737 ⌚ L & D daily **$$$** [p274, B1]
Emeril Lagasse dishes up delicious Creole flavors in his personal steakhouse.

International

Cravings
The Mirage ☎ 702-891-7374 ⌚ B, L & D daily **$$$** [p274, B1]
This is one of the best (and priciest) all-you-can-eat buffets on the Strip, with 11 cooking stations where everything from omelets and pizzas to Asian noodle dishes and stir fries is prepared to order. There's a sushi bar and an absolutely lavish dessert section.

Sushisamba
The Palazzo ☎ 702-607-0700 ⌚ L & D daily **$–$$$** [p276, B4]
The idea of a Japanese-Brazilian-Peruvian restaurant may sound odd, but it works at this big restaurant nestled deep in the Palazzo shopping zone. The menu does not distinguish between cuisines, and some dishes fuse influences from both sides of the Pacific.

Italian

Onda
The Mirage ☎ 702-791-7223 ⌚ D Thur–Mon **$$$** [p274, B1]
Regional and classic Italian dishes with North American innovations, featuring home-made pastas, breads, fresh seafood, and meats.

Postrio
Grand Canal Shoppes at The Venetian ☎ 702-796-1110 ⌚ L & D daily **$–$$$$** [p274, B1]
Wolfgang Puck's San Francisco-style eatery serves pasta entrées and pizzas topped with unusual ingredients like wild mushrooms, lamb chorizo, or duck confit.

Japanese

RA Sushi
Fashion Show Mall ☎ 702-696-0008 ⌚ L & D daily **$–$$** [p276, B4]
Always lively, this hip hangout has one of the most extensive sushi and sashimi menus in town, along with many kinds of sake. They even offer seminars on pairing sushi with the right sake. Or try a more unusual beverage such as the cucumber martini.

Spanish

Café Ba-Ba-Reeba!
Fashion Show Mall ☎ 702-258-1211 ⌚ L & D daily **$$–$$$** [p276, B4]
This restaurant specializes in tapas to share, allowing you to try a full range of tastes such as shrimp and squid salad, marinated manchego cheese, gazpacho soup, roast dates and bacon… Great paella, too.

Steak/Seafood

Kokomo's
The Mirage ☎ 702-339-4566 ⌚ D daily **$$$** [p274, B1]
Though lush with rain-forest vegetation, this restaurant has no noisy jungle beasts like the MGM's Rainforest Café – just soothing waterfalls and a small lagoon. Its surf-and-turf pairings include filet mignon with king-crab legs and lamb chops with lobster tails. Lighter appetites will enjoy the lobster bisque.

Vietnamese

Pho
T.I. (Treasure Island) ☎ 702-894-7223 ⌚ L & D daily **$** [p276, B4]
The only Vietnamese on the Strip is actually a section of the hotel coffee shop with a separate chef.

STRATOSPHERE

Recommended Restaurants on page 185

WYNN LAS VEGAS TO STRATOSPHERE TOWER

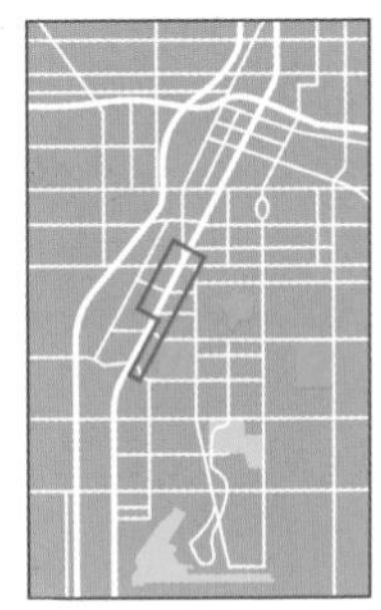

Enjoy casino action surrounded by world-class art, scare yourself silly on the tallest tower in the West, go to the circus for free, and enjoy the Sahara before it changes forever

The Stratosphere Tower has long been a Vegas landmark, but has struggled to attract trade from the centers of action on the Strip. Now, new centers are reaching north to join up with the Strat. The Miami Fountainebleau is coming to play in Sin City; Steve Wynn is spreading his Wynns with Encore; there's a new mini-city on the way, as well as a new kid in town – Sam Nazarian has plans for the veteran Sahara.

WYNN LAS VEGAS 6

3131 Las Vegas Boulevard South, www.wynnlasvegas.com
702-693-7871 or 877-321-9966

On the 200-acre (80-hectare) site of the old Desert Inn, north of The Venetian, is mega-entrepreneur Steve Wynn's most fabulous resort to date, Wynn Las Vegas.

The resort, accessible via a walkway crossing over the Strip, has a man-made "mountain" covered in pine trees that forms a natural barrier between the Strip and the casino; a coursing fall of water, and a lake spanning several acres. There's also a 50-story tower with 2,716 rooms, a beautiful casino and two huge showrooms. All of the rooms have floor-to-ceiling windows and views across the Strip, the lake and mountain, or the serene, manicured lawns of the only 18-hole, par-70 championship golf course (nearly) on the Strip.

Designed by Tom Fazio, the 6-mile (9km) course is exclusively for hotel guests, and tees are only a short stroll from the hotel. It features two marshland areas and a large, cascading waterfall.

Main attractions
WYNN LAS VEGAS
WYNN ESPLANADE
ENCORE
THE RIVIERA
ECHELON
FONTAINEBLEAU
CIRCUS CIRCUS
ADVENTUREDOME
SLOTS-A-FUN
THE SAHARA
NASCAR CAFÉ
LAS VEGAS CYBER SPEEDWAY
STRATOSPHERE TOWER
TOWER SHOPS

LEFT: the Stratosphere Tower.
RIGHT: a cigarette girl – smoking is allowed in the areas where gaming is played.

Wynn's Parasol Bar is a two-level casino lounge with a view of the lake. Entry is via a circular escalator (so not good for the very inebriated).

Water has always played a key role in Wynn's creations. For a while he contemplated flooding two Downtown streets and turning Fremont Street into a canal to create a Venice-like environment, a fantasy as yet unfulfilled.

Throughout the resort is a floral theme, which is echoed in the casino carpet. Within the Wynn is a boutique hotel-within-a-hotel: the luxurious **Tower Suites** is the first Vegas hotel to gain Mobil's prestigious 5-star award.

Wynn is probably the best-known personality in Las Vegas, and there was endless speculation about his new project – the first one to which he's given his name. He is incurably drawn to the spectacular, and to showmanship. After he appeared with Frank Sinatra in jokey commercials on US TV some years ago, his face became familiar to millions of Americans outside of Las Vegas.

RIGHT: Wynn's classy cashpoint. **BELOW:** the Wynn Esplanade is so upscale there is an on-site Ferrari-Maserati dealership.

The resort is a suitably stylish venue for the **Wynn Art Collection**, which hangs throughout the hotel. These include paintings by Picasso, Modigliani, Matisse, Cézanne, Monet, and Van Gogh. The shopping, too, is upscale, with Chanel, Cartier, John Paul Gaultier, and Manolo Blahnik lining the aisles of the **Wynn Esplanade**, in company with the Penske Wynn Ferrari-Maserati dealership and showroom.

Celebrity chefs

Restaurants bear all the familiar Steve Wynn hallmarks of opulent elegance. These include the prestigious Alex *(see page 185)* along with Bartolotta Ristorante di Mare, Daniel Boulud Brasserie, and SW Steakhouse.

The spa's 45 treatment rooms offer the very latest in anti-aging techniques, plus facial treatments including the Anakiri Active Enzyme Facial for super exfoliation and

Recommended Restaurants on page 185

nourishment, and the Naturopathica Custom Facial, based on traditional European deep-cleansing techniques.

The respected Belgian film and theater director, Franco Dragone, who worked to create Cirque du Soleil's *Mystère* and *O*, has produced the fire-and-water themed *Le Réve* especially for the resort.

Matching the signature trompe-l'oeil curve of Wynn Las Vegas and themed with butterflies is **Encore**. It has a casino, yet more famous-name retailers, and an indoor lake with an island, where the poker room is reached by a bridge. Encore adds two pools and another spa to the resort.

THE RIVIERA ❼

2901 Las Vegas Boulevard South, www.rivierahotel.com
702-734-5110 or 800-634-6753

In the 1980s, the Riviera shifted from headliners to broad-based stage shows. The first was *Splash*, which showcases performers and specialty acts, centered around a huge aquarium. Nine drag artistes perform shows and are led by Frank Marino with his renowned impersonation of Joan Rivers.

Following this was *An Evening at La Cage*, and the latest version is a rather tawdry skin show called ***Crazy Girls***, which begins with the audience being mooned by eight pairs of bare buttocks. Bronze Crazy Girls, their

Wynn's Encore added 2,000 more hotel rooms to the resort, along with eight bars and lounges, and six restaurants.

LEFT AND BELOW: inside and outside Vegas's most lavish resort (so far).

In true lottery fashion, room rates in many Vegas hotels change dramatically – often from hour to hour. If you're in town for a few days and not wedded to a particular hotel, it's worth calling around or visiting in person. Once you've found a rate you like, book it there and then, or risk it going up again.

ABOVE RIGHT: the Riviera's "crazy girls" sculpture has rear ends shined to perfection by the public. **BELOW:** an artist's drawing of Echelon.

rears shiny from being caressed by thousands of eager hands, flank the sidewalk entrance to the casino.

The fast-food court just off the sidewalk is a convenient and inexpensive place to eat with a choice of hot dogs, yogurt, burgers, Chinese dishes, sushi, pizza, espresso and pastries. There are half-a-dozen other restaurants including a hot-dog counter in **Nickel Town**.

Among the stores is one selling pearls right from the oyster; a magic shop; and one representing Pahrump Valley Vineyards, the state's commercial winery.

Movie location

The hotel, with its Olympic-sized swimming pool, exercise rooms, spa, tennis courts, and a video arcade, was the setting for Martin Scorsese's 1995 film *Casino*. Its own casino is slightly larger than that of Circus Circus, although it has fewer slot machines. When the Riviera first opened in 1955, it had only 116 one-armed bandits.

Liberace was a Las Vegas veteran with 10 years of performances behind him when he opened the Riviera in April 1955. He was accompanied by his own 23-piece orchestra, and Joan Crawford acted as his official hostess. Wearing a white tuxedo by avant-garde designer Christian Dior, the camp pianist was drawing $50,000 a week, an astonishing fee at a time when a house could easily be bought for less than a fifth of that figure.

The first high-rise hotel in Vegas had been planned to make an impact, and it quickly became known as entertainment central.

The Clover Room was headlined by 1950s' stars Marlene Dietrich, Milton Berle, Harry Belafonte, Orson Welles, Dinah Shore, Red Skelton, Ginger Rogers, Mickey Rooney, and Zsa Zsa Gabor. For the next three decades the hotel built more and more towers – up to the present five – and the stars kept right on coming. Carol Channing, Louis Armstrong, Cyd Charisse, George Burns, Eddie Fisher, Tony Bennett, and Dean Martin are just some of the people who played in the Riviera's impressive **Versailles Theatre**.

ECHELON 8

Echelon, owned by Boyd Gaming, is another of Vegas's glitzy new projects. But all is not well. Although ground was broken, construction was halted in 2008, and is planned

Recommended Restaurants on page 185

to resume in 2009. When the resort is completed, Echelon will have several boutique hotels – a Delano, a Mondrian, a Shangri-La, each with their own spa.

The 87-acre (35-hectare) resort will also encompass a 300,000-sq-ft (27,870-sq-meter) retail complex, 30 restaurants and bars, a 1,500-seat and a 4,000 seat theater, and with 140,000 sq ft (13,000 sq meters) of gaming floor space, one of the largest casinos in Las Vegas.

Fontainebleau Las Vegas ⑨

Arriving at the northeast corner of Las Vegas Boulevard and Riviera Boulevard late in 2009 is a sister to the famous Miami Beach landmark hotel. The Fontainebleau will be one of the tallest buildings on the Strip, at 60 floors, and will have over 1,000 hotel-condo apartments, 24 restaurants and lounges, nightclubs with cutting-edge sound and light technology, high-end retailing, a grand theater, and a luxury spa.

ABOVE: Riviera neon. **BELOW:** an artist's drawing of the soaring Fountainebleau, which will be one of the tallest buildings on the Strip.

CIRCUS CIRCUS ⑩

✉ 2880 Las Vegas Boulevard South, www.circuscircus.com
☎ 702-734-0410 or 800-444-2472

A Vegas classic, Circus Circus's Horse-A-Round Bar has "starred" in numerous movies. On the mezzanine overlooking the casino floor, this is the best seat in the house for watching the aerial circus acts.

Before Circus Circus, Jay Sarno had the vision for Caesars Palace, and everything since has progressed from there. The title of "Mr Las Vegas" has been casually awarded to quite a number of people in the town's history and several would seem to be worthy candidates, but few would argue that the kind of over-the-top spectacle that Vegas displays today owes more to the innovations of Jay Sarno than to any other individual.

Ahead of his time

How proud Sarno would be if he were able to see how his vision for palaces of fantasy, crafted around single themes, have grown. Bob Stoldal, a local TV writer said, "Sarno was ahead of his time. People said, 'Circus Circus just doesn't work. It's not Las Vegas.' Clearly that wasn't true."

With ample opportunities for inexpensive food, a vast family amusement park, bargain deals for hotel rooms, and 5,100 parking spaces – some making up an RV park called **Circusland** with its own pool, laundromat, and general store – Circus Circus rarely seems to run short of customers.

Aaron Betsky, the curator of architecture and design at San Francisco's Museum of Modern Art, said, "On the Strip, you are part of the most elaborate urban theater ever assembled. After four decades of trying, Las Vegas has finally managed

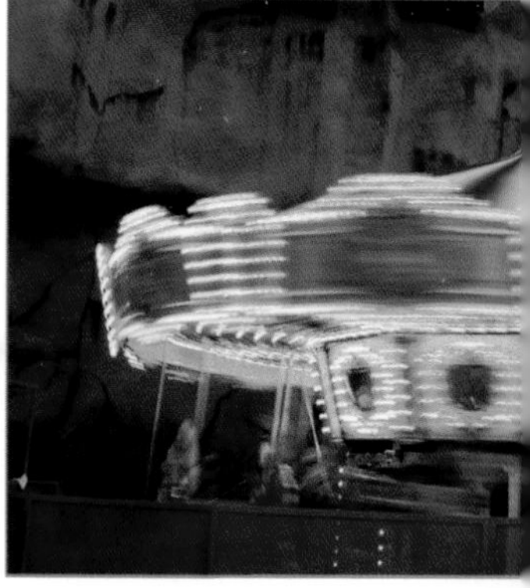

RIGHT: Circus Circus's Horse-A-Round Bar.
BELOW: the Riviera has hosted many top performers, including Louis Armstrong.

Map on page 166

Recommended Restaurants on page 185

to turn Hollywood into reality, and what we can learn from today's Vegas is that streets can also be theaters, buildings can become their own signs."

Preoccupied with the gaming, Circus Circus gamblers rarely look up to where another world is populated by crowds jamming the **Carnival Midway**. This is where acrobats, jugglers, aerialists, trapeze artists, and clowns perform in the world's largest permanent circus from 11am till midnight.

Miniature camels race along plastic tracks, children's faces are painted by a clown, and an endless line of hopefuls try to win prizes by bringing a big rubber mallet down heavily enough to propel a rubber chicken into a cooking pot.

"Act your age somewhere else," is the slogan here. And it seems to work.

Gambling fever

Every day for over 25 years, the resort has packed in the crowds, but this kind of success eluded Sarno himself. An inveterate gambler – he once won $10,000 betting that he could sink a long shot on a basketball toss – his instincts failed with Circus Circus, which took a long time to recover from opening with no hotel rooms. It was only after William G. Bennett and his partner Bill Pennington took over and concentrated on the then-untapped family market that it became a money machine.

One explanation for the turnaround comes from Mel Larson, a one-time VP of the casino. "I found out that half the people coming to

Jugglers, trapeze artists, and clowns perform here above the gaming hall from 11am until midnight.

BELOW: Circus Circus has the only RV park on the Strip.

ABOVE: play old-school slots at an old-school casino. **BELOW:** Vegas vacancies are easier to come by during the week than on weekends.

town did not have reservations and more than half were driving," he recalled. "So we just hammered on the radio on the stations that reached people on the freeway. We captured all this walk-in business, which was unheard of at the time. Everybody else was after the upper-income people but we just wanted a lot of folks." Sound strategy.

Now this aggressively successful down-market, family-oriented resort is owned by the MGM-Mirage group, which also operates Bellagio, Luxor, Monte Carlo, Excalibur, and the Mandalay Bay, and controls more hotels in the city than any of its competitors.

Thrill rides

Circus Circus has its own adventure park with thrill rides. **Adventuredome** attractions include Canyon Blaster, Rim Runner, Sling Shot, Chaos, Lazer Blast, and SpongeBob SquarePants 4-D Ride, as well as junior rides like Frog Hopper – all available on a day-pass ticket.

Stardust Memories

Until it was imploded in 2007 to make way for the new Echelon, the site was home to the Stardust Hotel, steeped in Las Vegas myth, lore, and legend. The casino was begun in 1955 by Tony Cornero, in his time a bootlegger, hijacker, rum-runner, and operator of offshore gambling boats before he started work on the Stardust. It was nearly three-quarters finished when he died of a heart attack after gambling at the Desert Inn. The Stardust was then owned for 10 years by former bootlegger and racketeer Moe Dalitz *(see pages 45–6)*, who had operated small gambling parlors in Cleveland and around the eastern United States before moving out West. Dalitz met future Teamsters boss Jimmy Hoffa through his laundry business and parlayed the use of Teamster pension funds to buy the Stardust.

Dalitz once said, "How was I to know those gambling joints were illegal? There were so many judges and politicians in them I figured they had to be all right."

Map on page 166

Recommended Restaurants on page 185

Next door, **Slots-A-Fun** ⓫ (2800 Las Vegas Boulevard South; tel: 702-734-0410) offers free beer to all players and has penny slot machines, but as they only take dollar bills you get to play 100 pennies at a time. There's a glass case near the door exhibiting Polaroid photos of earlier winners and usually somebody handing out free ticket booklets and offering a free pull. In some casinos you can find machines that take $500 tokens, but not in Slots-A-Fun, which is distinctly down-market.

Making money

Satellite casinos like this one are heavy on slot machines, which have been by far the biggest money-making sector in the casino gaming industry. The old one-armed bandits, now historical relics, have been replaced by electronic machines, increasingly devoted to video poker. Almost all machines now operate on multiple coins, or at least, coin multiple value, feeding into a master jackpot which any machine in the group can win. These jackpots can grow into astronomical amounts.

THE SAHARA ⓬

✉ 2535 Las Vegas Boulevard South, www.saharavegas.com
☎ 702-737-2111 or 888-696-2121

In 2008, the Sahara was bought by a Las Vegas outsider, whose approach seems radically different from that of the casino establishment. While Sam Nazarian does plan to open a redeveloped Sahara in 2011, he doesn't intend to implode the existing hotel. And he aims to appeal to a younger crowd,

ABOVE AND BELOW: young kids like Faces, etc, while older kids go for the Sahara's NASCAR Café.

In case you're in the mood for a midnight smoothie, the Grind Café at the Sahara is open 24 hours a day.

RIGHT AND BELOW: over the next few years, the Sahara hopes to shed its current image for a sharper one that attracts the LA crowd.

one he believes is not attracted by present-day Vegas. (Nazarian himself is in his early thirties.)

The Sahara's current entrance is a neon-lit rotunda with a motif of neon camels, and a **NASCAR Café** *(see page 185)* that features racing on giant projection screens with surround sound. Numerous authentic stock cars are on display, including the world's largest, Carzilla, a 3-tonne Pontiac Grand-Prix. At the rear is the **Las Vegas Cyber Speedway** (open summer only; charge), where visitors can choose a car and course for a virtual-reality adventure, in life-size racing cars, shaking and swaying as a fast-moving racetrack is projected onto a nearby and enveloping screen.

Speed

"Speed – The Ride" (open summer only; charge) is a roller coaster that lasts only 45 seconds, but riders are propelled from zero to 35mph (56kph) in two seconds, in what a local writer described as "an adrenaline junkie's crack pipe;" a loop skywards and then back down.

When the Sahara opened in 1952, it featured real camels and a North African theme. Marlene Dietrich and Tony Bennett made their Las Vegas debuts in the Congo Room, where Mae West and later George Burns appeared. Don Rickles debuted in the Casbar Lounge in 1959.

In 1963, Elvis Presley and Ann-Margret filmed segments of *Viva Las Vegas* at the hotel. The Sahara was also one of the first to have the video poker machines on which a pair of phantom hands "deal" the cards.

Map on page 166

Recommended Restaurants on page 185

The venerable hotel-casino was built by the Del Webb Corp. which later owned Downtown's The Mint, the Thunderbird, and the Lucky Club. When the owner wanted to extend the Sahara, he received the first Bank of Las Vegas casino loan.

Nowadays, the Sahara is cornering the market on the romance of the 1950s and the early 1960s rock 'n' roll and soul era. A mainstay act in its **Congo Room** is a show with performances of the Platters, the Coasters, and the Marvelettes, a 90-minute medley of moods, rooted in their "blasts from the past." The performers enjoy the work, and the (mainly middle-aged) audiences leave with new rhythms in their steps.

New-look Sahara

Sam Nazarian's plans are to change all of that. Having spent around $300 million buying the property, he aims to renovate the existing hotel, and with design assistance from uber-stylist Philippe Starck, to add a new tower to the site. "There is an alienation of the high-energy, youthful crowd," he said of the Las Vegas scene. Nazarian has experience as well as vision, as that same excitable celebrity set has followed him to various high-profile clubs and restaurants he's set up in Los Angeles.

STRATOSPHERE TOWER ⓭

✉ 2000 Las Vegas Boulevard South, www.stratospherehotel.com
☎ 702-380-7777 or 800-998-6937

This tower is the tallest building west of the Mississippi River and

ABOVE AND BELOW: when the Sahara opened in 1952, it featured real camels as part of its North African theme.

 Map on page 166

The Big Shot ride on top of the Strat Tower is truly terrifying.

RIGHT AND BELOW: on a clear day, visitors at the top of the Strat Tower can see as far away as Arizona and California.

one of the tallest free-standing observation towers in the country. Speedy elevators whisk visitors to a height of 1,149ft (345 meters) in an ear-popping 30 seconds, where on a clear day California and Arizona are visible. The deck is also a favorite nightspot for visitors, who relish the fine view of the world's best display of neon. The casino offers some of the most competitive odds available on the Strip.

The 1,500-room resort is topped by a revolving restaurant and offers rides hundreds of feet above ground. The thrilling **Big Shot** is a kind of reversed bungee jump that shoots riders high into the air. A recent rider said, "I didn't want to do it, my kids made me. It was the most terrifying thing I ever did. I couldn't wait to do it again." The Stratosphere also features the extreme **X Scream**, which thrusts riders out over the top and edge of the casino, then rocks them slowly back to safety.

Insanity has a massive mechanical arm that extends over the edge of the tower, 1,100ft (305 meters) in the air, and spins riders around at a force of 3Gs for what is guaranteed to be a truly memorable, face-bending – and most likely – lunch-loosening experience.

Rooms with a view

The resort has a showroom, a pool, and a spa, as well as a choice of restaurants, one with the best view on (and of) the Strip *(see right)*.

The **Tower Shops** is themed as an international marketplace with streets decorated to recall Paris, Hong Kong, and New York. Romantically inclined visitors who do not suffer from vertigo can get married near the top of the tower. ❑

Best Restaurants

Price includes dinner for one and a glass of wine, excluding tip:
$ = under $20
$$ = $20–$30
$$$ = $30–$40
$$$$ = over $40

American

NASCAR Café
The Sahara ☎ 702-737-2111 ◷ L & D daily **$** [p276, B1]
Two-level restaurant features NASCAR stock cars, sports screens, and auto merchandise.

Roxy's Diner
Stratosphere ☎ 702-383-5396 ◷ L & D daily **$** [p276, B1]
Every five minutes, one of the waitresses takes her turn singing 1950s oldies and dancing around the dining area. Retro kitsch decor sets the stage for giant hamburgers and shakes.

THE Steak House
Circus Circus ☎ 702-794-3767 ◷ D daily; champagne brunch Sun 9.30, 11.30am, 1.30pm **$$** [p276, B2]
Steaks, seafood, and chicken cooked over an open grill. A display case shows customers the variety of beef available.

Top of the World
Stratosphere Tower ☎ 702-380-7711 ◷ L & D daily **$$$** [p276, B1]
Revolving restaurant with the best view of the Strip in town. This can overshadow the menu, but the sunset is fabulous.

Asian

Red 8
Wynn Las Vegas ☎ 702-770-3380 ◷ L & D daily **$$** [p276, B3]
Mee goreng, sea bass *congee*, and Cantonese roast duck in plum sauce share the menu with Hong Kong-style dim sum at this bright casino-level eatery. Entrées are affordable, though beverages are expensive.

Buffet

Wynn Las Vegas Buffet
Wynn Las Vegas ☎ 702-770-3463 ◷ B, L & D daily **$$–$$$** [p276, B3]
The classiest all-you-can-eat buffet in town, featuring five kinds of ceviche, Indian tandoori items, sushi, and great desserts. Dine at off-hours. or you may be in for a long wait in line.

French

Alex
Wynn Las Vegas ☎ 702-248-3463 ◷ D Thur–Mon **$$$$** [p276, B3]
The creation of TV's "iron chef" Alessandro Strata, this warmly lit establishment offers extravagantly priced tasting menus with wine pairings and prix-fixe three-course dinners.

International

DJT
Trump International ☎ 702-982-0000 ◷ B & D Tue–Sun **$$$$** [p276, B3]
Not short on ego, Donald Trump gave this restaurant his initials instead of naming it for Joseph Isadori, Trump's personal cook. A signature entrée here is *miso-yaki* Tasmanian sea trout, served with steelhead roe, grapefruit, and *yuzu* emulsion.

Italian

Ristorante Italiano
The Riviera ☎ 702-794-9363 ◷ D daily **$** [p276, B3]
The decor recalls the mafioso opulence of 1950s Las Vegas. The menu features classic Tuscan and northern Italian cooking. You can build your own pasta plate, picking one kind of pasta, one kind of sauce, and your choice of sausage or meatballs.

Steak/Seafood

House of Lords Steak House
The Sahara ☎ 702-737-2111 ◷ D Mon–Sat **$$** [p276, B1]
Beautiful waterfalls and plush seating highlight the cozy ambiance, while the menu features prime beef and very good seafood.

Right: Stratosphere Tower, Top of the World.

HOLLY
ELVIS
VIVA LAS VEGAS!
C'MON EVERY BODY
THE LADY LOVES ME
MY RIVAL
WHAT'D I SAY
VIVA LAS VEGAS
IF YOU THINK I DON'T NEED YOU

Recommended Restaurants on page 197

BEYOND THE STRIP

The Hard Rock, the Hilton, Liberace's candelabra, and a spa that offers "fruity body slushes" in piña colada. There are plenty of attractions and experiences to be had beyond the Strip

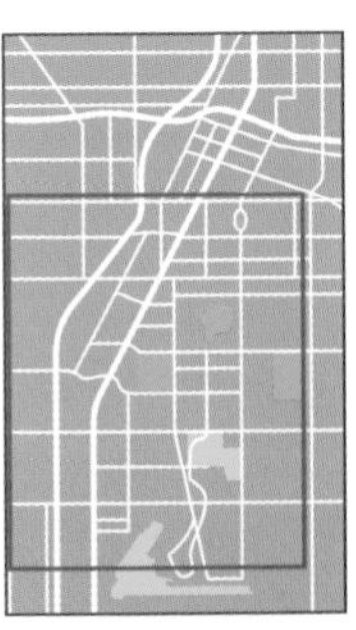

Main attractions

HOOTERS CASINO HOTEL
ALEXIS PARK
HARD ROCK HOTEL
FRUIT LOOP
MARJORIE BARRICK MUSEUM
LIBERACE MUSEUM
ATOMIC TESTING MUSEUM
LAS VEGAS HILTON
WEST OF THE STRIP
THE ORLEANS
THE PALMS
THE GOLD COAST
CHINATOWN
LAS VEGAS ART MUSEUM
LAS VEGAS PREMIUM OUTLETS

Off to the east and west of the Strip is a calmer Las Vegas; parts of town with resorts less pumped with the gleaming-theme steroids, less packed and thronged with families, and inebriated out-of-town thrill-seekers. There are stylish suites and hip hotels here, cool pools and sleek gaming rooms, plenty of places to go and games to play away from the main drag.

EAST OF THE STRIP

There is a lot to be said for the hotels in this area, especially if you're here for an event at the convention center, when a short journey in the morning can be very useful.

Two hotels just off the Strip offer different kinds of accommodations. **Hooters Casino Hotel** (115 East Tropicana Avenue, www.hooterscasinohotel.com, tel: 702-739-9000), behind the Tropicana, seems to be staffed mainly by young women in bikinis and sarongs, and has a loud, party atmosphere.

Behind the MGM Grand is the more up-market **Alexis Park** (375 East Harmon Avenue, www.alexispark.com; tel: 702-796-3330), set in attractively landscaped grounds. The Alexis is an all-suite hideaway with no gaming, although if that's what you're after, it's just a short stroll to the Hard Rock for some of the best action around.

Hard Rock Hotel ❶

4455 Paradise Road, www.hardrockhotel.com
702-693-5000 or 800-693-7625

About three blocks east of the Strip, the Hard Rock is a magnet to rock

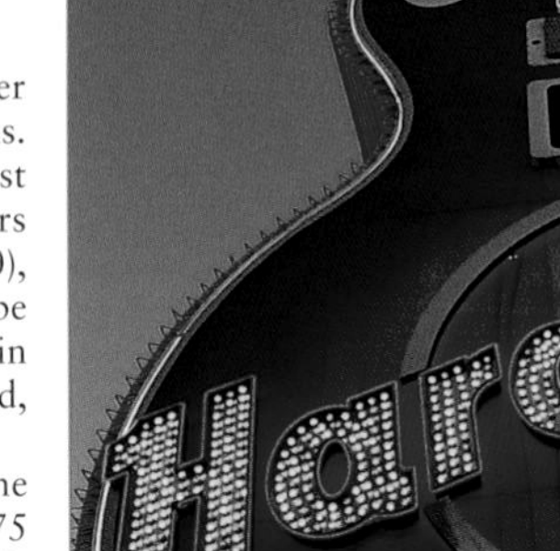

LEFT: viva Las Vegas, vintage-style.
RIGHT: rock legends are celebrated here, and a few are even created.

A straight run south along Paradise Road from the Hard Rock leads to the underrated McCarran International Airport. Its aviation museum, although small, is surprisingly interesting, and of course, you can always play the slot machines.

RIGHT: soft leather and easy money at the Hard Rock Hotel.

fans with its lively vibes, guitar-shaped chandeliers, and glass cases showing the ephemera of rock aristocracy. A Rolling Stones display has a couple of "Keef's" guitars and one of Mick's leopard-skin jackets. A massive expansion is underway, which should be complete sometime in 2009. Currently, there are luxury suites, a spa, and a huge **pool area,** with swim-up blackjack, and a sandy beach, where a huge style scene has evolved. Restaurants include the **Pink Taco,** plus an out-

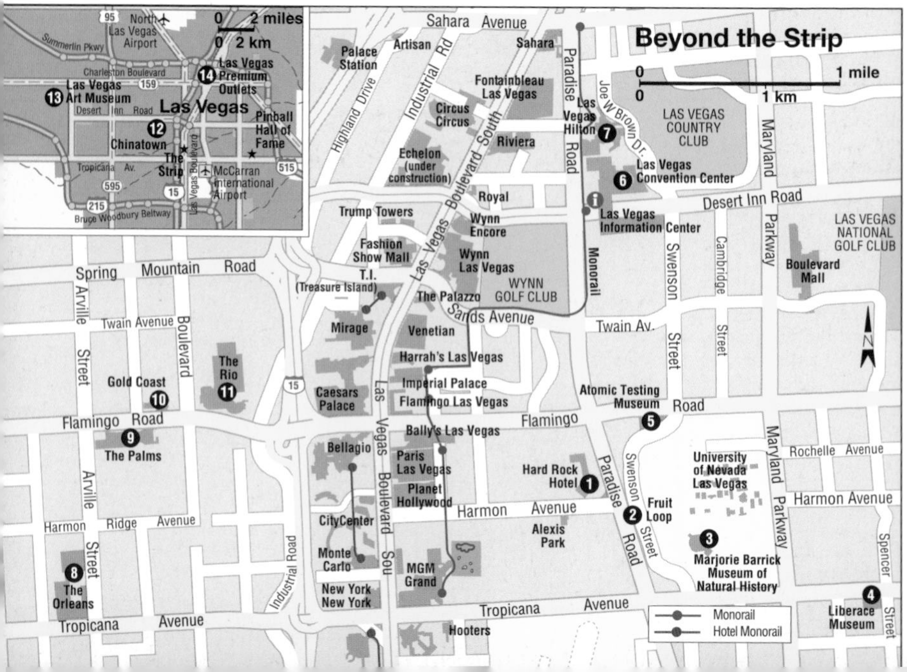

Beyond the Strip

0 – 1 mile
0 – 1 km

Sahara Avenue, Palace Station, Artisan, Sahara, Industrial Rd, Highland Drive, Fontainbleau Las Vegas, Circus Circus, Riviera, Las Vegas Hilton 7, Joe W Brown Dr., Las Vegas Country Club, Maryland, Echelon (under construction), Las Vegas Boulevard South, Las Vegas Convention Center 6, Royal, Desert Inn Road, Trump Towers, Wynn Encore, Las Vegas Information Center, Parkway, Las Vegas National Golf Club, Fashion Show Mall, Wynn Las Vegas, Monorail, Swenson, Cambridge, Boulevard Mall, T.I. (Treasure Island), The Palazzo, Wynn Golf Club, Sands Avenue, Twain Av., Street, Mirage, Venetian, Harrah's Las Vegas, Imperial Palace, Caesars Palace, Flamingo Las Vegas, Atomic Testing Museum 5, Road, Bally's Las Vegas, Flamingo, Bellagio, Paris Las Vegas, Planet Hollywood, Hard Rock Hotel 1, Paradise Road, Swenson Street, University of Nevada Las Vegas, Rochelle Avenue, Maryland Parkway, Harmon Avenue, Fruit Loop 2, CityCenter, Alexis Park, Monte Carlo, MGM Grand, Marjorie Barrick Museum of Natural History 3, Spencer Street, New York New York, Tropicana Avenue, Hooters, Liberace Museum 4, Monorail, Hotel Monorail

Spring Mountain Road, Arville Street, Twain Avenue, Boulevard, The Rio 11, Gold Coast 10, Flamingo Road, The Palms 9, Harmon, Ridge Avenue, Industrial Road, The Orleans 8, Tropicana Avenue, 15

North Las Vegas Airport, 95, Summerlin Pkwy, Charleston Boulevard, 159, Las Vegas Art Museum 13, Desert Inn Road, Las Vegas, Las Vegas Premium Outlets 14, Pinball Hall of Fame, Chinatown 12, The Strip, Las Vegas Boulevard, Tropicana Av., McCarran International Airport, 515, 595, 15, 215, Bruce Woodbury Beltway, 0 – 2 miles, 0 – 2 km

Recommended Restaurants on page 197

crop of the restaurant Nobu *(see page 197)*, and **AJ's Steak House,** with an aura of 1950s' Vegas.

The Joint is a live-performance venue that brought top rock acts to Vegas when it was known more for senior crooners. Steely Dan, the Rolling Stones, and The Who all played here. But a sad note in rock history: the day before a US tour was to begin, John Entwhistle, bass player of The Who, died at the Hard Rock, on June 27, 2002.

Although not a particularly gay city, the area around Paradise Road and Naples Drive has become known as the "**Fruit Loop**" ❷ for its gay or gay-friendly businesses and clubs.

Marjorie Barrick Museum ❸

4505 South Maryland Parkway, http://hrcweb.nevada.edu/Museum
702-895-3381 Mon–Fri 8am–4.45pm, Sat 10am–2pm
free, but suggested donation

Located on the nearby campus of the **University of Nevada**, this museum is best approached from Paradise Road on the east side. Live lizards, Gila monsters, a tortoise, and a thin, red snake greet visitors from their glass cases in the lobby, and in the museum are sandy dioramas of Mojave desert life. Stuffed birds from sandpipers to pelicans decorate an oasis of cholla cactus, desiccated wood, and a tiny kit fox. In another room are three large bears: black, polar, and grizzly.

There are also exhibits on the Southern Paiute Native Americans,

WHERE

About 30 blocks from the Strip straight down Tropicana is the Pinball Hall of Fame Museum. A labor of love for owner Tim Arnold, this free, not-for-profit venture is the perfect afternoon out for pinball wizards. For more information: www.pinballmuseum.org

LEFT: early artwork at the Marjorie Barrick Museum.
BELOW: a public branding operation.

Try to time your visit to the Marjorie Barrick Museum with a trip to the Las Vegas Arboretum, or a concert at the Thomas & Mack Center. Both share the University of Nevada campus with the Barrick Natural History Museum.

RIGHT: desert garden at the Marjorie Barrick Museum. **BELOW:** a portrait of Wladziu Valentino Liberace.

including turquoise belts, rugs and baskets, Navaho pottery, and an explanation of the weaving process with samples of natural dyes.

Alongside are Mexican masks, colorful Guatemalan *huipiles* (embroidered blouses), and Mayan ceramics whose jars resemble contemporary pottery. Pierced ears were common, one exhibit explains, because it was believed that without them passage to the "other world" would be impossible. There's an explanation of the pictures in a reproduction of the *Codex Barbonicus*, an ancient pictorial manuscript which stretches for several feet, and a display of prewar Vegas slot machines and Hoover Dam exhibits.

Behind the museum is the delightful **Xeric Garden** (from the Greek word *xeros*, meaning dry), a scene miles away in spirit from the jangling slots of the Strip, with cacti, desert plants, and a bird-watching verandah. Ask for the pretty free brochure which identifies and describes all the plants.

Liberace Museum ❹

✉ 1775 East Tropicana Avenue, www.liberace.org ☎ 702-798-5595 ⏲ Mon–Sat 10am–5pm, Sun 1–4pm $ charge

The brochure for the Liberace Museum says that "though the Strip may sparkle and the neon may shine, nowhere in Las Vegas can be found a more dazzling spectacle than the museum." Even today, a five-tiered violet cape of ostrich feathers with lavender sequins – as Liberace wore for a 1985 television show – is an extravagance that would turn

Liberace

In 1944, after Wladziu Valentino Liberace debuted at the Frontier casino, he got an offer he didn't know how to refuse. Mobster Bugsy Siegel said he would double the pianist's $2,000 weekly salary if he moved to the Flamingo. But Bugsy died, so Liberace stayed at the Frontier. His show featured his signature candelabra, copied from one he'd seen on the piano in the biopic of Frederic Chopin, *A Song to Remember*. He had a replica of the candelabra on the front of his Stutz Bearcat, an otherwise manly convertible. Liberace's flamboyance made him a Vegas legend and a tremendous draw with the ladies, despite or maybe because of his obvious gay mannerisms.

In England, *Daily Mirror* columnist William Connor said he was a "deadly, winking, sniggling, snuggling, chromium-plated, scent-impregnated, luminous, quivering, giggling, fruit-flavored, mincing, ice-covered heap of mother love." Liberace sued, and won $22,400 in damages. In the early 1960s his young companion, Scot Thorsen, sued for palimony (but lost) after being ejected from Liberace's home. In 1972, he opened at the Las Vegas Hilton for $300,000, played his last show at Caesars Palace in 1986, and died the next year, aged 67.

Recommended Restaurants on page 197

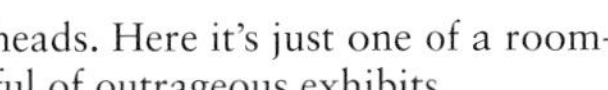
heads. Here it's just one of a roomful of outrageous exhibits.

A black-diamond mink bears 40,000 Austrian rhinestones and a separate display exhibits the world's biggest rhinestone, weighing in at 115,000 carats and 50lb (23kg). The entertainer was fond of jewelry – like the piano-shaped watch and a piano-shaped 260-diamond ring – antiques, including an inlaid, ormolu desk that belonged to Czar Nicholas II of Russia, as well as cars and musical instruments. A hybrid Rolls Royce Volkswagen (license plate RRVW) is one of the 19 cars on display (he owned more than 30).

Bedroom camp

Liberace had a Spanish-style home in Palm Springs, and the bedroom is recreated here, but for his Vegas career, he bought two adjoining homes on East Tropicana Avenue and had Michelangelo's ceiling from the Sistine Chapel in Rome reproduced above his bed.

As a complete contrast, at the northwest edge of the University of Nevada campus is the underrated **Atomic Testing Museum** ❺ (755 East Flamingo Road, www.atomictestingmuseum.org; tel: 702-794-5161; open Mon–Sat 9am–5pm, Sun 1–5pm; charge). Exhibits recall the time when Vegas locals packed picnics to watch the above-ground nuclear explosions at the Nevada test site north of the city. Visitors can also see a replica of an underground testing tunnel with a multisensory presentation, or a fragment of the Berlin Wall, old-time Geiger counters, and atomic kitsch.

BELOW: there are 19 cars, plus glitter galore, on show at the amusing Liberace Museum.

Convention central

Las Vegas is the convention capital of the US, hosting more than 3,500 each year. (This figure includes small conventions as well as large ones.) The **Las Vegas Convention Center** ❻ (3150 Paradise Road; tel: 702-892-0711) was financed in the 1950s with a hotel and motel room tax; now the convention business brings billions of dollars to the town each year.

ABOVE: the Las Vegas Convention Center is one of the largest in the US. **BELOW:** Hilton highlights include Barry Manilow in the showroom and a statue of Elvis by the entrance.

With continued expansion, the convention center now has 3.2 million sq ft (300,000 sq meters) of space, and Las Vegas has three of the country's seven largest convention centers. Between 2008 and 2011, another massive upgrade is taking place, bringing in the center's own on-site police substation.

Unsurprisingly, several hotels are located around the convention center. One is the **Courtyard Las Vegas Convention Center** at 3275 Paradise Road (tel: 702-791-3600). Nearby is the **Residence Inn Las Vegas** at 3225 Paradise Road (tel: 702-796-9300), both run by Marriott.

A hotel with a starry story connects to the convention center by an indoor walkway:

Las Vegas Hilton ❼

3000 Paradise Road,
www.lvhilton.com
702-732-5111 or 800-687-6667

The Hilton has a showroom where Elvis Presley famously performed 800 times. In honor of this, a statue of the King has been erected near the front entrance. Today, the Hilton is a pleasant hotel with green views, if you're lucky, of the golf course at the back, the (private) Las Vegas Country Club.

Well-connected to the monorail, this a pretty good place to stay even if you're not a high roller in one of the penthouse apartments with gold-plated bathroom fixtures. There are 13 restaurants, a pool, a spa, a spacious, low-key casino, and *Star Trek: The Experience* in which visitors can assume the identity of a Starfleet or alien crew member and participate in a series of virtual-reality and video escapades.

WEST OF THE STRIP

West of the Strip, the Palms is a virtual style scene, and often appears in reality TV shows. There are quieter, old-school resorts here, too, like the Orleans and the Gold Coast, as well as an art museum. As improbable as it sounds, there's even a Chinatown.

Recommended Restaurants on page 197

The Orleans ❽

✉ 4500 West Tropicana Avenue, www.orleanscasino.com
☎ 702-365-7111

New Orleans-style attractions here include the French Quarter, the Garden District, and Mardi Gras. Cajun and Mexican cuisines are available. The buffet is good value, especially at Tuesday lunch times when seafood from the previous night's buffet is carried over at half price – terrific if you're short of funds. Showroom tickets at the Orleans are inexpensive compared with Strip hotels, a bargain for acts like Frankie Valli; Frankie Avalon; Bobby Rydell; Peter, Paul and Mary; and Neil Sedaka. Other veterans still packing out the lounges include Paul Anka, Chuck Berry, Chubby Checker, Little Richard, and British rock group the Moody Blues.

The Palms ❾

✉ 4321 West Flamingo Road, www.palms.com
☎ 702-942-7777 or 866-942-7777.

From its beginning, the Palms was promoted as the hip place to be. Popular as a venue for TV reality shows and music shows, it attracts some of the coolest customers in Vegas.

Its owner, George Maloof, also owns the National Basketball Association's Sacramento Kings, and two dozen of the hotel's rooms have massive beds, 16ins (40cm) longer than usual. "Our players complain that they stay at hotels and the beds are too small," Maloof said. "We looked into it and there is actually such a thing as an NBA bed."

Be sure to book Vegas shows months in advance. When in town, call the box office directly, as there may be one or two seats left on the night that ticket-bookers do not know about. Many theaters are dark on Mondays.

LEFT AND BELOW: the Palms attracts a cool, hip crowd.

Signature cocktail in the Rio's popular VooDoo Lounge.

The five bars include the stylish 55th-floor **Ghostbar**, accessed by high-speed elevators, with spectacular views of the city's skyline and an open-air deck in whose floor is inset a plexiglass window, with nothing below it but 54 stories of space, then the asphalt of the parking lot.

One of the nightclubs, called **Rain Las Vegas**, has a color-changing wall of water and an electronic system that produces fog, haze, fireballs, and dancing fountains. Near the swimming pool, which is "the color of sapphires and amethysts," is a spa offering "fruity body slushes" in a yummy choice of amaretto sour, margarita, or piña colada.

The **Fantasy Tower** is the ultimate in sybaritic luxury. Choose from the Celebrity Suite, the hip-hop inspired Crib Suite, or the Erotic Suite. At the top are six Sky Villas, each with its own swimming pool overlooking the shimmering Strip.

BELOW: the Rio's *Show in the Sky* takes place in the evenings on weekends.

The Gold Coast ⑩

✉ 4000 West Flamingo Drive, www.coastcasinos.com
☎ 702-367-7111 or 800-331-5334

One of the earliest hotels to open west of the Strip, the Gold Coast has been renovated with a fitness center overlooking the pool area. Dixieland jazz has long been a mainstay in the lounge, and there's a bowling center with its own snack bar nearby. The seafood spread is particularly good at the Ports of Call buffet, which is popular with local Las Vegans.

The Rio ⑪

✉ 3700 West Flamingo Road, www.harrahs.com
☎ 702-252-7777 or 866-746-7671

West of the freeway is the extravagantly lit Rio, an all-suite hotel. The smallest suites are 600 sq ft (56 sq meters) and the largest, almost three times that size, with wraparound windows and great views. The hotel promotes a Latin American aura in its Samba Theater, Copacobana Showroom, and Ipanema Bar.

Try to catch the panoramic view from the Rio's 52nd floor where the specialty of the **VooDoo Lounge** is a bubbling, smoking concoction of five rums and three liqueurs by the name of Witch Doctor. The tropical lagoon has waterfalls, four pools, five whirlpool spas, and a sandy beach.

Life is a masquerade

The Rio's major spectacle, ***Show in the Sky,*** takes place every hour from 7pm until midnight Thursday through Sunday, performed above spectators' heads as a procession of gaily decorated floats moves steadily around a 950ft (290-meter) track. Exotically and scantily dressed performers sing and wave from a balloon, and from vehicles decked out as gondolas or ghostly riverboats.

On the other nights, a Latino band performs onstage, and the entire audience turns into one long conga line. All of this takes place in the lively **Masquerade Village**, complete with eating, shopping, and gaming facilities.

The Rio is one of the properties owned by Harrah's, and a free shuttle runs between all the Harrah's casinos every 30 minutes until midnight (until 1am on weekends).

Chinatown ⓬

4235 Spring Mountain Road
702-221-8448

Chinatown is easily spotted just west of the Strip by a long row of red pagoda-style roofs. They shelter shops and restaurants with cuisines including Filipino and Vietnamese (some of which have fresh seafood flown in daily). Chinatown culminates in a plaza with a gold-colored statue and an enclosed mall in which

> *Gambling is a way of buying hope on credit.*
>
> Alan Wykes

LEFT: the Gold Coast is popular with locals. **BELOW:** The Rio's sign is one of the most extravagant in Vegas.

is a central restaurant surrounded by shops with Chinese signs. There's a good shop for gifts, and, for more esoteric friends and family, try Great Wall Bookstore for the Chinese edition of *Time* magazine.

ABOVE AND BELOW: Vegas's Chinatown has only been around since 1995, but the Chinese population is booming.

Las Vegas Art Museum ⓭

9600 West Sahara Avenue, www.lasvegasartmuseum.org
702-360-8000 Tue–Sat 10am–5pm, Sun 1–5pm charge

This museum, situated about 10 miles (16km) west of the Strip in the Sahara West Library building, is an affiliate of the Smithsonian Institute. It was founded as the Las Vegas Art League in 1950 by a group of volunteers who believed in the need for a local arts venue.

It has since gone on to present a series of major exhibitions, including Marc Chagall, Salvador Dali, Dale Chihuly, and Auguste Rodin. With a changing series of temporary exhibits and programs, it aspires to be a leading visual-arts institution.

Life is a masquerade

On the way to downtown Vegas is **Las Vegas Premium Outlets** ⓮ (875 South Grand Central Parkway, www.premiumoutlets.com). With 150 stores and considerable savings, it's worth the trek to get here (think Burberry, Dolce & Gabbana, Polo Ralph Lauren), but it's not easy without a car.

A bus running to the Strat Tower stops nearby, but the stop is not well signposted and is distinctly unwelcoming after dark. A better idea is to use some of the money you save by shopping here and jump in a cab. ❑

BEST RESTAURANTS

Price includes dinner for one and a glass of wine, excluding tip:
$ = under $20
$$ = $20–$30
$$$ = $30–$40
$$$$ = over $40

Buffet

Carnival World Buffet
Rio All-Suite Hotel ☎ 702-777-7777 ⓒ B, L & D daily **$–$$** [p274, A2]
Acknowledged by many as the best buffet for the price, you can have a dozen international meals, and 70 different types of pastries.

French

Alizé
The Palms ☎ 702-951-7000 ⓒ D daily **$$$$** [p274, A3]
Celebrity chef André Rochat ascends to the top (literally) of the Palms Hotel to present his award-winning French cuisine and excellent wine list. Good views.

Pamplemousse
400 East Sahara Ave ☎ 702-733-2006 ⓒ D daily **$$$** [p276, C1]
For generations, local couples have been celebrating special occasions at this romantic version of a French country inn. There are no menus – the waiter recites the fare from memory. A gourmet feast for a minimum of 10 diners is available by advance order.

German

Hofbräuhaus
4501 Paradise Rd ☎ 702-853-2337 ⓒ L & D daily **$$** [p275, E1]
This grandiose restaurant across the street from the Hard Rock Hotel is a replica of Munich's famed brewery dating back to the 1600s. Bratwurst and sauerkraut, imported beer, and oompah bands make for a Bavarian Oktoberfest atmosphere all year round.

Italian

Battista's Hole in the Wall
4041 Audrie Street ☎ 702-732-1424 ⓒ D daily **$$** [p274, C1]
This restaurant has more than 30 years' worth of celebrity photos and mementoes. The menu features one-price meals of pasta, seafood, or veal, which includes all the wine you can drink. The wandering accordion player is a local legend.

Japanese

Benihana Village
Las Vegas Hilton ☎ 702-732-5111 ⓒ D daily **$$** [p277, C2]
Chefs cook *hibachi* chicken and *sukiyaki* steak table-side in this dimly lit, perennially popular restaurant. The atmosphere is dominated by special-effects thunder and lightning and "rain" that falls from the ceiling into pools, and streams that flow throughout.

Nobu
Hard Rock Hotel ☎ 702-693-5090 ⓒ D daily **$$–$$$** [p275, D1]
A Nobu Matsuhisa restaurant. The sashimi has South American flair, and the menu features inventive Japanese fare like Kobe beef carpaccio and *tiradito* with chili paste and cilantro.

Mexican/Seafood

Blue Agave
The Palms ☎ 702-942-7777 ⓒ L & D daily **$$** [p274, A3]
Named for the plant from which tequila is made, this casual eatery specializes in oysters, pan-fried shellfish, and bowls of red or green chili. It has been named Best Mexican Restaurant by the *Las Vegas Journal* every year since it opened in 1994.

Steak/Seafood

Golden Steer Steak House
308 West Sahara Ave ☎ 702-384-4470 ⓒ D daily **$$$** [p276, B2]

Frank Sinatra, John Wayne, and Elvis were regular customers here. Twenty-ounce T-bones and chateaubriand share the menu with jumbo Australian lobster tails. Decor recalls San Francisco's Gold Rush era.

Thai

Lotus of Siam
953 East Sahara Ave ☎ 702-753-3033 ⓒ L weekdays, D daily **$–$$** [p277, C1]
Called "the single best Thai restaurant in North America" by *Gourmet*, the menu features over 130 items, including roast duck in pineapple curry sauce, *tub wharn* (charbroiled beef liver with chili and lime), and *plar dook o-cha* (deep-fried whole catfish with peanuts and cashews).

RIGHT: Hofbräuhaus, Paradise Road.

18b Arts District

Few associate Las Vegas with cultural sophistication, but the city is emerging as one of the top art destinations in the Southwest

The 18b Arts District got its name when the city declared this run-down 18-block area between the Strip and Downtown to be its official art studio zone. Still dominated by car repair shops and used furniture stores, it doesn't look like much unless you know which doors to peek behind – or during the monthly event, First Friday. This sees all the studios in the district throw open their doors for receptions, and is also the time when other local artists display their works out on the streets. The Arts Factory is the de facto center of this creative melting pot: in an old brick warehouse you'll find around 15 small studios sharing space with a graphic arts firm and an architect.

A new festival, ArtAbout, held on the third Saturday of each month from 10am until 10pm, includes not only studio receptions but also street performers, children's activities, and a farmers' market.

Above: vase on display at Wynn Las Vegas.

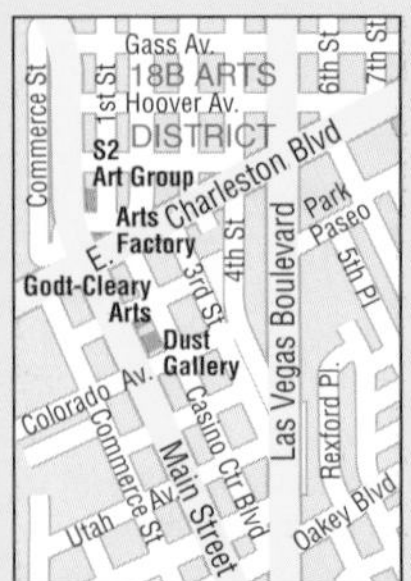

The Essentials

Main Street and Charleston Boulevard

First Friday festival information 702-384-0092

First Friday festival, each month, 6–10pm

free

First Friday trolleys from 6pm, El Cortez casino, 600 East Street

FINE ART AND STEVE WYNN'S PICASSO

Until billionaire casino mogul Steve Wynn put his art collection on display at Bellagio, it had never occured to anyone that resorts could draw customers with culture. This revelation inspired other casino art museums and moved the city to create an arts district. Today, the Strip has several major galleries, and artists' studios have proliferated throughout the city. Many of the paintings on display at Bellagio Gallery of Fine Art *(see page 145)* are acknowledged to be among the individual artists' greatest masterpieces: Rubens, Degas, and Gauguin are among those represented.

Godt-Cleary Arts, a leader among the galleries in the 18b Arts District, exhibits works by contemporary artists inclding David Hockney, Jasper Johns, and Andy Warhol. About 10 miles west of the Strip, in the Sahara West Library building, is the Las Vegas Art Museum *(see page 196)*, a Smithsonian affiliate showing the Institute's touring exhibits.

In 2006, Wynn agreed to sell his PIcasso blue-period portrait, *Le Rêve*, for a record $139 million. Shortly before the sale was completed, while gesticulating to cocktail party guests, Wynn poked a hole in the canvas with his elbow. As reported by guest Nora Ephron, Wynn commented "Oh shit, look what I've done. Thank God it was me." The dream deal was called off and Wynn kept his favorite Picasso.

ABOVE AND BOTTOM: celebrating the diverse works of local artists, the 18b Arts District First Friday festival attracts some 15,000 visitors each month.

FAR LEFT: crammed with antiques and vintage collectibles, The Funk House is a popular stop on the First Friday circuit.

LEFT: ArtAbout has children's activities for budding culture buffs.

Recommended Restaurants on page 217

DOWNTOWN

Downtown is where gaming began and myths were made. Gambling odds are good, as is the Fremont Street Experience, but the Street of Dreams still struggles against its big brother, the Strip

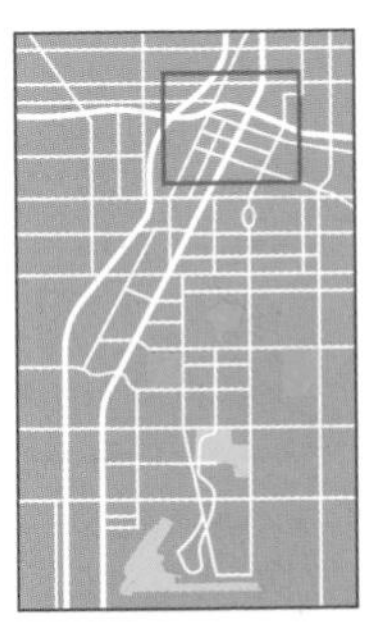

The area between the Stratosphere Tower and Downtown is often overlooked by visitors as they speed from one part of the Strip to another. The emergence of the Arts District *(see page 198)* will, planners hope, bridge this gap between "old" (Downtown) and "new" Vegas (the Strip). But in fact, its lower profile contributes to the charm, as this part of the Strip retains a pleasantly funky feel more reminiscent of 1950s Vegas than any *faux* re-creation. Popular chapels like the **Little White Chapel** (tel: 702-382-5943) and inexpensive, neon-signed motels are a respite from the hurly-burly that swarms around the rest of the city.

Downtown is Vegas

Farther along, **Downtown** is where gambling started in Las Vegas. In fact, Downtown *is* Las Vegas. The Strip is actually outside the city limits, so those who don't visit Downtown may not have actually been to Las Vegas.

Downtown, the neon beats brightly in a dense concentration of billboards and marquees with the iconic signs that made Las Vegas famous, like "Vegas Vickie," the cowgirl fronting **Glitter Gulch**, and her equally well-known and photogenic sweetheart, "Vegas Vic."

Nowadays, Downtown is fighting for a slice of the action that the Strip has grabbed for itself.

FREMONT STREET ❶

Over 100 years old, this is where Las Vegas's first casino was located, the site of the first city traffic signal, the city's first paved street, and the city's

Main attractions

FREMONT STREET
FREMONT STREET EXPERIENCE
NEONOPOLIS
BINION'S GAMBLING HALL
GOLDEN NUGGET
FOUR QUEENS
PLAZA LAS VEGAS
MAIN STREET STATION
UNION PARK
FREMONT EAST DISTRICT
OLD MORMON FORT
LAS VEGAS NATURAL HISTORY MUSEUM
LIED DISCOVERY CHILDREN'S MUSEUM

LEFT: performance art is often part of the Fremont Street Experience.
RIGHT: Vegas Vickie of Glitter Gulch, one of Vegas's iconic symbols.

first telephone. The first gaming license was issued to the long-defunct Northern Club at 13 East Fremont. Tony Cornero's Meadows Club was the place to be when gambling was legalized in 1931, with its

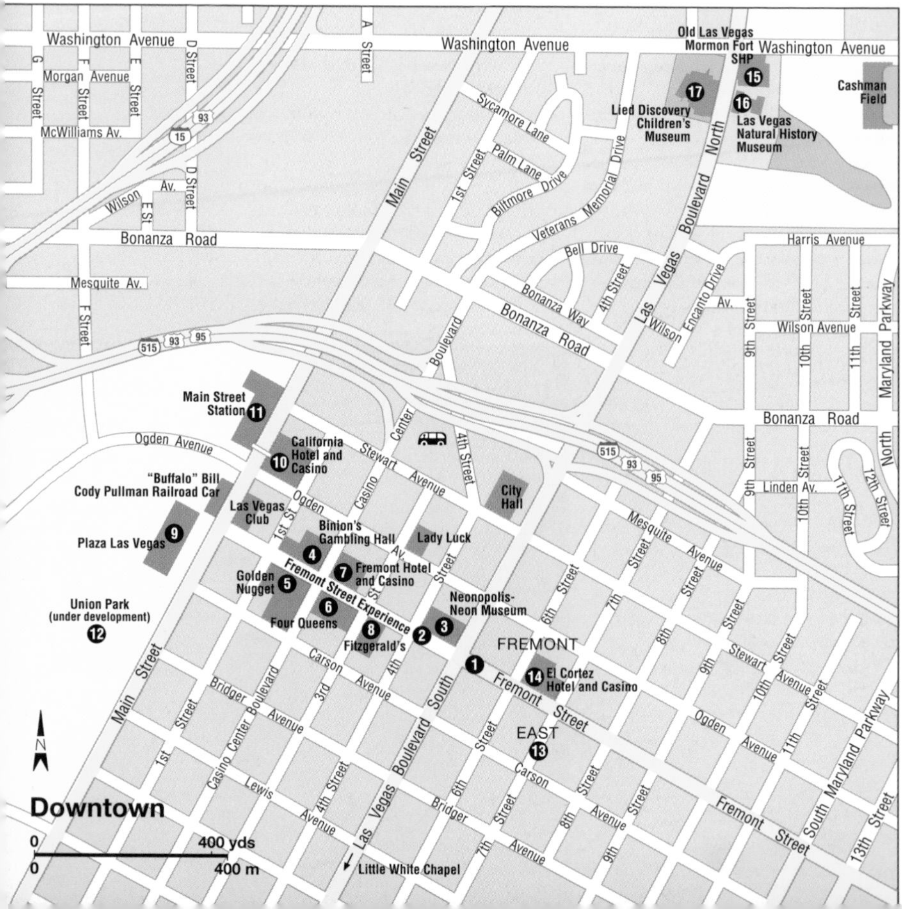

Downtown

0 400 yds
0 400 m

Washington Avenue
Morgan Avenue
McWilliams Av.
Wilson Av.
Bonanza Road
Mesquite Av.
Ogden Avenue
Stewart Avenue
Carson Avenue
Bridger Avenue
Lewis Avenue
Fremont Street
Main Street
Las Vegas Boulevard North
Las Vegas Boulevard South
Casino Center Boulevard
Veterans Memorial Drive
Sycamore Lane
Palm Lane
Biltmore Drive
Bell Drive
Bonanza Way
Encanto Drive
Harris Avenue
Linden Av.
Maryland Parkway
South Maryland Parkway
Cashman Field

1 FREMONT EAST
2 Fremont Street Experience
3 Neonopolis-Neon Museum
4 Binion's Gambling Hall
5 Golden Nugget
6 Four Queens
7 Fremont Hotel and Casino
8 Fitzgerald's
9 Plaza Las Vegas
10 California Hotel and Casino
11 Main Street Station
12 Union Park (under development)
13 EAST
14 El Cortez Hotel and Casino
15 Old Las Vegas Mormon Fort SHP
16 Las Vegas Natural History Museum
17 Lied Discovery Children's Museum

"Buffalo" Bill Cody Pullman Railroad Car
Las Vegas Club
Lady Luck
City Hall
Little White Chapel

Recommended Restaurants on page 217

Examples from the Neon Museum can be found on many Downtown streets.

rooms providing hot water and electricity. The next year the Apache Hotel on Fremont Street was the first in Las Vegas with an elevator, and Binion's *(see page 207)* innovated carpets, leading to the quaint term "carpet joint," slang for an up-market gambling establishment. Fueling even more interest in Downtown, the Vegas residency requirement for divorce was reduced to six weeks and people flocked here, but the law didn't last for long.

Today, Fremont Street throws off enough neon to read by, but it's all switched off before each performance of the main reason people come here.

FREMONT STREET EXPERIENCE ❷

nightly every hour, on the hour
free

This is an eye-popping computer-generated light spectacular that spans several city blocks. Twelve million lights and 550,000 watts of quality sound blast a ten-minute moving picture show across the biggest overhead screen in the world, VistaVision, projecting squadrons of jet fighters, thundering herds of buffalo, a tropical jungle with exotic birds and flora, that morph into a space odyssey, a cartoon orchestra, thunder and lightning, the rock band Queen, and rows

LEFT AND BELOW: the Fremont Street Experience uses 12 million lights.

ABOVE: downtown Vegas has lots of souvenir shops.
BELOW: Downtown loses allure in the daylight hours.

of dancing girls kicking to a samba beat. (Players working for a payoff should keep their eye on their slots if they step outside to watch the show because there are those who wait for just such a chance to jump in.) It costs millions of dollars each year to operate the show, but it has disappointed its backers: the show is not doing enough to reverse the decline in Downtown players. What may help is the Downtown extension of the monorail, but no firm date has been set for its completion.

While there is consensus on the need for a revival, there is little agreement over how to bring it about. Some want the big buildings that pull tourists to the Strip. Others see a solution in developing Downtown on a small scale from what's already there, creating, "a neon, desert version of New Orleans, naughty but eminently livable," as *Las Vegas Life* puts it.

Vegas villages

With this end, the eastern stretch of Fremont Street has been developed with new bars and cafés in a pedestrian-friendly zone *(see page 213)*.

"When I came here in 1964," says Oscar Goodman, the city's ebullient mayor and Downtown booster, "we had a place called Vegas Village, a marketplace where everyone came and did their shopping. The politicians were there, the gangsters, the actors. That's the kind of feel I want to reinvent for Downtown."

Mayor Goodman, who steps down from office in 2011, sees as his legacy another revitalized area west of the railroad tracks, called Union Park *(see page 212)*.

City planners are also pinning their hopes for revival on adventurous urban pioneers moving into the aforementioned Arts District. This is the area between Charleston Boulevard and Bonneville Avenue, where a group of young architects aim to develop lofts in existing buildings. "In many ways architecture reflects a community's cultural standards and sense of identity," Goodman said. "We are not content to settle for mediocrity."

So that's the future. For now, away from the main streets and the attractions listed here are liquor stores, strip joints, and junk-filled souvenir shops with dollars-in-a-bottle and T-shirt slogans like "if I can't win, I don't want to play."

Neon central

A previous rejuvenation attempt was the **Neonopolis** ❸ complex, at the junction of Fremont Street and Las Vegas Boulevard, but since it opened in 2002, it stayed mostly empty. In 2007, a name change to **Fremont Square** was proposed to link it more closely with the Fremont Street Experience, but the three-level mall with shops, a food court, a (good) multiscreen movie theater, and underground parking for 600 cars, has never really caught on.

The **Neon Museum** (tel: 702-229-5366) is not actually a building, but a collective title for the old neon signs displayed all around Downtown. Some of the more colorful exhibits hang on an 85ft (26-meter) tower in Neonopolis's interior plaza. These recall the 1920s era of Thomas Young's Electric Sign Company (YESCo) where clients included those of the now-defunct Thunderbird and Hacienda hotels as well as the Tropicana, the Aladdin, and the Sands.

"It was a town known for its neon," reminisces Mark Laymon, foreman of what is today the country's largest sign company, still deriving one-third of its income from casinos. Today, however, many of the best neon signs are indoors, having been snapped up and moved elsewhere, beckoning gamblers to the slot machines.

Many of the historic signs that are here have been "curated" from other cities; Hunick's Lounge was an Orange biker bar back in the 1950s, the Hunt's Red Car motel sign came from Compton, California.

Young, who leased his neon signs to smaller businesses to make them affordable, was obliged to deal with mobsters who were behind many of the original casinos.

"People would say, 'You're really in a hotbed down there,' but I can honestly say that was never apparent

ABOVE: the culinary specialty of Mermaids is deep-fried Twinkies.
BELOW: Neonopolis.

Pawn Shops

With gold, silver, and precious stones, minks and automobile pink slips, you'll never be stuck for a loan

More than one Las Vegas taxi driver will tell a tale of driving an unfortunate gambler to McCarran International Airport only to be told on arrival that his fare has no money – and been obliged to accept a watch or a wedding ring as payment. For many of Vegas's big losers there is a stop before that taxi ride: the pawn shop. The Las Vegas *Yellow Pages* lists seven pages of pawn shops, some with half a dozen branches or more, and many emphasizing that they are open 24 hours a day: just what a down-on-his-luck gambler might least want, but most need to know.

Pawnbroker ads invariably include a long list of what they'll loan money on, ranging from rifles and shotguns to tools, camcorders, and paintings. A few specialize in automobiles, with one firm promising that you can drive your car away – just so long as you leave them the title.

But jewelry tops the charts at most shops. "Watches, rings, necklaces, you name it," said one dealer. "We had one gent in here along with his girlfriend. Made her take off her earrings and then even an ankle bracelet. It was gold. Truth is, I wasn't feeling happy about serving him, but well, you know, that's the way it is in business."

Surprisingly, between 80 and 90 percent of pawnshop customers do return to redeem their items. By law, items must be kept by the shops for 120 days before disposing of them, allowing the customer to redeem them within that grace period. The standard interest charged is 10 percent, although some places take more – and a few establishments will charge as much as they can.

Generally pawn shops the world over have a negative reputation, but one local dealer said that he was merely performing a service for his needy clients, making money on somebody else's money "the same way a bank makes interest on a loan."

In most places in the US, pawn shops are found in poorer neighborhoods because that's where the most customers are, but in Las Vegas not only is there at least one pawn shop a mere stone's throw from the Strip, but the customer base cuts across all income levels and social classes. Habitual gamblers are more likely to face ups and downs than ordinary people, hence their need for this 24-hour service industry.

Pawnbroking is a profession so old that it is mentioned in the Bible, which warns Christians against usury, and forbids the taking of the necessities of life as security or any pledge whose loss would severely injure the borrower. "If you take a neighbor's cloak in pawn, you shall return it to him by sunset," admonishes the text in *Exodus* (xxii, 25–26), "because... it is the cloak in which he wraps his body; in what else can he sleep?"

No local pawnbroker admits to taking his neighbor's cloak, but fur coats have occasionally turned up (in the desert) as well as hand-tooled leather boots, ivory-topped walking sticks, and bicycles. ❑

LEFT AND ABOVE: gold jewelry is always a good bet if you need to visit a pawn shop.

Recommended Restaurants on page 217

in our dealings. We had something they needed and we were the only ones who could produce it. And they paid their bills. They were people of honor so far as we knew."

Some signs that haven't been restored yet are in a 3-acre (1.2-hectare) site called **The Boneyard**. Tours are available by advance booking at www.neonmuseum.org or by calling 702-387-6366. In 2009, construction begins on a permanent **visitor's center**, housed in the whimsical, swooping curves of the old La Concha Motel Lobby.

Downtown's blazing emblem is the four glittering casinos at the main intersection of Fremont Street and Casino Center Boulevard.

Binion's Gambling Hall ❹

128 Fremont Street, www.binions.com
702-382-1600 or 800-237-6537

Benny Binion arrived in the 1940s, a colorful Texas gambler with a trademark buffalo-hide overcoat and a big, white cowboy hat. He took over the Eldorado Club, renamed it Binion's and began a remarkable 40-year career which endeared him to his customers.

Binion's offers late-night gamblers a New York Steak Dinner for practically nothing (11pm–7am), which the *Las Vegas Advisor* called "the greatest Las Vegas meal deal of all time." Downtown's older casinos have always had a battle to woo the punters from the Strip, so they give free food to almost three quarters of them. In contrast, the Strip casinos give nearly half their customers free drinks, which is a slightly better ratio than Downtown.

TIP

Veteran Vegas writer Deke Castleman recommends visiting slot machines around seven in the morning when the crew empties the change buckets; the ones with the least quarters might be the loosest.

LEFT: Binion's security. **BELOW:** exhibition of vintage cars under the covered canopy of Fremont Street.

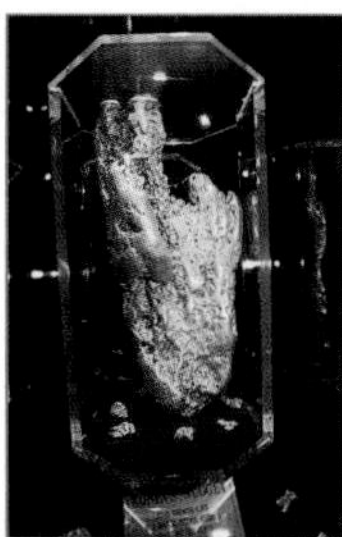

See the world's biggest gold nugget, the Hand of Faith, at the Golden Nugget.

In early 2004, the Becky Binion-run casino startled the gaming community by closing its doors overnight. It reopened in a deal with the Harrah's group, but has since changed hands again. Although the World Series of Poker moved from its birthplace, and is now played around various Harrah's-owned resorts on the Strip, the tournament will always be associated with Binion's, and with Benny Binion.

Golden Nugget ❺

✉ 129 Fremont Street,
www.goldennugget.com
☎ 702-385-7111 or 800-634-5336

The Golden Nugget stands out against the neon crassness of many of its neighbors, with its classy white exterior trimmed in soft gold lights. The Golden Nugget retains the style from when it first opened as a saloon more than 60 years ago, making it one of the earliest casinos. Crystal chandeliers reflect off polished brass and marble in the lobby.

Brass and granite squares shine from the surrounding sidewalk. Its buffet always has long lines, especially for champagne brunch on Sundays. An outdoor pool sits in landscaped gardens with tall palm trees, the terrace is lined with white alabaster swans and bronze sculptures of fish. In the Spa Suite Tower (which has a separate check-in lounge), the Grand Court is modeled on a room in the Frick Museum of New York. On display in the casino is the world's biggest gold nugget called the Hand of Faith, weighing a staggering 59.84lb (27.2kg). It was discovered in Australia.

Recreation business

In 1972, Steve Wynn's career more or less began at the Golden Nugget, and he was the youngest corporate chairman in Las Vegas history at the age of 31. He added hotel rooms and suites, of which there are now almost 2,000. *Time* magazine once said that Wynn was on a mission to gentrify gambling, removing its associations with high life and low life and delivering it to the suburbs as an innocuous middle-class weekend recreation. Wynn said, "What I do for a living and what keeps me

BELOW: the Golden Nugget is one of the classiest joints on Fremont Street.

Recommended Restaurants on page 217

young and happy is creating places where people go 'Wow!' and have fun. It's not that I'm insatiable, it's just that I love the exercise."

TIP

For studious gamblers who can forgo the showbiz excitement, Downtown's odds are almost always better than those offered in casinos on the Strip.

Four Queens ❻

✉ 202 East Fremont Street, www.fourqueens.com
☎ 702-385-4011 or 800-634-6045

The Four Queens casino claims that some of its slots have a 97.4 percent payback, higher than the Downtown average of 95.6 percent. Downtown slots, according to *Casino Player*'s Jim Hildebrand, pay almost two percent more than the 25¢ machines on the Strip. The difference doesn't look huge from the 95–97 percent end of the telescope, but the shift reduces the house "take" by 23 percent.

Largest blackjack table

The gambling bargain in downtown casinos, like El Cortez or the Golden Gate, are the inexpensive craps tables, and drinks are often free. Justifiably or not, the Four Queens calls itself "the jackpot capital of the world." The Queens boasts of the world's largest blackjack table and the world's largest slot machine, which can be played by six people at a time. Magnolia's Veranda offers views of the casino as you eat, and Hugo's Cellar has glowing reviews

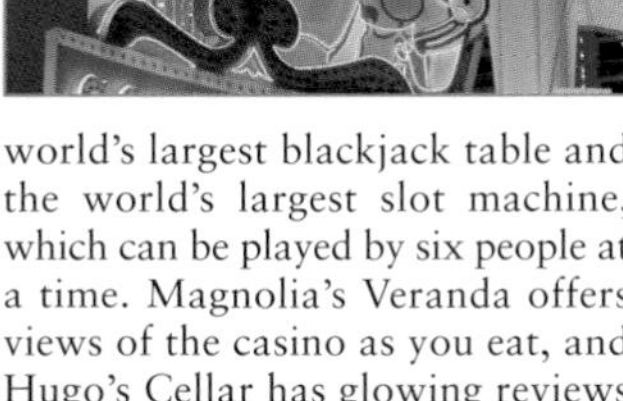

LEFT: Vegas Vic.
BELOW: the neon nirvana of Glitter Gulch.

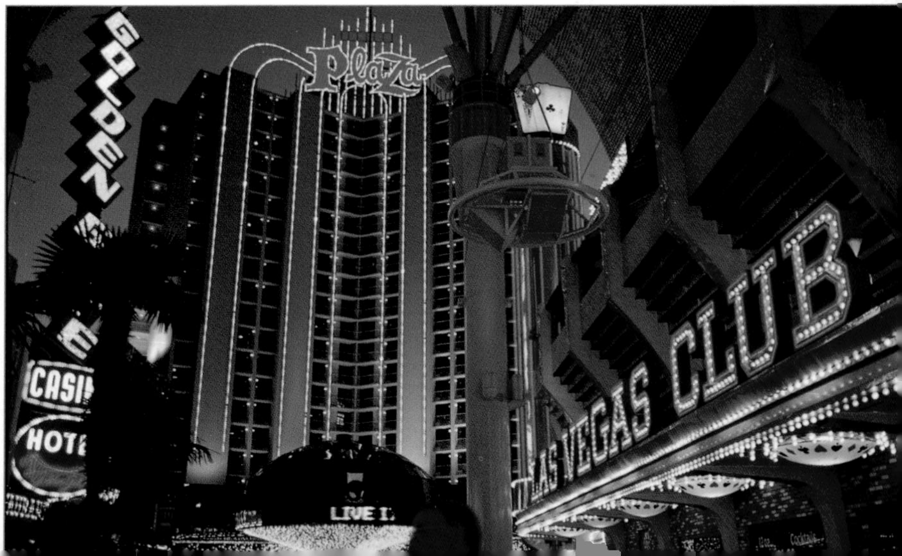

from guests. The Queens is one of the few casinos which invites visitors to take photographs, although not of people.

The Fremont Hotel and Casino ❼ (200 East Fremont Street; tel: 702-385-3237 or 800-634-6460) completes the neon quadrant of hotels. The 450 seats in its garden buffet prevent would-be diners getting stuck in the usual long line-ups, and the hotel has three other restaurants, including a Tony Roma's and the 24-hour Lanai Café. For a $100 hit on the slots, there's a free T-shirt.

BELOW: queen and king for a night.

Nickel zone

Next door to the Four Queens is **Fitzgerald's** ❽ (301 Fremont Street, www.fitzgeraldslasvegas; tel: 702-388-2400 or 800-274-5825), which has 200 slot machines in its Nickel Zone. They claim to have paid out over a billion nickels. Fitzgerald's offers a free O'Lucky Bucks card to improve your gambling chances, and trinkets like key chains, beanie animals, autographed sports memorabilia, and free meals.

Displaying shamrocks everywhere, Fitzgerald's is so Irish in theme that it has instituted a "Halfway to St Patrick's Day" celebration in mid-September, with green beer and Irish stew.

One way for casinos to promote loyalty is with free club membership. Members get a card to use in slot machines allowing them to play for credit, and tracking their play. Even small-time players can earn bonuses like $10-a-night motel rooms or 1–2 percent of their gambling money returned in gifts. Near the buffet is a British red telephone booth, equipped with a modern phone.

Recommended Restaurants on page 217

Towering at the top end of Fremont Street, the neon-lit, 1,000-room **Plaza Las Vegas** 9 (1 Main Street, www.plazahotelcasino.com; tel: 702-386-2110 or 800-634-6575) was the first downtown casino to install cashless slot machines. There are eight daily sessions of bingo upstairs, and free music in the Omaha Lounge.

About a block from the plaza is the **California Hotel** 10 (Ogden and 1st Street, www.thecal.com; tel: 702-385-1222 or 800-634-3484), promoting "an aloha spirit," derived from previous owner Sam Boyd's five years in Hawaiian bingo parlors where contacts with travel agents brought visitors from across the Pacific. "Dad worked the Hawaiian market like you couldn't believe," his son Bill said.

Aloha, cowboy

The hotel's arcade has shops for food, souvenirs, clothes, and other items from the 49th state. At the **California's Market Street Café**, the inexpensive breakfast buffet features tropical fruit, eggs, and Spam. The big draw is the ox-tail soup, but that's only served at night.

Sam Boyd was described by author and screenwriter Jack Sheehan as "an urban cowboy with the ever-present Stetson hat and string tie." A nonstop worker, even as a multimillionaire he cleared tables, dealt craps, or worked in the casino cage. He began work in an amusement park as a carny and pitchman for games of chance. For a time he was a pit boss at the Thunderbird.

Sam Boyd died in 1995. Based in Las Vegas, Boyd Gaming Corporation (listed on the New York Stock Exchange) is a leading casino entertainment company, operating 14 gaming entertainment properties across six states.

Main Street

A bridge crossing the street beside the **Aloha Cafe** leads to the **Main Street Station** 11 (200 North Main Street, www.mainstreetcasino.com; tel: 702-387-1896 or 800-713-8923), which claims "turn-of-the-century opulence." There are Belgian streetlamps from 1870, century-old chandeliers from the opera houses of Paris and

> *Most Las Vegans agree "if it's worth doing, it's worth overdoing."*
>
> John Smith

BELOW: where could you be but Vegas?

San Francisco, and bronze doors from a Kuwaiti bank.

Along the sidewalk, passers-by can peer into the Pullman Bar and Grille, situated in a beautifully preserved and antique-filled railroad car in which "Buffalo" Bill Cody lived as he toured the country more than a century ago. Its guest quarters were occupied, separately, by Teddy Roosevelt and Annie Oakley.

ABOVE AND BELOW: Downtown is the place to come for cheap drinks, and chips with everything.

Here also is the downtown area's only microbrewery, which produces a range of beers from light German-style ale to dark malty porter. In the bar, screens show sports and music videos, and the pub serves food from lunch through to late-night suppers.

UNION PARK ⓬

Mayor Goodman describes the 61-acre (25-hectare) site of a former railway switching yard, sandwiched between current Downtown and the two major freeways, as "the greatest piece of urban real estate in the country. A blank slate on which to create a whole new environment." Ground was broken in 2008 for the energetic mayor's pet project.

Architect Frank Gehry has designed the **Lou Ruvo Alzheimer's Institute**, which will be an extraordinary landmark, even in this town of architectural theater.

There are also plans for a 60-story international center for the jewelry trade. Chef Charlie Palmer, known locally for his Aureole restaurant at Mandalay Bay *(see page 125)* plans a hotel at Union Park, and the centerpiece of the development is a $360-million project for the **Smith Center for the Performing Arts**. Other projects

Gamblers' Book Shop

There's hardly any aspect of gambling that the Gamblers' Book Shop (630 South 11th Street, tel: 702-382-7555) doesn't have covered on its shelves, and if Brooklyn-born manager Howard Schwartz can't find a book on a subject, he will usually commission somebody to write one. "I have a lot of respect for people who buy books so they can understand the games," he says.

Many titles were written by John Luckman, who founded the store in 1964 with his wife Edna. He wrote little paperback books including *The Facts of Blackjack* and *The Facts of Craps*, which they sold by mail order and in casino gift shops. Casino bosses weren't keen on "wising up the suckers," but sales of the 50¢ books soared. About half of the store's sales derive from a mailing list of 25,000 customers, who increasingly want computer games and DVDs. Whatever the subject, Schwartz emphasizes the importance of study. Gamblers who don't bother to educate themselves, he said, "might as well mail in their wallets."

Recommended Restaurants on page 217

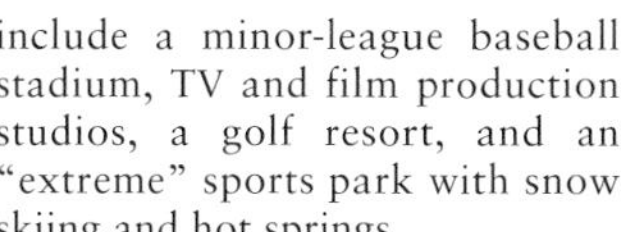

include a minor-league baseball stadium, TV and film production studios, a golf resort, and an "extreme" sports park with snow skiing and hot springs.

Around the park, a $3-billion **World Market Center** is underway with an outlet mall, which is due to be followed by an exposition space dedicated to promotion and showcasing for the furniture industry.

FREMONT EAST DISTRICT ⓭

Through a bright, illuminated gateway, another hopefully up-and-coming area of Downtown is the Fremont East District. In late August 2007, the city of Las Vegas completed a $5.5-million streetscape effort for this new entertainment quarter. More than a dozen new nightclubs, bars, and restaurants have been attracted to the Fremont East District, all in the drive to swell the numbers of Downtown's 18.7-million annual visitors.

But it's been a rocky start. A new nightclub with an alternative-music auditorium, the Hive, is expected, and family-friendly mid-priced eateries are opening. Long notorious for lowlife, the sleazier and more dangerous species of street life are being successfully encouraged to leave, but it's still not an area for incautious dalliance.

Newcomers

A couple of the newcomers do merit mention: the Griffin at 511 Fremont Street has fireplaces, deep red-leather booths, and a well-stocked jukebox to provide a cozy setting for their cool clientele. A young, arty crowd enliven Beauty Bar a few doors farther along at 517 Fremont Street. There's a dance floor inside, and live bands in the garden. The fittings are from a New Jersey hair salon.

Right in the middle of all this is the **El Cortez Hotel and Casino** ⓮ (600 East Fremont Street, www.elcortezhotelcasono.com; tel: 702-385-5200 or 800-634-6703), an old-style establishment started by Jackie Gaughan that is still popular for its penny slot machines (a man once won $76,000 playing them).

Gaughan is an expert on slot machines, and especially on where to site them to maximize their yield. About positioning the penny slots he said, "You use them to make a place look alive because people stay there longer playing them. They collect the pennies people have in their pockets and want to get rid of, and they make a little money."

ABOVE AND BELOW: everyday life in Sin City, Downtown-style.

ABOVE: El Cortez is old-style Vegas. **BELOW:** these boots were made for walking – and drinking.

Old-time gambler

Bill Boyd called Jackie Gaughan "one of the few old-time gamblers left in Las Vegas. He grew up in the business and his word is his bond." In 1946, Gaughan arrived in Vegas and bought 3 percent of the downtown Boulder Club then, a few years later, 3 percent of the Flamingo.

Jackie's son Michael trained at El Cortez, ran a school for dealers, and opened the Gold Coast Casino on West Flamingo, popular with Las Vegas locals, partly for the bowling alley, dancehall, and movie theater. Beginning with El Cortez in 1963, Gaughan acquired the Union Plaza, the Gold Spike, the Las Vegas Club, and the Western Hotel and Bingo Parlor. All Gaughan casinos have now merged with Boyd Gaming.

BEYOND DOWNTOWN

At the corner of Las Vegas Boulevard and Washington Avenue in what is technically the **Old Las Vegas Mormon Fort State Historic Park,** is one of the state of Nevada's most venerable buildings.

Old Mormon Fort ⑮

✉ 500 East Washington Avenue, www.parks.nv.gov/olvmf.htm ☎ 702-486-3511 ◷ daily 8.30am–4.30pm Ⓢ charge

Built in 1855 by Brigham Young's pioneers to protect missionaries and the mail route to California, inside the adobe walls a reconstructed tower looks over a plaza, deserted but for a broken-down wagon and iron pegs for throwing horseshoes.

The only surviving part of the original structure is the building nearest to the little creek that irrigated potatoes, tomatoes, squash,

Recommended Restaurants on page 217

grapes, peaches, barley, and wheat. Similar plants are grown today in a demonstration garden.

After the Mormons left, miner Octavius D. Gass assembled a sizable ranch around the fort. Helen Stewart subsequently sold the ranch to the railroad *(see page 36)*.

Las Vegas Natural History Museum ⓰

900 Las Vegas Boulevard North, www.lvnhm.org 702-384-3466 daily 9am–4pm charge

Near to the old fort is another site for history, the local natural history museum. A sign in the museum's hallway proclaims, "a walk through time in which each foot represents a million years." The animated dinosaurs are convincing and a huge Tyrannosaurus Rex growls when a button is pressed.

Interactive exhibits include an African Rainforest ("To Africa" says the sign on the elevator) where a button creates a thunderstorm on Mount Kilimanjaro, and a savannah has zebra, gazelle, rhino, hippo, baboon, and cheetah, at the waterhole.

Striped baby sharks

Lions, bison, leopard, antelope, musk ox, ibex, peacock, ostrich, geese, vultures, and flamingos fill a large room, while the next has striped baby sharks swimming in an open aquarium. The sharks are fed at 2pm on Monday, Wednesday, and Saturday. Other fish are in a separate tank, and all similarly sized, so they don't eye each other for dinner.

Bonnie and Clyde, two sleepy Burmese pythons, sprawl behind glass. They have highly developed heat sensors to detect warm-blooded animals. Pythons naturally grow to a length of 24ft (7 meters) and can devour creatures as big as leopards.

ABOVE: hopes to lure bright young things to Downtown are anchored on Fremont East.
BELOW: the Old Mormon Fort dates to 1855.

Not many museums have exhibits dedicated to pre-walkers. At Downtown's Lied Discovery Children's Museum features are cleverly designed to stimulate the senses of the very youngest visitors to the museum.

Leaflets are available for parents, with questions and suggestions to stimulate interest for younger visitors. In the **Young Scientists Center,** exhibits challenge children to identify familiar aromas and teach them about different tastes.

There's plenty to engage the attention of adults as well as kids in the next attraction, which shares the ground floor of the city's library.

Lied Discovery Children's Museum ⑰

✉ 833 Las Vegas Boulevard North, www.ldcm.org ☎ 702-382-3445 🕒 Tue–Fri 9am–4pm, Sat 10am–5pm, Sun noon–5pm. Summer open Mon Ⓢ charge

If you ever wondered what a million pennies ($10,000) looks like, here's an exhibit that will show you. Also in the make-believe post office, young, would-be customers can sort, weigh, and mail packages.

Irresistible to all ages is the Discovery Grocery Store, which makes shopping a game and a musical pathway with which you can play a tune by jumping on different panels. There's a tube stretching up several floors, in which you can put your head and talk to hear the echo; an overhead ropeway with moving buckets that can be filled and emptied; sand in which to move rubber cacti around; a place to pump bubbles up viscosity tubes or to draw a picture of yourself on grid sheets while looking in a mirror.

A common mistake is in the pronunciation of the name of the museum. It is pronounced "leed," not "lied."

Planet Walking

Heavy boots can be donned for the installation called Planet Walking, which demonstrate the difference in gravity. What weighs 80lb (36kg) on Earth would weigh 95lb (43kg) on Saturn, Uranus, and Neptune; 188lb (85kg) on Jupiter; and 2,232lb (1,01kg) on the Sun. And maybe they'll have that delightful Language Map in operation. It speaks, and lights up, to show the locations around the world where a particular language is spoken. ❑

BELOW: exterior of the excellent Lied Discovery Children's Museum.

BEST RESTAURANTS

Price includes dinner for one and a glass of wine, excluding tip:
$ = under $20
$$ = $20–$30
$$$ = $30–$40
$$$$ = over $40

American

Triple 7 Restaurant and Brewery
Main St Station, 200 North Main St ☎ 702-385-7111 🕒 B, L, & D daily; until 7am **$–$$$** [p278, B1]
Among copper-clad brewing pots, choose between five kinds of burger, gourmet pizzas, barbecue ribs, or pale ale-battered shrimp. There's also a sushi bar, but the real attraction is the beer.

Asian

Lillie's Noodle House
Golden Nugget ☎ 702-385-7111 🕒 D daily **$–$$** [p278, B2]
Considered by many to be Downtown's best Asian restaurant, Lillie's extensive (but not expensive) menu features house specialties like Korean marinated *kalbi* steak.

Barbecue

Tony Roma's
Fremont Hotel ☎ 702-385-3232 🕒 D daily **$** [p278, B2]
With over 200 restaurants on five continents, Tony Roma's Las Vegas location may be predictable, but it also offers some of the most affordable, reliably tasty fare in the area. Barbecued baby back ribs are a specialty.

Delicatessen

Shrimp Bar and Deli
Golden Gate Hotel, 1 Fremont St ☎ 702-385-1906 🕒 24 hours daily **$** [p278, B2]
Located in the oldest hotel in town, this eatery has long been famous for its shrimp cocktails for 99¢ (for players' club members; otherwise $1.99).

French

André's Las Vegas
401 South Sixth St ☎ 702-385-5016 🕒 D daily **$$$$** [p278, B2]
This converted historic home (*c*.1930) is rustic and friendly, with small rooms for intimate dining. André Rochat serves classics such as sole Véronique, rack of lamb, and *magret* of duck. In a part of town not known for fine dining, this branch consistently wins "best Vegas food" awards.

Italian

Chicago Joe's
820 South 4th St ☎ 702-382-5637 🕒 L & D daily **$$** [p278, B3]
This homey little red-checkered-tablecloth restaurant in the Arts District has been a local favorite for more than 30 years. The "Chicago-style" menu emphasizes pastas, veal, and seafood. Best bet: *cioppino*, a thick seafood stew.

Mexican

El Sombrero Café
807 South Main St ☎ 702-382-9234 🕒 L & D Mon–Sat **$–$$** [p278, B3]
This small family-run restaurant has been serving authentically Mexican tacos, chile *rellenos*, burritos, and enchiladas smothered in piquant chile *colorado* since 1950. Even if you're staying nearby, take a taxi – the neighborhood is not the best, and the cab company is right next door.

Steakhouse

Binion's Ranch Steakhouse
Binion's Gambling Hall ☎ 702-382-1600 🕒 D daily **$$$** [p278, B2]
Casino owner and rancher Benny Binion, who dominated the downtown casino scene for years, prided himself on the quality of beef he raised and served in his establishments. The tradition is kept alive at this restaurant with its spectacular view of the city.

Hugo's Cellar
Four Queens ☎ 702-385-4011 🕒 D daily **$$$** [p278, B2]
Red brick walls and romantic lighting set the mood for chateaubriand, aged steaks, and dishes such as duckling anise flambé. Salads are prepared table-side.

RIGHT: El Sombrero Café.

246

367

RED ROCK CANYON LOOP

Leave Sin City behind, visit an old Western town, hike in a geological phenomenon, and be back in time for a night on the Strip

Main attractions

- LAS VEGAS OUTLET CENTER
- BONNIE SPRINGS OLD NEVADA
- SPRING MOUNTAIN RANCH
- RED ROCK CANYON NATIONAL CONSERVATION AREA
- RED ROCK CASINO RESORT & SPA
- SUMMERLIN
- NEVADA STATE MUSEUM & SPRINGS PRESERVE

A 40-mile (63km) loop from the Las Vegas Strip will take in most of the sites immediately to the south and west of the city. Begin with a drive south down Las Vegas Boulevard, past the Mandalay Bay casino to the first destination, the **Las Vegas Outlet Center** ❶ (7400 Las Vegas Boulevard, www.premiumoutlets.com; tel: 702-896-5599; open 10am–9pm, Sun 10am–8pm). Aisles are lined by familiar names like Liz Claiborne, Nike, Reebok, and Waterford Wedgwood among the 130 stores.

Savings are promised with the "no middlemen, no mark-up" outlet philosophy. There is ample parking space and a central food court. A fleet of taxis lines up outside, ready to take passengers and their purchases back to the Strip.

Wild West

Only a few hundred yards beyond the outlet, SR160 heads west to the community of **Blue Diamond**, a company town for a gypsum producer, where SR159 curves right through Red Rock Canyon.

On the way is **Bonnie Springs Old Nevada** ❷ (1 Gunfighter Lane, www.bonniesprings.com; tel: 702-875-4191; hours vary, charge). The *faux* Olde Western town has a motel with themed rooms ranging from Covered Wagon to Chinese. Most places are covered with dust and sport an old and probably intentionally decrepit appearance.

There was a ranch here in 1843, used as a stopover to refresh passengers and horses on wagon routes to California by the old Spanish Trail. Today's visitors throng to the

PRECEDING PAGES: sailing on Lake Mead.
LEFT: Summerlin, with the Stratosphere Tower in the background.
RIGHT: take a bike to Bonnie Springs.

zoo or the subterranean wax museum, which has crude figures representing a mountain man, a missionary, a prospector, and a native Paiute. Abraham Lincoln's lips move almost in synch with a recorded speech. Brigham Young, the explorer Jedediah Smith, and President James Buchanan are among the motley group. Lining the main street are a disused opera house and the dingy shacks of a sheriff's office, a shaving parlor ("teeth pulled here"), and a store doubling as a museum. Exhibits include an 1897 washing mangle and medicine bottles. Horseback riding is available, too.

Don't have a car? Anyone staying in Vegas who wants to visit the Bonnie Springs ranch should call Star Land Tours, tel: 702-493-0416.

Spring Mountain Ranch ❸

✉ Blue Diamond Drive, http://parks.nv.gov/smr.htm
☎ 702-875-4141 ⏲ house daily 10am–4pm Ⓢ charge

Not far from Bonnie Springs is another ranch, the former home of wealthy Vera Krupp, who raised cattle on thousands of adjoining acres. The ranch dates to the time when mountain man Bill Williams, one of explorer John Fremont's guides, camped here. The sandstone cabin and blacksmith's shop, built in 1876, are open to visitors. Along with the Old Mormon Fort in downtown Las Vegas, these are some of the oldest buildings in the valley.

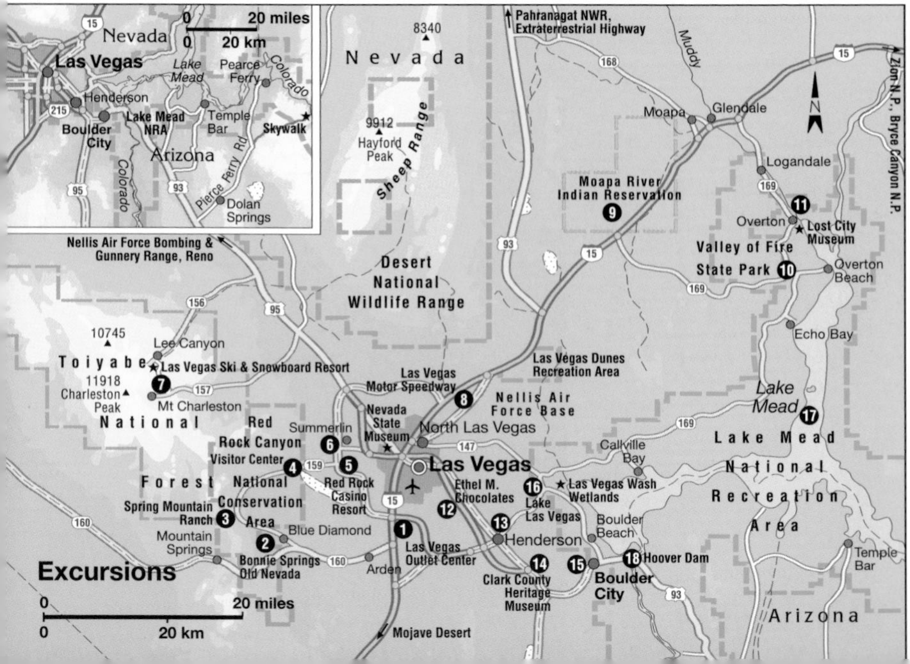

Today's visitors begin their tour at the attractive modern ranch house built by Chester Lauck who played Lum in a famous early radio show, *Lum and Abner*.

He built the 3-acre (1.2-hectare) reservoir (which is still used for irrigation), naming it Lake Harriet after his wife, and bred racehorses on the ranch with his partner, the 1950s screen actor Don Ameche.

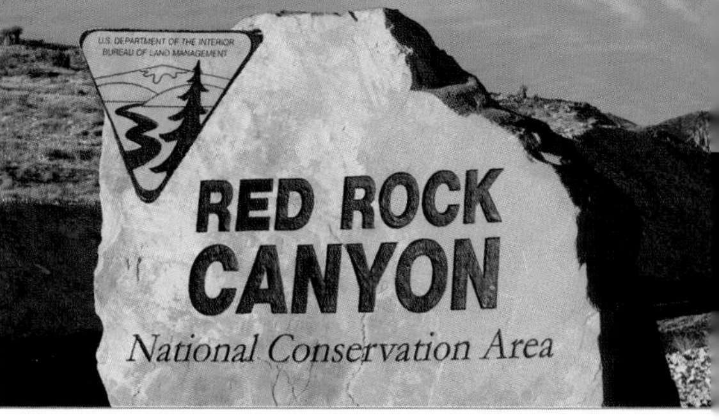

The Krupp diamond

Additions to the property, including the swimming pool, were added by Mrs Krupp, wife of the notorious German "cannon king," Alfred Krupp. In 1959, Vera was robbed at gunpoint in her living room, and a ring set with a 33.6-carat diamond was taken. The ring was recovered a few weeks later, and, after her death, it was bought by Richard Burton for Elizabeth Taylor for $305,000. The living room in question now serves as the **visitor center**.

In 1967, Howard Hughes bought the ranch as part of his Las Vegas spree, but probably never visited, although his deputy, Robert Maheu, occasionally entertained guests here. After one more owner, Spring Mountain Ranch was bought for $3.25 million by the Nevada State Parks Department, and is now a site for summer concerts and other activities. There are guided tours, beginning at noon, and the picnic grounds are open until dusk.

RED ROCK CANYON NATIONAL CONSERVATION AREA ❹

www.redrockcanyonlv.org
702-515-5350 visitor center daily 8.30–4.30pm
charge to enter the park

ABOVE: the nearest national conservation area to Vegas.
BELOW: Summerlin and other green suburbs are within reach of the Strip.

Red Rock Canyon really ought to be called "red-rock and green-tree canyon," because the far side is green and fertile compared to the arid beauty of the near side of the canyon. Along the way are sculpted vistas, hidden waterfalls, and desert vegetation, as well as bighorn sheep, coyotes, antelope, wild horses, and donkeys. (Please remember not to feed the animals.)

More than a million visitors a year travel SR159 to explore this dramatic 197,000-acre (80,000-hectare) desert area, managed by the Bureau of Land Management.

The **Red Rock Visitor Center** is at the end of a spectacular 13-mile (21km) loop if you come from Bonnie Springs, or at the beginning if you enter from West Charleston Boulevard. The center is part of an expansion program, due to be completed in 2010.

Despite its desert appearance, the canyon is often a few degrees cooler that the Vegas streets, and has a tiny breeze, very welcome in summer.

ABOVE AND BELOW: Pink Jeep Tours are just one of the companies that visit Red Rock from Las Vegas.

Sculpted vistas

There are trails, both long and short, for hikers and cyclists; picnic areas; a campground (permits required); and a rock-climbing center which offers classes. Red Rock is great for climbers, as the ascents range from easy to very difficult.

Traces of the Paiute tribe have been found at **Willow Spring**, where a well-preserved panel of five petroglyphs survives. Archeologists say that they "reflect the belief that the rock face was a permeable boundary between the natural and supernatural worlds... the door the shaman entered to visit the spirits."

Magnificent morning colors

The magnificent colors of the ochre and gray morning landscape come from ferrous minerals in the rocks, and change as the day progresses. When evening shadows grow long, the canyon turns a deep terracotta red. After heavy winter rains, wildflowers are abundant, and in late spring the air is filled with the scent of blossoming cliffrose, a tall, attractive shrub covered with tiny, cream-colored flowers.

Mojave Desert flora and fauna are displayed both inside and outside the visitor center (the only place in the park where water is sold, so be sure to buy a bottle). Dominant shrubs like the creosote bush sprout yellow flowers whose nectar and pollen sustain the area's bees, as does the rabbit brush which blooms from August to October. The roundish,

woody saltbush shrub is a common desert plant that sustains wildlife; and groundsel, the weedy, yellow sunflower, is valued in Native American traditional medicine.

The **Red Rock Casino Resort & Spa** ❺ (1011 West Charleston, www.redrocklasvegas.com; tel: 702-797-7777) is a new, upscale property for those craving the glitz of the Strip but also the calm of the countryside. With on-site gaming and good food, there's little reason to leave. The pool area is particularly popular, a refuge from the oppressive desert heat.

SUMMERLIN ❻

Heading back toward Vegas on SR159, just north of the road, is a chance to drive through the lush acres of **Summerlin**. A self-contained, planned suburb with around 85,000 residents, it has tropical landscaping and well-appointed golf courses. Developed by the Howard Hughes Corporation, the town is named for the elusive tycoon's grandmother.

The manicured grounds of the **JW Marriott Las Vegas Resort & Spa** (Rampart Boulevard and Summerlin Parkway; tel: 702-702-869-7777) are bordered by lavish pools, lagoons and waterfalls, a spa, restaurants, and a casino. The October **Fall ArtWalk** is one of the Vegas valley's largest, where artists join jewelers, weavers, and other craftspeople for a weekend of demonstrations and displays.

Summerlin is a tranquil stop for a late lunch or early dinner before heading back and hitting the frenetic tables of the Strip. ❑

The Red Rock Loop Road is a one-way lane open 6am–8pm in the summer (closes earlier in the winter), where wildlife, waterfalls, and petroglyphs can be seen from designated viewing spots. Bicycles are allowed on the Loop Road, but all-terrain vehicles are not.

LEFT: a desert bighorn ewe. **BELOW:** the mineral-rich rocks of Red Rock Canyon.

Nevada State Museum and Springs Preserve

The well-respected Nevade State Museum has decamped from its old, cramped premises in downtown Las Vegas to this bright, new, and extensive campus, which opened in 2009 to house and display its superb collection of fossils and bones. These include relics from the Cretaceous period – the last era of the dinosaurs – including the femur from a dromaeosaur (raptor), a tooth from a tyrannosauroid (ancestor to the Tyrannosaurus rex), a tooth from a sauropod (a long-necked dinosaur), and an iguanodontid's tooth.

The museum's new $36-million facility is set in the 180-acre (73-hectare) Las Vegas Springs Preserve, which includes four trails of Nevada's cultural and environmental history, plants and wildlife, and gardens showing exhibits of desert and non-native flora and aboreculture. An instructive "watering-can theater" gives visitors hands-on opprtunities to learn about the importance, the use, and the conservation of precious water in the desert.

LOUIS L'AMOUR
KID RODELO
BEEF

NORTH OF LAS VEGAS

Northwest of Las Vegas there are snow-covered mountains and blazing desert; northeast, a lost civilization and sandstone cliffs. But hey – what's that hovering overhead?

Outside Las Vegas, things can be as strange as they are on the Strip. Mount Charleston is a great place for outdoor pursuits, including summer and winter sports, of course, but there's also the whacky world of NASCAR, the nuclear testing range of Yucca Flat, and the nuclear waste-dump-to-be at Yucca Mountain. Other-worldly landscapes are ringed with fire or studded with ancient stone carvings. And then there are the aliens…

NORTHWEST OF LAS VEGAS

To reach the invigorating slopes of **Mount Charleston ❼**, head north on US95 and then west on SR157. In the distance and rising to a peak of around 12,000ft (4,000 meters), rugged, craggy **Charleston Peak** is high enough to support both summer and winter activities – skiing and sleigh rides during the cold season, horseback riding, wagon rides, and hiking during the hotter months.

The temperature is typically in the 70s°F (21°C), one of the reasons Mount Charleston is such a popular summer day trip from the sweltering streets of Sin City, which is usually much hotter. At other times of the year, people head for the **Las Vegas Ski and Snowboard Resort** (www.skilasvegas.com; tel: 702-385-2754), which has ski trails spread over 40 acres (16 hectares) in the delightful **Lee Canyon**. Skis and clothes can be rented, and lessons are available for both adults and children. The season starts in late November and runs until the snow melts in early spring.

Mount Charleston captures enough westerly precipitation to support varied vegetation. Sagebrush, crimson blooming cactus, yellow

Main attractions

- MOUNT CHARLESTON
- LAS VEGAS SKI AND SNOWBOARD RESORT
- TOIYABE NATIONAL FOREST
- YUCCA MOUNTAIN
- LAS VEGAS MOTOR SPEEDWAY
- NELLIS AIR FORCE BASE
- EXTRATERRESTRIAL HIGHWAY
- MOAPA RIVER INDIAN RESERVATION
- VALLEY OF FIRE STATE PARK
- OVERTON
- LOST CITY MUSEUM

LEFT: flying the flag.
RIGHT: cabins in snowy Mount Charleston, a ski area in the desert.

Take to the slopes at the Las Vegas Ski and Snowboard Resort.

wildflowers, and bristle cone pines are among 30 species of plants native to the region.

Named after two brothers who ran a sawmill more than a century ago, **Kyle Canyon** has a campground and RV site; there are other camping sites and picnic areas around, too. On top of the mountain is the **Mount Charleston Lodge** (tel: 702-872-5408), which rents log cabins.

Elevated elegance

The formerly low-key **Hotel on Mount Charleston** (tel: 702-872-5500) was recently remodelled as a classy resort ("elegance at a higher level"), with a convention center and a spa. Mountain views and huge fireplaces with roaring fires make this an ideal spot for a honeymoon if you happened to have gotten hitched in one of Vegas's chapels earlier in the day. The vast dining room offers grand mountain views, and there are "movies under the stars" on late summer evenings.

To explore the **Toiyabe National Forest**, a unique landscape of forested mountains surrounded by desert, there are scenic drives, hiking trails, and horses for rent. Thousands of years ago, as the water that once covered the valley dried up, plant and animal life retreated to the higher ground which today still supports deer, elk, wild turkey, wild horses and donkeys, bighorn sheep, and even some mountain lions.

ABOVE RIGHT: a statement on the license plate of the Silver State.
BELOW RIGHT: courting Lady Luck in Reno.

Pioneer territory

Continuing north on US95, the road skirts the western border of the 3.5 million-acre (1.5 million-hectare) **Nellis Air Force Bombing and Gunnery Range**, in an area known as Pioneer Territory. Originally built to train B-29 gunners during World War II, it eventually became the training ground for the nation's ace fighter pilots. Many key military personnel assigned to Nellis during

Reno – a Mini Vegas and More

Reno (446 miles/718km northwest of Las Vegas) trumpets itself as "The Biggest Little Town in the World," with a neon arch Downtown. And this little town does pack in a pretty hefty range of entertainment and recreation, with excellent opportunities for hiking, biking, climbing, golf, water sports, skiing, and snowboarding.

The green-baize tables and shiny slots still have big pulling power, and just as Las Vegas is the gambling mecca for Angelenos, Reno is the gaming resort of choice for San Franciscans. Two old-school Las Vegas casino hotels are represented by sibling establishments here, Circus Circus and Harrah's. The Eldorado is a favorite with many visitors for its atmosphere, service, and value. But as well as the fun of gambling, shows, and the trademark super-swift divorce, Reno also has a cultural calendar. There is an opera society, and at least two groups of players who appear at the outdoor summer Shakespeare festival.

The Downtown arch is, in fact, the Little Town's second; the original arch from 1926 is displayed on Lake Street near the National Automobile Museum.

World War II returned as civilians to take up residence in Las Vegas. Today, thousands of active-duty personnel, civilian employees, military dependents, and military retirees are connected to Nellis. The base is not open to the public.

Yucca Flat was a major nuclear test region, and the Federal government has selected **Yucca Mountain** as the lucky repository for 77,000 tonnes of radioactive waste. Given how near Las Vegas is, the decision is a controversial one. Some opposition comes from worries about the hazards of transporting the waste from all over the country to Nevada. The waste will be stored in supposedly safe canisters, in concrete-lined chambers. But nobody knows quite how safe this will be, particularly since the discovery that the mountain's interior is not as waterproof as it had been assumed to be. The plan was vetoed by Nevada's governor but his veto was overridden by a vote in the Senate. The project has been delayed until 2013.

Northeast of Las Vegas

The fastest route from Las Vegas northeast is via Interstate 15, which soon passes the **Las Vegas Motor Speedway** ❽ (www.lvms.com; tel: 1-800-644-4444). The Speedway features celebrity races, NASCAR events, and country-music festivals.

The Speedway underwent a major renovation in 2007, and added the "NASCAR Disneyland" of the **Neon Garage**. Great sight lines gear up the racing excitement, and between races, rock and tribute bands play on a big stage. There's a bird's-eye view of the Winner's Circle.

If the idea of all that speed starts a thrill in your veins, the track has been known to offer "test and time"

ATVs (all-terrain vehicles) are a great way to explore the Nevada Desert.

LEFT: take care when traveling in the desert. **BELOW:** Nevada's Highway 375 is the site of many UFO sightings.

Track tours of the Las Vegas Motor Speedway are offered from Monday to Saturday 9am–4pm, Sunday 11am–4pm. Tours leave on the hour. Laps around the track are dependent on the schedule of races.

events. Show up with a street-legal car that passes a technical inspection and you can try it on the track and get an official report. It's advisable to arrive with an alternate ride home – your car may not be quite so technically excellent after you've thrashed it around the track. The Speedway sometimes hosts training courses, too.

Alien landscape

Flanking both sides of I-15 are the grounds of **Nellis Air Force Base.** A left turn north off I-15 leads to US93, which runs along the eastern border of the Nellis Air Force Bombing and Gunnery Range *(see page 228)*.

Beyond the **Pahranagat National Wildlife Refuge**, US93 bumps into what may be the strangest feature of this landscape, SR375. Also known as the **Extraterrestrial Highway**, dusty, arrow-straight SR375 has been the site of many more than the average number of UFO sightings, and has its coterie of devoted fans.

The little community of **Rachel**, barely more than some trailers (which can be rented by the night or longer) and a funky-but-fun restaurant called the **Little A'e'Inn**, is a rallying point for UFOlogists from around the world.

RIGHT AND BELOW: different ways to travel through Valley of Fire State Park.

Their credibility is strengthened by rumors of Air Force alien studies at nearby Groom Lake, but of course, the existence of any such thing is officially denied. Needless to say, the top-secret aircraft test base is heavily guarded, and intruders are detained if not arrested.

Back down on I-15 and still heading northeast, the road slices through the **Moapa River Indian Reservation** ❾, or technically, a corner of it. The community is not open to the public, but Native Americans often man a truck stop where souvenirs, liquor, cheap cigarettes, and gas can be purchased.

Valley of Fire State Park ❿

A right-hand turn off the highway along SR169 loops through this fine park, Nevada's oldest and largest state park. The name comes from the jagged sandstone cliffs which appear to blaze in the sunlight, a sight much appreciated by moviemakers. A leaflet is available from the toll booth at the entrance and

also from the wonderfully sited **visitor center** (tel: 702-397-2088; daily 8.30am–4.30pm; charge to enter the park) about midway through the route. Take plenty to drink as it can get hot and rugged around here.

Mouse Tank, a trek of almost ½ mile (1km) from the road, is where the indigenous Paiute tribe used to drink rainwater collected in the stone basin. Carvings and petroglyphs can be seen, mostly around **Atlatl Rock**. One of the most impressive is that of the atlatl itself, a prehistoric forerunner of the bow and arrow. For an additional fee, camping is allowed.

AROUND OVERTON ⓫

Overton is where SR169 leaves Valley of Fire State Park, a small town in which the **Lost City Museum** (tel: 702-397-2193; daily 8.30am–4.30pm; charge) documents the long-lost Native American Anasazi. Living in the area for centuries, the tribe left as long as 800 years ago, probably because of a prolonged drought. Ironically, the area that was inhabited by the Anasazi is now deep beneath the waters of Lake Mead.

The museum, established in 1935, exhibits some of the beads, polished shells, pottery, baskets and, intriguingly, bone gaming counters, that were found by archeologists before the lake and Hoover Dam were built. In Overton on North Moapa Valley Boulevard are the Overton Motel (tel: 702-397-2463) and a Best Western (tel: 702-397-6000).

If there's time, the meandering **Northshore Scenic Drive** offers attractive scenery, and occasional sightings of bighorn sheep. Following it south, the drive curves around the lake and eventually ends up near Lake Mead marina and closer to Hoover Dam *(see page 244.)*

On the way are smaller roads to **Overton Beach** (good for fishing), **Echo Bay**, or to **Callville Bay**, originally established by Anson Call in 1864 as a freight outlet for Colorado River steamboats.

But many years of drought are taking a toll on the area's marinas. Due to low water levels, Lake Mead marina has been forced to move 3 miles (5km) south of its previous location, and the marina at Overton Beach is currently closed. ❑

Overton's Lost City Museum traces the history of the indigenous Anasazi.

BELOW: Valley of Fire is the largest state park in Nevada.

THE COFFEE CUP
CAFE
GREAT AMERICAN FOOD
The Coffee Cup Ca

HENDERSON AND BOULDER CITY

Two different towns lie just a short distance from Vegas. Henderson is fast-growing and fast-moving, while Boulder City feels like a sleepy community in the Midwest

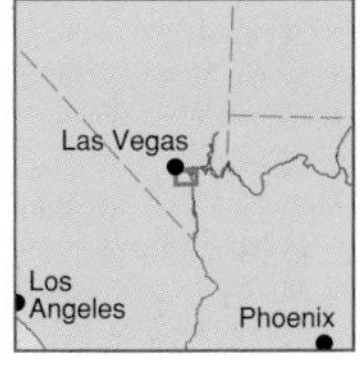

Henderson and Boulder City could hardly be more different – from each other or from Las Vegas. Henderson, for years one of the US's fastest growing cities, is now primarily a suburb servicing Vegas. The desert scrubland gives way to small communities so fast that maps are updated almost every year, and taxi drivers are perpetually lost. Many hotel and other service staff make the 13-mile (21km) commute to the Strip or Downtown every day. Boulder City is older and distinctly more genteel, with growth restricted to 120 inhabitants per year by city ordinance. Both towns are popular with retirees.

ON THE WAY TO HENDERSON

About 9 miles (14km) southwest of Las Vegas, the casino-resort **Sam's Town** (5211 Boulder Highway; tel: 702-456-7777) has rooms decorated in a southwestern theme, two huge RV parks, a swimming pool, a laundry, and a casino that spreads over three levels.

The resort also has an 18-screen movie theater, a bowling alley, Billy Bob's Steakhouse and Saloon, and a free shuttle to and from Bill's Gamblin' Hall on the Las Vegas Strip.

LEFT: Boulder City bike and diner.
RIGHT: waitresses at Mel's Diner.

Ethel M. Chocolates ⓬

1 Cactus Garden Drive 888-627-0990 daily 8.30am–7pm (self-guided tours) free

Northwest of Henderson is an enterprise guaranteed to bring a smile to the lips of any chocoholic. Around 60 different varieties of Nevada's yummy local candy are made in this factory, including a "chocolate postcard" bearing your own photograph. Visitors can watch some of the chocolate production on a self-

Main attractions

- SAM'S TOWN
- ETHEL M. CHOCOLATES
- GREEN VALLEY RANCH
- THE DISTRICT
- HENDERSON
- SUNSET STATION HOTEL CASINO
- CLARK COUNTY MUSEUM
- BOULDER CITY
- BOULDER HISTORIC DISTRICT
- BOULDER THEATRE
- BOULDER DAM HOTEL
- BOULDER CITY-HOOVER DAM MUSEUM

guided tour. A tonne and half of chocolates are typically enrobed in the course of a shift. Employees are given sensory training that includes learning which flavors are tasted on which parts of the tongue.

Life is sweet

The company was founded by "Mr Mars Bar," Forrest Mars. He built up the worldwide chocolate business starting with his parents' candy store in Tacoma, Washington.

Mars was described by author Joel Glenn Brenner as "the Howard Hughes of candy." In his book, *The Emperors of Chocolate: Inside the Secret World of Hershey and Mars*, Brenner says that Forrest spent about two months of the year in a penthouse above his Las Vegas factory – and watched the employees through one-way mirrors. Mars, who lived to the age of 95, decided to establish the candy business in Nevada because it was one of the few US states to allow the sale of liqueur-filled cordials.

Behind the factory is Nevada's largest **Botanical Cactus Garden** (also free). In 4 acres (1.6 hectares) of desert, about 300 species of plants grow. It's a good place to learn about them, since so many of these prickly plants look alike to an untrained eye.

North of Henderson, the hill-top **Green Valley Ranch** (2300 Paseo Verde Parkway; tel; 702-617-7777) has a casino, a music venue, and a spa. More interesting to casual visitors is probably **The District**, a shopping mall with brand names like Coach and J. Jill. Most summer weekends there are free movies under the stars or free concerts in the outdoor theater. If it's too hot, there are screenings at the air-conditioned multiplex.

ABOVE: a world away from the Vegas Strip. **BELOW:** hard-working employee at the Ethel M. Chocolate Factory.

Map on page 222

HENDERSON ⓭

The city of Henderson began as a Las Vegas satellite when the latter's population was just 8,500. For awhile, Henderson's infrastructure couldn't keep up with the expansion (though lately it has slowed down).

Henderson's early development was spawned by Cleveland entrepreneur Howard Eells' contract to produce magnesium for the US Defense Department. Many of the 13,000 workers lived in shacks, trailers, and tents along the Boulder Highway, but the company town of Henderson sprang up after a Senate bill was passed that allowed residents to buy their homes.

Thousands of panes of stained glass are subtly lit to denote the passing day in the ceiling of **Sunset Station Hotel Casino** (1301 West Sunset Road, Henderson; tel: 702-547-7777). Iron balconies, windows, and weathered brick give a sense of strolling in a Spanish village. The Mediterranean architecture is enhanced by a bar in the style of Modernist architect Antoni Gaudí. The hotel has a 13-screen movie theater, a bowling alley, and an outdoor amphitheater where fairly big-name rock acts perform. The latter is a treat for the locals, who don't always relish a drive to Vegas.

Clark County Museum ⓮

1830 South Boulder Highway; www.accessclarkcounty.com/departs/parks/museum
702-455-7955 daily 9am–4.30pm small charge

Between Henderson and Boulder City was southern Nevada's first museum, started in 1949 by Anna

SHOP

Visitors who have overdosed on rich food or casino buffets will be relieved to hear that Henderson hosts a Farmer's Market on Water Street every Thursday from 9am–4pm. There's also a branch of Whole Foods in The District shopping mall at Green Valley Ranch.

LEFT AND BELOW: take the trolley to do the shopping, Green Valley Ranch.

ABOVE AND BELOW: in southern Nevada, you can shop for Old West, Native American, or Mexican souvenirs.

Parks. That was the forerunner of the present museum, which is reached by the Boulder Highway.

The history of southern Nevada is shown in exhibits beginning with a diorama of the desert as it was 12,000 years ago, with petrified logs on sandy wastes, turtles, cacti, and a tall extinct beast described as a camelope. A Pauite camp is displayed with baskets, rabbit pelts woven into a blanket, and other finely detailed craftwork.

The pioneer life of trappers, farmers, and ranchers is represented by a woman sitting in her kitchen beside a big spinning wheel along with a baby in a rocker. Sin City's naughty 1940s and '50s are repesented by two of singer Ella Fitzgerald's dresses. The collection also includes items from the Tropicana, the Hacienda, and the Thunderbird casinos.

On **Heritage Street**, part of the grounds of the museum, are a group of old, restored, or recreated buildings that depict southern Nevada's recent history. Among them are a newspaper printshop (showing life from the 1890s), an antiques shop (1924), the Boulder City train depot (1931), a mobile home (1948), and a big, red barn (1955).

BOULDER CITY ⑮

Boulder City came into existence mainly because the US Government wanted to keep the men building the Hoover Dam away from hard liquor, gambling, and prostitution. The secretary of the interior appointed Tennessee-born Sims Ely, a former newspaper editor, to be city manager, and he proved to be a strict guardian of the city's morals. Cars were searched at the entrance to town, and impounded if liquor was

Hiking, Biking, and Birdwatching

A recent survey established that about 8 million of Las Vegas's annual visitors visit public lands and recreational areas around the Las Vegas Valley. What might sound like an unlikely stop is Henderson's 147-acre (60-hectare) Water Reclamation Facility (2400 B Moser Drive, near where Sunset intersects the Boulder Highway; tel: 702-566-2940; daily 6am–3pm), which has been designated a Bird Viewing Preserve, and where a branch of the Audubon Society has documented 200 different species. Early morning is the best time to visit.

The hills north of Boulder City are a mecca for mountain bikers. Established trails now have formal approval from the city, which maintains a road to the top of what locals call Radar Mountain. The International Mountain Biking Association has certified Bootleg Canyon as a rare "epic" ride.

Hikers can explore the Historic Railroad Trail from the visitor center at US93 and Lakeshore Drive, east of Boulder City. Part of the trail runs through tunnels built to ferry materials to Hoover Dam.

found. Alcoholic beverages were not legalized until 1969, and prostitution is banned to this day.

Off Duty

Off-duty workers went to Vegas for entertainment – although one casino west of town, called the **Railroad Pass** (tel: 702-294-5000), was quickly opened in 1931, and is still open, making it one of the state's oldest gaming houses. Sims had totally dictatorial powers – a "little Hitler" – one disgruntled worker called him, giving orders to the police and granting or refusing all commercial or residential leases.

Today, this pretty city (pop: 15,000) still has no gaming, no neon, and a strictly controlled growth policy. It is proud of its history and strives to preserve its small-town atmosphere; Boulder City is one of only two major places in Nevada that does not allow gaming. Upon entering the town, the speed limit counts down – from 65 miles an hour on the main road down to 15 in town – announced in ever-decreasing increments.

The town's charm is best appreciated in the **Boulder Historic District**. The **Boulder Theatre** (1225 Arizona Street; tel: 702-293-3171), built in 1931, is the town's former cinema. Restored by local resident, musician Desi Arnaz, Jr, it is home to the Boulder City Ballet, and the Dam Short Film Festival *(see page 88)*.

Down the street is the **Boulder Dam Hotel** (1305 Arizona Street, www.boulderdamhotel.com; tel: 702-293-3510). It has the atmosphere of a bed-and-breakfast inn, and over the years has hosted Bette Davis, Henry Fonda, James Cagney, and Shirley Temple. The rooms are charming.

ABOVE AND BELOW: a bar in the Sunset Station is modeled in the style of the Spanish Modernist architect, Antoni Gaudí.

Fans of culinary Americana should check out Boulder City's great diners. Mel's Diner, 558 Nevada Highway, has friendly staff, terrific hash browns, and chicken steak to die for. The Coffee Cup, 512 Nevada Highway, is family-run and has the best chilli *verde* around.

RIGHT: Bob's is now called Bradley's, but try the BBQ anyway. **BELOW:** the old Boulder City train depot.

Boulder City-Hoover Dam Museum

✉ 1305 Arizona Street, www.bcmha.org ☎ 702-294-1988 ⏲ Mon–Sat 10am–5pm, Sun noon–5pm $ charge

This is a pleasant little museum inside the Boulder Dam Hotel where the age-old debate over the name "Hoover Dam" or "Boulder Dam" is kept alive. One exhibit is an ancient switchboard, set up for visitors to plug in and hear residents reminiscing about the old days of Boulder City. A film shows how hard the men worked – "muckers" did the most dangerous work, shovelling out rock after each blast with short-handled spades called banjos, for just $4 a day.

Tree-lined streets

Other parts of Boulder's Historic District are as attractive as the theater and the hotel. The little houses with red-tiled roofs and stuccoed walls on nearby Cherry and Birch streets were built to house employees of the dam's power companies. The area looks much the same now as it did then, a leafy enclave far away in every repect to Sin City only 23 miles (36km) away.

By 9pm all is quiet – even the McDonalds on the strip mall outside town shuts early. One thing about keeping all that sin out of town is that you'll be guaranteed to get a good night's sleep. ❑

Grand Canyon West

East of Las Vegas and hovering over the Grand Canyon like a ghostly glass footbridge is an extraordinary man-made creation. No wonder they call it the Skywalk.

Over 70ft (21 meters) out from the precipice, the clear view straight down the canyon wall for 4,000ft (1,200 meters), takes visitors by surprise. People with no history of vertigo step out onto the plexiglass Skywalk – and then spring back. The downward view is so clear – and it's such a very long way down – that many people take a moment or two, and then a much more cautious second step. "It took a little while to get used to that sheer drop," a recent visitor said, "then I was fine. It was thrilling."

Shuffling in the soft paper slippers provided (to keep the plexiglass pristine), visitors keep mostly to the reassuring steel sides and venture across the transparent void only now and then. As well as their shoes, everyone must surrender cameras (official photographers are on hand), cellphones, wallets – anything that might drop into the canyon. Views across the quiet, still air to the horizon of the canyon's far side, 3 miles (5km) away, are uninterrupted by human structures, other than those rising up behind the Skywalk itself.

The cantilever glass walk is the result of a partnership between the Hualapai, "People of the Tall Pines," and Las Vegas-based businessman David Jin, and is said to be strong enough to support a dozen 747 airplanes. Jin, who conceived the idea, collects almost half of the (fairly steep) entrance fee for the first 25 years of operation.

The Hualapai's remote location 120 miles (190km) east of Las Vegas had previously meant that after the 2½-hour drive, visitors only stayed long enough to drop a few quarters in their casino's slot machines. "Now," operations manager Robert Bravo said, "this is what's going to feed our tribe."

Arrival is best timed early in the morning, before buses start to disgorge their tour groups at about 9am. (This is one reason to splurge on a helicopter or air tour from Vegas, as the solitude of being alone on the walk is superb.) The canyon rim is unsheltered, and gets pretty hot as the sun heaves up in the sky, so be sure to bring sunblock and a hat.

When the Skywalk opened in March 2007, one of the first to step out onto it was Buzz Aldrin, the second man to step on the surface of the moon. The height here probably didn't trouble him too much. ❑

ABOVE: Grand Canyon West is co-owned and operated by the Hualapai tribe. **RIGHT:** the Skywalk.

LAKE MEAD AND HOOVER DAM

The giant lake in the desert offers recreational opportunities all year round, made possible by a masterpiece of 1930s engineering

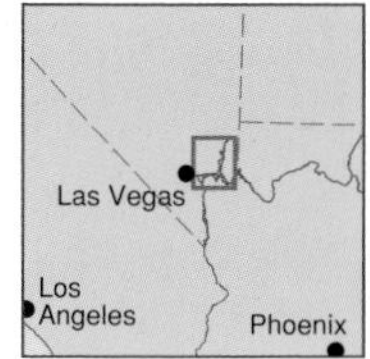

Main attractions

LAKE LAS VEGAS
LOEWS LAKE LAS VEGAS RESORT
RITZ-CARLTON HOTEL
LAS VEGAS WASH
DUCK CREEK TRAIL
HACIENDA
LAKE MEAD
LAKE MEAD CRUISES
HOOVER DAM

The most popular day trip from Las Vegas is to Lake Mead and Hoover Dam, about 35 miles (56km) to the southeast. Sightseeing excursions can be arranged from Las Vegas by light airplane, by helicopter, or by bus if you don't have a car. If you're traveling by road, stops can be made at Henderson and Boulder City *(see pages 235 and 236)*, where the local museums are put into context after a trip to the dam.

LAKE LAS VEGAS ⓰

Only 17 miles (27km) from the Strip and on the way to Hoover Dam is this opulent resort, a $7-billion development. The entrance is off SR147, locally known as Lake Mead Drive. The resort centers around the huge, sparkling, man-made Lake Las Vegas, and has 19 residential neighborhoods, two fine hotels, and two championship golf courses. Singer Celine Dion lived here during her residency at Caesars Palace.

The 493-room **Loews Lake Las Vegas Resort** (tel: 702-567-7000) is decorated in hues of cayenne and gold with two-story arched windows. Upper galleries overlook the Mediterranean-style courtyard. It has a spa, a fitness center, two swimming pools with cabanas, and five places to eat. Julia Roberts and Billy Crystal's movie *America's Sweethearts* was filmed here.

Ritz-Carlton

Montelago Village, at the west end of the lake, is near the **Ritz-Carlton Hotel** (tel: 702-567-4700). About 65 of the Ritz-Carlton's rooms are on a bridge over the lake, styled after the Ponte Vecchio in Florence, and with a classy shopping arcade. There are 47 suites with lake or mountain

LEFT: parking lot at Lake Mead.
RIGHT: angling is encouraged.

Time for a cruise; drinks are served onboard, but be sure to bring sunscreen.

views, and four larger apartments, each with a private entrance. The beach area, with a lawn and picnic areas, has 350 tonnes of imported white sand. A popular choice for wedding couples is the decorative pier that juts out into the lake.

Two golf courses adjoin the hotels. **Reflection Bay Golf Club,** designed by golf champion Jack Nicklaus, has lovely views of the lake. The first nine holes of **The Falls Golf Club** are desert, and the 12th hole has a great view of the Vegas Strip, glittering on the horizon.

Bird-watching

The **Las Vegas Wash**, wetlands between Lake Las Vegas and Lake Mead, is a prime spot for nature-viewing, providing a desert oasis for birds and other creatures. At the eastern end of Tropicana Avenue, a parking area gives access to the **Duck Creek Trail**, the part of the preserve that is dotted with "sitting shelters" to watch waterfowl. Bring water and sunscreen. The visitor's center is open daily 10am–4pm.

Four miles (6km) before Lake Mead, a casino-hotel called the **Hacienda** (Highway 93, Boulder City; tel: 702-293-5000 or 800-245-6380) is popular with locals, especially those from Boulder City, where gambling is not allowed.

RIGHT: Lake Mead's *Desert Princess*. **BELOW:** go boating, fishing, swimming, hiking, and camping here.

LAKE MEAD ⓱

After dusty Las Vegas, the first glimpse of Lake Mead is exhilerating.

Map on page 222

From the road and turning off just before Boulder City, the hot, desert landscape softens. A sudden curve, a hill, and from the top, the lake is ice-blue against brown rolling hills. The drive to the marina is through the fragrant national park, with more coyotes and mountain goats than people.

Warm waters

With a jagged 550-mile (885km) shoreline, for years the lake had enough water to cover the state of New York to a depth of a foot. Since the late 1990s, though, the area has been in severe drought, falling many feet in depth. It is expected to reduce still further before the drought ends.

The recreation areas on and around the lake attract 9 million visitors each year. **Lake Mead Cruises** (www.lakemeadcruises.com; tel: 702-293-6180) offers a variety of appealing excursions, and many of them will include a pick-up from a Las Vegas hotel.

The *Desert Princess* is a triple-decked paddle wheeler, and the largest boat on the lake. Throughout the year she sails on 90-minute cruises, as well as weekend dance cruises, and dinner cruises. The two-hour dinner cruise is particularly pleasant, with appetizing entrées and a well-stocked bar. After a turn-around at Hoover Dam, the return is timed for a view of the setting of the sun behind the ochre-and chocolate-colored hills.

Lake Mead's water has an average daytime temperature of 86°F (30°C) in summer, so visitors who hang beer and soda to cool over the side of a boat find that the drinks come up warmer than they went in.

ABOVE: living with water and desert. **BELOW:** ladies of the lake.

The least-crowded time to visit Hoover Dam is 9–10.30am and 3–4.45pm. January and February have the fewest tourists. Food is available near the parking garage; note there is a fee to enter the visitor center, even if you do not take a tour.

Nevada Highway 169, which is also called the **Northshore Scenic Drive**, runs for miles along the shore, then heads north toward Overton Beach and Valley of Fire State Park *(see pages 230–1)*. There are no roads on the south side.

Angling on the lake goes on year-round but a license is required. The lake has a number of camping spots and there are several businesses offering boats to rent, as well as provisions for overnight camping. Houseboats can also be rented.

HOOVER DAM ⑱

✉ www.usbr.gov/lc/hooverdam ☎ 702-494-2517 ⏲ tours 9.15am–5.15pm (summer), 9.15am–4.15pm (winter) $ charge

RIGHT: "best food by a dam site."
BELOW: Hoover Dam was dedicated by President Franklin D. Roosevelt in 1935.

Right on the Arizona-Nevada border, the Hoover Dam is anchored to the rugged volcanic walls of the Black Canyon and towers 726ft (221 meters) above the Colorado River. It was for years, and occasionally still is, known as Boulder Dam.

The reason for both names was antipathy to the 31st president, Herbert Hoover, who was instrumental in the delicate negotiations to get the project underway.

Dedicated by President Franklin D. Roosevelt in 1935, the Hoover Dam was built primarily as a flood-control measure, but with 17 generators it was able to produce enough energy to supply a million residences. The lake that resulted from filling the deep canyons behind it now supplies nearly 25 million people with water, including Las Vegans.

After the snow melts in the Rocky Mountains, the runoff pours into the 1,400-mile (2,250km) -long Colorado River, roaring through the Grand Canyon before beginning its 100-mile (160km) journey into Lake Mead. This is where the Hoover Dam halts its flow. The river heads

Map on page 222

south, providing the state border with Arizona all the way into Lake Mohave, which is blocked at the southern end by the Davis Dam.

A masterpiece of engineering, the dam has striking sculptures by Oskar J.W. Hansen, possibly the largest monumental bronzes ever cast in the US. On the two-hour **Powerplant Tour**, a million visitors a year are treated to a talk in the circular, state-of-the-art **visitor center**. After a 10-minute movie (with vintage film of the dam's construction), visitors take an elevator to a scenic viewing platform. Tickets may be purchased in advance. But tickets for the **Hoover Dam Tour** can only be purchased on-site on a first-come, first-served basis. This tour involves a lot of walking, journeying into lesser-known parts of the dam.

Colorado River Compact

Before the river could be managed, its waters had to be divided among the seven states it serves by the Colorado River Compact in 1922; Mexico was allocated a share in 1944. More than 1½ million acres (607,000 hectares) of land are irrigated in the US and Mexico by the water management.

The dam is still one of the engineering and technological wonders of the modern world. Be alert, though, that at certain times of the year, Nevada and Arizona are on different time zones. ❑

Hoover Dam took fewer than five years to complete – a remarkable feat of engineering and construction.

LEFT: the dam straddles two states which may be in different time zones.
BELOW: water roars through the Grand Canyon before arriving at Hoover Dam.

INSIGHT GUIDES

LAS VEGAS

Travel Tips

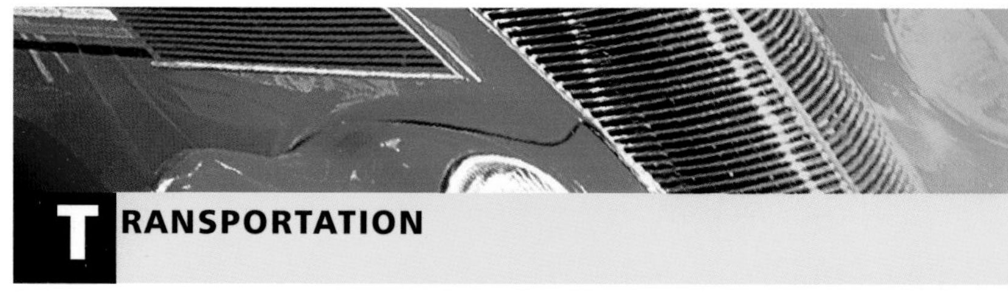

TRANSPORTATION

GETTING THERE AND GETTING AROUND

With around 39 million out-of-town visitors a year, Las Vegas offers a full range of options for getting around, including a rental-car fleet so large that it fills a vast new $167-million facility several miles from the airport. Still, fewer than one out of every 20 visitors rents a car, and if you plan to stay on the Strip or Downtown, you may not need one. Taxis, limousines, double-decker buses, and the monorail will get you around just fine any time of the day or night.

GETTING THERE

By Air

McCarran International Airport, 5757 Wayne Newton Boulevard, tel: 702-261-5211, is the hub for air travel into and out of southern Nevada. It becomes particularly busy on weekends.

By Train

There are no trains, but there are rumors that eventually high-speed services will be resumed to and from Los Angeles.

By Bus

Greyhound (tel: 800-231-2222) operates daily services to Las Vegas from most parts of the country. The Downtown depot of Greyhound is at 200 South Main Street (tel: 702-384-9561). There are several inexpensive hotels and motels within walking distance.

By Car

Around 26 percent of Las Vegas visitors are from southern California. Those who come by car usually follow Interstate 10 from LA (or I-215 from San Diego) to join I-15 north of Riverside. At Barstow, I-15 is intersected by US 58 which takes travelers from the northwest. Traffic on I-15 is fast moving, mainly through desert, and there are many accidents. From the north, the most direct route is US 95.

GETTING AROUND

Orientation

Although casinos, hotels, attractions, and activities are spread throughout the Las Vegas Valley, there are essentially two main areas where visitors will find the highest concentration of places to stay, sights to see, and things to do – the Las Vegas Strip and downtown Las Vegas. To reach the Strip, tourists need only travel south on Las Vegas Boulevard, which becomes the Strip at Sahara Avenue. Travelers from the west arrive at the Strip first.

Downtown starts at Jackie Gaughan's Plaza Hotel Casino and runs east on Fremont Street. Five blocks from the Plaza, Fremont Street intersects with Las Vegas Boulevard.

From the Airport

McCarran Airport is about 1 mile from the Strip and about 5 miles (8km) from downtown Las Vegas. A taxi ride from McCarran to the Strip costs about $10; the fare to Downtown can run up to $20. A shuttle bus service runs continually from the airport and costs much less.

Some airborne sightseeing excursions to the Grand Canyon and elsewhere take off from the

North Las Vegas Airport, 2730 Airport Drive, tel: 702-261-3800. Public transportation is limited and the North Las Vegas Airport is best reached by cab.

Taxis

All taxi service in Las Vegas is heavily regulated by the Nevada Taxicab Authority (tel: 702-486-6532). There are a limited number of companies and the service is metered. Unlike in most cities, Las Vegas cabs are prohibited by law from picking up hailing customers on the street. Not that it doesn't occasionally happen, but visitors shouldn't feel snubbed if they hail an empty cab but it doesn't stop to pick them up

However, there are nearly always lines of taxis at the airport, or by major hotels on the Strip and Downtown; also at some restaurants. Taxis can also be ordered by telephone 24 hours a day. Services include:

A Cab. Tel: 702-369-5686.
A-North Las Vegas Cab. Tel: 702-643-1041.
Ace Cab. Tel: 702-736-8383.
Checker Cab. Tel: 702-736-2227.
Deluxe Taxicab Service. Tel: 702-568-7700.
Desert Cab. Tel: 702-386-9102.
Designated Drivers. Tel: 702-531-6959.
Henderson Taxi. Tel: 702-384-2322.
Lucky Cab Company of Nevada. Tel: 702-732-4400.
Nevada Yellow Cab Corporation. Tel: 702-873-2000.
Star Cab Co. Tel: 702-873-8012.
Union Cab. Tel: 702-736-8444.
Western Cab Company. Tel: 702-736-8000.
Whittlesea Blue Cab. Tel: 702-384-6111.

Trolleys and Buses

A trolley on wheels connects many of the Strip resorts with each other but this is not well publicized; look for a sign or a bench at the side or even the back of a particular casino. The trolley operates from 9.30–1.30am on a 2-hour loop system and a trolley (supposedly) arrives every 15 minutes. Be sure to have the exact fare when you board.

Public transportation is provided by Citizen's Area Transit (CAT) buses, which can be found in the Las Vegas Valley including the towns of Boulder City, Mesquite, and Laughlin. A guide detailing routes, scheduling, and service is available by calling CAT-RIDE (tel: 702-228-7433).

CAT operates 5.30am–1.30am daily on residential routes. Some routes run 24 hours a day, and some only during peak-service hours Monday to Friday, except major US public holidays.

Helpful CAT phone numbers are 702-228-7433 (CAT-RIDE; www.catridecom) for transit information; 702-676-1500 for RTC (Regional Transportation Commission; www.rtc.co.clark.nv.us) offices; and 702-228-7433 for lost and found.

All buses have electronic fareboxes that accept dollar bills and coins, but do not give change. If you plan to transfer to another bus to complete your one-way trip, ask the driver for a transfer.

Monorail

The RTC's much-anticipated monorail system is now under construction. The first phase, completed in early 2004, extends from Tropicana Avenue to Sahara Avenue. The second, which will run from the airport to The Strip, will be completed in 2011. There is a charge to ride the monorail, and day passes are also available.

On the other side of the Strip, there is a free private monorail system that connects the Excalibur, the Luxor, and the Mandalay Bay casinos.

Sightseeing

Limousines

Cruising the Las Vegas Strip in a limousine is an exciting way to see the sights. As with taxis, the limousine service in Las Vegas is strictly regulated. However, limousines are not metered. The cost is agreed at the time of rental.

A Luxury Limo Referral Service. Tel: 702-737-8899.
Ambassador Limousine. Tel: 702-362-6200.
Bell Transportation. Tel: 702-739-7990.
BLS Limousine. Tel: 702-221-5555.
Fox Limousine Inc. Tel: 702-597-0400.
Larson's Van Service. Tel: 702-454-7335.
Las Vegas Limousines. Tel: 888-650-8383.
Lucky 7 Limousines. Tel: 702-740-4545.
On Demand Sedan and Limousine Service. Tel: 702-386-2709.
Presidential Limousine. Tel: 800-731-5577.
Star Limousine. Tel: 702-871-1112.
Western Limousine. Tel: 702-382-7100.

ABOVE: Maverick helicopter flying over the Grand Canyon.

Charters and Tours

ATV Action Tours, 180 Cassia Way, Henderson. Tel: 702-566-7400 or 888-288-5200. Off-road vehicle tours to Red Rock Canyon, Death Valley, and others.
Bell Trans/Limousines and Buses, PO Box 15333. Tel: 702-385-5466 or 800-274-7433. www.bell-trans.com.
Coach USA, 795 East Tropicana. Tel: 702-384-1234 or 800-634-6579. www.paulina.salen @coachusa.com
Greyhound Charter Service, 200 South Main Street. Tel: 800-454-2487.
Lake Mead Cruises, 490 Horsepower Road #B, Boulder City. Tel: 702-293-6180.
Pink Jeep Tours, 3629 West Hacienda Avenue. Tel: 702-895-6777 or 888-900-4480.
Sweetours, 6363 South Pecos, Suite 106. Tel: 702-456-9200.
Travelways, 1455 East Tropicana Avenue. Tel: 702-739-7714.
Triple J Tours, 4455 Cameron Street. Tel: 702-261-0131.

Air Tours

Air Vegas Airlines, 2642 Airport Drive, North Las Vegas. Tel: 702-736-3599 or 800-255-7474. www.airvegas.com
Grand Canyon Discount, 2990 East Oquendo Road. Tel: 702-629-7776 or 800-871-1030. www.gcflight.com
Heli USA Flights, 275 East Tropicana Avenue, Suite 200. Tel: 702-736-8787 or 800-359-8727. www.heliusa.com. Tours over the Strip, to the Grand Canyon, and other destinations.
Look Tours, 2642 Airport Drive. Tel: 702-233-1627 or 800-566-5868. www.atour4u.com
Maverick Helicopters, 6075 Las Vegas Blvd South. Tel: 702-261-0007. www.maverickhelicopter.com. Custom flights over the Strip and the Grand Canyon.
Papillon Grand Canyon Helicopters, 245 East Tropicana Avenue. Tel: 702-736-7243 or 888-635-7272. www.papillon.com
Scenic Airlines, 2705 Airport Drive, North Las Vegas. Tel: 702-638-3300 or 800-634-6801. www.scenic.com
Sundance Helicopters, 5596 Haven. Tel: 702-736-0606 or 800-653-1881. www.helicoptour.com

Car Rental

Many rental-car companies have outlets at McCarran International Airport on the aptly named Rent A Car Road.

There is little difference between Nevada driving regulations and other places in the US. All speed limits are posted, seat belts are required and their use is strictly enforced, and drivers can turn right on a red light.

One major difference about Nevada roads is the center lane, which is not used for travel but for left-hand turns only. Nearly every major hotel has free valet parking with an attendant who, although optional, is usually rewarded with a tip of $1 or $2 per car every time you park.

Alamo Rent-A-Car, 6855 Bermuda Road. Tel: 702-263-3030 or 800-327-9633. www.goalamo.com
Avis, 5164 Rent A Car Rd. Tel: 702-261-5595 or 800-831-2847.
Budget Car and Truck Rental, 5188 Paradise Road. Tel: 702-736-1212 or 800-527-0770. www.budgetvegas.com
Dollar Rent-A-Car, 5301 Rent A Car Road. Tel: 702-739-8408 or 800-800-4000. www.dollarcar.com
Enterprise Rent-A-Car, 5032 Palo Verde Dr. Tel: 702-795-8842 or 800-736-7222.
Express Rent A Car, 3200 South Rancho Dr. Tel: 702-795-4008.
Hertz Rent A Car, 5300 Rent A Car Road. Tel: 702-736-4900 or 800-654-3131. www.hertz.com
Lloyd's Rent-a-Car, 3951 Las Vegas Blvd South. Tel: 702-736-2663 or 800-654-7037. www.xpressrac.com
National Car Rental, 5233 Rent A Car Road. Tel: 702-261-5391 or 800-227-7368. www.nationalcar.com
Rent-A-Vette, 5021 Swenson St. Tel: 702-736-2592.
Rent A Wreck, 2310 Las Vegas Boulevard South. Tel: 702-474-0037 or 800-227-0292.
Thrifty Car Rental, 376 East Warm Springs Rd. Tel: 702-896-7600 or 800-367-2277.

Motorcycles

Eagle Rider-Las Vegas Motorcycle Rentals, 5182 South Arville St. Tel: 702-876-8687. www.lasvegas.eaglerider.com
Las Vegas Harley-Davidson, 2605 South Eastern Avenue. Tel: 702-431-8500. www.lvhd.com
Street Eagle Las Vegas, 6330 South Pecos Road. Tel: 702-346 8490 or 877-373-2601. www.streeteagle.com

ACCOMMODATIONS

WHERE TO STAY

Las Vegas hotel rooms come in all sizes, price ranges, and degrees of luxury. In general, the best (and priciest) rooms are in large resorts on or near the Strip, with every amenity imaginable, while more basic and affordable accommodations are available Downtown and in suburban areas such as Henderson. Lower-priced rooms can also be booked in the few older hotels that survive from Las Vegas's early days, including the Riviera, the Tropicana, the Imperial Palace, and the Flamingo.

What to Know

Las Vegas hotel rates vary enormously but one constant is that hotel rooms cost more on weekends. Rates also go up and down depending on demand; it's possible for a room rate to vary between the time you call in the morning and later on that same day, so if you're staying on the Strip, for example, you might want to inquire several times.

Astonishing deals are available, but if you're not on-site, it may be necessary to consult the travel pages of a US newspaper – the Sunday edition of the *Los Angeles Times* is good – to find them. This is also where you will find ads listing free 800 telephone numbers and such websites as vegas.com and hotels.com which can offer a choice of as many as 100 hotels from $45 per night. It's definitely worth shopping around.

BELOW: Caesars Palace.

Booking a Room

Hotels are designed for different demographics. A few places, such as Circus Circus and Excalibur, cater especially to families with young children; others, like the Hard Rock Hotel, draw a rowdy young adult crowd; still others, like the Bellagio, appeal to a more mature, dignified clientele. In the convention center and airport areas, hotels tend to appeal to business travelers and offer fewer frills like spas. Most hotels have smoking and non-smoking rooms. Other factors to think about are on what floor you prefer to stay and whether you want a view of, say, the Strip or the distant mountains.

ACCOMMODATIONS LISTINGS

THE STRIP

HOTELS

As room rates vary, the dollar signs here are an approximate guide only; sometimes it's possible to bargain on the spot before check-in. For more details on individual casino hotels, *see pages 115–217.*

Bally's Las Vegas
3645 Las Vegas Boulevard South
Tel: 702-739-4111 or 800-634-3434
[p274, C2] **$$$**
www.ballyslv.com

Bellagio
3600 Las Vegas Boulevard South
Tel: 702-693-7111 or 888-987-6667
[p274, B2] **$$$$**
www.bellagio.com

Bill's Gamblin' Hall and Saloon
3595 Las Vegas Boulevard South
Tel: 702-732-2100 or 888-227-2279
[p274, C1] **$$$**
www.billslasvegas.com

Caesars Palace
3570 Las Vegas Boulevard South
Tel: 702-731-7110 or 800-634-6661
[p274, B1] **$$$**
www.caesars.com

Circus Circus
2880 Las Vegas Boulevard South
Tel: 702-734-0410 or 800-444-2472
[p276, B2] **$$**
www.circuscircus.com

Excalibur
3850 Las Vegas Boulevard South
Tel: 702-597-7777 or 800-937-7777
[p275, C3] **$$**
www.excaliburcasino.com

Flamingo Las Vegas
3555 Las Vegas Boulevard South
Tel: 702-733-3111 or 888-902-9929
[p274, C1] **$$$**
www.flamingolv.com

Four Seasons
3960 Las Vegas Boulevard South
Tel: 702-632-5000 or 877-632-5000
[p275, D4] **$$$$**
www.fourseasons.com

BELOW: most resorts have at least two pools.

Harrah's
3475 Las Vegas Boulevard South
Tel: 702-369-5000 or 800-HARRAHS
[p274, B1] **$$**
www.harrahs.com

Imperial Palace
3535 Las Vegas Boulevard South
Tel: 702-731-3311 or 800-634-6441
[p274, B1] **$$**
www.imperialpalace.com

Las Vegas Hilton
3000 Paradise Road
Tel: 702-732-5111 or 800-732-7117
[p277, C2] **$$$**
www.lv-hilton.com

Luxor
3900 Las Vegas Boulevard South
Tel: 702-262-4000 or 800-288-1000
[p275, C4] **$$**
www.luxor.com

Mandalay Bay
3950 Las Vegas Boulevard South
Tel: 702-632-7777 or 877-632-7800
[p275, D4] **$$$**
www.mandalaybay.com

MGM Grand
3799 Las Vegas Boulevard South
Tel: 702-891-7777 or 877-880-0880
[p275, C3] **$$$**
www.mgmgrand.com

The Mirage
3400 Las Vegas Boulevard South
Tel: 702-791-7111 or 800-374-9000
[p274, B1] **$$$**
www.mirage.com

Monte Carlo
3770 Las Vegas Boulevard South
Tel: 702-730-7777

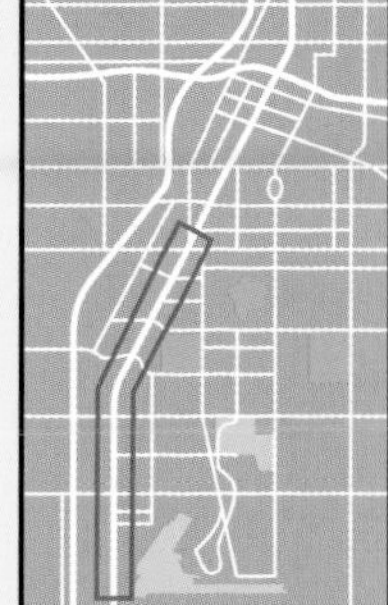

[p274, C3] **$$$**
www.monte-carlo.com

New York New York
3790 Las Vegas Boulevard South
Tel: 702-740-6969 or 800-689-1797
[p275, C3] **$$$**
www.nynyhotelcasino.com

Paris Las Vegas
3655 Las Vegas Boulevard South
Tel: 702-946-7000 or 888-266-5687
[p274, C2] **$$$**
www.paris-lv.com

The Palms
4321 West Flamingo Road
Tel: 702-942-7777
[p274, A3] **$$$**
www.palms.com

Planet Hollywood
3667 Las Vegas Boulevard South
Tel: 702-785-5555 or 866-919-7472
[p274, C2] **$$$**
www.planethollywoodresort.com

Riviera Hotel and Casino
2901 Las Vegas Boulevard South
Tel: 702-734-5110 or 800-634-6753
[p276, B3] **$$**
www.theriviera.com

Stratosphere Tower Hotel and Casino
2000 Las Vegas Boulevard South
Tel: 702-380-7777 or 800-998-6937
[p276, B1] **$$**
www.stratlv.com

(TI) Treasure Island
3300 Las Vegas Boulevard South
Tel: 702-894-7111 or 800-944-7444
[p276, B4] **$$$**
www.treasureisland.com

Tropicana Resort and Casino
3801 Las Vegas Boulevard South
Tel: 702-739-2222 or 800-634-4000
[p275, C3] **$$**
www.tropicanalv.com

Trump International Hotel
2000 Fashion Show Drive
Tel: 702-982-0000
[p276, B3]
$$$$
www.trumplasvegashotel.com

The Venetian
3355 Las Vegas Boulevard South
Tel: 702-414-1000
[p274, B1] **$$$$**
www.venetian.com

Wynn Las Vegas
3131 Las Vegas Boulevard South
Tel: 702-770-7000 or 877-321-WYNN
[p276, B3] **$$$$**
www.wynnlasvegas.com

MOTELS

Howard Johnson
1401 Las Vegas Boulevard
Tel: 702-388-0301 or 800-325-2344
[p278, B4]
Near the convention center; with a pool. **$–$$**

King Albert Motel
185 Albert Avenue
Tel: 702-732-1555 or 800-553-7753
[p275, C1]
Pool, kitchenettes, and a laundromat. **$**

Motel 6
195 East Tropicana Avenue
Tel: 702-798-0728
[p275, D3]
Three blocks from the Strip, near the airport. Pool, plenty of parking, and a food shop. **$**

DOWNTOWN

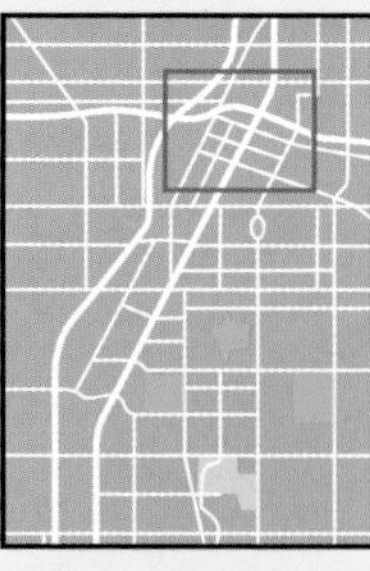

CASINO HOTELS

Binion's Gambling Hall
129 Fremont Street
Tel: 702-392-1600 or 800-237-6537
[p278, B2]
www.binions.com
Shopping, pool, seven restaurants, buffet, room service, and cable TV. **$**

California Hotel and Casino
12 Ogden Avenue
Tel: 702-385-1222 or 800-634-6505
[p278, B1]
www.thecal.com
Hawaiian decor. Shopping, swimming pool, concierge desk, three restaurants, room service, and cable TV. **$**

El Cortez Hotel and Casino
600 East Fremont Street
Tel: 702-385-5200 or 800-634-6703
[p278, B2]
www.elcortezhotelcasino.com
Salon, huge casino, concierge desk, restaurant, and room service. One of the last places in Vegas with penny slot machines. **$**

Fitzgeralds Casino and Hotel
301 Fremont Street
Tel: 702-388-2400 or 800-724-5824
[p278, B2]
www.fitzgeralds.com
Rooms with computer ports, safe, and 25-inch TVs with cable and movies, airport shuttle, four eating places, buffet, room service. **$**

Four Queens Casino and Hotel
202 East Fremont Street
Tel: 702-385-4011 or 800-634-6045
[p278, B2]
www.fourqueens.com
Two restaurants, room service, and cable TV. Good slot machines. **$**

Fremont Hotel and Casino
200 East Fremont Street
Tel: 702-385-3232 or 800-634-6460
[p278, B2]
www.fremontcasino.com
Shopping, five restaurants, room service, and cable TV. **$**

PRICE CATEGORIES

Rates are for a hotel room, using the lowest standard rate. Suites start at a higher rate.
$ = under $50
$$ = $50–$100
$$$ = $100–$150
$$$$ = over $150

TRANSPORTATION
ACCOMMODATIONS
SHOPPING
ACTIVITIES
A – Z

Golden Gate Hotel and Casino
1 Fremont Street
Tel: 702-385-1906 or 800-426-1906
[p278, B2]
www.goldengatecasino.com
Built in 1906, the Golden Gate dates back to the early days. Noted for its 99¢ shrimp cocktails. Two restaurants, cable TV, and a coffee-maker in each room. Sun–Thur **$**, Fri–Sat **$$**

Golden Nugget
129 East Fremont Street
Tel: 702-385-7111 or 800-864-5336
[p278, B2]
www.goldennugget.com
The most upscale of all the Downtown properties. Shopping, salon, exercise facilities, swimming pool, airport shuttle, five restaurants, buffet, room service, cable TV. **$$**

Las Vegas Club Casino Hotel
18 East Fremont Street
Tel: 702-385-1664 or 800-634-6532
[p278, B2]
www.vegasclubcasino.net
Sports-themed hotel at the corner of Main Street. Concierge desk, three restaurants, room service, cable TV. **$**

Main Street Station Brewery and Hotel
200 North Main Street
Tel: 702-387-1896 or 800-713-8933
[p278, B1]
www.mainstreetcasino.com
Casino with antique woodwork and stained-glass windows. Concierge desk, three restaurants, cable TV. **$**

Plaza Las Vegas
1 Main Street
Tel: 702-386-2110 or 800-634-6575
[p278, B1]
www.plazahotelcasino.com
The Plaza is a few steps from the Greyhound station. Exercise facilities, swimming pool, wedding chapel, airport shuttle, concierge desk, three restaurants, and cable TV in every room. **$**

MOTELS

Crest Budget Motel
207 North 6th Street
Tel: 702-382-5642
[p278, B1]
Complementary coffee and breakfast, cable TV, free and pay-for movies, microwave oven. **$**

Days Inn Downtown
707 East Fremont
Tel: 702-388-1400
[p278, B2]
Slot parlor, elevated pool, sundeck, and a restaurant. 24-hour front desk. **$**

Downtowner Motel
129 North 8th Street
Tel: 702-384-1441
[p278, C1]
http://downtownermotellv.com
Newly remodeled motel; kitchenettes; free donuts and coffee, and friendly service. **$**

BELOW: the Golden Gate is the oldest hotel and casino in Las Vegas.

BEYOND THE STRIP

HOTELS

Alexis Park
375 East Harmon Avenue
Tel: 702-796-3330 or 800-582-2228
[p275, D2]
www.alexispark.com
This non-gambling all-suite hotel is quiet and elegant, with 20 acres (8 hectares) of beautifully landscaped grounds, three swimming pools, a fitness center, and a day spa. **$$$**

Amerisuites Hotel
4520 Paradise Road
Tel: 702-369-3366 or 800-833-1516
[p275, E1]
www.amerisuites.com
Located half a mile from the airport, amenities include exercise facilities, business services, a pool, airport shuttle, concierge desk, cable television and VCR, data port, and a coffee maker in each room. **$$**

Arizona Charlie's Hotel and Casino
740 South Decatur Boulevard
Tel: 702-258-5200 or 800-342-2695
[off map]
www.azcharlies.com
The original Arizona Charlie's (there's another on the way to Boulder City), located about a mile west of the Strip and about 11 miles (18km) from the airport. Wedding chapel, swimming pool, airport shuttle, five restaurants, buffet, and cable TV. **$**

The Artisan
1501 West Sahara Avenue
Tel: 702-214-4000 or 800-554-4092
[p276, A2]
www.theartisanhotel.com
Small, elegant European-style boutique hotel has posh suites individually decorated with original artwork. No casino nearby, but there's a swimming pool, café and bar. **$$$**

Best Western Mardi Gras Inn
3500 Paradise Road
Tel: 702-731-2020 or 800-634-6501
[p277, C3]
www.mardigrasinn.com
About 3 miles (4km) from the airport, the hotel has a casino, salon, business services, swimming pool, airport shuttle, concierge desk, cable TV, and data port. **$$**

Cancun Resort
8335 Las Vegas Boulevard South
Tel: 702-614-6200 or 800-597-2914
[location off map]
http://pacificmonarchresorts.com
A non-gaming property located 5 miles (8km) from the airport south of the Strip, Cancun Resort has a penthouse suite and villas with private balconies. Services include exercise facilities, swimming pool, concierge desk, cable TV, VCR, Jacuzzi, and data port. Call for rates.

The Carriage House
105 East Harmon Avenue
Tel: 702-798-1020 or 800-221-2301
[p275, C2]
www.carriagehouselasvegas.com
Condominium suite hotel, one block from the Strip near the MGM Grand. This non-gaming hotel has in-room movies, kitchenettes, pool, whirlpool, sports court, airport shuttle, concierge desk, restaurant, room service, and cable TV. **$$$**

Convention Center Marriott Suites
325 Convention Center Drive
Tel: 702-650-2000 or 800-228-9290
[p276, C3]
www.marriott.com
A comfortable hotel for business travelers and tourists who prefer suites. Three miles (5km) from the airport, it has exercise facilities, business services, swimming pool, concierge desk, cable TV, restaurant, and data port. **$$$**

Courtyard Las Vegas Convention Center
3275 Paradise Road
Tel: 702-791-3600 or 800-661-1064
[p277, C3]
www.marriott.com

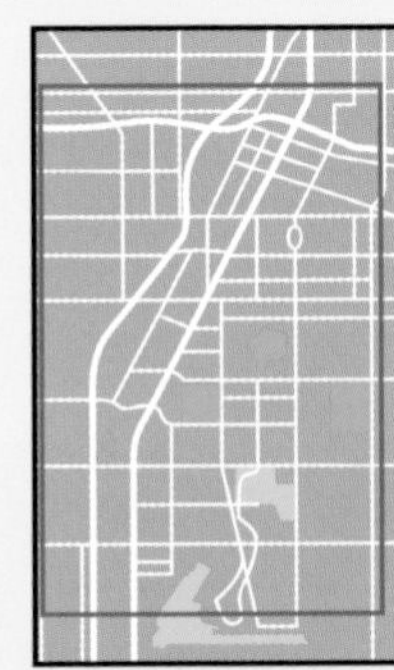

Opposite the convention center, this Marriott offers meeting rooms, exercise facilities, business services, pool and spa, concierge desk, cable TV, and a restaurant. It has no gaming. **$$$**

Doubletree Club
7250 Pollock Drive
Tel: 702-948-4000 or 800-222-TREE
[off map]
www.doubletree.com
Non-gaming hotel with free shuttle to the Strip and airport. Fitness center, pool, on-site bakery, café. **$–$$**

Embassy Suites Convention Center
3600 Paradise Road
Tel: 702-893-8000 or 800-362-2779
[p277, D3]
www.eslvcc.com
Located just three blocks from the

PRICE CATEGORIES

Rates are for a hotel room, using the lowest standard rate. Suites start at a higher rate.
$ = under $50
$$ = $50–$100
$$$ = $100–$150
$$$$ = over $150

convention center, this non-gaming, all-suites venue has a restaurant, room service, shopping, exercise facilities, swimming pool, cable TV and data port. **$$$**

Emerald Springs – Holiday Inn
325 East Flamingo Road
Tel: 702-732-9100 or 800-732-7889
[off map p277, D4]
www.holidayinnlasvegas.com
An attractive boutique non-gaming hotel, 2 miles (3km) from the airport; with exercise facilities, business services, pool, airport shuttle, restaurant, cable TV. **$$**

Gold Coast Hotel and Casino
4000 West Flamingo Road
Tel: 702-367-7111 or 800-331-5334
[p274, A2]
www.coastcasinos.com
At the Gold Coast, there's a bowling center, three lounges, a dancehall, and a theater. The guest rooms are comfortable and affordable. **$$**

Greek Isles Hotel and Casino
305 Convention Center Drive
Tel: 702-952-8000 or 800-633-1777
[p276, C3]
www.greekislesvegas.com
Attractive Greek decor with a taverna. There's a showroom and comedy lounge, wedding chapel, exercise facilities, business services, pool, airport shuttle, restaurant, cable TV, and data port. **$$**

Hampton Inn
7100 Cascade Valley Court
Tel: 702-360-5700 or 800-426-7866
[off map]
www.hamptoninn.com
Tucked away in the northwest portion of Las Vegas, about 15 miles (8km) from the airport. A non-gaming venue, it has business services, pool, and cable TV. **$$**

Hard Rock
4455 Paradise Road
Tel: 702-693-5000 or 800-693-7625
[p275, D1]
www.hardrockhotel.com
Three blocks from the Strip. Everyone knows the Hard Rock. This one has a beach club, spa, some luxury suites, and music memorabilia. **$$**

Hooters Casino Hotel
115 East Tropicana Avenue
Tel: 702-739-9000 or 866-584-6687
[p275, D3]
www.hchvegas.com
In keeping with the identity of its chain of restaurants, Hooters employs lots of big-breasted women, makes visual jokes about the same, and offers poolside events. **$$**

Las Vegas Hilton Hotel and Casino
3000 South Paradise Road
Tel: 702-732-5111 or 888-732-7117
[p277, C2]
www.lv-hilton.com
Popular with conventioneers, as the hotel is attached to the convention center by a walkway. **$$$**

The Orleans Hotel and Casino
4500 West Tropicana Avenue
Tel: 702-365-7111 or 800-675-3267
[p274, A4]
www.orleanscasino.com
Mardi Gras-themed hotel, offering New Orleans style with salon, exercise facilities, business services, pool, Jacuzzi, concierge desk, eight restaurants and buffet, room service, cable TV, and data port. **$$**

Renaissance Las Vegas
3400 Paradise Road
Tel: 702-784-5700 or 800-750-0980
[p277, C3]
www.renaissancelasvegas.com
Big, bright-colored rooms with generous work spaces make this hotel near the convention center a good choice for business travelers. No casino.

The Rio All-Suites Hotel and Casino
3700 West Flamingo Road
Tel: 702-252-7777 or 866-746-7671
[p274, A2]
www.harrahs.com
Good value off the Strip, this huge casino-hotel has large, spacious rooms and one of the best buffets in town, the Carnival World. Be sure to ask for a room in the Masquerade Tower. **$$$**

St Tropez – All Suite Hotel
455 East Harmon Avenue
Tel: 702-369-5400 or 800-666-5400
[p275, D1]
www.sttropezlasvegas.com
A luxurious non-gaming all-suites hotel near the airport. Shopping, exercise facilities, business services, pool, airport shuttle, concierge desk, a restaurant, cable TV, VCR, data port, and coffee hour. **$$$$**

BELOW: the Rio has one of the best buffets in town.

Silverton Hotel and Casino
3333 Blue Diamond Road
Tel: 702-263-7777 or 800-588-7711
[off map]
www.silvertoncasino.com
Near the airport, a Western-themed hotel with cocktail lounge and entertainment. Pool, restaurants and buffet, room service, and cable TV. Kitchenettes, laundromat. **$**

BEYOND LAS VEGAS

HOTELS

Towards Boulder

Arizona Charlie's Boulder Hotel and Casino
4575 Boulder Highway
Tel: 702-951-5900 or 800-362-4040
www.azcharlies.com
East of Las Vegas, part way to Boulder City and Hoover Dam. About 6 miles (10km) from the airport, amenities include a casino, airport shuttle, buffet, five restaurants, and cable TV in each room. **$**

Boulder Station Hotel Casino
4111 Boulder Highway
Tel: 702-432-7777 or 800-683-7777
www.boulderstation.com
Boulder Station is about 15 miles (25km) from the airport. It has movie theaters, childcare, business services, swimming pool, airport shuttle, concierge desk, 12 restaurants, buffet, room service, and cable TV. **$$**

Sam's Town Hotel and Gambling Hall
5111 Boulder Highway
Tel: 702-456-7777 or 800-634-6371
www.samstown.com
On Boulder Highway 7 miles (11km) east of the airport. A beautiful, huge atrium offers patio dining, waterfalls, and a nightly laser show. Pool, eight restaurants and buffet, cable TV, and childcare. **$$**

Boulder City

Boulder Dam Hotel
1305 Arizona Street
Tel: 702-293-3510
www.boulderdamhotel.com
This quaint, historic and centrally located hotel offering bed and breakfast has a restaurant, room service, shop, a charming museum, exercise facilities, cable TV, and data ports. **$$**

Hacienda Hotel and Casino
US Highway 93
Tel: 702-293-5000 or 800-245-6380
www.haciendaonline.com
Three restaurants, 24-hour shop, buffet, swimming pool, theater, Jacuzzi, and helicopter rides. **$$**

Henderson

Fiesta Henderson Casino Hotel
777 West Lake Mead Drive
Tel: 702-558-7000 or 888-899-7770
www.fiestacasino.com
South-of-the-border theme hotel about 10 miles (16km) from the airport. The Fiesta has a swimming pool, Jacuzzi, three bar-lounges, restaurants and buffet, cable television, and data port in each room. **$**

Residence Inn – Henderson Green Valley
2190 Olympic Avenue
Tel: 702-434-2700 or 800-331-3131
www.marriot.com
This is an all-suite hotel with no gaming facilities located 5 miles (8km) from the airport. There's an excellent sports court suitable for basketball, tennis, or volleyball; exercise facilities; a swimming pool; airport shuttle; cable television and

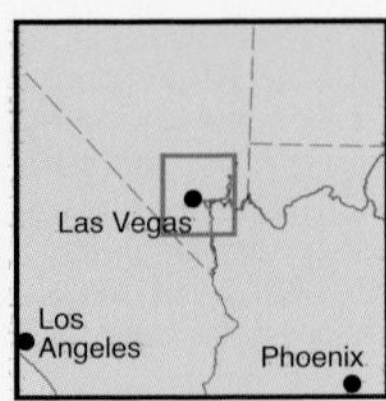

VCR; as well as a data port in each room. **$$$**

Sunset Station Hotel
1301 West Sunset Road
Tel: 702-547-7777 or 888-786-7389
www.sunsetstation.com
Mediterranean style with a bar based on the style of Spanish architect Gaudí. Eight miles (13km) from the airport, this hotel has a casino, a microbrewery, multiscreen movie theater and an outdoor amphitheater. **$$–$$$**

PRICE CATEGORIES

Rates are for a hotel room, using the lowest standard rate. Suites start at a higher rate.
$ = under $50
$$ = $50–$100
$$$ = $100–$150
$$$$ = over $150

Shopping

Best Buys

In earlier times, Las Vegas offered few shopping opportunities for fear these would distract visitors from the gaming tables. But eventually, casino resort managers realized the wisdom of giving winners plenty of opportunities to spend their newly won cash. Now, with hundreds of designer boutiques and several malls, Vegas has become one of the best places for upscale shopping. It's hard to beat the city's variety, either, as there are budget-conscious outlet malls and chain stores, too. *For more shopping, see pages 100–1.*

Shopping Malls

Some of the best shopping in Las Vegas can be found in the huge malls, many of which include entertainment and dining facilities. At the time of going to press, all the stores here have premises in the mall or shopping arcade listed, but if you're interested in a specific shop, be sure to call ahead first or check the web to make sure the place has not moved. Opening hours are approximate, as they vary store by store.

Boulevard Mall
3528 South Maryland Parkway (between Flamingo and Desert Inn roads)
Tel: 702-732-8949
www.boulevardmall.com
10am–9pm. This standard shopping mall has 140 stores, anchored by Macy's, Sears, JC Penney and Dillards.

Chinatown Plaza
4255 Spring Mountain Road
Tel: 702-221-8448
www.lvchinatown.com
Chinese background music and Tong Dynasty architecture set the stage for browsing at jade jewelry, arts and herbs. There are also a large Asian supermarket, a Chinese bookstore, and 10 restaurants.

Fashion Outlets of Las Vegas
Primm, Nevada (around 35 miles/56km south of Las Vegas on Interstate 15)
Tel: 702-874-1400
www.fashionoutletlasvegas.com
10am–8pm. Free shuttles take shoppers from the MGM Grand, Miracle Mile, and Fashion Show Mall to this mall with over 100 designer outlets.

Fashion Show Mall
3200 Las Vegas Boulevard South (at Spring Mountain Road)
Tel: 702-784-7000
www.thefashionshow.com
10am–9pm. Right on the Strip, Las Vegas's largest shopping complex has 240 quality shops and department stores as well as 10 restaurants.

Forum Shops
3500 Las Vegas Boulevard South (by Caesars Palace)
Tel: 702-893-4800
www.simon.com
10am–11pm. This visually spectacular mall with huge Roman columns and an aquarium houses 160 upscale boutiques and shops.

Galleria at Sunset
1300 West Sunset Road (intersection of Sunset/Stephanie roads, Henderson)
Tel: 702-434-0202
www.galleriaatsunset.com
10am–9pm. This suburban mall has JC Penney and Mervyn's department stores and a standard array of shops from Eddie Bauer to Victoria's Secret.

Grand Canal Shoppes
3355 Las Vegas Boulevard South (in The Venetian Hotel/Casino)
Tel: 702-414-4500
www.venetian.com
10am–11pm. Lavish Italian Renaissance decor sets the stage

for a wide selection of stores including several fine-art galleries and no less than 14 jewelers.

Hawaiian Marketplace
3743 Las Vegas Boulevard South
Tel: 702-795-2247
10am–10pm. Though there's not much Polynesian except the decor at this theme mall, kids will like the animatronic birds and the Tahitian dance troupe.

Las Vegas Outlet Center
7400 Las Vegas Boulevard South at Warm Springs Road
Tel: 702-896-5599
www.lasvegasoutletcenter.com
10am–8pm. One of the world's largest indoor factory outlet malls has more than 130 famous-name stores. The double-decker Deuce city bus will take you there from the Strip.

Las Vegas Premium Outlets
875 S. Grand Central Parkway
Tel: 702-474-7500
www.premiumoutlets.com/lasvegas
10am–9pm. Under the same management as the Las Vegas Outlet Center but with surprisingly little overlap, this upscale outdoor mall recently expanded to 150 shops.

Miracle Mile Shops
3667 Las Vegas Boulevard South
Tel: 702-866-0710
www.harmongrp.com
10am–11pm. Adjoining the Planet Hollywood Hotel, this modernistic steel and glass mall has 170 stores, including many from European chains and others whose names are not instantly familiar.

Town Square
6605 Las Vegas Boulevard South
702-269-5005
www.townsquarelasvegas.com
10am–9.30pm. Architecture modeled after great American and European cities is the star at this recently opened mall with an outstanding kids playground, a picnic area, and a concert stage. Voted Best Mall, 2008 by the *Las Vegas Review-Journal*'s readers.

RESORT SHOPPING

Most of the larger resort casinos have shopping areas that provide guests with almost everything they'll need, but a boutique in a hotel other than your own may have the perfect souvenir to remind you of your Las Vegas visit. Most of the shops open at 10am, and close 8–10pm.

Appian Way
Caesars Palace, 3570 Las Vegas Boulevard South
Tel: 702-731-7110
Some of the finest boutiques and shops, including Cartier jewelry.

Avenue Shoppes
Bally's, 3645 Las Vegas Boulevard South
Tel: 702-739-4111
www.ballyslv.com.

BELOW: the Forum Shops at Caesars Palace.

ABOVE: Grand Canal serenade.

Specialty clothing and jewelry stores. There's also a wedding chapel and three restaurants.

Carnaval Court
Harrah's, 3475 Las Vegas Boulevard South
Tel: 702-369-5000
www.harrahs.com
The Art of Gaming, Carnaval Corner, Jackpot, and Ghirardelli Chocolates.

Castle Walk
3850 Las Vegas Boulevard South
Tel: 702-597-7777
www.excaliburcasino.com
Excalibur Shoppe, Castle Souvenirs, Gifts of the Kingdom, Spirit Shoppe, Dragon's Lair, and Desert Shoppe. Good for children's souvenirs.

Circus Circus Shops
2880 Las Vegas Boulevard South
Tel: 702-734-0410
www.circuscircus.com
Marshall Rousso, and other stores featuring gifts, clothing, ceramics, jewelry, and souvenirs. Good for kids' stuff.

Las Vegas Hilton Stores
3000 Paradise Road
Tel: 702-732-5111
www.lvhilton.com
Kidz Clubhouse, Candy Mania, Paradise Gift Shop, Landau Jewelers, Charisma Apparel and Footwear, Sports Zone Arcade, Ozone Business, and Regis Salon.

Clothes Chart

The chart listed below gives a comparison of United States, European, and United Kingdom clothes sizes. It is always a good idea, however, to try on any article before buying it, as sizes between manufacturers can vary enormously.

• Women's Dresses/Suits

US	Continental	UK
6	38/34N	8/30
8	40/36N	10/32
10	42/38N	12/34
12	44/40N	14/36
14	46/42N	16/38
16	48/44N	18/40

• Women's Shoes

US	Continental	UK
4½	36	3
5½	37	4
6½	38	5
7½	39	6
8½	40	7
9½	41	8
10½	42	9

• Men's Suits

US	Continental	UK
34	44	34
—	46	36
38	48	38
—	50	40
42	52	42
—	54	44
46	56	46

• Men's Shirts

US	Continental	UK
14	36	14
14½	37	14½
15	38	15
15½	39	15½
16	40	16
16½	41	16½
17	42	17

• Men's Shoes

US	Continental	UK
6½	—	6
7½	40	7
8½	41	8
9½	42	9
10½	43	10
11½	44	11

Palms Promenade
JW Marriott Las Vegas Resort, 221 North Rampart Boulevard
Tel: 702-869-8777
www.marriott.com
Jewelry by Berger and Son, eyewear by Occhiali, the Markman Gallery, and Tolstoys.

The Shoppes at The Palazzo
The Palazzo, 3377 Las Vegas Boulevard South
Tel: 702-414-4500
Upscale and vast, with almost ½ million sq ft (46,450 sq meters) of high-end retail space, the Shoppes are anchored by a second location of Barney's New York. There's live music and a 20ft (6-meter) waterfall.

Shopping le Boulevard
Paris Las Vegas, 3655 Las Vegas Boulevard South
Tel: 702-967-7000
www.parislasvegas.com
Upscale French retail outlets fronting quaint cobblestoned streets.

The Shopping Promenade
(TI) Treasure Island, 3300 Las Vegas Boulevard South
Tel: 702-894-7111
www.treasureisland.com
Toiletries to designer fashions.

Starlane Walk
MGM Grand, 3799 Las Vegas Boulevard South
Tel: 702-891-7777
www.mgmgrand.com
Emerald City, Houdini Magic, Harley-Davidson, Pearl Factory.

The Street of Dreams
Monte Carlo, 3400 Las Vegas Boulevard South
Tel: 702-791-7777
www.montecarlo.com
Fine jewelry, designer clothing, eyewear, and souvenir boutiques.

The Street of Shops
Mirage, 3400 Las Vegas Boulevard South
Tel: 702-791-7111
www.mirage.com
Childrenswear, swimwear, jewelry, casual wear, and designer attire.

Tower Shops
Stratosphere, 2000 Las Vegas Boulevard South
Tel: 702-380-7777
Everything from gifts to clothing, souvenirs to novelties.

Via Bellagio
Bellagio, 3600 Las Vegas Boulevard South
Tel: 702-693-7111
www.bellagio.com
Chanel, Armani, Prada, Tiffany, Moschino, Hermes, Gucci.

Wynn Esplanade
Wynn Las Vegas, 3131 Las Vegas Boulevard South
Tel: 702-770-7000
This may not be the only ultra-elite shopping complex on the Strip, but it's the only one with its own Ferrari-Maserati dealership.

Specialist Shops

The Attic
1018 South Main Street
Tel: 388-4088
Massive collection of vintage clothes and knick-knacks,and located in the up-and-coming Arts District.

Bonanza Gifts
2460 Las Vegas Boulevard South
Tel: 702-385-7359
www.worldslargestgiftshop.com

Left over from classic 1950s Las Vegas, the "World's Largest Gift Shop" is the place to chuckle over unbelievably tacky curios, like fake bullet holes, $1 million bills, and rubber chickens.

Cactus Joe's Blue Diamond Nursery
12740 Blue Diamond Road
702-875-1968
A must-see stop near Red Rock Canyon, the 9-acre (3.6-hectare) desert garden is filled with native Southwestern cactuses, succulents, agaves, and Joshua trees. You can buy a cactus and have it shipped home.

Gamblers' Book Shop
630 South 11th Street
Tel: 702-382-7555
See page 212.

Gamblers General Store
800 South Main Street
Tel: 702-382-9903
Slot machines, videos, and everything the not-so-discerning gambling fanatic might desire.

The Manilow Store
Las Vegas Hilton,
3000 Paradise Road
Tel: 702-732-5755
Barry Manilow fans can buy memorabilia ranging from DVDs and sheet music to bobblehead dolls at this shop in the hotel where the crooner performs. There's a sound booth where you can record your own version of a Manilow song, too.

Rainbow Feather Company
1036 South Main Street
Tel: 702-598-0988

Specializing in the feather boas, fans, and headpieces worn by Las Vegas showgirls, this feather-dying factory and retail shop also sells feather jewelry and angel wings.

Serge's Showgirl Wigs
953 East Sahara Avenue
Tel: 702-732-1015
www.showgirlwigs.com
The largest wig emporium in the US stocks everything from unbelievable big-hair to fine European-made human hair wigs.

Showcase Slots and Antiquities
6672 Spencer Street, Suite 600
Tel: 702-740-5722
www.showcaseslots.com
Here you can buy a vintage slot machine to take home. Laws vary by state, but many allow possession of one-armed bandits if you are over a certain age.

Toys of Yesteryear
2028 East Charleston Boulevard
Tel: 702-598-4030
Aimed more at adults than kids, this antique toy store is the place to look for hula hoops, Etch-a-Sketches, vintage Barbie dolls and other nostalgic playthings.

WOW! Multimedia Superstore
4580 West Sahara
Tel: 702-364-2500
Out-of-the-way but huge electronics and CD emporium.

ART GALLERIES

Arts Factory
107 East Charleston Boulevard
Tel: 702-676-1111
www.theartsfactory.com
The hub of the 18b Arts District is a converted warehouse containing a maze of artists' studios. Few visitors except during the district's monthly First Friday festivals.

Dust
900 South Las Vegas Boulevard
Tel: 702-880-3878
www.dustgallery.com
This chic downtown gallery represents postmodern painters, sculptors, photographers and installation artists – some local, others from New York, Boston, and Los Angeles.

S^2 Art Center
1 East Charleston Boulevard
Tel: 702-868-7880
Owner Jack Solomon was the exclusive lithographer for the late Norman Rockwell. With antique flatbed presses on site, you can often watch artists printing and drying art-quality lithographs.

High Stakes Art
S^2 Art Center, 1 East Charleston Boulevard
Tel: 702-868-7880
This unique studio-gallery specializes in art prints on gambling themes by top area artists, as well as reproductions of old gambling-theme movie posters.

ACTIVITIES

NIGHTLIFE AND SPORT

Las Vegas entertainment comes in so many forms that the biggest challenge facing many visitors is choosing how to spend an evening – showgirl (or male stripper) extravaganzas, magic acts, celebrity impersonators, big-production stage spectaculars, and headliner concerts, to mention just a few. It's also the place to go for spectator sports from boxing to rodeo, as well as participation thrill sports like mountain biking, skydiving, and even auto racing lessons. For all shows, reserve tickets well in advance.

NIGHTLIFE

Vegas's nightlife is the heartbeat of the city. Aside from gaming and the shows at the hotels and resorts, there are many lounge acts, nightclubs, and dance halls. In Las Vegas, you must be 21 or older to frequent nightclubs, casinos, and bars. For a select list of gay clubs, *see page 270. For more on Stage Shows and Magic, see page 162–3.*

Comedy

Carrot Top
Luxor, 3900 Las Vegas Boulevard South
Tel: 702-262-4000
One-man show relies on crazy props and sight gags.

Comedy Stop at the Trop
Tropicana Resort and Casino, 3801 Las Vegas Boulevard South
Tel: 702-739-2714 or 800-634-4000
www.comedystop.com
Nightly. Some of the best comedians in the country.

Improv Comedy Club
Harrah's, 3475 Las Vegas Boulevard South
Tel: 702-369-5111 or 800-392-9002
www.harrahs.com
Tuesday–Sunday nights. Presenting some of the new faces in comedy.

Rita Rudner
Harrah's, 3475 Las Vegas Boulevard South
Tel: 702-785-5555
Soft-spoken comic pokes fun at marriage, relationships, and shopping.

Riviera Comedy Club
Riviera Hotel and Casino, 2901 Las Vegas Boulevard South
Tel: 702-794-9433
www.theriviera.com
This is the original comedy showcase in Las Vegas.

The Second City
Flamingo Las Vegas, 3555 Las Vegas Boulevard South
Tel: 702-733-3333
www.flamingolasvegas.com

Tuesday–Sunday, plus additional shows some evenings. Second City has been a starting point for many US comedy actors, writers, and directors including Joan Rivers, Dan Akyroyd, John Candy, and John Belushi. Enjoy some of the finest improvisational comedians.

Headliners

Barry Manilow
Las Vegas Hilton, 3000 South Paradise Road
Tel: 702-732-5111

TICKETS

Tickets for big shows can be purchased online at:
www.vegas.com
www.lasvegas.com
www.lasvegasshows.com

The crooner came out of retirement when the Hilton built him his own theater.

Bette Midler
Caesars Palace, 3570 Las Vegas Boulevard South
Tel: 702 731-7110
The Divine Miss M is one of the long-term headliners, alternating with Cher in Caesars' Colosseum concert venue.

Cher
Caesars Palace, 3570 Las Vegas Boulevard South
Tel: 702 731-7110
The ageless vamp alternates with Bette Midler on Caesars' huge concert stage.

Live Entertainment

The Bar at Times Square
New York New York, 3790 Las Vegas Boulevard South
Tel: 702-740-6969.
Features dueling pianos.

Carnival Court
Harrah's, 3475 Las Vegas Boulevard South
Tel: 702-369-5111.
Admission free. Enjoy live bands throughout the day and into the wee small hours.

Cleopatra's Barge
Caesars Palace, 3570 Las Vegas Boulevard South
Tel: 702-731-7110
Listen or dance nightly to live acts.

House of Blues
Mandalay Bay, 3950 Las Vegas Boulevard South
Tel: 702-632-7600
Nightly live entertainment including high-class performers like the Blues Brothers, Sheryl Crow, and Bob Dylan. Book early for big stars.

The Joint
Hard Rock Hotel, 4475 Paradise Road
Tel: 702-693-5000
Big-name entertainment and the Hard Rock Center Bar.

Le Cabaret
Paris Las Vegas, 3655 Las Vegas Boulevard South
Tel: 702-946-7000
Live entertainment show lounge.

Napoleon's
Paris, 3655 Las Vegas Boulevard South
Tel: 702-946-7000
Enjoy live music as well as the cigar and pipe lounge.

Octane Lounge
Excalibur, 3850 Las Vegas Boulevard South
Tel: 702-597-7777
Live rock bands Thursday–Saturday.

The Railhead
Boulder Station, 4111 Boulder Highway
Tel: 702-432-7777
Live headline entertainment with free blues on Monday.

Rain
The Palms, 4321 West Flamingo Road
Tel: 702-942-7777
This impressive, enormous venue is a concert hall, a nightclub and a special-events facility.

VooDoo Lounge
Rio Hotel, 3700 West Flamingo Road
Tel: 702-777-7800
Wednesday–Saturday. Live entertainment and celebrity DJs at one of Las Vegas's hottest clubs.

Wasted Space
Hard Rock Hotel, 4475 Paradise Road
Tel: 702-693-5000
Chic new rock club introduces hot up-and-coming bands.

Nightclubs

Coyote Ugly Bar and Dance Saloon
New York New York, 3790 Las Vegas Boulevard South
Tel: 702-212-8804.
Nightly from 6pm to 3am. Hot nightspot with bar-top dancing and fire-breathing coyotes.

LAX
Luxor, 3900 Las Vegas Boulevard South
Tel: 702-262-4591
Huge two-story club has two dance floors with different DJs.

Mix
Mandalay Bay, 3950 Las Vegas Boulevard South
Tel: 702-632-9500
Futuristic, dressy penthouse disco with a view of the Strip from the 64th floor.

Playboy Club
The Palms, 4321 West Flamingo
Tel: 702-942-7777
The last Playboy Club on earth.

PURE
Caesars Palace, 3570 Las Vegas Boulevard South
Tel: 702-731-7873
Four dance floors, four DJs, and the legendary Pussycat Dolls Lounge.

Rumjungle
Mandalay Bay, 3950 Las Vegas Boulevard South
Tel: 702-632-7408
From 11pm. Interactive entertainment and dining, with volcanic mountains of rum rising in the illuminated bar. Various music from salsa to romantic, techno to hip hop. "Tasteful" attire only.

Shadow
Caesars Palace, 3570 Las Vegas Boulevard South
Tel: 702-731-7110
Afternoons during the week and weekend evenings. Enjoy cocktails, appetizers, and top-shelf liquor while viewing silhouetted dancers performing behind a screen.

Studio 54
MGM Grand, 3799 Las Vegas Boulevard South
Tel: 702-891-7254

Tuesday–Saturday until the early mornings, enjoy a two-story dance club blending cutting-edge house music with the latest pop and rock. Beautiful women swing over the dance floor releasing a shower of glitter on dancers below.

Cocktail Lounges

All the Las Vegas hotel and casino venues have a lounge, as do most of the restaurants. These are a few with different atmospheres.

Caramel
Bellagio, 3600 Las Vegas Boulevard South
Tel: 702-693-8300
Ultrachic cocktail lounge overlooks the casino floor. Dress code.

Ghostbar
The Palms, 4321 West Flamingo
Tel: 702-492-3960
An indoor and outdoor lounge on the 55th floor with tremendous views attracting a stylish crowd.

J.C. Wooloughan
J.W. Marriott,
221 North Rampart
Tel: 702-869-7725
Irish pub open all day Saturday and Sunday as well as each evening.

Minus 5 Experience
Mandalay Bay, 3950 Las Vegas Boulevard South
Tel: 702-632-9500
This unique new lounge made entirely of ice has an Arctic/Antarctic exploration theme.

Peppermill's Fireside Lounge
2985 Las Vegas Boulevard
Tel: 701-735-7635
Locals say this longtime favorite is the most romantic lounge in Las Vegas.

V Bar
The Venetian, 3355 Las Vegas Boulevard South
Tel: 702-414-3200
The world's finest liquors are served to the strains of cool jazz early and hot reggae later.

Tribute Shows

American Superstars
Stratosphere Hotel and Casino, 2000 Las Vegas Boulevard South
Tel: 702-380 7777
Celebrity impersonators do Michael Jackson, Britney Spears, and Elvis.

An Evening at La Cage
Riviera, 2901 Las Vegas Boulevard South
Tel: 702-734-5110
Drag queens mimic Joan Rivers, Judy Garland, Bette Midler, and others in this curiously wholesome drag-queen show.

An Evening With Dean and Friends
Riviera, 2901 Las Vegas Boulevard South
Tel: 702-734-5110
Tom Stevens performs as Dean Martin, Sammy Davis Jr, Jerry Lewis, and others.

Barbra and Frank
Riviera, 2901 Las Vegas Boulevard South
Tel: 702-734-5110
Uncanny impersonations of Streisand and Sinatra in a "concert that never was."

Legends
Imperial Palace Hotel and Casino, 3535 Las Vegas Boulevard South
Tel: 702-731 3311
One of Las Vegas's longest-running celebrity impersonation shows features look-and-sound-alikes of Elvis, Madonna, and James Brown.

The Rat Pack Is Back
Plaza Hotel, 1 Main Street
Tel: 702-386-2110
Re-creates a performance by "Old Vegas" superstars Frank Sinatra, Dean Martin, Joey Bishop, and Sammy Davis Jr.

SPORT

Las Vegas is a sports enthusiast's playground. Lake Mead's deep blue waters and 550 miles (885km) of shoreline provide a recreation center for all types of outdoor activities including scuba diving, swimming, boating, water skiing, and fishing.

Golf

Golf is almost as much a part of Las Vegas history as gaming. There are enough challenging courses to make the sport, for some, the main reason for visiting. Here is a selection of those open to the public:

Angel Park
100 South Rampart Boulevard
Tel: 702-254-4653 or 888-446-5358
www.angelpark.com
Two 18-hole Arnold Palmer courses and one par-3 course featuring holes with similar shot values as at the world's most famous par 3s.

BELOW: Coyote Ugly Bar.

Badlands
9119 Alta Drive
Tel: 702-363-0754
www.badlandsgc.com
Two-time PGA winner Johnny Miller designed Badlands in consultation with Chi Chi Rodriguez, with three nine-hole courses.

Bali Hai
3220 East Flamingo Road
Tel: 702-450-8000 or 888-397-2499
www.waltersgolf.com
Near the south end of the Las Vegas Strip, the course has numerous water features, towering palms, and tropical plants.

Bear's Best
1111 West Flamingo Road
Tel: 702-385-8500
Jack Nicklaus recreated 18 of his most famous holes worldwide.

Black Mountain
500 Greenway Road, Henderson
Tel: 702-565-7933
www.golfblackmountain.com
In the shadow of Black Mountain, this par-72 course is one of the oldest in the city.

Callaway Golf Center
6730 Las Vegas Boulevard South
Tel: 702-897-9500
www.cgclv.com
This facility features a 113-stall driving range, Callaway performance center, St Andrews golf shop, and a lit par-3 golf course.

Craig Ranch
628 West Craig Road,
North Las Vegas
Tel: 702-642-9700
With thousands of trees, this 72-par course is a local favorite.

Desert Pines
3415 East Bonanza Road
Tel: 702-450-8000 or 888-397-2499
www.waltersgolf.com
Just 15 minutes from the Strip, Desert Pines offers a country-club experience with more than 4,000 pines and white-sand bunkers.

Desert Rose
5483 Club House Drive
Tel: 702-431-4653
www.americangolf.com
A county facility with narrow fairways and smooth greens.

ABOVE: playing golf within sight of the Strip.

Eagle Crest
2203 Thomas Ryan Boulevard
Tel: 702-240-1320
www.golfsummerlin.com
Perfect for quick rounds in under three hours, the Summerlin course has an executive layout.

Las Vegas Golf Club
4300 W. Washington Avenue
Tel: 702-646-3000
There are several reachable par 5s on this par-72 layout. The oldest in Las Vegas – and busy too.

Las Vegas National
1911 East Desert Inn Road
Tel: 702-734-1796
www.americangolf.com
This par 71 has hosted several LPGA and PGA Tour events. It is a traditional-style course with a lit range and lessons available.

Las Vegas Paiute Resort
10325 Nu-Wav Kaiv Boulevard
Tel: 702-658-1400 or 800-711-2833
www.lvpaiutegolf.com
Owned and operated by Southern Paiute Native Americans at the base of Mount Charleston, three nationally acclaimed courses.

Legacy
130 Par Excellence Drive,
Henderson
Tel: 702-897-2187 or
888-851-4114
www.thelegacygc.com
The Devil's Triangle, a three-hole series on the back nine, can make or break the round on this par 72.

Painted Desert
5555 Painted Mirage Road
Tel: 702-546-2570
www.americangolf.com
A rugged and arid 18-hole desert-style course.

Reflection Bay
75 Montelago Boulevard,
Henderson
Tel: 702-740-4653
www.lakelasvegas.com
A Jack Nicklaus-designed par-72 course on the shore of the man-made Lake Las Vegas.

Revere at Anthem
2600 Evergreen Oaks Drive,
Henderson
Tel: 702-259-4653
Designed by Billy Casper and Greg Nash, the Revere flows down a natural desert canyon.

Rio Secco
2851 Grand Hills Drive
Tel: 702-889-2400 or 888-867-3226
www.playrio.com
Said to be one of the world's top golf resorts, the 7,000-yd (6,700-meter) course is frequented by Tiger Woods and is home to the Butch Harmon School of Golf.

TPC Las Vegas
9851 Canyon Run Drive
Tel: 702-256-2000
This beautiful desert course is host to the Invensys Classic at Las Vegas, the first professional PGA tournament won by ace golfer Tiger Woods.

CAMPING AND HIKING

Hiking and camping are a wonderful way to experience southern Nevada outside the dark gaming dens of Sin City.

Some of the larger casinos in Las Vegas maintain RV parking lots in town where visitors driving RVs are encouraged to stay, but there are also some spectacular camping areas around Las Vegas that highlight the desert side of the city. Most of the marinas at Lake Mead also operate camping areas for a nominal fee.

The United States Forest Service on Mount Charleston maintains some outstanding camping areas and trails that can take adventurous guests up to heights of 11,819ft (36,000 meters).

The temperature on Mount Charleston is generally much, much cooler than in Las Vegas and so can be a welcome retreat from the heat. The mountain is home to unique vegetation and animal life. During a stay on the mountain, it's not uncommon for campers to spot deer, elk, coyote, squirrels, or a number of different types of birds.

Tennis

There are hundreds of tennis courts in Las Vegas. Andre Agassi, who was born and raised here, learned how to play in the desert heat of southern Nevada. Many casinos have courts and offer lessons, while numerous courts throughout the metropolitan area are free.

Casino Courts

Bally's/Paris
3645 Las Vegas Boulevard South
Tel: 702-739-4111
Eight illuminated outdoor courts. Non guests pay slightly more than guests.

Flamingo Las Vegas
3555 Las Vegas Boulevard South
Tel: 702-733-3111
Four lit outdoor courts to the northeast of the hotel. Reasonable fees considering it's the Strip.

Las Vegas Hilton
3000 Paradise Road
Tel: 702-732-5648
Six courts with four lit on the pool deck area. For guests only.

Monte Carlo
3770 Las Vegas Boulevard South
Tel: 702-730-7777
Three lit courts, all open to the public. The fee is fairly reasonable.

Plaza Las Vegas
No. 1 Main Street
Tel: 702-386-2110
Four lit courts Downtown. Call for reservations and fees.

Riviera Hotel
2901 Las Vegas Boulevard South
Tel: 702-734-5110
Lit courts. Guests of the hotel play for free; non guests allowed for a fee.

Public Courts

There are numerous public parks around the metropolitan area that have tennis courts available to the public. Many are free of charge when the park is open (generally 7am–11pm daily). They are usually on a first-come first-served basis, and players simply drive around and look for an open court.

Lorenzi Park Courts
3075 West Washington Avenue
Tel: 702-229-4867
Reservations are recommended for these eight lit courts. There is a fee charged.

Paradise Park
4775 McLeod Drive
Tel: 702-455-7513
Two free lit courts on Tropicana Avenue just east of Eastern Avenue.

Paul Meyer Park and Community Center
4525 New Forest Drive
Tel: 702-455-7723

Sunrise Park/Community Center
2240 Linn Lane
Tel: 702-455-7600

Sunset Park
2601 East Sunset Road
Tel: 702-260-9803
Located east of Las Vegas Boulevard South, there are eight lit courts. Call for opening hours, reservations, and cheap prices.

Whitney Park, Community and Senior Center
5700 Missouri Street
Tel: 702-455-7573.

Winchester Park and Community Center
3130 South McLeod Street
Tel: 702-455-7340.

YMCA
4141 Meadows Lane
Tel: 702-877-9622
Lessons are available at this public facility which has five lit courts; small fee.

Car Racing

For the adrenaline junkies:

600 Racing Inc
6825 Speedway Boulevard
Suite B 102
Tel: 702-642-4386

Richard Petty Driving Experience
6975 Speedway Boulevard
Tel: 702-643-4343

Freddie Spencer's High Performance Driving School
7055 Speedway Boulevard
Tel: 702-643-1099

Cycling

Downhill Bicycling Tours
7943 Cadenza Lane
Tel: 702-897-8287
A bus drives riders up to the 8,000-ft (2,438-meter) mark on Mount Charleston, and you ride 18 miles (30km) back down the mountain through several different layers of desert and mountain environments.

Escape Adventures Mountain Bike and Hiking Tours
8221 West Charleston Suite 101
Tel: 702-596-2953
www.escapeadventures.com
Provides rental bikes and guides, and conducts tours to Mt Charleston and Red Rock Canyon.

Horseback Riding

Bonnie Springs Old Nevada
1 Gunfighter Lane, Blue Diamond
Tel: 702-875-4191
Red Rock riding stables with desert tours available.

Cowboy Trail Rides
800 North Rainbow Suite 204
Tel: 702-387-8778
Fax: 248-9336
www.cowboytrailrides.com
Singles to large groups guided on horseback to breathtaking views of Red Rock Canyon.

Hot-Air Ballooning

Adventure Balloon Tours
PO Box 27466
Tel: 702-247-6905
www.smilerides.com

D and R Balloons
3275 Rosanna St
Tel: 702-248-7609
www.lasvegasballoonrides.com

The Ultimate Balloon Adventure
2013 Clover Path Street
Tel: 702-869-9999
www.lvhd.com

Rafting

Western River Expeditions
7258 Racquet Club Drive,
Salt Lake City, Utah, 84121
Tel: 800-453-7450
www.westernriver.com

ABOVE: Las Vegas offers plenty of outdoor sports.

Skiing

Las Vegas Ski and Snowboard Resort
Office: 9501 Tule Springs Road Suite 110. Resort: Highway 156 Lee Canyon, Mount Charleston
Tel: 702-645-2754
Snow report: 702-593-9500
www.skilasvegas.com
Around 35 miles (56km) north-east of Vegas off Highway 95, this resort is open from around Thanksgiving to Easter. Fees and hours vary.

Cedar Breaks Lodge
PO Box 190248, Brian Head, Utah 84719
Tel: 888-282-3327
www.cedarbreakslodge.com
A major ski resort in southern Utah around four hours' drive north of Vegas on Interstate 15. Lifts, resort area, and hotel rooms.

Skydiving

Skydive Las Vegas
1401 Airport Road, Suite 4, Boulder City
Tel: 702-759-3483 or 800-875-9348
www.skydivelasvegas.com
Specializes in first-time jumpers and tandem jumps with a 46-second freefall.

Las Vegas Gravity Zone
Jean Sport Aviation Airport, Jean
Tel: 702-456-3802
A family-owned school for first-time jumpers. Member of the U. Parachute Association.

Flyaway Indoor Skydiving
200 Convention Center Drive
Tel: 702-731-4768
www.flyawayindoorskydiving.com

Water-Skiing/Sailing

In winter it is possible to ski in the morning, then water-ski in the afternoon. Most, however, prefer to leave water-skiing until the water warms up to 85°F (30°C), generally around the first of June.

Forever Resorts
Callville Bay, Lake Mead, Cottonwood Cove, Lake Mohave
Tel: 800-255-5561
Renting everything from luxurious houseboats to powerboats. Prices very greatly.

Lake Mead Houseboats
322 Lakeshore Rd, Boulder City
Tel: 702-293-3484.

Lake Mead Marina
Las Vegas Bay, Lake Mead Drive
Tel: 702-565-9111
Houseboats, tracker patio boats, Bayliner ski boats and personal watercraft can be rented. There is a restaurant and lounge.

A–Z

AN ALPHABETICAL SUMMARY OF PRACTICAL INFORMATION

A Admission Charges 268
B Budgeting For Your Trip 268
Business Hours 268
C Climate 268
Crime and Safety 269
Customs Regulations 269
D Disabled Travelers 269
E Electricity 269
Emergency Numbers 270
Entry Requirements 269
G Gay Travelers 270
H Health Care 270
I Internet 270
M Maps 270
Media 270
Money Matters 270
P Photography 271
Postal Services 271
Public Holidays 271
R Religious Services 271
S Smoking 271
T Telephone Numbers 272
Time Zones 271
Tipping 272
Tourist Information 272
W Weights and Measures 272
What to Read 272

Admission Charges

Museums and attractions have hefty admission prices, often around $15. The best shows in town are expensive, too, usually over $100. To see a major star, expect to pay much more.

Budgeting For Your Trip

Almost everything except for admission and show prices can be done cheaply, from dining at a $6.99 all-you-can-eat buffet, to staying in a decent motel for as little as $25. Sin City is also a place that likes to do deals, and car-rental firms and even major casinos offer extremely low prices, usually in the hot summer months. It's always worth bargaining.

Business Hours

Las Vegas is a 24-hour city. Casinos, hotels, many liquor stores, bars, numerous restaurants, grocery stores, and other shopping outlets never close. Banks keep regular hours, generally 9am to 5pm, but some branches are open on Saturday and a few even on Sunday. Major shopping malls are open from 10am to 9pm, while malls in casinos are often open until 9pm.

Climate

Located in the Mojave Desert, Las Vegas has relatively hot and dry weather most of the year. Most of the city's annual rainfall of about 4.13ins (10.64cm), comes in winter. The monsoon period in the Mojave Desert falls from July through September with frequent thunderstorms bringing lightning and heavy downpours. The drenching rains, though fleeting, can create dangerous flash floods, and motorists and pedestrians are cautioned never to cross running water, flooded washes, or roads after a storm.

The average monthly temperature is 56–80°F (13–27°C). Summer temperatures are often over 100°F (38°C) in the day and 75–85°F (26–30°C) at night, but

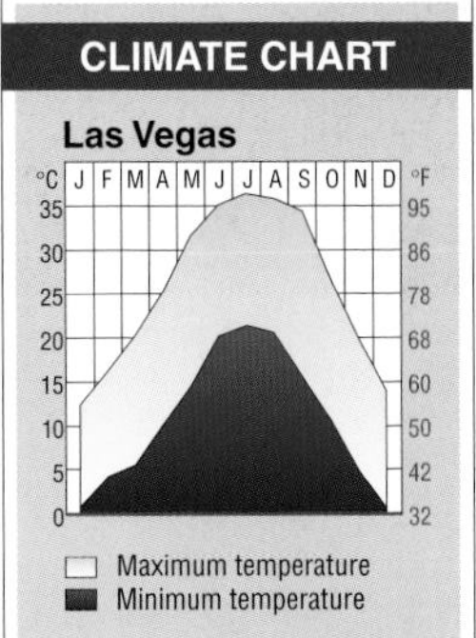

heatwaves of 117°F (47°C) can occur in Las Vegas. The heat is dry as the city has low humidity.

Although it rarely drops much below freezing, the Las Vegas Valley occasionally has snow. An average year sees 212 clear days, 82 partly cloudy days, and 71 cloudy days. The mildest Las Vegas weather is generally from October through April or May.

What to Bring

Dress is almost universally casual, although some upscale restaurants require smart attire. While cool clothes are essential for summer, coats and sweaters are needed in winter, and a jacket may be advisable for cooler summer nights. Rain can be expected in winter and spring. During the hot season, wear a hat and sunglasses.

Crime and Safety

Las Vegas is a relatively safe city despite the fact that it is awash in cash. In addition to the Metropolitan Police Department, which patrols nearly all areas, there are separate police departments in North Las Vegas, Henderson, and Boulder City.

Every casino has its own armed security force to protect customers and the casino's interests. If you have any problem inside the hotel, your first stop should be with security, although the chances of retrieving lost property are not good.

At no time should you leave cash or belongings unattended. For the most part, visitors to Las Vegas are safe in all casino areas including the street in front of the resorts, but as in most cities, it is unwise to travel at night in areas that are not well lit.

Customs Regulations

Meat or meat products, illegal drugs, firearms, seeds, plants, and fruits are among prohibited goods. Also, do not bring in any duty-free goods worth more than $400 (US citizens) or $100 (foreign travelers). Visitors over 21 may import 200 cigarettes, 3lb (1.3kg) of tobacco or 50 cigars; and 34 fl oz (1 liter) of alcohol.

Non-residents may import, free of duty and internal revenue tax, articles worth up to $100 for use as gifts for other persons, as long as they remain in the US for at least 72 hours and keep the gifts with them. This $100 gift exemption or any part of it can be claimed only once every six months. It can include 100 cigars, but no alcohol. Do not have the articles gift wrapped, as they must be available for customs inspection.

If you are not entitled to the $100 gift exemption, you may bring in articles worth up to $25 free of duty for your personal or household use. You may include any of the following: 50 cigarettes, 10 cigars, 150 ml of alcohol, or 5 fl oz (150ml) of alcoholic perfume or proportionate amounts. Articles bought in duty-free shops in foreign countries are subject to US customs duty and restrictions but may be included in your exemption. However, if you stop off in Vegas for a couple of days "in-transit," these may be confiscated.

For a breakdown of customs allowances contact the United States Customs Service, PO Box 7407, Washington, DC 20044. Tel: 202-514-4316.

Disabled Travelers

If you have a physical disability and need special accommodation requirements, your reservation agent or hotel ADA coordinator can help you find a room. Most showrooms have assistive listening devices and wheelchair-accessible accommodations, as do quite a few restaurants and hotel lounges.

For more information you should contact the properties concerned directly. Many casinos have slot machines and table games with wheelchair access.

If you rent a car, you should bring your hometown parking permit, or request a free 90-day permit through the city of Las Vegas at the Parking Permit Office, tel: 702-229-6431.

Lift-equipped shuttles are available to and from McCarran International Airport, which also has TTYs for the hearing impaired.

Entry Requirements

A passport, a passport-sized photograph, a visitor's visa, proof of intent to leave the US and, depending on your country of origin, an international vaccination certificate are required of most foreign nationals. Visitors from a few European countries staying less than 90 days do not need a visa. Vaccination certificate requirements vary, but proof of immunization against smallpox or cholera may be necessary. Canadian and Mexican citizens, and British residents of Canada and Bermuda, are normally exempt but it is wise to check.

Since September 11, 2001, security measures are in place,

ELECTRICITY

The US uses a 110–120-volt 50-cycle alternating current (AC). Transformers or plug adaptors can be bought in many Las Vegas shops.

EMERGENCY NUMBERS

- **All emergencies**: 911
- **Police:**

Metropolitan Police Department, 400 Stewart Avenue. Tel: non-emergency 702-795-3111 or 229-3111.
North Las Vegas Police Department, 1301 East Lake Mead Boulevard, North Las Vegas. Tel: 702-633-9111.
Henderson Police Department, 240 South Water Street, Henderson. Tel: 702-565-8933.
Boulder City Police Department, 1005 Arizona Street, Boulder City. Tel: 702-293-9224.
Nevada Highway Patrol Tel: 702-486-4100.

- **Ambulance Dispatch Center** Tel: 702-384-3400.
- **Alcoholics Abuse Hotline** Tel: 800/222-0199.
- **Alcoholics Anonymous**, 1431 East Charleston Avenue. Tel: 702-598-888.
- **Domestic Violence Hotline** Tel: 702-646-4981.
- **Drug Abuse Prevention** Tel: 702-799-8402.
- **Gamblers Anonymous** Tel: 702-385-7732.
- **Rape Crisis Hotline** Tel: 702-366-1640.

and are subject to change without notice. Foreign nationals should always carry photo ID.

Gay Travelers

The **Gay and Lesbian Center**, 953 East Sahara Avenue, Suite B31, tel: 702-733-9800, is generally staffed seven days a week. The office provides a guide to local bars which includes:
Badlands Saloon, 953 East Sahara Avenue, tel: 702-792-9262. An easy-going neighborhood bar with very friendly staff.
FreeZone, 610 East Naples Drive, tel: 702-794-2300. The most popular bar for women, but also a hit with men on boys'

nights and weekends. Check out the *What a Drag* show.
Gipsy, 605 Paradise Road, tel: 702-731-1919. One of the longest-established gay clubs in town and still the best.
Hamburger Mary's, 4503 Paradise Road, tel: 702-735-4400. A great place to grab some food and hang out for both the gay and straight crowd. Holds tons of special events.
KRAVE, 3663 Las Vegas Boulevard South, tel: 702-836-0830; www.kravelasvegas.com. The only gay and lesbian club on the Strip.
Las Vegas Eagle, 3430 East Tropicana Avenue, tel: 702-458-8662. Home of the "infamous" Underwear Nights on Wednesday and Friday.
Las Vegas Lounge, 900 Karen Avenue, tel: 702-737-9350. Las Vegas's only transgender bar. Has fantastic, splashy shows and a great crowd.
Spotlight Lounge, 957 East Sahara Avenue, tel: 702-696-0202. A favorite with locals. Lots of community events, and friendly laid-back staff.

Health Care

Health care is extremely expensive, so visitors should always have comprehensive travel insurance to cover any emergencies, including repatriation.

Hospitals

Desert Springs Hospital Medical Center, 2075 East Flamingo Road, tel: 702-369-7610.
St Rose Dominican Hospital, 102 East Lake Mead Drive, Henderson, tel: 702-564-2622.
Summerlin Hospital Medical Center, 657 Town Center Drive, tel: 702-233-7000.
Sunrise Hospital and Medical Center, 3186 South Maryland Parkway, tel: 702-731-8000.
Valley Hospital, 620 Shadow Lane, tel: 702-388-4000.

Internet

Most resorts have in-room wireless internet access; a few of the best have business centers. Local libraries and a few 24-hour supermarkets also have computers for basic surfing.

Maps

Flexi-maps, available from Insight Guides, provide key sites and a handy, laminated finish.

Media

Print

There are two major daily newspapers in Las Vegas, the *Las Vegas Review-Journal* and the smaller *Las Vegas Sun*. Although the papers are editorially separate, they share advertising and printing facilities. Several other publications are available, most of which are free.

Television

There are numerous TV stations in Vegas as well as the national CBS, NBC, and ABC. There is also the FOX network, and the UPN network, an entertainment channel; a local government channel; and a few Spanish channels.

Money Matters

Credit cards are accepted almost everywhere, although not all cards at all places. Along with out-of-state or overseas bank cards, they can also be used to withdraw money at ATMs (automatic teller machines), which are commonplace in casinos. These are marked with the corresponding stickers (ie Cirrus, Visa, MasterCard, American Express, Plus, etc.). Service charges at casino ATMs can be very high.

If you plan to cash traveler's checks, be sure to bring along your passport. Proof of identification (some sort of photo ID) may also be required when using credit cards in stores. Las Vegas supposedly has one of the highest numbers of identity fraud in the US, hence the precautions.

Currency

US dollars (US$). Automated teller machines (ATMs) are located throughout the city and in most major casinos, many of which also accept traveler's checks and cash foreign currency. Note that the charge on an ATM in a casino can be hefty. There are many check-cashing services, which accept foreign checks. If you're making a purchase in a store by credit card, you may be required to show identification; identity theft is rampant in Sin City.

Tax

Shoppers in Clark County pay about 7.75 percent in taxes for all non-food items, or for food items purchased already prepared such as in a restaurant. There is often a slight difference between the tax in Clark County, the city of Las Vegas, Henderson, North Las Vegas, Boulder City, Mesquite, Laughlin, and other areas of the state. The lodging tax on hotel rooms is 11 percent within the city limits (including Downtown but not the Strip) and 9 percent in Clark County (including the Strip).

Photography

Taking photographs is an imperative for most visitors who otherwise find it hard to explain Las Vegas to friends and family back home. There are numerous camera shops that handle all types of film and equipment, and there are places to have film developed in an hour on almost every street corner and in most supermarkets Downtown or on the Strip.

Photography inside casinos or showrooms is strictly prohibited. In the early days there was such a stigma attached to gaming that customers would get upset if anyone took photographs, in case a picture of them sitting at a blackjack table appeared in their newspaper. Particularly obliging pit bosses or security guards might give you a wink and turn their backs *if you ask first*.

In showrooms, the performers and casino big shots believe that while customers have paid for the right to watch a live performance, it doesn't give them the right to take pictures, or, a big fear, perhaps sell the photo to others. Many showbusiness people have spent large sums of money registering the right to make money off their faces, and they don't want just anyone taking their picture.

In some shows, like the daredevil Cirque du Soleil performances, a photographic flash going off at a critical moment could be hazardous for the acrobats themselves, so cameras are banned. However, some performers, such as Wayne Newton at the Stardust, will walk through and greet the audience, and photography is positively encouraged.

Postal Services

Postal authorities are available to respond to questions or concerns 24 hours a day, seven days a week by calling 800-275-8777. There are branches of the post office throughout the Las Vegas Valley, but the main post office is located at 101 East Sunset Road, a stone's throw from McCarran Airport.

Religious Services

There are more than 500 churches and synagogues in Las Vegas representing more than 40 faiths. Ask the concierge of your hotel for more information.

Casino gaming chips are found in donation baskets nearly every day at two Roman Catholic churches a few hundred yards from the Strip.

Smoking

Smoking tobacco products is prohibited in all indoor public areas except casinos, strip clubs, brothels, and bars that do not serve food. Larger hotels usually provide smoking and non-smoking room options.

Time Zones

Pacific Standard Time (Pacific Daylight Time in summer). Vegas is in the same time zone as California; 8 hours behind London and 3 hours behind New York.

Public Holidays

Although Las Vegas recognizes all major public holidays in the US, it makes little difference to the casual visitor. Most government offices, including Federal, county, and city, close on holidays, but the majority of businesses that cater to tourists never close. Most major holidays occur on the Monday closest to the celebration date. On most three-day weekends, Vegas becomes very crowded.

- **New Year's Day** January 1
- **Martin Luther King Day** Third Monday in January
- **President's Day** Third Monday in February
- **Labor Day** First Monday in September
- **Independence Day** July 4
- **Veterans' Day** November 1
- **Christmas Day** December 25

TELEPHONE NUMBERS

Unless otherwise stated, all telephone numbers in this book begin with the code **702**. When calling outside Las Vegas – to Henderson or Boulder City, for instance, where the code is still 702 – you must dial the number in full. The area code throughout most of the rest of Nevada is **775**.

Tipping

Far more than in other US cities, tipping is the grease that keeps the machine of Las Vegas operating. Most tipping (bellman per bag; cocktail waitress; daily maid service) is in the $1–3 range, but sometimes a larger tip will move things along. No table at a big hotel restaurant? Try a $10 or $20 bill. Valet parking full? Start with $5 and work upwards, but always discreetly.

Restaurant tipping is between 15 and 20 percent of the total bill before taxes. Be aware that some restaurants add this to the bill automatically, so check first.

Tourist Information

There are public tourist offices throughout Clark County. These provide excellent information for Las Vegas travelers and often have discount coupons for activities in the area. They can be accessed at www.lasvegas24hours.com, the website of the Las Vegas Convention and Visitors Authority (LVCVA). Everything you need to know about Las Vegas can be found here including an events calendar, detailed maps of the area, and visitor and convention information.

The tourist offices are:

Las Vegas Visitor Information Center, 3150 Paradise Road; tel: 702-892-7575 or 877-VISITLV (877-847-4858). Open daily 8am–5pm.

Nevada Welcome Center @ Boulder City, US 93, Boulder City; tel: 702-294-1252. Open daily 8am–4.30pm.

For 24/7 pre-recorded visitor information call the **Las Vegas Chamber of Commerce Info Center**, tel: 702-735-1616.

BELOW: tipping gets better service.

Weights and Measures

The US uses the Imperial system of weights and measures.

What to Read

American Billionaire by Richard Hack. Millennium Press, 2001.
The Anza Borrego Desert Region by Lowell and Diana Lindsay. Wilderness Press, 1978.
Behind the Tables by Barney Vinson. Gollehon, Grand Rapids, 1986.
Chip-Wrecked in Las Vegas by Barney Vinson. Mead Publishing, 1994.
The Dirt Beneath the Glitter: Tales from Real Life Las Vegas edited by Hal K. Rothman and Mike Davis. University of California Press, 2002.
Dummy Up and Deal by H. Lee Barnes. University of Nevada Press, 2002.
The First 100, edited by A.D. Hopkins and K.J. Evans. Huntington Press, 1999.
Hiking Southern Nevada by Bruce Whitney. Huntington Press, 2000.
How to Win at Gambling by Avery Cardoza. Cardoza Publishing, 1993.
In the Desert of Desire by William L. Fox. University of Nevada Press, 2007.
The Las Vegas Pauites: A Short History by John Alley. Las Vegas Tribe of Pauite Indians, 1977.
Loaded Dice by John Soares. Taylor Publishing, 1985.
The Man Who Invented Las Vegas by W.R. Wilkerson III. Ciro's Books, 2000.
The Money and the Power: the Making of Las Vegas and its Hold on America by Sally Dention and Roger Morris. Vintage Books, 2002.
The New Gambler's Bible by Arthur S. Reber. Three Rivers Press, 1996.
The Players: The Men Who Made Las Vegas edited by Jack Sheehan. University of Nevada Press, 1997.
Saints in Babylon: Mormons in Las Vegas by Kenric F. Ward, 2002.
Sharks in the Desert by John L. Smith. Barricade Books, 2005.
When the Mob Ran Vegas by Steve Fischer. Berkline Press, 2005.
Wilderness Emergency by Gene Fear. Survival Education Association, 1972.
Winner Takes All by Christina Binkley. Hyperion, 2008.

Other Insight Guides

Insight Smart Guides are a new series with a unique A–Z approach to each destination.

Insight Step-by-Step Guides are self-guided walks and tours produced by local writers. Each book comes with a free pull-put map.

Las Vegas Street Atlas

The key map shows the area of Las Vegas covered by the atlas section. An index of street names and places of interest shown on the maps can be found on the following pages. For each entry there is a page number and grid reference

Map Legend

- Freeway with Exit
- Freeway (under construction)
- Divided Highway
- Main Road
- Secondary Road
- Minor Road
- Track
- International Boundary
- State Boundary
- National Park/Reserve
- Airport
- Church (ruins)
- Monastery
- Castle (ruins)
- Archaeological Site
- Cave
- Place of Interest
- Mansion/Stately Home
- Viewpoint
- Beach
- Freeway
- Divided Highway
- Main Roads
- Minor Roads
- Footpath
- Railroad
- Pedestrian Area
- Important Building
- Park
- Monorail
- Bus Station
- Tourist Information
- Post Office
- Cathedral/Church
- Mosque
- Synagogue
- Statue/Monument
- Tower

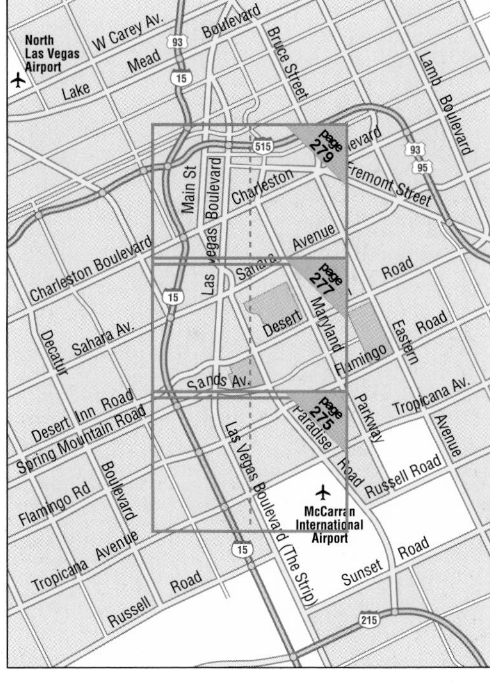

276

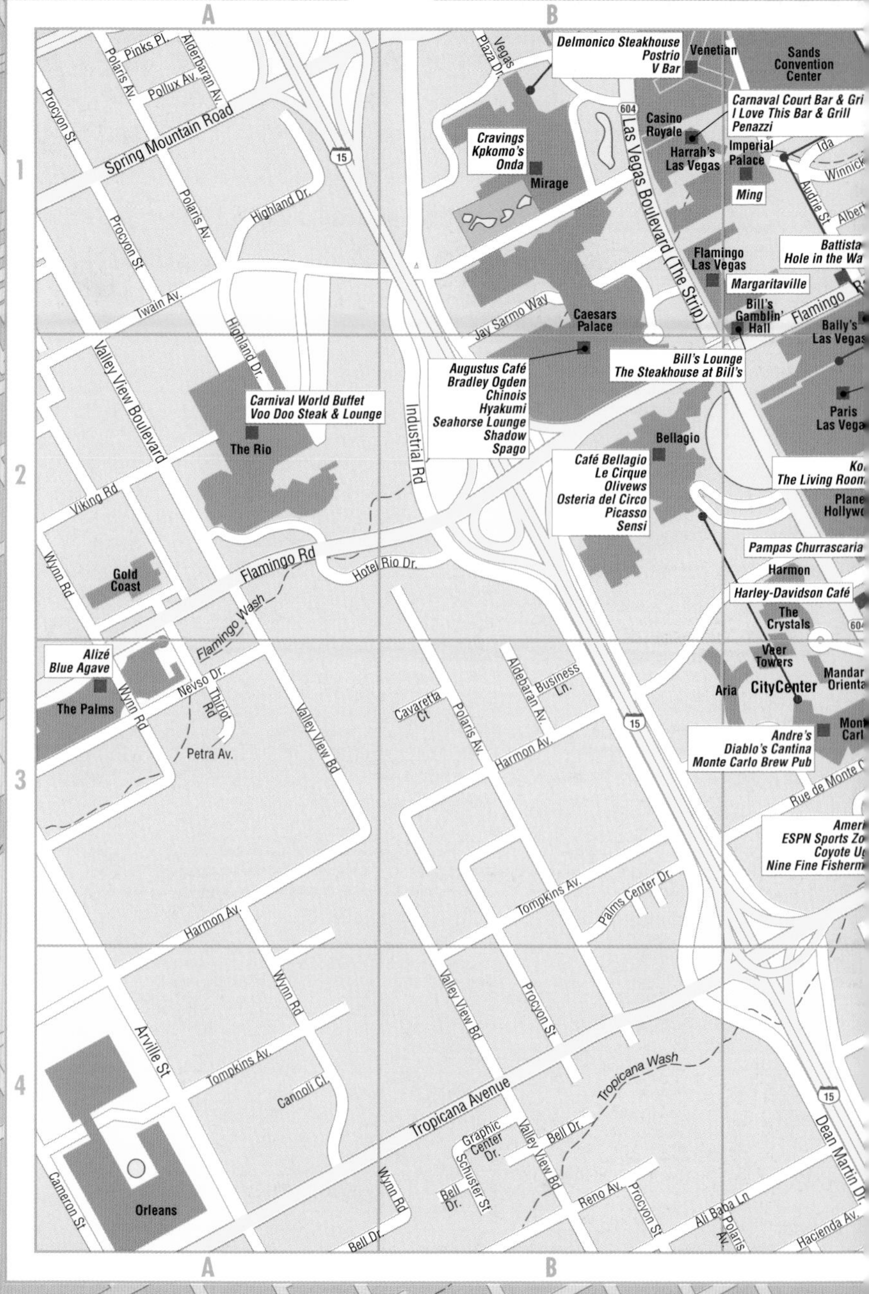

Delmonico Steakhouse
Postrio
V Bar
Venetian
Sands Convention Center
Carnaval Court Bar & Gri
I Love This Bar & Grill
Penazzi
Casino Royale
Harrah's Las Vegas
Imperial Palace
Ming
Cravings
Kpkomo's
Onda
Mirage
Spring Mountain Road
Las Vegas Boulevard (The Strip)
Flamingo Las Vegas
Margaritaville
Battista
Hole in the Wa
Caesars Palace
Bill's Gamblin' Hall
Bally's Las Vegas
Bill's Lounge
The Steakhouse at Bill's
Augustus Café
Bradley Ogden
Chinois
Hyakumi
Seahorse Lounge
Shadow
Spago
Carnival World Buffet
Voo Doo Steak & Lounge
The Rio
Paris Las Vega
Bellagio
Café Bellagio
Le Cirque
Olivews
Osteria del Circo
Picasso
Sensi
The Living Room
Pampas Churrascaria
Harmon
Harley-Davidson Café
The Crystals
Gold Coast
Flamingo Rd
Alizé
Blue Agave
The Palms
Veer Towers
Aria
CityCenter
Andre's
Diablo's Cantina
Monte Carlo Brew Pub
ESPN Sports Zo
Coyote Ug
Nine Fine Fisherm
Tropicana Avenue
Tropicana Wash
Orleans
Dean Martin Dr.
A
B
1
2
3
4

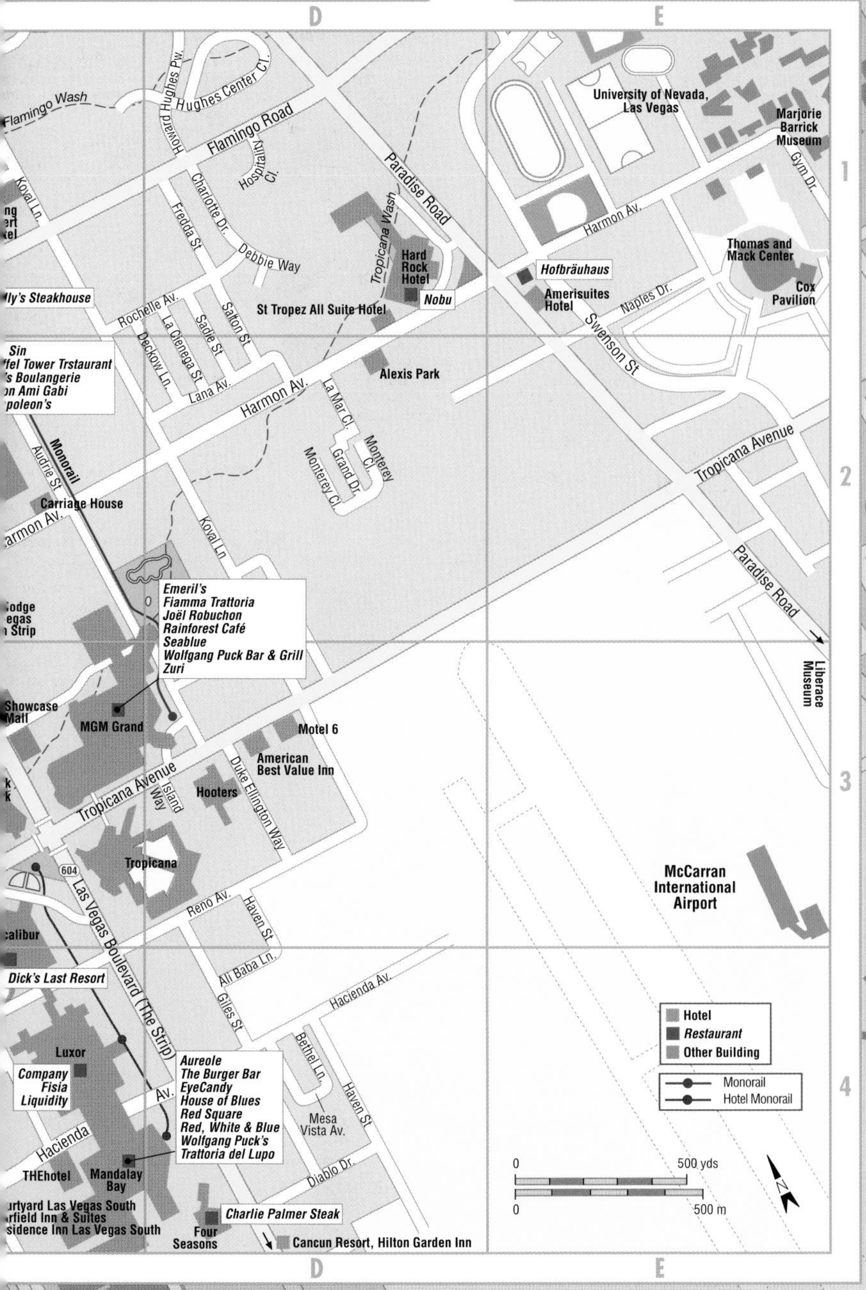

277
D
E
1
2
3
4
University of Nevada, Las Vegas
Marjorie Barrick Museum
Thomas and Mack Center
Cox Pavilion
Hofbräuhaus
Amerisuites Hotel
Hard Rock Hotel
Nobu
St Tropez All Suite Hotel
Alexis Park
Flamingo Wash
Hughes Center Cl.
Howard Hughes Pw.
Flamingo Road
Hospitality Cl.
Paradise Road
Tropicana Wash
Koval Ln.
Charlotte Dr.
Fredda St
Debbie Way
Harmon Av.
Naples Dr.
Swenson St
Gym Dr.
Rochelle Av.
La Cienega St
Sadie St
Salton St
Deckow Ln.
Lana Av.
La Mar Cl.
Monterey Cl.
Grand Dr.
Tropicana Avenue
Monorail
Audrie St
Carriage House
Emeril's
Fiamma Trattoria
Joël Robuchon
Rainforest Café
Seablue
Wolfgang Puck Bar & Grill
Zuri
Liberace Museum
Showcase Mall
MGM Grand
Motel 6
American Best Value Inn
Hooters
Island Way
Duke Ellington Way
Tropicana
604
Las Vegas Boulevard (The Strip)
Reno Av.
Haven St
Ali Baba Ln.
Hacienda Av.
Giles St
Bethel Ln.
Mesa Vista Av.
McCarran International Airport
Dick's Last Resort
Luxor
Company
Fisia
Liquidity
Aureole
The Burger Bar
EyeCandy
House of Blues
Red Square
Red, White & Blue
Wolfgang Puck's
Trattoria del Lupo
Hacienda Av.
THEhotel
Mandalay Bay
Diablo Dr.
Charlie Palmer Steak
Four Seasons
Cancun Resort, Hilton Garden Inn
Hotel
Restaurant
Other Building
Monorail
Hotel Monorail
0
500 yds
0
500 m
N

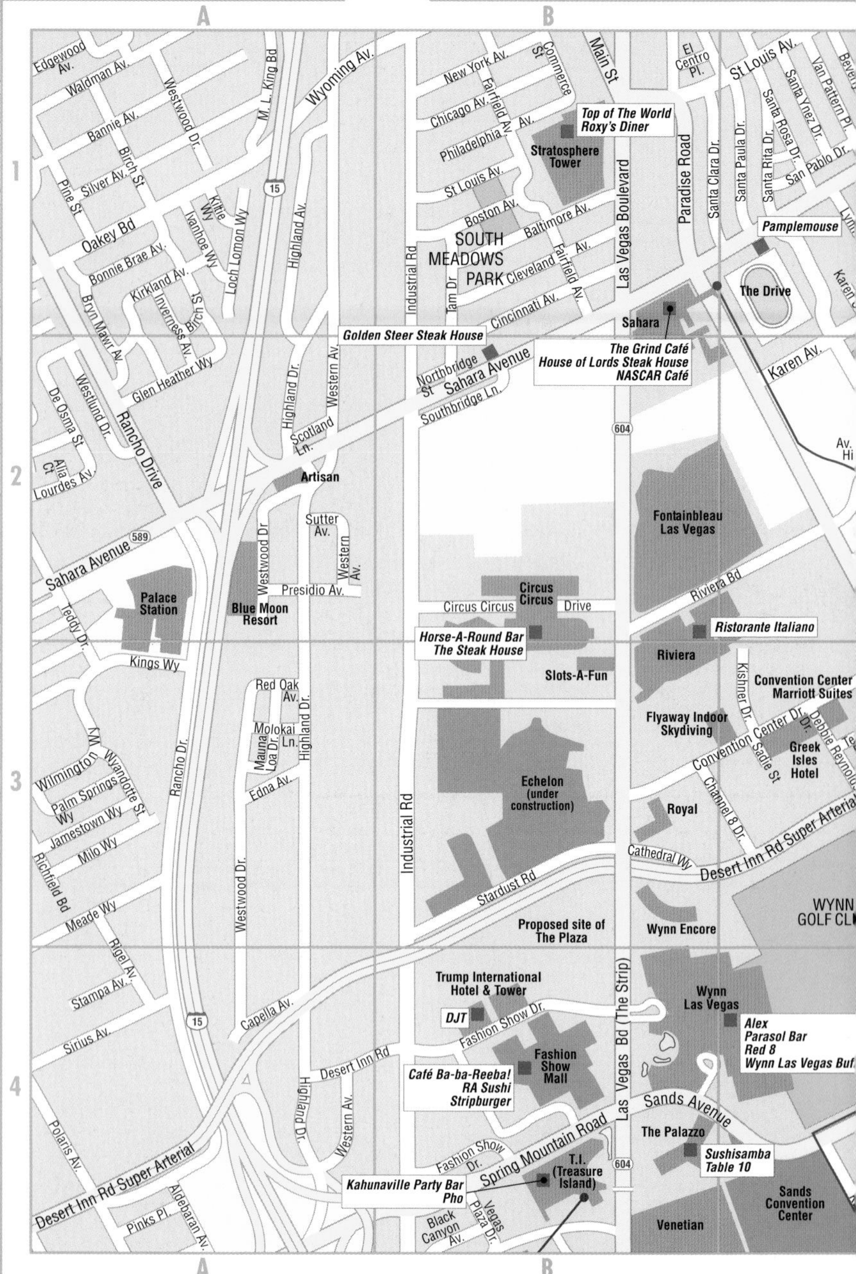
278
274
Top of The World
Roxy's Diner
Stratosphere Tower
SOUTH MEADOWS PARK
Pamplemouse
The Drive
Sahara
Golden Steer Steak House
The Grind Café
House of Lords Steak House
NASCAR Café
Artisan
Fontainbleau Las Vegas
Palace Station
Blue Moon Resort
Circus Circus
Horse-A-Round Bar
The Steak House
Ristorante Italiano
Riviera
Slots-A-Fun
Convention Center Marriott Suites
Flyaway Indoor Skydiving
Greek Isles Hotel
Echelon (under construction)
Royal
Proposed site of The Plaza
Wynn Encore
WYNN GOLF CL
Trump International Hotel & Tower
DJT
Wynn Las Vegas
Alex
Parasol Bar
Red 8
Wynn Las Vegas Buf
Fashion Show Mall
Café Ba-ba-Reeba!
RA Sushi
Stripburger
The Palazzo
Sushisamba
Table 10
Kahunaville Party Bar
Pho
T.I. (Treasure Island)
Venetian
Sands Convention Center
Sahara Avenue
Las Vegas Boulevard
Las Vegas Bd (The Strip)
Paradise Road
Industrial Rd
Rancho Drive
Desert Inn Rd Super Arterial
Spring Mountain Road
Sands Avenue
Riviera Bd
Convention Center Dr.
Circus Circus Drive
Stardust Rd
Fashion Show Dr.
Desert Inn Rd
Main St
Wyoming Av.
M. L. King Bd
Highland Av.
Oakey Bd
Westwood Dr.
Western Av.
Highland Dr.
Karen Av.
St Louis Av.
Kings Wy
Presidio Av.

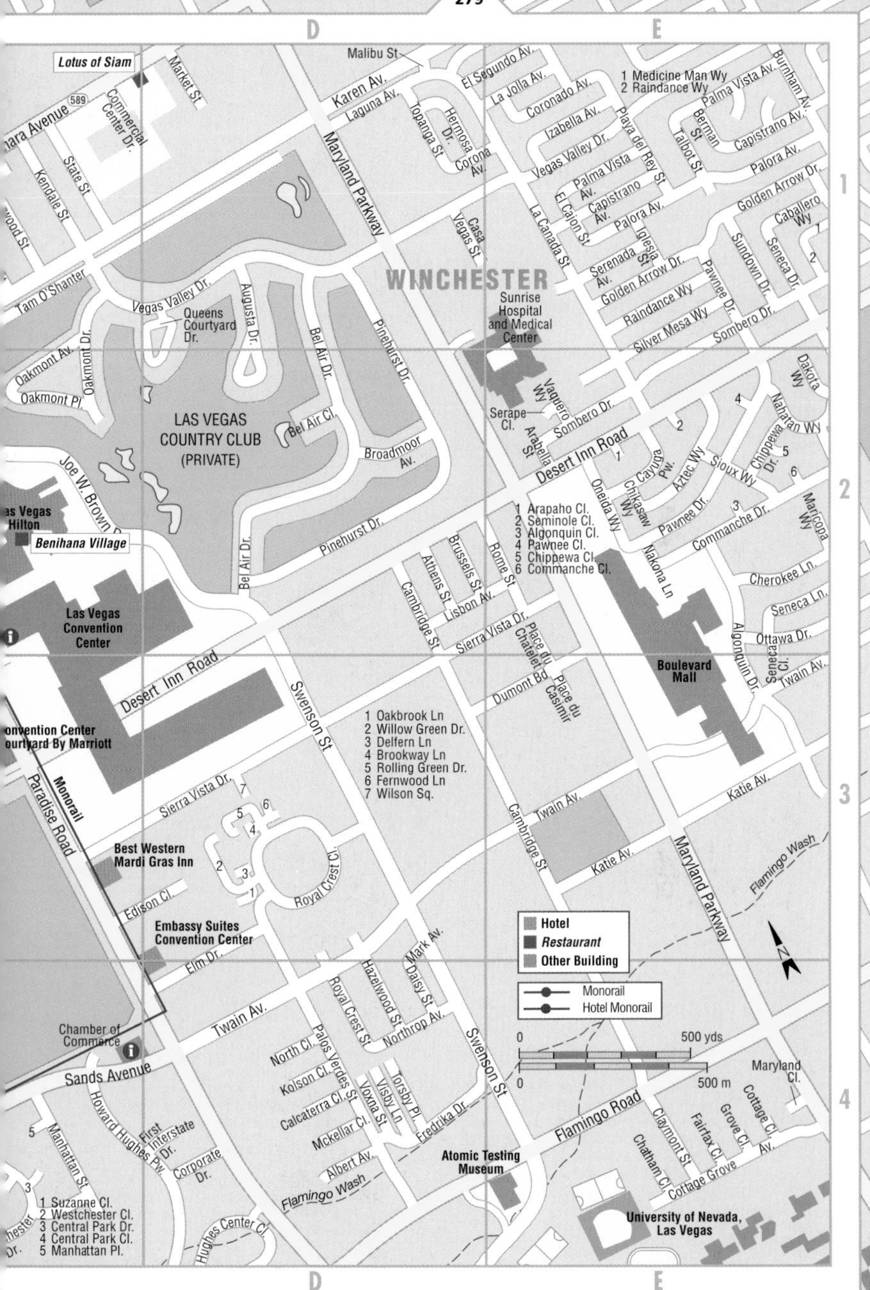
279
D
E
1
2
3
4
275
Lotus of Siam
WINCHESTER
Sunrise Hospital and Medical Center
LAS VEGAS COUNTRY CLUB (PRIVATE)
Las Vegas Hilton
Benihana Village
Las Vegas Convention Center
Convention Center Courtyard By Marriott
Best Western Mardi Gras Inn
Embassy Suites Convention Center
Chamber of Commerce
Boulevard Mall
Atomic Testing Museum
University of Nevada, Las Vegas
Maryland Parkway
Desert Inn Road
Paradise Road
Swenson St
Twain Av.
Sands Avenue
Flamingo Road
Flamingo Wash
Monorail
1 Medicine Man Wy
2 Raindance Wy
1 Arapaho Cl.
2 Seminole Cl.
3 Algonquin Cl.
4 Pawnee Cl.
5 Chippewa Cl.
6 Commanche Cl.
1 Oakbrook Ln
2 Willow Green Dr.
3 Delfern Ln
4 Brookway Ln
5 Rolling Green Dr.
6 Fernwood Ln
7 Wilson Sq.
1 Suzanne Cl.
2 Westchester Cl.
3 Central Park Dr.
4 Central Park Cl.
5 Manhattan Pl.
Hotel
Restaurant
Other Building
Monorail
Hotel Monorail
0
500 yds
0
500 m
N

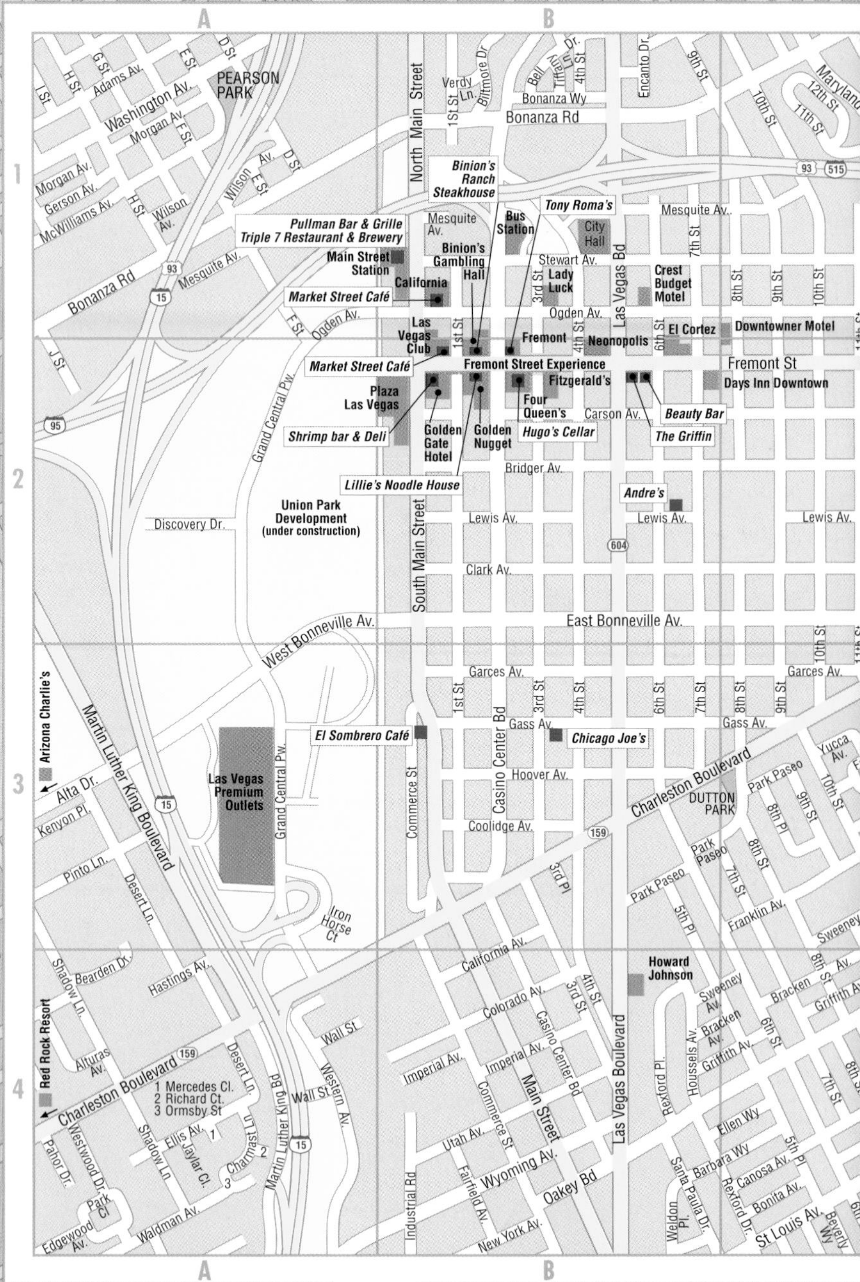

Binion's Ranch Steakhouse
Tony Roma's
Pullman Bar & Grille
Triple 7 Restaurant & Brewery
Main Street Station
California
Market Street Café
Binion's Gambling Hall
Bus Station
City Hall
Lady Luck
Crest Budget Motel
Las Vegas Club
Fremont
Neonopolis
El Cortez
Downtowner Motel
Market Street Café
Fremont Street Experience
Plaza Las Vegas
Fitzgerald's
Four Queen's
Days Inn Downtown
Beauty Bar
Shrimp bar & Deli
Golden Gate Hotel
Golden Nugget
Hugo's Cellar
The Griffin
Lillie's Noodle House
Andre's
Union Park Development
(under construction)
El Sombrero Café
Chicago Joe's
Las Vegas Premium Outlets
Arizona Charlie's
Red Rock Resort
Howard Johnson
PEARSON PARK
DUTTON PARK
1 Mercedes Cl.
2 Richard Ct.
3 Ormsby St

D
E
1
2
3
4
HADLAND PARK
1 Stamos Dr.
2 Builders Av.
3 Contract Av.
Charleston Boulevard
Fremont Street
Eastern Avenue
27th Avenue
Charleston Plaza
HUNTRIDGE CIRCLE PARK
JAYCEE PARK
BAKER PARK
Maryland Parkway
Sahara Avenue
Oakey Bd
St Louis Av.
Hotel
Restaurant
Other Building
500 yds
500 m
N

277

Street Index

1st St **278** B3–B1
3rd Pl. **278** B3
3rd St **278** B3–B2
4th St **278** B3–B1
5th Pl. **278** B3–C4
6th St **276** C1
6th St **278** C4–B3–B2
7th St **278** C4–C3 B3–B2
8th Pl. **278** C3–C4
8th St **278** C4–C3–C3
9th St **278** C3–C2–B1
10th St **278** C1–C3, **279** C4
11th St **278** C1–C3, **279** C3–C4
12th St **278** C1
13th St **278** C1, **279** C2–C3
14th St **279** C1–C2
15th St **279** C1–C2–D3–D4
16th St **279** C1–C2–D3
17th St **279** D1–D4
18th St **279** D1
19th St **279** D1
20th St **279** D1
21st St **279** D1
23rd St **279** D1
26th St **279** E1
27th Av. **279** E1
27th St **279** E1
28th St **279** E1
29th St **279** E1
30th St **279** E1

A

Adams Av. **278** A1
Albert Av. **274** C1, **277** D4
Aldebaran Av. **274** B3
Alderbaran Av. **274** A1
Algonquin Cl. **277** E2
Algonquin Dr. **277** E2–E3
Alhambra Cl. **279** C4
Alhambra Dr. **279** C4
Ali Baba Ln. **274** B4–C4
Alia Ct **276** A2
Almond Tree Ln. **279** D4
Alta Dr. **278** A3
Alturas Av. **278** A4
Ambler Pl. **279** E1
Arabella St **277** E2
Arapaho Cl. **277** E2
Ardmoor St **279** E3
Armory Ln. **279** D1
Artisan **276** A2
Arville St **274** A4
Ash Av. **279** D1
Athens St **277** D2
Atlantic St **279** E2
Atomic Testing Museum **277** E4
Audrie St **274** C1, **275** C2
Augusta Dr. **277** D1
Aztec Way **277** E2

B

Balboa Av. **279** E4
Ballard Dr. **279** D2
Bally's Las Vegas **274** C1
Baltimore Av. **276** B1
Bannie Av. **276** A1
Barbara Way **278** B4–C4
Bearden Dr. **278** A4
Becke Cl. **279** D3
Bel Air Cl. **277** D2
Bel Air Dr. **277** D2
Bell Dr. **274** A4–B4, **278** B1
Bellagio **274** B2
Berkley Av. **279** D1
Berman St **277** E1
Bethel Ln. **275** D4
Beverly Way **276** C1
Bill's Gamblin' Hall **274** C1
Biltmore Dr. **278** B1
Binion's Gambling Hall **278** B1
Birch St **276** A1
Blue Moon Resort **276** A2
Bonanza Rd **278** A1–B1
Bonanza Way **278** B1
Bonita Av. **279** C4–D4–D3–E3
Bonneville Av., East **278** B2
Bonneville Av., West **278** A3–B2
Bonnie Brae Av. **276** A2–A1
Boston Av. **276** B1
Boulevard Mall **277** E3
Bracken Av. **278** C4, **279** C3–D3
Bridger Av. **278** B2, **279** C2
Brisa Av., La **279** E4
Broadmoor Av. **277** D2
Brookway Ln. **277** D3
Brown Dr., Joe W. **277** C2
Bruce St **279** C1–D2–D3–E4
Brussels St **277** D2
Bryn Mawr Av. **276** A2
Builders Av. **279** E1
Burnham Av. **279** D2–E3–E4
Business Ln. **274** B3

C

Caballero Way **277** E1
Caesars Palace **274** B1
Cajon St, El **277** E1
Calcaterra Cl. **277** D4
California **278** B1
California Av. **278** B4
Cambridge St **277** D2–E4
Cameron St **274** A4
Canada St, La **277** E1
Cannoli Cl. **274** A4
Canosa Av. **279** C4–D4–E3
Capella Av. **276** A4
Capistrano Av. **277** E1
Carson Av. **278** B2, **279** C2
Casa Vegas St **277** D1
Casimir, Place du **277** E3
Casino Center Bd **278** B3–B4
Casino Royale **274** B1
Cathedral Way **276** B3
Cavaretta Ct **274** B3
Cayuga Pw. **277** E2
Cedar Av. **279** C1
Central Park Cl. **277** C4
Central Park Dr. **277** C4
Centro Pl., El **276** B1
Cervantes St **279** D1
Channel 8 Dr. **276** C3
Chapman Dr. **279** D3
Charleston Bd **278** A4–B3, **279** D2–E1
Charleston Plaza **279** D2
Charlotte Dr. **275** D1
Charmast Ln. **278** A4
Chatelet, Place du **277** E2
Chatham Cl. **277** E4
Cherokee Ln. **277** E2
Chicago Av. **276** B1
Chikasaw Way **277** E2
Chippewa Cl. **277** E2
Chippewa Dr. **277** E2
Cholla Way **279** C2
Cienega St, La **275** D1
Cincinnati Av. **276** B2
Circle Dr. **279** D2
Circus Circus **276** B3
Circus Circus Dr. **276** B2
CityCenter **274** C2–C3
Clark Av. **278** B2, **279** C2
Claymont St **277** E4
Cleveland Av. **276** B2
Clifford St. **279** E2
Cochran St **279** D3–D4
Colorado Av. **278** B4
Commanche Cl. **277** E2
Commanche Dr. **277** E2
Commerce St **278** B3–B4
Commercial Center Dr. **277** C1
Concordia Pl. **279** D3
Contract Av. **279** E1
Convention Center Dr. **276** C3
Coolidge Av. **278** B3
Cordova St **279** C4
Corona Av. **277** D1
Coronado Av. **277** E1
Corporate Dr. **277** D4
Cortez, El **278** B2
Cottage Cl. **277** E4
Cottage Grove Av. **277** E4
Cottonwood Pl. **279** C3
Crestwood Av. **279** D2
Curtis Dr. **279** D3–D2

D

D St **278** A1
Daisy St **277** D4
Dakota Way **277** E2
Danville Ln. **275** D4
De Osma St **276** A2
Debbie Reynolds Dr. **276** C3
Debbie Way **275** D1
Deckow Ln. **275** D2
Del Mar Av. **279** D4
Delfern Ln. **277** D3
Desert Inn Rd **277** C3–D3–E2
Desert Inn Rd Super Arterial **276** A4–B3–C3
Desert Ln. **278** A3–A4
Diablo Dr. **275** D4
Discovery Dr. **278** A2
Duke Ellington Way **275** D3
Dumont Bd **277** E3

E

E St **278** A1
Earl St **279** C2
Eastern Av. **279** D1–E3
Eastwood Dr. **279** E2
Echelon **276** B3
Edgewood Av. **276** A1
Edison Cl. **277** C3
Edna Av. **276** A3
Ellen Way **278** C4
Ellis Av. **278** A4
Elm Av. **279** D1
Elm Dr. **277** D3
Encanto Dr. **278** B1
Euclid Av. **279** E2
Excalibur **275** C3
Exley Av. **279** D4–E3

F

F St **278** A1
Fairfax Cl. **277** E4
Fairfield Av. **276** B1
Fashion Show Dr. **276** B4
Fashion Show Mall **276** B4
Fernwood Ln. **277** D3
First Interstate Dr. **277** D4
Fitzgerald's **278** B2
Flamingo Las Vegas **274** B1
Flamingo Rd **274** A2–B2–C1, **275** D1
Flower Av. **279** D1
Flyaway Indoor Skydiving **276** B3
Fontainbleau Las Vegas **276** B2
Four Queen's **278** B2
Four Seasons **275** D4
Francis Av. **278** C3
Franklin Av. **279** C3–D2
Fredda St **275** D1
Fredrika Dr. **277** D4
Fremont **278** B2
Fremont St **278** B2, **279** D2–E2
Fremont Street Experience **278** B2

G

G St **278** A1
Garces Av. **278** B3–C3
Gass Av. **278** B3–C3
Gerson Av. **278** A1
Giles St **275** D4
Glen Heather Way **276** A2
Gold Coast **274** A2
Golden Arrow Dr. **277** E1
Golden Gate Hotel **278** B2
Golden Nugget **278** B2
Grand Central Pw. **278** A3–A2
Grand Dr. **275** D2
Graphic Center Dr. **274** B4
Greek Isles Hotel **276** C3
Griffith Av. **279** C3–D3
Grove Cl. **277** E4
Gym Dr. **275** E1

H

H St **278** A1
Hacienda Av. **275** C4–D4
Hard Rock Hotel **275** D1
Harley Way **279** C1
Harmon Av. **274** A3–B3, **275** C2–D2–E1
Harrah's Las Vegas **274** B1
Hartke Pl. **279** D3
Hassett Av. **279** C4–E3
Hastings Av. **278** A4
Haven St **275** D3, D4
Hazelwood St **277** D4
Hermosa Dr. **277** D1
Highland Av. **276** A1
Highland Dr. **274** A1, **276** A2–A4
Hillside Pl. **279** D2–D3
Hiltons, Av. of the **276** C2
Hooters **275** D3
Hoover Av. **278** B3
Hospitality Cl. **275** D1
Hotel Rio Dr. **274** A2–B2
Houssels Av. **278** C4–B4
Houston Dr. **279** E2
Howard Av. **279** C4–E3
Howard Hughes Pw. **277** C4–D4
Hughes Center Cl. **275** D1

I

I St **278** A1
Ida Av. **274** C1
Iglesia St **277** E1
Imperial Av. **278** B4
Imperial Palace **274** C1
Industrial Rd **274** B2–B3–C4, **276** B2–B3
Interstate Bus Terminal **278** A2
Inverness Av. **276** A2
Iron Horse Ct **278** B3
Isabelle Av. **279** D1
Island Way **275** D3
Ivanhoe Way **276** A1
Izabella Av. **277** E1

J

J St **278** A2
Jamestown Way **276** A3
Jaylar Cl. **278** A4
Jessica Av. **279** C3
Jolla Av., La **277** E1
Joshua Way **279** C2

K

Karen Av. **276** C2, **277** D1, **279** E4
Karen Ct **276** C1
Kassabian Av. **279** D3
Katie Av. **277** E3
Kendale St **277** C1
Kenyon Pl. **278** A3
Kiltie Way **276** A1
Kings Way **276** A3
Kirkland Av. **276** A2–A1
Kishner Dr. **276** C3
Kolson Cl. **277** D4
Koval Ln. **275** C1–D2

L

Lady Luck **278** B1
Laguna Av. **277** D1
Lamplighter Ln. **279** D3
Lana Av. **275** D2
Las Vegas Bd **276** B2, **278** B1–B4
Las Vegas Bd (The Strip) **274** B1, **275** C3, **276** B4
Las Vegas Club **278** B2
Las Vegas Premium Outlets **278** A3
Las Vegas Convention Center **277** C2
Las Vegas Hilton **277** C2
Lewis Av. **278** B2–C2, **279** C2–D2
Linden Av. **279** C1
Lisbon Av. **277** D2
Loch Lomon Way **276** A2
Lon Gene Ct. **279** C2
Lourdes Av. **276** A2
Luxor **275** C4
Lynnwood St **276** C1

M

Main St **278** B4
Main Street Station **278** B1
Malibu St **277** D1
Malta Pl. **279** E1
Mandalay Bay **275** C4

Manhattan Pl. **277** C4
Manhattan St **277** C4
Manzanita Way **279** C2
Mar Cl., La **275** D2
Maria Elena Dr. **279** D3
Maricopa Way **277** E2
Mariposa Av. **279** E3
Mark Av. **277** D3
Marjorie Barrick Museum **275** E1
Market St **277** D1
Marlin Av. **279** C1–D1
Maroney Av. **279** D4
Martin Luther King Bd **278** A3–A4
Maryland Cl. **277** E4
Maryland Pw. **277** D1–E3, **279** C2–C3–D4
Mauna Loa Dr. **276** A3
Mayfair Pl. **279** C2–D2
McCarran International Airport **275** E4
McKellar Cl. **277** D4
McWilliams Av. **278** A1
Meade Way **276** A3
Meadows Av. **279** E2
Medicine Man Way **277** E1
Menlo Sq. **279** E1
Mercedes Cl. **278** A4
Mesa Vista Av. **275** D4
Mesquite Av. **278** A1–B1, **279** C1
MGM Grand **275** C3
Milo Way **276** A3
Mirage **274** B1
Mojave Rd **279** E1
Molokai La. **276** A3–B3
Monte Carlo **274** C3
Monte Carlo, Rue de **274** C3
Monterey Av. **279** E3
Monterey Cl. **275** D2
Morgan Av. **278** A1

N

Nahatan Way **277** E2
Nakona Ln. **277** E2
Naples Dr. **275** E1
Neonopolis **278** B2
Nevso Dr. **274** A3
New York Av. **276** B1
New York New York **274** C3
Norman Av. **279** C3
North Cl. **277** D4
North Main St **278** B2
Northbridge St **276** B2
Northrop Av. **277** D4

O

Oakbrook Ln. **277** D3
Oakey Bd **279** C4–D3–E2
Oakmont Av. **277** C2
Oakmont Dr. **277** C2
Oakmont Pl. **277** C2
Ogden Av. **278** B2, **279** C1–D1
Olive St **279** E2
Oneida Way **277** E2
Orleans **274** A4
Ormsby St **278** A4
Ottawa Dr. **277** E2

P–Q

Pacific St **279** E2
Pahor Dr. **278** A4
Palace Station **276** A2
Palazzo, The **276** B4
Palm Springs Way **276** A3
Palma Vista Av. **277** E1
Palms Center Dr. **274** B3
Palms, The **274** A3
Palora Av. **277** E1
Palos Verdes St **277** D4
Paradise Rd **275** D1–E2, **276** B1, **277** C3
Pardee Pl. **279** D4
Paris Las Vegas **274** C2
Park Cl. **278** A4
Park Paseo **278** B3–C3
Pauline Way **279** D2
Pawnee Cl. **277** E2
Pawnee Dr. **277** E1–E2
Petra Av. **274** A3
Peyton Dr. **279** D2
Philadelphia Av. **276** B1
Phillips Av. **279** D4
Pico Way **279** D2
Pine St **276** A1
Pinehurst Dr. **277** D2
Pinks Pl. **276** A4
Pinto Ln. **278** A3
Planet Hollywood **274** C2
Plaza **278** B2
Polaris Av. **274** A1, B3, C4
Pollux Av. **274** A1
Poplar Av. **279** C1
Presidio Av. **276** A2–B2
Procyon St **274** A1, B4
Queens Courtyard Dr. **277** D2

R

Raindance Way **277** E1
Rancho Dr. **276** A2–A3
Red Oak Av. **276** A3
Reno Av. **274** B4, **275** D3
Rexford Dr. **278** C4
Rexford Pl. **278** B4
Rey St, Playa del **277** E1
Richard Ct **278** A4
Richfield Bd **276** A3
Rigel Av. **276** A3
Rio, The **274** A2
Riviera **276** B3
Riviera Bd **276** B2
Rochelle Av. **275** C1
Rolling Green Dr. **277** D3
Rome St **277** E2
Royal **276** B3
Royal Crest Cl. **277** D3
Royal Crest St **277** D4

S

Sadie St **275** D1, **276** C3
Sahara **276** B2
Sahara Av. **276** A2–B2, **277** C1, **279** D4–E3
Salton St **275** D1
San Jose Av. **279** E3
San Pablo Dr. **276** C1
San Pedro St **279** D4
Sands Av. **276** B4–C4, **277** C4
Sands Convention Center **276** C4
Santa Clara Dr. **276** D1
Santa Paula Dr. **276** C1
Santa Rita Dr. **276** C1
Santa Rosa Dr. **276** C1
Santa Ynez Dr. **276** C1
Santiago St **279** C4
Schuster St **274** B4
Scotland Ln. **276** A2
Segundo Av., El **277** E1
Seminole Cl. **277** E2
Seneca Cl. **277** E3
Seneca Dr. **277** E1
Seneca Ln. **277** E2
Serape Cl. **277** E2
Serenada Av. **277** E1
Shadow Ln. **278** A4
Sherwood St **277** C1
Showcase Mall **275** C3
Sierra Vista Dr. **277** D3–E2
Silver Av. **276** A1
Silver Mesa Way **277** E2
Sioux Way **277** E2
Sirius Av. **276** A4
Slots-A-Fun **276** B3
Sombero Dr. **277** E2–E1
South Main St **278** B2
Southbridge Ln **276** B2
Spencer St **279** D2–D3
Spring Mountain Rd **274** A1, **276** B4
St Louis Av. **279** D4–E3
St Joseph Cl. **279** D3
St Jude Cl. **279** D3
Stamos Dr. **279** E1
Stampa Av. **276** A3
Stardust Rd **276** B3
State St **277** C1
Stewart Av. **278** B1, **279** C1–D1
Stockton Av. **279** E3
Stratosphere Tower **276** B1
Sundown Dr. **277** E1
Sunrise Av. **279** D1–E1
Sutter Av. **276** A2
Suzanne Cl. **276** C4
Sweeney Av. **278** C3, **279** D1–D2
Swenson St **275** E1–E2, **277** D3–D4

T–U

T.I. (Treasure Island) **276** B4
Talbot St **277** E1
Tam Dr. **276** B2
Tam O'Shanter **277** C2
Teddy Dr. **276** A2
Terry Dr. **276** C3
THEhotel **275** C4
Thelma Ln. **279** D2
Thiriot Rd **274** A3
Thomas and Mack Center **275** E1
Tiffany Ln. **278** B1
Tompkins Av. **274** A4, B3
Topanga St **277** D1
Torsby Pl. **277** D4
Tropicana **275** C3
Tropicana Av. **274** B4, **275** C3–D3–E2
Trump International Hotel and Tower **276** B4
Twain Av. **277** D4–E3
University of Nevada, Las Vegas **275** E1
Utah Av. **278** B4

V

Valley St **279** E1
Valley View Bd **274** A2–A3, B4
Van Patten St **276** C1
Van Pattern Pl. **276** C1
Vante Av., La **279** E4
Vaquero Way **277** E2
Vegas Plaza Dr. **276** B4
Vegas Valley Dr. **277** D1–E1
Venetian **274** B1
Verdy Ln. **278** B1
Viking Rd **274** A2
Visby Ln. **277** D4
Voxna St **277** D4

W–Y

Waldman Av. **278** A4
Wall St **278** A4
Washington Av. **278** A1
Weldon Pl. **278** B4
Wengert Av. **279** C3–D3–E2
Westchester Cl. **277** C4
Westchester Dr. **277** C4
Western Av. **276** A2–A4
Westlund Dr. **276** A2
Westward House **276** B3
Westwood Dr. **276** A1–A3
Wet 'n' Wild **276** B2
Willow Green Dr. **277** D3
Willow St **278** A4
Wilmington Way **276** A3
Wilson Av. **278** A1
Wilson Sq. **277** D3
Winnick Av. **274** C1
Wyandotte St **276** A3
Wynn Encore **276** B3
Wynn Las Vegas **276** B4
Wynn Rd **274** A2–A3, A4, B4
Wyoming Av. **278** B4
Yucca Av. **278** C3

Art and Photo Credits

All photography by APA/Team Nowitz except:

Courtesy of Access Vegas 137
AKG Images 87TL, 87M
Alamy 30T
ATV 229T
Courtesy of Bellagio 145T
Bob Brye 31B, 114
Courtesy of the Chapel of the Flowers 91TR
Courtesy of Cirque du Soleil 9CL, 72/73all
Corbis 86
Richard Cummins 59, 126, 129B, 192T
Courtesy of Fremont Street Experience 6T, 9TL, 10B, 22, 23, 62/63, 108, 200, 202/203T, 203B, 207B, 214B
APA/Glyn Genin 7T, 11C, 56B, 76TL, 84, 131TL, 132T & B, 134TL, 140T, 160TL, 166T, 179T, 184TL, 201, 209B, 225T, 228T, 231T, 236BR, 245TR & TL, 248
Getty Images International 50B
Lindsay Hebbard 139 all
Phillip Hughes 215T
Catherine Karnow 3, 14/15, 16/17, 18, 19, 25, 28C, 58TR, 64, 67, 70, 71, 74, 79, 83T, 85, 92, 94, 104/105, 106/107, 123B, 133B, 140B, 146T & B, 162/163T, 164, 167B, 181B, 186, 187, 196B, 204B, 205B, 208T, 220, 221, 223B, 226, 234B, 241, 246
Courtesy Las Vegas Monorail 60TL, 241
Courtesy of the Las Vegas News Bureau, LVCVA 12T, 20, 27TR, 38B, 38TL, 38/39T, 40TL, 40TR, 40B, 41T, 44TL, 45, 46, 47TR, 48T, 50T, 51TL, 51TR, 52TL, 53TL, 54, 55, 56, 57, 60TR, 102/103, 124B, 128B, 134B, 142T, 142B, 151T, 152B, 155T & B, 157B, 161, 170, 175TR, 194T, 195B, 212BR, 253, 257, 265
Courtesy of Las Vegas Town Square 120TL, 120BR, 120BL
Courtesy of the Liberace Museum 190B, 191L & R
Courtesy of the Luxor 118B, 119B
Courtesy of Mandalay Bay 117TR, 117TL
Mary Evans Picture Library 32, 34, 37
Kevin Mazur 61
Courtesy of Monte Carlo 134CT
Courtesy of the Neon Museum 6B, 154, 157T, 203T
Nevada Commission on Tourism 205
Peter Newark's American Pictures 36L, 36R, 43, 52TR
Rex Features 12C
Courtesy of the Riviera 178
Ronald Grant Archive 42, 87TR, 88, 89
Topham Picturepoint 28B, 44TR, 49, 53TR, 53CL, 93, 96, 97, 98, 99
Denise Truscello 130B

Picture Spreads

Pages 72/73
All images courtesy of Cirque du Soleil except Getty Images International 73TR

Pages 100/101
All images by APA/Team Nowitz

Pages 162/163
Courtesy of the Las Vegas News Bureau 162C, 163B, 163C; Catherine Karnow 162/163T; APA/Team Nowitz 162B, 163CL

Pages 198/199
All images APA/ Team Nowitz except Catherine Karnow 199TR

Picture Research: Steven Lawrence

Map Production: Stephen Ramsay

General Index

A

Academie National de Musique 141
accommodations 251–7
Adelson, Sheldon 167
admission charges 268
Adventuredome 180
Agassi, Andre 23–4, 99
air tours 250
air travel 248
Albright, George 48
Alexis Park **187**, 255
Ali, Muhammad 96, 97, 152
Alvarez, Al 79
The Amazing Colossal Man 88
Anasazi tribe 33, 231
animals *see* **wildlife**
Ann-Margret 86, 182
Anthony, Greg 24
Appian Way **149–50**, 259
Arc de Triomphe 140
architecture 65
Arden, Donn 47, 67
Armijo, Antonio 33–4
art galleries *see* **museums and galleries**
the arts
performing 26
visual 27
Arts District 27, **198–9**
Arum, Bob 23
Atlatl Rock 231
ATM machines 144, 270–1
Atomic Energy Commission 44
Atomic Testing Museum 191
Auto Collections 157–8
Aviation Museum 188

B

Bacall, Lauren 49
backstage tours 143
Bailey, Bob 46
Baldwin, Alex 89
ballet 26
Bally's Las Vegas **142–4**, 252
Bally's Paris Promenade 142
Barrett, Marty 24
basketball 82, 83
Beatty, Warren 89
Bellagio **144–6**, 252
Conservatory and Botanical Gardens 146
creation of 58, 65
Fountains 70, 145
Gallery of Fine Art 145–6
Big Shot 184
Bill's Gamblin' Hall & Saloon **153–5**, 252
Bill's Lounge 153–5
Binion, Benny 41, 44, 79
Binion, Ted 56
Binion's Gambling Hall **207–8**, 253
Binion's Horseshoe 41, 44, 56, 159
birdwatching 236, 242
Bishop, Joey 49
black Americans 39, 46
Black Book 47
Black Canyon 244
blackjack 77–8, 84
Blue Diamond 221
"Bodies" 120
Bogart, Humphrey 49
Boneyard 207
Bonnie Springs Old Nevada 221–2
Bootleg Canyon 236
bootleggers 45
Botanical Cactus Garden 234
Boulder City 39, 233, **236–8**
accommodations 257
Boulder City-Hoover Dam Museum 238
Boulder Dam *see* **Hoover Dam**
Boulder Dam Hotel **237**, 257
Boulder Theater (Boulder City) 88, 237
Le Boulevard **141**, 260
boxing **96–7**, 152
Boyd, Sam 211
Brenner, David 25
Bringhurst, William 35
Bringing Down the House, 21 87
Brooklyn Bridge 128
budgeting 268
Bugsy 89, 155
Bugsy Celebrity Theater 155
Burton, Lance 25, 133–4
bus travel 159, 248, 249
business hours 268

C

Caesar salads 151
Caesars Palace 60, **149–53**, 252
history 55–6
Cage, Nicholas 87
California Hotel **211**, 253
Callville Bay 231
Campanile Bell Tower 167–8
camping 266
Canyon Ranch 167
car racing 266
car rental 250
Cardini, Caesar 151
Caribbean Stud 78
Carnaval Court **159**, 259, 263
Carnival Midway 179
Casino 89, 176
Casino Royale 75, **160**
Casino War 78
Cassidy, David 24
Castle Walk **122**, 259
CBS Television City 131
celebrities
resident 24–5
weddings 90–1
Century building 127
Champs Elysées 141
cheating 70–1, 77–8, 83
Cheney-Coker, Syl 27
Cher 25, 152, 263
Chihuly, Dale 58, **144**
children 59, 68, 120
Chinatown 195–6
chips, commemorative 82, 83
Chrysler building 127
CineVegas festival 88
Circus Circus 56, **178–80**, 252
Circusland 178
Cirque du Soleil 59, **72–3**
see also ***Love***; ***Mystère***; ***O***; ***Zumanity***
CityCenter 134, **154**
Clark County Museum 235–6
Clark, Wilbur 45
Clark, William 36, 37
Cleopatra's Barge 152, 263
climate 268–9
Clinton, Bill 98
clothing 269
size chart 260
The Cloud 170
clubs 263
cocktail lounges 264
Collins, Joan 91
Colorado River 244, 245
Colosseum 150–1, **152**
Colton, George 36
comedy 262
conferences and conventions 66, 192
Congo Room 182, 183
The Cooler 89
Cordova, Marty 24
Costello, Frank 43
Courtyard Las Vegas Convention Center **192**, 255
Coward, Noel 49
Cragin, Ernie 39
craps 78–9, 84
Crawford, Cindy 91
Crazy Girls 175–6
credit cards 270
crime 59, 269
Cross, Craig 70
cruises, Lake Mead 242, **243**
culture 26
currency 271
Curtis, Tony 24
customs regulations 269
cycling 236, 267

D

Dalitz, Moe 45–6, 53, 180
Dam Short Film Festival 88
Dandridge, Dorothy 67
dates, wedding 92

Davis, Sammy, Jr 43, 49, 86
de la Hoya, Oscar 96, 97
de Niro, Robert 89
Dealertainer's Pit 158
Denton, Ralph 39
Depp, Johnny 87
Desert Inn 45, 52–3, 58
Diamonds Are Forever 86
dice 82
Dickenson, Angie 49
Diederich, Harvey 44
Dion, Celine 25, 151, 152, 241
disabled travelers 269
The District (Green Valley Ranch) **234**, 235
divorces 93
Doges Palace 168
Dorfman, Alan 43
Downtown **201–17**
accommodations 253–4
Dragone, Franco 175
drive-thru weddings 93
Duck Creek Trail 242

E

Easton, Sheena 25
Echelon 60, 61, **176–7**
Echo Bay 231
eco-friendly design 154
Eiffel Tower 59, 92, **140**
El Cortez Hotel and Casino 40, **213**, 253
El Rancho Vegas 39–40
electricity 269
Elster, Kevin 24
Ely, Sims 236, 237
emergency numbers 270
Empire State Building 127
Encore 175
energy problems 154
Entratter, Jack 48
entry requirements 269
ESPN Zone 128
Ethel M. Chocolates 233–4
Excalibur 92, **121–3**, 252
EXTRA Lounge 138–9
Extraterrestrial Highway 230

F

Fall ArtWalk (Summerlin) 225
Falls Golf Club 242
Fantasy 120
Fantasy Tower 194
Fashion Show Mall 169–70
FBI 47, 50–1
Fear and Loathing in Las Vegas 87
festivals
film 88
high-season days and holidays 24
Fitzgerald's **210**, 253
Flamingo Las Vegas **155–6**, 252
Flamingo Garden 155, **156**
history 40, 41, 58
Folies Bergère 124
Fontainebleau Las Vegas 177
Foreman, George 96, 97
Forum Shops 152
Forum Tower 151
Four Queens **209–10**, 253
Four Seasons **117–18**, 252
Foyt, Larry 25
Fremont, John C. 35–6
Fremont East District 213–14
Fremont Hotel and Casino **210**, 253
Fremont Street 201–3
Fremont Street Experience 58, **203–4**
Frey, Charles 39, 79
Frontier 40, 61

G

Gable, Clark 86
Gabor, Zsa Zsa 90
Gamblers' Book Shop **212**, 261
gambling **75–85**
compulsive 78–9
history 37–48, 55–8
how to win **84–5**, 207
and Mormons 34
regulation 48
slot machines 39, 76, 79–81, 207
Sports Books 82, **85**, 120–1
surveillance 70–1
Gameworks 132
Garden of the Gods 150
gardens *see* **parks and gardens**
Gardner, Ava 90
Garland, Judy 49
Gaughan, Jackie 213–14
gay travelers 270
Gere, Richard 91
Ghostbar **194**, 264
Giancana, Sam 50, 51
Gibson, Jim 34
Glitter Gulch 201
The Godfather 89
Gold Coast **194**, 256
Golden Nugget 41, **208–9**, 254
Goldwyn, Sam 40
golf **97–8**, 242, **264–5**
Goodman, Oscar 204–5, 212
Gorme, Eydie 25
Grable, Betty 90
Graf, Steffi 23–4, 99
Grand Canal 168
Grand Canal Shoppes 25–98, **168**
Grand Canyon West 239
Great Depression 38
Green Valley Ranch 234
Greene, Shecky 51
Griffith, R.E. 40
Griffith, Robert 37
Guin, Kenny 61

H

Hacienda **242**, 257
Hand of Faith 208
Hannagan, Steve 44
Hard Rock Hotel **187–9**, 256
Harrah, William 158, 160
Harrah's 81, **158–60**, 252
Hawkins, Frank 24
Hayworth, Rita 90
health 270
helicopter flights 250
Henderson 233, **235**
accommodations 257
hiking 236, 266
Hill, Virginia 41
Hilton *see* **Las Vegas Hilton**
Hilton, Paris 90–1
history 28–61
Hoffa, Jimmy 51, 53, 180
Hoffman, Dustin 86
Holmes, Larry 96, 152
Holyfield, Evander 96, 151
Honey I Blew Up the Kid 88–9
Honeymoon in Vegas 87, 96, 132
Hooters Casino Hotel **187**, 256
Hoover, Herbert 244
Hoover Dam 37, **38**, 238, **244–5**
Hope, Bob 97
horseback riding 267
hospitals 270
hot-air ballooning 267
Hotel on Mount Charleston 228
hotels 251–7
House of Blues **116**, 263
Hualapai people 239
Hughes, Howard 48, 57
Auto Collections 157
Desert Inn **52–3**
Spring Mountain Ranch 223
Hull, Tom 39

I

illusion **65–6**, 86
Imperial Palace **156–8**, 252
impersonators **132**, 157
Improv Comedy Club **159**, 262
Indecent Proposal 87
Independence Day 88
Insanity 184
International 51, 58
internet 270
Irving, Clifford 52

J

jackpots 83
Jackson, La Toya 25
James, Harry 90
jazz 26
JJ's Boulangerie 141
John, Elton 25, 152
Johnson, Jody 26
The Joint **189**, 263
Jolie, Angelina 91
Jones, Cliff 43
Jones, Tom 52
Jordan, Michael 91
Jubilee! 142
JW Marriott Las Vegas Resort & Spa (Summerlin) 225

K

Kahunaville Party Bar 168
Kefauver, Estes 43–4
Kelch, Maxwell 40
Kellar, Charles 39
Kennedy, John F. 50, 67
Kennedy, Joseph 50
keno 81–2, 84–5
Kerkorian, Kirk 41, 51, 55
  MGM Grand 58, 79
  MGM-Mirage 130
King, BB 25
King, Don 23
Knievel, Evel 95
Knievel, Robbie 95–6, 98
Knight, Gladys 25
Krupp, Vera 222, 223
Kyle Canyon 228

L

Lady Luck 86
Lake Las Vegas 61, 241
Lake Mead 231, **242–4**
Lance Burton Theater 133–4
Lansky, Meyer 40, 41, 47
Las Vegas Arboretum 190
Las Vegas Art Museum 144, **196**
Las Vegas Club 41, 254
Las Vegas Convention Center 192
Las Vegas Cyber Speedway 182
Las Vegas Hilton **192**, 252, 256
  history 51, 58
  themed weddings 92
Las Vegas Motor Speedway 229–30
Las Vegas Natural History Museum 215–16
Las Vegas Outlet Center 122, **211**, 259
Las Vegas Philharmonic 26
Las Vegas Premium Outlets **196**, 259
Las Vegas Ski and Snowboard Resort 227
Las Vegas Sports Consultants 82
Las Vegas Springs Preserve 225
Las Vegas Wash 242
Last Frontier 40
Lawford, Peter 49, 50, 86
Lawrence, Steve 25
LAX **120**, 263
Lazar, Swifty 49
Le Réve 175
Leaving Las Vegas 87
Lee Canyon 227
Legends in Concert **157**, 264
Legends Deli 123–4
Leonard , Sugar Ray 96, 97, 151
Let It Ride 78
Levinson, Ed 47
Lewis, Jerry 25
Lewis, Lennox 97
Liberace 176, **190**
  Auto Collections 157
  Liberace Museum 190–1
Lied Discovery Children's Museum 216
limousines 249
Lion Habitat 130
Liston, Sonny 96
Little Church of the West 90, 91
Little, Rich 25
Little White Chapel 90–1, 201
Loews Lake Las Vegas Resort 241
Lost City Museum (Overton) 231
Lou Ruvo Alzheimer's Institute 65, **212**
Louis, Joe 46, 47, 97, 152
Louvre 141
Love 167
Lower East Side street 128
Luxor **119–21**, 252

M

M&M's World 132
McCarran, Pat 43–4
McCarran International Airport 60, 76, 188, **248**
McGuire, Phyllis 51
Macy, Warren H. 89
Madame Tussaud's 168
Mafia *see* **Mob**
magic 163
Maheu, Robert **52–3**, 223
Main Street Station **211–12**, 254
malls 258–9
Maloof, George 193
Mama Mia 116
Mandalay Bay 59, **115–17**, 252
Mandalay Bay Events Center 116
Mandra Spa 139
Manilow, Barry 25, 262–3
maps 270
Marchese, Patricia 26
Marjorie Barrick Museum 189–90
Marriott Corporation 34
Mars Attacks 88
Mars, Forrest 234
Martin, Dean 49, 86
Marz, John 34
Masquerade Village 195
media 270
Mexican War 35
MGM Garden Arena 130–1
MGM Grand **129–31**, 252
  history 58, 143–4
Midler, Bette 25, 152, 263
Milestone, Lewis 50, 86
Miller, Arthur 86
Miller, Bill 51
Mina, Michael 146
mining 36
Miracle Mile Shops 61, 139
Mirage 59, **165–7**, 252
  history 57
The Misfits 86
Moapa River Indian Reservation 230
Mob 41, 43–8, 50–1, 53
money 270–1
monorail 60–1, 249
Monroe, Marilyn 50–1, 86
  Auto Collections 158
Monte Carlo 41, 58, **132–4**, 252
Monte Carlo Pub and Brewery 133
Montelago Village 241
Montgolfier balloon 140
Mormons 35, 214–15
  and casinos 34
motels 157, 253, 254
motor racing 152
motorcycles 250
Moulin Rouge 46–7
Mount Charleston 227–8
Mount Charleston Lodge 228
movie locations 86–8
Murphy, Sandy 56
museums and galleries
  art galleries 261
  Atomic Testing Museum 191
  Auto Collections 157–8
  Aviation Museum 188
  Bellagio Gallery of Fine Art 145–6
  Boulder City-Hoover Dam Museum 238
  Clark County Museum 235–6
  Guggenheim Hermitage Museum 169
  Las Vegas Art Museum 144, **196**
  Las Vegas Natural History Museum 215–16
  Liberace Museum 190–1
  Lied Discovery Children's Museum 216
  Lost City Museum (Overton) 231
  Madame Tussaud's 168
  Marjorie Barrick Museum 189–90
  Neon Museum 205
  Nevada State Museum 225
  Pinball Hall of Fame Museum 189
  Wynn Art Collection 174
music 26
Mystère 169

N

Napoleon's Champagne Bar **140**, 263
NASCAR racing 98–9, 229
Native Americans 33–5
  see also **Anasazi tribe**; **Paiute tribe**
  casinos 75–6
  Marjorie Barrick Museum 190
  Moapa River Indian Reservation 230
Nazarian, Sam 181, 183
Nellis Air Force Base 230

Nellis Air Force Bombing and Gunnery Range 228–9
Neon Museum 205
Neonopolis 205–7
Nevada Desert 228–31
Nevada Gaming Commission 47, 48, 51
Nevada Gaming Control Board 48, 49, 50, 51, 71, 82
Nevada State Museum 225
New York New York 58, **127–9**, 252
newspapers 270
Newton, Wayne 25
Nickel Town 176
nightlife **162–3**, **262–4**
Niven, David 49
Northshore Scenic Drive 231, 244
nuclear testing 44–5, 46, 61
  Atomic Testing Museum 191
nuclear waste 61, 229

O

O 146
Ocean's 11 **50**, 86, 144
Ocean's 13 86
Octavius Tower **151**, 154
Old Las Vegas Mormon Fort State Historic Park 214
Old Mormon Fort 214–15
O'Neal, Shaquille 23
orientation 248
Orlando, Tony 25
Orleans **193**, 256
Overton 231
Overton Beach 231, 244

P

Pahranagat National Wildlife Refuge 230
Paiute tribe 33, 34–5
  Mouse Tank 231
  Willow Spring 224
Palace Tower 151
Palace of Versailles 141
Palazzo 60, 168
The Palms **193–4**, 252
Paris Las Vegas **140–2**, 252
  Eiffel Tower 59, 92, **140**
Paris Opéra 141
Parker, Colonel Tom 51, 52
parks and gardens
  Bellagio Conservatory and Botanical Gardens 146
  Botanical Cactus Garden 234
  Flamingo Garden 155, **156**
  Garden of the Gods 150
  Las Vegas Arboretum 190
  Xeric Garden 190
Patterson, Floyd 96
pawn shops 206
Penn & Teller 25
people 23–7
petroglyphs 33, 224, 231
photography 271
Piazza San Marco 168
Picasso, Pablo 199
Pinball Hall of Fame Museum 189
Planet Hollywood **137–9**, 252
Planet Hollywood group 61
Planet Hollywood Towers 139
playing cards 80, 82–3
Plaza Las Vegas **211**, 254
Pleasure Pit 137
poker 78, 79, 85
police 270
population, shifting 26
postal services 271
Presley, Elvis 48, **51–2**
  Auto Collection 158
  impersonators **132**, 157
  Las Vegas Hilton 192
  Viva Las Vegas 86
Presley, Priscilla 51
prostitution 68–70
public holidays 271
Pure 153
Puzo, Mario 75, 83

R

Race for Atlantis 153
Rachel 230
rafting 267
Railroad Pass (Boulder City) 237
railroads 36, 37
Rain Las Vegas **194**, 263
Rain Man 86
Rainbow Company 26
Rainforest Café 130
Rat Pack 43, **48–51**, 86
Red Rock Canyon National Conservation Area 223–5
Red Rock Casino Resort & Spa 225
Red Rock Loop Road 225
Redford, Robert 87
Reed Whipple Center 26
Reflection Bay Golf Club 242
religious services 271
Reno 228
Residence Inn Las Vegas 192
Reynolds, Debbie 25
Rialto Bridge 168
rides
  Adventuredome 180
  Big Shot 184
  Insanity 184
  Race for Atlantis 153
  Roller Coaster at New York New York 128
  "Speed – The Ride" 182
  X Scream 184
Rio **194–5**, 256
Ritz-Carlton Hotel 241–2
Rivera, Rafael 33–4
Riviera 46, **175–6**, 252
road travel 248
rodeos 99
Rolling Stones 82, 188
room rates 176, 251
Rooney, Mickey 90
Rosselli, John 53
roulette 85
Rudner, Rita 25, 159, 262
Rush Hour 2 89

S

safety 269
Sahara 181–3
sailing 267
St John of Las Vegas 88
Sam's Town 233
Sarno, Jay **55–7**
  Caesars Palace 150
  Circus Circus 178, 179
Sawyer, Grant 39, 46–7
Searchlight 36
sex trade 68–70
Shark Reef 66, **115–16**
Shaw, Don 34
Sherwood Forest Café 121
shopping **100–1**, **258–61**
  Appian Way **149–50**, 259
  Le Boulevard **141**, 260
  Carnaval Court **159**, 259
  Castle Walk **122**, 259
  The District (Green Valley Ranch) **234**, 235
  Farmer's Market (Henderson) 235
  Fashion Show Mall **169–70**, 258
  Forum Shops **152**, 258
  Gamblers' Book Shop **212**, 261
  Grand Canal Shoppes 25–98, **168**
  Las Vegas Outlet Center 122, **211**, 259
  Las Vegas Premium Outlets **196**, 259
  Miracle Mile Shops 61, **139**, 259
  Shoppes at The Palazzo **168–9**, 260
  Street of Dreams **133**, 260
  Tower Shops **184**, 260
  Town Square **120**, 259
  Via Bellagio **145**, 260
  World Market Center 213
  Wynn Esplanade **174**, 260
Show in the Sky 195
Showcase Mall 132
showgirls 47, 67–8, 124
  backstage tours 143
Showgirls 87, 89
shuttle buses 159
Siegel, Benjamin "Bugsy" **40–1**, 79, 155–6
Siegfried & Roy 25, 165–6
Siegfried & Roy's Secret Garden & Dolphin Habitat 166–7
sightseeing tours 249–50
Signature at MGM Grand 129